Conservation Education and Outreach Techniques

SECOND EDITION

Techniques in Ecology and Conservation Series

Series Editor: William J. Sutherland

Conservation Education and Outreach Techniques

SECOND EDITION

Susan K. Jacobson
Mallory D. McDuff
and Martha C. Monroe

OXFORD
UNIVERSITY PRESS

Great Clarendon Street, Oxford, OX2 6DP,
United Kingdom

Oxford University Press is a department of the University of Oxford.
It furthers the University's objective of excellence in research, scholarship,
and education by publishing worldwide. Oxford is a registered trade mark of
Oxford University Press in the UK and in certain other countries

First Edition published in 2006
Second Edition published in 2015

Impression: 1

Published in the United States of America by Oxford University Press
198 Madison Avenue, New York, NY 10016, United States of America

British Library Cataloguing in Publication Data
Data available

Library of Congress Control Number: 2015938277

ISBN 978–0–19–871668–6 (hbk.)
ISBN 978–0–19–871669–3 (pbk.)

Printed and bound by
CPI Group (UK) Ltd, Croydon, CR0 4YY

This book is dedicated to those who have nourished, guided, and inspired us over the years—our families, colleagues, mentors, and students—and to the natural world that sustains us all.

Acknowledgments

We are grateful to the many conservation educators around the world who have contributed wonderful examples and inspiration for this book. For expert review of various chapters we are deeply thankful to: Alice Cohen, Julie Ernst, Tom Harris, Jeff Hardesty, Trina Hofreiter, Perry Jacobson, Margaret Kinnaird, Shelby Krantz, Lawrence Lowry, Lisa Marks, Susan Marynowski, Lily Maynard, Lindsey McConnell, Lauren McDonell, Douglas McKenzie-Mohr, Katie Monroe, O. Gene Myers, Molly Nicholie, Michelle Prysby, W.J. "Rocky" Rohwedder, Susan Sachs, Ricky Telg, and Richard Wilke. For research and secretarial assistance we thank Beida Chen, Rebecca Soodeen, Deidra Brown, Eric Carvallo, Elaine Culpepper, Lisa Pennisi, and Sarah Tarrant. We thank students in the Methods and Materials in Environmental Education class at Warren Wilson College who reviewed early drafts of chapters: Lev Ben-Ezra, Kylie Kraus, Jessica Mosher, Ryan Nepomuceno, Joy Proctor, Annie Ross, Tucka Saville, and Greg Traymar. We are grateful for the collegiality at the University of Florida and Warren Wilson College. In honor of our parents, Betty and Perry Jacobson, Ann and Larry McDuff, and Helen and John Monroe, the proceeds from the book will be used to support conservation education activities.

Contents

Introduction

Think of a challenging conservation problem you have encountered—protecting a rare species, winning support for legislation, cleaning up a river, or sustainably managing a forest. Inevitably, people are part of the problem and public education and outreach will be part of the solution. Effective education and outreach are essential for promoting conservation policy, creating knowledgeable citizens, changing people's behaviors, garnering funds, and recruiting volunteers. The fate of our ecosystems and the plants, animals, and people that depend on them lies with our ability to educate children and adults, in settings as diverse as schools, communities, farms, and forests. Findings from the Millennium Assessment Reports and the Intergovernmental Panel on Climate Change have documented that the vital ecosystem services that support life on earth—such as fresh water, fisheries, biodiversity, air and water cycling, and the regulation of natural hazards and regional climate—are being degraded and threatened. Conservation education and outreach programs are a critical component in changing course toward a more sustainable future.

The goal of this book is to present the many techniques available for creating effective education and outreach programs for conservation. Chapter 1 presents a framework for designing programs and Chapters 2 and 3 provide the theoretical and practical background for understanding the learning process, and therefore how to effectively teach and support behavior change among adults and youth. Subsequent chapters introduce the reader to an exciting array of education and outreach techniques. These include techniques for classrooms and enhancement of school resources focused on students and developing written materials, from blog posts to guidebooks, for all ages. Marketing conservation messages, using mass media, and using the arts for conservation provide a range of innovative techniques. Many on-site techniques, such as exhibits, guides, and demonstrations are critical for natural areas, parks, and community centers. The planning, implementation, and evaluation processes are described for each technique.

What is in the book?

Chapter 1: Designing successful conservation education and outreach

Systematic planning, implementation, and evaluation are the foundation of effective education and outreach. This chapter begins the planning process with guidelines for identifying the needs, objectives, and target audiences of a program. Possible strategies

Conservation Education and Outreach Techniques. Second Edition. Susan K. Jacobson, Mallory D. McDuff & Martha C. Monroe © Susan K. Jacobson, Mallory D. McDuff & Martha C. Monroe 2015. Published 2015 by Oxford University Press.

are compared based on resources and constraints of time, money, and staff. Planning helps to ensure that educators target the right audience and use appropriate messages and delivery systems. Implementation involves pilot-testing activities and monitoring the ongoing operations. Monitoring and assessment allows educators to modify materials and strategies based on timely feedback and new information. Evaluation of the outcomes reveals whether the techniques worked. Eight tools, from quantitative surveys to qualitative observation, are described. These allow decision-making about the worth of the program.

Chapter 2: Learning and teaching

Theories about learning and teaching form the basis for designing effective programs and marketing them to their audiences and administrators. This chapter provides program planners with a foundation in how people learn and a suite of theories, such as constructivism, inquiry learning, experiential learning, activity theory, social learning, and cooperative learning, that can be used to design effective interactive programs. Critical thinking, creative thinking, and systems thinking skills are important to help learners address conservation issues and can be practiced and promoted through well-designed programs.

Chapter 3: Changing conservation behaviors

The road to behavior change is paved with many theories. The disciplines of education, sociology, and psychology offer a number of ideas about human behavior that can be used to design programs that influence people's conservation-related behaviors. This chapter organizes many of the most commonly used theories concerning the development and research of conservation program around key purposes: providing information, addressing social influences, building self-efficacy, exploring motivation, designing supportive environments, and organizing an effective program sequence. Some are designed to influence how people gain information and learn skills to become responsible citizens, while others explore ways to orchestrate changes in specific behaviors. Both types of theories have important roles to play in the development of conservation education and outreach programs.

Chapter 4: Conservation education in schools

Partnerships with environmental organizations and agencies can help create effective conservation education in schools. This chapter presents strategies for building successful programs in schools, including the effective use of communication, serving as a resource to the schools, supporting academic standards, and integrating conservation education into legislation and policy. Education in schools should include learning about the local environment, but too often academic demands preclude the chance to study the natural world outside the classroom door. When conservation education links academic standards to the study of natural and social systems and their interactions, students, teachers, administrators, and the environment are all winners. A variety of successful approaches to the implementation of conservation education within schools are described, such as environment-based education and education for sustainability.

Chapter 5: Making conservation come alive

Making conservation come alive can mean, for example, discovering the natural world through a neighborhood scavenger hunt or researching the perspectives of an industry group for a role-play. Techniques in this chapter, such as hands-on activities, field trips, and backcountry skills, immerse participants in exploring the outdoors or an environmental concept. Other techniques bring conservation alive through a minds-on approach, such as storytelling, games, case studies, role-playing, and contests. Conservation educators can combine these techniques, such as using a role-play to teach backcountry skills. Most of the techniques in this chapter involve an element of fun, from a field trip exploring a wetland to a storytelling session on forests. This chapter contains helpful hints for implementation, including tips for engaging an audience in a story or developing a role-play. Every technique engages the audience in learning through direct experience.

Chapter 6: Using the arts for conservation

Using the arts for conservation can help attract new audiences, increase understanding, introduce new perspectives, and create a dialogue among diverse people. The arts—painting, photography, literature, theatre, and music—offer an emotional connection to nature. This chapter provides examples of using the arts to increase environmental awareness and inspire people to take action. Planning art activities requires reaching out to artists and the arts community, audiences with whom scientists and educators may seldom interact. Using aesthetic, kinesthetic, and philosophical approaches can help young people and adults understand their environment. Conservation problems require creative solutions. It makes sense to access more ways of knowing the world in order to take care of it.

Chapter 7: Connecting classes and communities

Effective conservation aims to integrate, rather than compete with, the needs of the human communities that share landscapes with biological communities. This chapter focuses on techniques to connect classrooms and communities with conservation. Conservation education techniques, such as service-learning, issue investigation, and project-based learning, can involve students, teachers, and community members in finding creative approaches to issues such as reducing carbon emissions and building community gardens. In addition, public participation in scientific research involves collaboration between members of the public and scientists, and includes both citizen science and community-based research as examples. Finally, this chapter describes mapping as a technique which allows individuals or groups to create visual representations of resources, a community, or a region. The techniques described in this chapter bring real conservation issues to the forefront of communities and classrooms and ultimately help achieve conservation goals.

Chapter 8: Networking for conservation

Networking involves aligning your interests with other individuals, groups, and communities to increase the success of a conservation effort. Talking with festival attendees at an information booth or forming a long-term partnership between organizations both require making connections. Networking can create or use existing environmental groups or clubs, as well as promote conservation objectives through workshops, public presentations, and professional posters. The skills needed to organize conferences and special events are necessary for developing connections among larger audiences to promote conservation messages and ultimately achieve conservation objectives. The techniques in this chapter provide opportunities to network and attain success both within and beyond the conservation community.

Chapter 9: Marketing conservation

A number of marketing techniques can help increase conservation-related behavior if they specifically target a behavior or action and if they help people overcome the barriers they were experiencing. Sometimes people need information, awareness, and reminders. Signs, billboards, advertisements, press releases, and prompts help people learn and remember information. However, these are rarely sufficient for supporting a new behavior. Techniques involving the use of feedback and demonstrations or models help people realize whether this behavior has become a norm in their community. Incentives and disincentives can help launch a new behavior, and asking for a commitment can help sustain it. Working with local leaders to identify behaviors and consider the barriers that deter each behavior helps educators choose the most effective combinations of techniques. This chapter provides many examples of how a variety of techniques have been used and evaluated to achieve behavior change.

Chapter 10: Getting your message out using the written word

Using the written word for education and outreach is an essential technique for accomplishing the conservation objectives of many organizations and agencies. Harnessing the power of mass media through editorials, news releases, and blog posts provides the means to reach vast numbers of people with information in a reliable format. This type of free advertising is valuable to everyone dealing with critical conservation issues and tight budgets. Guidelines on the structure and format for producing these materials are presented to ensure success in the competitive mass and social media arena. Fact sheets, flyers, brochures, and guidebooks are used by conservation organizations to build audience awareness, increase knowledge, and foster new conservation skills. The tips presented for clear writing and attractive graphic design help guarantee the production of effective written materials.

Chapter 11: Taking advantage of technology

Educational technology, such as radio, television, and the Internet, can dramatically increase the number of people we reach with conservation messages. It also allows audiences to vicariously experience natural events and places they might never see in person. Websites, social media, videos, and distance learning allow conservation agencies and organizations to go beyond traditional face-to-face programming. They can establish new ways to effectively reach their audience and open the door for audience members to share information with others. Whether these technologies are successful depends in part on the degree to which they incorporate relevant learning theories. Strategies for evaluating websites, videos, and online programs help ensure good-quality output.

Chapter 12: Designing on-site activities

On-site activities can enhance first-hand experiences in natural areas and community centers by orienting, informing, and stimulating visitors. The development of on-site activities considers the visitor experience, the resources of the site, and the education and outreach objectives of the organization. An initial planning process at a site paves the way for developing trails, guided walks, exhibits, demonstrations, nature awareness activities, and visitor centers. Guidelines provided in this chapter for implementing and evaluating these techniques help achieve conservation and education goals.

The challenge

Abundant examples illustrate the techniques described throughout this book. They represent the hard work and wisdom shared by conservation educators around the world. We hope these will inspire creative thinking and new ideas to fit the needs of the students, educators, environmentalists, program designers, resource managers, conservation biologists, and policy-makers reading this book. We hope the book will help people speak and act more effectively for wildlife and the environment. We hope it will help conservation programs amplify their results to bring about a more sustainable future for us all.

Designing successful conservation education and outreach

"A goal without a plan is just a wish."

Antoine de Saint-Exupery

We all recognize that careful planning is critical for success. As the need for conservation education and outreach grows, systematic planning will ensure it succeeds. This chapter describes the development of education and outreach programs following guidelines for the planning–implementation–evaluation (PIE) process. It provides a design for identifying education and outreach goals, targeting specific audiences, selecting appropriate media and content, and evaluating the results. These guidelines will help you effectively use the many education and outreach techniques needed to safeguard the environment and promote sustainable communities. Whether teaching a class, giving a public presentation, or designing a website, you can follow this systematic framework for success.

1.1 The need for conservation education and outreach

The need for improved education and outreach about the environment is growing as conflicts over natural resources increase (Fig. 1.1). The public affects the success or failure of environmental management efforts. Public opposition can prevent the implementation of plans to manage natural resources, and public collaboration can be key to success (Wondolleck and Yaffee 2000). The protection of endangered panthers in Florida or snow leopards in Nepal is a social as well as a biological challenge. People decide whether to allocate the required funds, coexist with carnivores, or preserve enough land to sustain them. The fate of the big cats depends, in part, on how well natural resource managers communicate with the public and policy-makers to raise concern and support for conservation. In essence, researchers could spend years studying biological processes but fail to achieve conservation goals without adequate public support. Failure to accurately assess and target public knowledge and concerns can result in opposition to conservation initiatives and costly political battles. When the public is informed and involved, however, conservation goals can be achieved. Successful outreach programs have helped to increase populations of wolves in the USA and endangered primates in Brazil. They have improved wetland restoration and farmland management. The importance of an informed public is critical given the high stakes of conservation challenges such as

Conservation Education and Outreach Techniques. Second Edition. Susan K. Jacobson, Mallory D. McDuff & Martha C. Monroe © Susan K. Jacobson, Mallory D. McDuff & Martha C. Monroe 2015. Published 2015 by Oxford University Press.

Fig. 1.1 Human interactions with wildlife range from recreation and economic benefits to concerns about disease and safety. Education is needed to better manage wildlife and people. (Photo by S. Jacobson.)

climate change, with its wide-ranging impacts on biodiversity, food security, human health, water supply, immigration, ocean waters, and ecosystems.

Programs like the Global Rivers Environmental Education Network (GREEN) demonstrate the power of education and outreach. GREEN is a program for monitoring water quality (GM GREEN 2009). Through participation in the program, students explore their local rivers, present their findings to government officials, and exchange data and insights with students from other cultures throughout the world. GREEN has developed a global communication network including countries as diverse as Bangladesh, Argentina, Australia, Italy, Kenya, and the USA. While these countries differ culturally, many face similar conservation issues concerning the pollution and degradation of aquatic systems. Through our common need for healthy rivers and watersheds, GREEN has helped learners take action to address local watershed issues in more than 49 participating country programs, 26 of which received media coverage totaling over 14 million mentions from Internet, television, and print sources.

The public is exposed to conservation issues through print and social media, radio, television, and the Internet. An international survey revealed that 82% of consumers in Latin America, 56% in Asia, 49% in the USA, and 48% in Europe showed concern for the environment (Bishop 2012), and a 2012 Associated Press poll found that 80% of US respondents think global warming could pose serious problems, up from 73% in 2009.

Although people report that they care about the environment, public knowledge and concern about conservation are uneven. Support for wildlife focuses on attractive and emotionally appealing species. Among US citizens, 89% believe endangered bald eagles (*Haliaeetus leucocephalus*) should be protected, yet only 24% believe the similarly endangered Kauai wolf spider (*Adelocosa anops*) deserves protection (Kellert 1996). Most people view invertebrates with indifference or dislike, despite their crucial role in pollinating our crops or maintaining ecosystems.

Many school curricula include environmental topics, but too few offer comprehensive programs or focus on achieving conservation goals (see Chapter 4). Although innovative extracurricular materials have been developed, teachers may not find the time or have the training or motivation to use them. Yet the need for conservation education continues to increase as problems become more complex. From cumulative impacts on wetland restoration to declines in biodiversity and the impacts of climate change, a knowledgeable public is needed to effectively protect the environment and address the goals of sustainable development.

Many conservation agencies and organizations have education and outreach programs. These programs focus on nature and the interface between natural resources and human well-being. They emphasize capabilities for solving environmental problems. Conservation education shares many goals with the broader field of environmental education. These include giving learners opportunities for:

- awareness—to acquire an awareness of and sensitivity to the environment and its associated problems;
- knowledge—to gain a variety of experiences in and acquire a basic understanding of the environment and its associated problems;
- attitudes—to acquire a set of values and feelings of concern for the environment and the motivation for actively participating in environmental improvement and protection;
- skills—to acquire the skills for identifying and solving environmental problems; and
- participation—to encourage citizens to use their knowledge to become actively involved at all levels in working toward resolution of environmental problems (UNESCO 1978).

Conservation education and outreach programs also share goals with newer programs like education for sustainable development. These are an outgrowth of the United Nations Conferences on Environment and Development held in Rio de Janeiro, Brazil, in 1992 and 2012. Education for sustainability emphasizes the need to solve problems by addressing three goals: protecting the environmental systems that sustain life, enhancing social justice for all people, and ensuring appropriate economic development (Pigozzi 2003). Some conservation education programs, particularly those that focus on community resources, address issues of sustainability and explore local concerns to develop solutions, promoting this broad mission.

Education is often defined as a process of imparting or acquiring general knowledge, developing the powers of reasoning and judgment, and preparing oneself or others intellectually for mature life. Conservation education techniques include issue investigation, citizen science, nature awareness, service-learning, and interactive websites. In classrooms, teachers use inquiry learning, experiments, simulations, debates, and other techniques that employ the environment as a classroom. First-hand experiences help students understand natural systems, their community, and environmental issues. Infusion of environmental themes into the curriculum stimulates effective creative writing and language arts studies. The outdoors can serve as a laboratory for the study of mathematics, science, and other subjects.

Conservation outreach programs encompass approaches to promote both communication and information. Unlike organized, formal education programs, outreach programs often target a non-captive audience in social and novel settings. Outreach programs are designed to increase understanding of conservation issues, exchange opinions and experiences, and establish a dialogue among sectors of the community (Fien et al. 2002). Outreach programs use techniques like publications, presentations, exhibits, and the Internet to improve awareness and knowledge of conservation problems. Outreach also includes techniques from the field of public relations. This involves marketing conservation products or services to meet the needs and interests of identified audiences: techniques include public meetings, social media, advertisements, and television, targeting young people and adults.

Researchers have shown that appropriate education and outreach can foster sustainable behavior, improve public support for conservation, reduce vandalism and poaching in protected areas, improve compliance with environmental regulations, increase recreation-carrying capacities, and influence policies and decisions that affect the environment and natural resources (e.g., Day and Monroe 2000; Knudson et al. 2003; Jacobson 2009). The goal of this book is to present the many techniques available for creating effective education and outreach programs.

1.2 Designing education and outreach programs

Education and outreach programs help conservation organizations and agencies to address public needs, solve environmental problems, and increase resilience in communities. Some programs target a broad audience with an awareness campaign, such as providing information about recycling to homeowners in a city or introducing wetlands ecology themes into a curriculum. Other programs target groups practicing specific behaviors that the organization wishes to change, for example providing information about harvest regulations to deer hunters or collecting shorebird monitoring data in a citizen science program. Some programs teach young people problem-solving skills or how to investigate an issue. To succeed, organizations and agencies must respond to the existing needs, interests, and behaviors of their audience(s).

To be successful, program development should follow a systematic framework. Planning involves identifying goals and objectives, audiences, and educational strategies. Implementation concerns the operation of activities. Monitoring and evaluation of the results help identify successful activities as well as components in need of improvement. This interactive process—PIE—leads to an education and outreach program that avoids common problems like targeting the wrong audience or using an inappropriate message or medium. It's as easy as pie!

The expression "As easy as pie" connotes a simple and pleasurable experience, like eating pie. Yet, if you have ever baked a pie you know that careful measuring, cooking, and monitoring are required for success. During the planning process, decisions must be made about the ingredients to be included and measured. What kind of pie is required—a vegetable pie for supper or a berry pie for dessert? Who will eat the pie and what are their dietary requirements or preferences? What kind of crust? Is there time to make a topping or money to buy blueberries? It is a good idea to test a new recipe out on your family or neighbors—a pilot test—before inviting many guests to a banquet. The implementation phase involves preheating the oven, baking the pie, serving the pie, maintaining the equipment, and other operational activities. Evaluation includes how the pie looks and tastes. Did your oven cook evenly? Did your guests eat a slice and ask for seconds? Even though the outcome appears easy, a lot of hard work goes into the production.

In a similar way, you might envision designing a conservation education or outreach program. Box 1.1 outlines an "easy as pie" plan for guiding just about any conservation education and outreach program. Most conservation concerns are urgent. These guidelines help avoid wasting time and resources on ineffective practices or programs.

Box 1.1 As easy as PIE—questions to guide the design of an education and outreach program

---

Planning

- What is the conservation problem or issue you want to address?
- What are your goals and objectives?
- What audiences or stakeholders are involved in the issues to be communicated?
- What are their backgrounds, needs, interests, and actions?
- For each audience, what changes or actions are desired?
- How can audience members be involved in the planning process?
- What constraints and resources are there?
- What messages must be sent?
- What channels and activities will most efficiently result in the desired changes in knowledge, attitudes, or behaviors?

Implementation

- What modifications are indicated by pilot tests of activities and materials?
- Are scheduling, funding, and staffing adequate and efficient?

Evaluation

- How will you know if the strategy worked?
- What are the outputs and outcomes of the program?
- Are there unanticipated outcomes?

1.3 Planning

Planning starts with a review of the mission of your organization or agency and the goals for the education and outreach program. With this foundation you then can identify target audiences and develop objectives for each audience. Based on the audience and objectives, you then devise specific activities to attain your goal. An inventory of your resources in terms of staff, materials, and funds shapes the design of realistic activities. The entire planning process assesses and then narrows the menu of activities, media channels, and messages for the education or outreach campaign. A number of approaches can be followed in the planning process, but all of them should include the development of goals, objectives, and actions in response to the conservation issues that are important to your organization.

1.3.1 Review the mission

The mission of an organization, agency, or school is the reason for its existence. A mission statement articulates the guiding principles for the institution's actions and long-term goals—it defines "Who we are, what we do, and why." The answers will circumscribe the range of activities and opportunities to be pursued in an education and outreach program. The mission statement provides overall direction in light of audience needs, the organization's resources, and external constraints and opportunities. Like a beacon in the night, the mission illuminates your path so you can get where you want to go. Without a clear mission, you risk wandering in the darkness of an ineffective program. Examples of mission statements include:

- The Nature Conservancy—"To conserve the lands and waters on which all life depends" (<http://www.nature.org/>): their activities accordingly include land purchase, resource management, policy, and public outreach programs.
- The Royal Society for the Protection of Birds in the UK "works for a better environment rich in birds and wildlife" (<http://www.rspb.org.uk/>) (Fig. 1.2).
- The Institute for Ecological Research (IPÊ) in Brazil "develops innovative models for biodiversity conservation that promote socio-economic benefits through science, education and sustainable business," reconnecting precious remnants of Brazil's Atlantic forest (<http://www.ipe.org.br>)

These mission statements describe why each group exists and their mission helps them define a path to success. If a proposed education or outreach activity does not help an organization achieve its mission, then it probably should not be implemented.

1.3.2 Identify goals and objectives

Examples of the goals of conservation organizations include to protect endangered species, manage a community forest, increase energy conservation, or improve sustainable farming practices. Education and outreach goals generally address problems. Conversely, the identification of specific conservation problems is a good way to formulate goals. One of the Save the Manatee Club's goals, for example, is the recovery of manatees (*Trichechus manatus*), also called sea cows, in the wild. The more clearly

Fig. 1.2 Attractive brochures and other outreach activities help promote the mission of the Royal Society for the Protection of Birds.

the problem is stated, the more targeted a goal will be. The problem, "Manatees are an endangered species," is less helpful for identifying potential education and outreach-based solutions than "Collisions with motorboats are a major cause of manatee deaths." This problem statement helps to identify a specific goal: "Reduce the number of boat collisions with manatees." It also helps identify specific audiences such as boat owners, marina operators, or coastal regulators.

With the goal clearly in mind, specific objectives can be identified for each audience. In a school setting, teachers may have specific goals, for example to teach the scientific method or develop students' skills using maps. Research on manatee ecology or distribution can provide a real-life example for students. While goals are broad, objectives are specific and measurable for each target audience. Thinking at both levels helps you form a bridge from the mission statement to the activities you eventually conduct. Later the objectives can serve as benchmarks for measuring a program's performance.

Education and outreach objectives may be related to changing the knowledge, attitudes, or behaviors of a target audience. Commercial advertisers view objectives in the form of a staircase leading up to their goal of selling a product. The first step is building consumer awareness—the consumer's ability to recognize and remember the product. The next step piques the consumer's personal interest. This increases the consumer's desire to learn about some of the features of the product and to evaluate these attributes. The remaining steps lead to the consumer's first purchase. If all goes according to plan, the consumer will continue to purchase and use the product.

This same process can be duplicated in conservation education and outreach programs, where each objective focuses on one or several steps. An initial message may just try to increase awareness about a conservation issue or agency service. A further objective may focus on increasing concern or shifting an attitude, and a final objective may encourage conservation action. A program that only increases general awareness about a problem or product does not guarantee action. Chapter 3 offers a number of theories that can provide the foundation for moving people from awareness to action.

To assess whether your education and outreach objectives are met, they must be SMART (Box 1.2). Objectives often specify the number of people who will display the desired concern or behavior and the dates by which these changes will be achieved (e.g., a 10% increase in visitors to a wildlife reserve per month or 80% passing scores on a classroom test). All objectives should identify the audience, the media and message, the desired effect, and the time frame to facilitate the implementation and evaluation of the strategy. When objectives are specific, program results can be compared with anticipated outcomes to judge success and make decisions about its continuation. Educators write objectives in terms of what they hope their intended audience will do. Consider the manatee example: "As a result of receiving a safe-boating flier while on the water, a certain percent of Florida boaters will obey voluntary speed zones by the end of the year" (Morris et al. 2007). A workshop to educate urban residents about invasive species, in particular the Amur honeysuckle plant, had the following objectives: to have 100 people attend a 1-day workshop with 80% of the attendees reporting intentions to remove invasive species from their yards, and a 50% reduction in Amur honeysuckle in the community after 1 year (Audubon 2011). Keep in mind that you may not anticipate all the positive results of your program—the evaluation phase will also help uncover unexpected outcomes.

Box 1.2 A SMART program objective meets the following criteria

- *Specific*: describes a behavior or outcome that is observable.
- *Measurable*: provides quantifiable indicators of progress toward achieving the objective.
- *Audience-focused*: identifies the audience and describes outcomes in terms of what the audience will be able to do.
- *Relevant*: details a meaningful and realistic task and impact for the audience.
- *Time-limited*: gives a definite time frame for achieving the objective.

1.3.3 Identify target audiences

Understanding and involving your target audience is vital in designing and selecting media and messages. You must address the concerns of your audience, whether it is hikers using a protected area, homeowners living at the wildland–urban interface, farmers testing integrated pest management, or students investigating environmental problems in their neighborhood. Audience research can help orient your conservation education and outreach program to meet the needs of your audiences while promoting the "conservation products" of your organization. You must know how audiences are connected to the issue, what actions you wish them to take, and their current knowledge about the topic. Understanding factors such as audience demographics, lifestyles, and media use will help you select appropriate educational approaches and objectives.

Methods for identifying and targeting audiences include collecting data through public surveys, interviews, public meetings, and workshops. Networking with organizations that already serve the audience can offer additional insights. To help a wildlife agency tailor messages to the needs of its audience, researchers might use demographic information, psychological profiles, consumer behaviors, geographic residence, and a host of other social variables (Fig. 1.3). Unobtrusive measures, such as observation of your audience, content analysis of Internet sources, Tweets, or documents, and analysis of similar cases allow you to study the problem with minimal influence on the audience. In a classroom setting, understanding the background and cognitive development of students is critical.

These methods for collecting data can be used not only to better understand the target audience but also to test assumptions about techniques, media, materials, and messages for the audience. Audience research allows you to assess alternative strategies for education and outreach channels and messages. It provides a foundation for building support for a program or influencing audience behaviors. Audience research also provides baseline information for evaluating the results of your conservation education and outreach efforts.

The Canadian Yukon Department of Renewable Resources developed an education program to reduce the number of female grizzly bears (*Ursus arctos*) killed by hunters. Their program targeted outfitters and hunting guides. Their baseline research about this audience suggested that the most critical message for the campaign was the information that gave guides the ability to judge the age and sex of a grizzly bear. This information was delivered using a video of a workshop by a respected Alaskan bear guide. He demonstrated that guides could judge the age and sex of a bear, leading clients to kill only male bears. The video also took advantage of motivational factors for the outfitters by including the symbolic value of the bear as a lone, powerful, wild figure, an image the baseline research revealed would greatly appeal to their audience (Smith 1995). In Japan, a bear education program focused on reducing conflicts between bears and rural residents. The Nature Preservation Division of Tochigi Prefecture launched a program that helped homeowners reduce the likelihood of attracting bears to their villages. They used survey and observational research to establish baseline needs and evaluate success in developing community participation to reduce damage to agriculture by bears (Sakurai et al. 2014).

In a similar manner, programs designed for school students must consider their needs and backgrounds. For example, nature programs designed for urban students must first make students comfortable in a novel setting in order for learning to occur.

Fig. 1.3 A researcher interviews boaters to obtain baseline information for an education program promoting safe boating with manatees. (Photo by S. Aipunjiguly.)

An understanding of your audience's baseline knowledge and beliefs is a prerequisite for creating effective conservation education. In traditional classroom settings this information is often readily available from student testing, but research is often needed for addressing controversial subjects among adults. A long-term controversy in the Pacific Northwest USA surrounding the conservation of old-growth forests and endangered spotted owls (*Strix occidentalis*) offers a classic example. Some residents framed the conservation debate as being between extremist groups that cared more about useless animals than human needs. Audience research revealed that only 8% of people understood why habitat loss was a cause of species extinction (Beldon and Russonello 1995, cited in Jacobson 2009). Some of those surveyed believed that spotted owls were simply being stubborn by refusing to move from old-growth forests to other places where they would cause less trouble. Therefore, effective outreach programs here needed to address knowledge about the owls' habitat needs as well as the value of conserving the animal and its habitat to support human needs. Obviously, messages framed for a specific audience must address their current knowledge and beliefs. Audience research can help by revealing people's beliefs and attitudes toward a conservation issue.

A leading environmental organization, the World Wide Fund for Nature (WWF), conducted audience research to better understand the public in the many countries in which they have national members. They wanted to examine people's attitudes and behaviors with respect to the environment and their willingness to support WWF initiatives. They conducted a series of focus groups and broad public surveys in 25 countries. The results allowed WWF to understand the wide range of attitudes and support within and across nations and helped them design a two-pronged approach for promoting sustainable environmental behaviors.

For countries where environmental awareness was relatively low (e.g., Greece, Italy, and Spain), WWF developed 30-second television advertisements with light-hearted messages that conveyed the need to curb consumption and wasteful habits like leaving the tap running or the lights on. One advert depicted an elderly woman, in comical fast motion, knitting a sweater to stay warm rather than turning up the thermostat. In contrast, for countries with high levels of environmental awareness (e.g., the Netherlands, New Zealand, and Sweden), WWF used advertising to convey a more sophisticated environmental message. They focused on issues such as the protection of tropical forests, which they found to be of high public concern (Klingemann and Rommele 2002). In these countries, their research suggested that people were already aware that rainforest destruction contributes to global warming and reduction in biodiversity, and that this audience would not require an explanation. Rather, they needed a reminder, or prompt, to examine their own consumer behavior to avoid buying furniture made from tropical hardwood that was unsustainably harvested (Jacobson 2005). WWF (2013) premiered a web series "Stop Wildlife Crimes" on their YouTube channel to build public awareness about the crisis of illegal wildlife trafficking. The 6-minute episodes explore the illegal trade in endangered species and actions to stop the crisis. In an episode entitled "I am not a rug," the images of magnificent tigers are depicted and the threats to their existence exposed. Other groups, such as Splash! Animals (Box 1.3), have joined the WWF "Stop Wildlife Crimes" campaign.

Box 1.3 Splash! Animals

Splash! Animals produced a series of videos providing a live art experience to entertain the audience and connect them with endangered animals (Splash! Animals 2014). The project uses art as a bridge for the audience to make an emotional connection to endangered species and associated wildlife crimes. Each 60-second public service announcement begins with a speed painter standing in front of a blank black canvas and ends with a full image of an endangered animal featuring characteristics that make it special. Christina Grenard, co-founder of Splash! Animals says, "You start with the animal and bring that animal to life, all the while [the audience] is thinking about the plight of the animal. What needs to be done? How can we stop what's happening to this animal? The completed art piece reveals a message. As we stare into the image of the endangered animal, it still exists and we have the potential to stop what's happening and save the magnificent beauty. The goal is to make the audience realize that they need to learn more and take action to stop the criminal action, and improve the situation."

Audience research forms the backbone of a conservation education or outreach program. It guides the development of activities and techniques. Audience research helps you orient your conservation program to meet your audience's needs and to market your organization's products. Knowledge of your target audience can facilitate diffusion of environmental information to opinion leaders and help you spread the message through social media to a broader public. It allows you to assess alternative communication channels and messages for building support for a program or influencing audience behaviors. This type of research is known as formative evaluation. It occurs during planning and implementation of a program to provide feedback for improvements in the "formation" of early stages of the program. The collection of baseline data about your audience also provides information for the later summative evaluation of your education efforts, assessing your end results. Research conducted before and after your program will reveal if your objectives have been achieved and if you had unanticipated or secondary impacts. This allows you to make decisions about whether your program should be modified, cut, or expanded.

1.3.4 Include audience members and potential partners

Effective programs involve audience members and program partners during all stages of a program to meet the mutual needs of the audience and the organization. The involvement of target audience members and other stakeholders in the planning process helps ensure relevance, and promotes a commitment to the implementation and long-term sustainability of the program. Involving a diverse range of people provides different perspectives and ideas for enhancing the development of a program. Their involvement in the planning process also helps to create a sense of community participation, ownership, and interest in the program. It can generate additional resources to assist with labor or funding. For example, the involvement of landowners in planning a native plant workshop helps ensure that the content and format will be appropriate for other landowners who participate in the program. Involvement of parents and community members in schools improves student learning. Involvement of teachers in planning programs for schools ensures that the programs will address education standards and specific curriculum objectives.

Potential partners might include local businesses, resource users, teachers, parents, community leaders, landowners, and agency staff. The planning process will help identify potential audience members and partners as you assess the needs of the program. To develop a group of people to serve in an advisory capacity, think about the ultimate users of the program. The following questions can help guide the process (Seng and Rushton 2003):

- In what specific ways can audience members or potential partners work with you?
- What do you or your program have to offer them?
- Who are the end users for your program?
- Who has special expertise to contribute to the design or content?
- Which groups and individuals should be represented on your advisory committee?
- What are the specific roles and responsibilities of the committee members?

A program in Fez, Morocco, was designed to improve solid waste collection through better outreach and technology and involved many stakeholders in the planning process. These included policy-makers, neighborhood residents, community leaders, municipal truck drivers, sanitation engineers, health professionals, and solid waste experts. During the 2-week planning meeting, the group researched the solid waste system as well as the social structure of the community. The end result was a program that represented a broad consensus and investment from all groups concerned with implementing it (Grieser 2000).

1.3.5 Make an inventory of resources and constraints

A realistic view of the strengths and constraints of time, personnel, money, and other resources provides a basis for selecting activities. Constraints limit the activities you can consider. For example, television advertisements may be beyond your budget, emails may not reach your intended audience, or the lack of enough trained staff may turn a wilderness field trip into a nightmare.

Timing of your activities may correspond to the annual calendar, seasonal occurrences, natural phenomena, school schedules, or special days. Other activities may be required at a moment's notice to respond to an unexpected opportunity or problem. No matter what the timing, the schedule for any activity requires careful planning to provide sufficient days to successfully complete each task.

Staffing requirements must be realistically gauged. Who will do what? If many people are needed to help with events, where will they come from? Empty niches can be filled by volunteers from the community, scouts, club members, interns from local colleges, or temporary hires. Each alternative has advantages, but may require additional resources for training, or stipends.

Accurate assessment of the funds needed versus the funds available is critical for planning an education and outreach program. Resources must be allocated efficiently, focusing on priority activities. How much money should be spent on your public programs? Budgeting involves determining your educational objectives, identifying the tasks needed to accomplish the objectives, and determining the costs of these activities. If your budget is too small, consider substituting alternative activities, redefining the objectives, or finding partners to share the costs. If funds are unavailable you may be able to get grants or donations of money, goods, or services in support of the program. Fundraising may often be an objective in itself.

1.3.6 Select activities and messages

The final stage of the planning process identifies appropriate activities to meet the objectives for each target audience. This book provides a selection of techniques, from personal interactions to mass media. In developing materials and choosing delivery systems for your program, consider the background, needs, and interests of your learners in order to determine which teaching or outreach techniques will work best under your conditions. For example, abstract ideas are fine for older teenagers, yet nonsensical for young children (see Chapter 2). Activities must be attuned to the situation, and should depend on the results of your inventory of budgets, personnel, time frames, and other constraints and opportunities. Your own experience and observation of similar effective programs can provide a wellspring of ideas for specific activities.

How do you choose techniques that will effectively reach the target audience? Using a variety of techniques may be the way to reach sufficient numbers of people segmented by factors such as age, education, occupation, recreation activities, or geographic location. Different audience characteristics may call for different techniques—speeches, demonstrations, emails, texting, or placement of messages in specialized newsletters. Knowing the media habits of your audience is one obvious way to target a message. For example, an article in *The Times* of London may effectively reach policy-makers' eyes, but few farmers may ever read it. An article in an agricultural newsletter may better target farmers. The use of more than one technique increases the likelihood of reaching a greater audience; repetition reinforces the message. When selecting techniques for teaching about conservation, evaluate factors such as potential impact, the expense of production and dissemination, and audience size (Box 1.4). Other chapters in this book describe the strengths of various techniques.

As you are identifying techniques and activities to meet your objectives, research other programs that have used similar techniques. Do not waste time reinventing the wheel if good-quality materials are already available or could be adapted to your use. Just as you involved your target audience in planning, invite key stakeholders and experts to participate in program development, such as gathering resources, writing lesson

Box 1.4 Factors that influence decisions about appropriate messages and media

Factors	Questions to ask
Background and habits of the audience	What are the interests and media sources of your target audiences?
Attributes of the message	Does it require background knowledge, maps, graphics, color, or sound?
Urgency of the message	Do you need a response today or next month?
Complexity of the message	Is a 30-second soundbite or 140 characters adequate for the message or is a detailed educational technique necessary?
Frequency of the message	Is repetition needed regularly, seasonally, infrequently? Do new people keep joining the target audience?
Personnel required	Is staff time available for personal contact, developing materials, providing outreach activities, training volunteers, and interfacing with media representatives or social media platforms?
Cost	How many in your target audience can be reached, for how long, with what detail, at what price?

Source: Jacobson (2009)

plans, reviewing drafts, creating graphics, and sharing experiences on social media. Environmental extension or agency staff or other experts can provide good data and feedback for program development and teachers can help develop curriculum supplements. Offering free materials, stipends, or recognition helps provide stakeholders with incentives to participate in the development of your program. You may need to raise funds to pay for outside experts or materials to complete your program development.

1.4 Implementation

1.4.1 Pilot test activities

Once your activities have been developed, you are ready to pilot test and implement your program. Just like a rehearsal before a theater production, practicing your activities with an audience before implementing them allows you to fine-tune your performance or postpone the opening day while changes are made. This is called piloting or pretesting the activities. Pilot tests are a form of evaluation conducted as a program is being developed, and also part of formative evaluation. Pilot tests involve subjecting a small group of the target audience to your planned activity or materials. Pilot tests answer questions such as:

- How do members of the audience react to the activity?
- Which alternative versions of the activities are most successful?
- Does the activity communicate the appropriate message for achieving the objective?
- What feedback do people give about the activity?

Pilot tests are conducted before a program is fully implemented. They help ensure that the activities are effective, and allow the needed changes to be made before the expense of implementing the entire program is incurred.

Methods for collecting data about an activity include focus groups or surveys with members of the target audience as they are exposed to your program and monitoring of social media sites. For written materials, approaches include a portfolio review, which entails placing new educational material in a folder alone or with alternative material and asking the test subjects from the target audience for their reactions. The audience can relay their impressions of the materials verbally, or they can complete a questionnaire using ratings or scales (e.g., very attractive/attractive/neutral/unattractive/very unattractive). Impressions about the main message, level of detail, appropriate audience, illustrations, graphics, and relevance guide decisions about the need for modification. Once feedback is obtained, the activity or materials can be revised, if needed, and pilot tested again before the campaign is executed. Pilot testing ensures that the best materials and activities are implemented (Fig. 1.4).

Pilot tests were critical for the Florida Wildlife Federation. Before the Federation embarked on a new magazine for its members they wisely pilot tested it. They sent a trial magazine issue with a written survey to a sample of 240 members. The survey asked the members what they liked most and least about the publication, and how much they might pay to receive such a magazine. Based on the negative responses to

Fig. 1.4 During pilot testing, a visitor provides feedback on the design for conservation messages embedded on park picnic tables. (Photo by S. Jacobson.)

the survey and the high cost of the project, the Federation rejected the entire activity of publishing a magazine (Jacobson 2009). Local teachers participating in a pilot test of a teaching resource guide about pine forests in the Bahamas helped identify unclear directions and several student activities that would not work in large classrooms. The resource book was completely revised before distribution to schools throughout the islands.

1.4.2 Program operations

During implementation, develop a final schedule and budget and formalize the responsibilities of project staff. The establishment of a system for oversight of program operations ensures that the activities you select will continue to achieve your objectives. Monitoring tells you when your program activities are running smoothly or if modifications are needed.

The remainder of this book provides examples and inspirational models of the implementation of more than 50 techniques for education and outreach programs. Experiential approaches such as field trips and hands-on activities engage participants through direct experiences (Chapter 5). Using the arts for conservation can elicit emotional responses and attract new audiences (Chapter 6). Project-based learning connects schools and communities and leads to creative solutions to local problems (Chapter 7). Forming partnerships with other organizations and audiences will increase the success of your conservation efforts (Chapter 8). Social marketing approaches are useful for targeting specific audience behaviors. The adoption of new behaviors like recycling or composting frequently occurs as a result of friends, family members, or colleagues introducing people to them (Chapters 3 and 9). Using mass media, educational technologies, and social media can have a powerful role in setting the public agenda and reinforcing opinions (Chapters 10 and 11). Long-term educational activities or interpersonal methods are often needed to change an audience's fundamental knowledge, or shift their attitudes, as described in a number of chapters. Activities conducted in natural areas and community centers can provide profound experiences in nature, or foster social interaction to effectively reach your audience (Chapter 12). The many examples in each chapter help demonstrate effective implementation of the exciting techniques available to support conservation goals.

1.5 Evaluation

During and after any education and outreach program, conservation educators must ask if their objectives are being met:

- Did the target audience receive the message?
- Were the materials recognized; was the message remembered?
- Was the audience interested, satisfied, or engaged with the activity?
- Are there changes in audience knowledge, attitudes, or skills?
- Are there long-term changes in resource use or participant behavior, or increased concern for environmental management or conservation legislation?
- Are there improvements in the wildlife, ecosystem, or other conservation target?

Evaluation reveals if the program is worth the time, money, and resources. Is it cost-effective? Does it need modification? Should it be continued or cut? Are there unanticipated results? Evaluation is the only systematic means of finding the answers to these questions. It is key to providing feedback for improving conservation education and outreach programs in general, and for providing accountability to funding agencies, staff, and audiences of specific programs. Without evaluation, ineffective outreach can harm the natural resources that your efforts seek to protect. A program may fail to reach the target audience, the message may be misunderstood, or the wrong behavior may be targeted. Without evaluation, hope of recognizing or improving a failed program is small.

Program outcomes may be immediate or long term, and expected or unanticipated. Methods for evaluating education and outreach include a wide range of techniques from formal before-and-after surveys to direct observations of the target audience or their impacts on the environment. To measure the effectiveness of an education and outreach program to conserve a rare wildlife species, you might count the number of new members who join your organization, funds donated to purchase key habitat, legislators' votes to pass protective measures, increases in public awareness after your campaign, and, ultimately, the status of a wildlife population or conservation target after a certain time period. You can also design controlled experiments, where, for example, you might test radio adverts versus an interactive website for a specific audience. Results can then be compared to evaluate the efficacy of different media. Continuous assessment allows you to modify activities based on timely feedback and new information. Results often are evaluated in terms of changes in public awareness, attitudes, or behaviors, and the cost-effectiveness and efficiency of the program. Evaluation of outcomes tells whether your educational strategy has worked and allows you to make decisions about the fate of the program—whether it should be continued, cut, or expanded.

1.5.1 Designing an evaluation

A popular method for planning an evaluation uses a logic model to guide program design and assessment (Box 1.5). Program inputs are the materials, staff, funds, facilities, and environmental and community resources identified during the planning process. Program throughputs include the techniques and activities that were implemented and the participants involved. Program objectives target specific outputs and outcomes. All facets of the logic model are influenced by external environmental, and social factors, for example political, economic, or institutional constraints.

The model requires that *logic* be used to align program activities with the desired outcomes stated in your objectives. If your program focuses on factual information, you would expect participants to display a short-term outcome of learning. If the goal is action, your program may need to provide similar information, but also incorporate experiential activities that develop the skills required for participants to take action. Your evaluation will measure whether these outputs and outcomes have been achieved. Reviewing evaluation results from similar programs can help practitioners anticipate likely outcomes. A number of online resources share evaluation results, for example MEERA (My Environmental Education Evaluation Resources Assistant, <http://www. meera.snre.umich.edu/>), and guides like the *Rare Pride Handbook* (Rare 2007) are available.

Planning an evaluation requires choices to be made regarding the evaluation design, data collection, analysis, and use of the evaluation results. The answers to the questions in Box 1.6 are derived from negotiation among the evaluator, program staff, audiences, and administrators. In schools, standardized tests dictated by educational institutions may set benchmarks that should be included in the evaluation of your program. Other large organizations may have existing benchmarks, or metrics, to help measure success.

1.5.2 Evaluation objectives

Evaluation methods range from experimental and quantitative methods (e.g., before-and-after tests) to informal qualitative measurement indices (e.g., focus groups, observation, and direct interview techniques). The type of evaluation questions you ask will guide your data collection; for example, the level of detail in your evaluation will be based on your educational objectives. You will probably want to assess both outputs and outcomes of your program as detailed in your logic model.

Outputs

The easiest level of impact to evaluate simply measures the activities and products of the education or outreach campaign. What did you produce and how much exposure did your activities receive? How many people attended your program? Who participated

Box 1.5 The logic model diagrams elements of program planning, implementation, and evaluation

Planning	Implementation	Evaluation				
Inputs	*Throughputs*	*Outputs*		*Outcomes*		
Resources	Activities	Participation	Counts/feedback	Short-term (learning)	Medium-term (action)	Long-term (conditions)
Teachers Staff Volunteers Curricula clinics Donors Time Money Materials Equipment Technology Partners	Curriculum design Product development Workshops Meetings Events Facilitation Assessments Media work Training	Participants Customers Stakeholders Volunteers Trainers Teachers Youth Families Students	Numbers reached Experiences Surveys Feedback Service units Cost per unit Service quality Aspirations	Awareness Motivations Knowledge Values Attitudes Opinions Skills	Practice Decisions Action Behavior Stewardship Policies	Social Political Civic Environmental

CONTEXT/INFLUENTIAL ENVIRONMENTAL FACTORS AND ASSUMPTIONS.

Adapted from Seng and Rushton (2003).

Box 1.6 Key questions for evaluation

Design of the evaluation

- What are the evaluation questions or objectives?
- What are the evaluation criteria or indicators of success?
- Who will be involved in the evaluation? If an experimental design is selected, how will random assignment to control and treatment groups be done?
- How will the results from the evaluation be used?

Data collection

- What are the information sources?
- Which data collection methods are most appropriate for the evaluation questions?
- How large is the sample? What sampling methods, if any, are needed?
- How will the quality of the data be ensured?
- Will data collection instruments need to be pilot tested?
- When will the data be collected?

Data analysis

- How should the data be analyzed?
- Are software and expertise available for statistical analyses, if needed?
- What is the most useful format for the data?

Source: Jacobson (2009).

---

and who did not? Was the content suitable for the audience? How many events, press releases, publications, followers on social media, and other outputs were produced? Did they reach your target audience? Outputs include the number of students participating in a schoolyard ecosystem program, the number of workshops on biological corridors provided to journalists, or the number of brochures or blog posts provided to farmers on adapting to climate change. Thorough records of activities, schedules, and participants are used to measure these outputs.

Short-term learning outcomes

Measurements of outcomes are often more complex. Measurements attempt to determine whether or not the target audience received, paid attention to, understood, and retained your conservation message, and in what form. You can conduct public opinion surveys to find out if your target audience has been exposed to your conservation message. Data collection tools such as focus groups, in-depth interviews, and polling of target audiences are necessary to answer these types of evaluation questions. Before-and-after tests and portfolio reviews are used in school contexts. Students' knowledge about ecological principles is evaluated in a science test, or their field journals are reviewed for their understanding of a class on pond ecology.

Medium-term action outcomes

The next level of impact seeks to measure changes in the opinions, attitudes, and behaviors of the target audiences, and improvements in conservation targets. Are audiences using new knowledge and skills to help protect the environment? Are more people removing exotic plants from their landscapes or participating in recycling programs? To determine these outcomes, techniques like surveys and experimental designs and unobtrusive methods such as observation and role-playing may be used. Behavioral changes can also be measured through secondary indicators. For example, targeted homeowners may be expected to use less fertilizer in order to protect local water bodies, which could be measured as reduced sales at local garden centers.

Long-term condition outcomes

The last level of impact measures changes in the environment that are due to changes in the behaviors of target audiences. Have populations of threatened species recovered? Is the environment cleaner? Are resources being used sustainably? Have communities implemented plans to build resilience to the impacts of climate change? On-the-ground measurement of environmental, economic, and social indicators is necessary to monitor impacts in the field, and to identify additional programs needed beyond education and outreach activities.

1.5.3 Data collection for an evaluation

This subsection describes useful tools for collecting the data needed to answer evaluation questions (adapted from Jacobson 2009). The advantages and disadvantages of the methods are outlined. These techniques also are useful for collecting baseline data to guide program planning.

Production of activities and participant counts

Simple measurements of outputs of your program are useful for evaluating impacts. These include monitoring the number of products and activities produced, as well as the number of participants. Such documentation provides a simple and inexpensive means of recording activities. It is useful for long-term monitoring of activities and audiences. Baseline data from such indicators can provide comparison for measuring increases in program products, audience size, and new activities. Other monitoring methods, such as monitoring mass media to determine coverage of a press release or followers on Twitter to document increased audience numbers, are used to assess outputs. Keep in mind, however, that measurement of outputs does not measure actual impacts and may sometimes be misleading. Thirty people may attend your workshop on sustainable forest management, but none may implement new practices.

Tests of attitudes, knowledge, skills, and behavior

This method measures a sample of the target population with attitude questionnaires, or knowledge or skills tests that address the objectives of the conservation education program. The evaluator tests the sample before implementation, but after program completion, to measure specific impacts of the education intervention. Tests are easy to administer and score, particularly in a school setting. They also make it easy to obtain a large sample. Tests may involve an experimental or a time series design. In an experimental design, subjects are randomly assigned to a treatment (i.e., educational activity) or a control group, while in a time series design the evaluator measures subjects on some indicator before a program and at several data collection points during and after the program to assess changes over a period of time. The results of the tests can be compared statistically to determine changes resulting from the education program (Fig. 1.5). A disadvantage of tests is that they may be threatening to participants, and are often not appropriate outside of school. They also miss unexpected program outcomes.

Surveys

A survey is a systematic way of collecting information from a sample of people. The results of surveys are used to make generalizations about a target population. Survey research is used commonly during the planning stage of a program to measure public attitudes and knowledge, and to characterize a target audience, where they live, and what their concerns are. Surveys of voters' attitudes about conservation legislation can tell promoters what types of benefits to emphasize, for example, the benefit of clean drinking water rather than recreational opportunities resulting from legislation about

Fig. 1.5 Students take a test after visiting a demonstration about medicinal plants at Kinabalu Park in Sabah, Malaysia. (Photo by S. Jacobson.)

wetlands protection. Surveys can be conducted on site, through the mail, telephone, or Internet. Insight provided about the levels of knowledge of your audience and their opinions and attitudes toward conservation issues can be used to successfully reach them with appropriate programs. Surveys are useful both for collecting information on broad societal issues and for detailed site- or program-specific problems. Specific objectives of a survey might be to describe:

- the social and political make-up of your target audience
- sources of information for audience members
- audience opinion about current issues such as new ecosystem management practices
- priorities of conservation problems for the audience
- compromises people may be willing to make on environmental or economic issues
- current levels of knowledge among the audience, for example, which specific aspects of ecosystem management do park neighbors not understand
- possible audience reactions to a new policy or communications campaign message
- the willingness of the audience to support or pay for new initiatives.

Many books are available for designing valid and reliable surveys (e.g., Dillman 2007; Vaske 2008; Ernst et al. 2009). Results of systematic surveys conducted before and after a program help measure changes in audience knowledge or attitudes that can be associated with the program.

Surveys are cost-effective for collecting factual data from large groups. Results from random samples surveyed can be generalized to the larger population. Problems with surveys are created by bias from small numbers of respondents or the inability to probe the target audience for complex information.

Interviews with participants

In an evaluation, interviews provide immediate data regarding a program's effectiveness. The personal contact between the evaluator and the respondent allows for the collection of more detailed information than a written survey. Participants in interviews can provide data on the strengths and weaknesses of a program and suggestions for improvement. Interviewers can ask for opinions about specific learning or skill outcomes. Common interview questions that participants might be asked include:

- What did you like most about the program?
- What did you like least about the program?
- How would you improve the program for the future?

Interviews may focus on other stakeholders besides the target audience, including donors, program staff, parents, government officials, and community members. Interviews can be structured or unstructured, either following a preset interview guide or allowing the interviewee to digress from the initial questions. Interviews with visitors to an environmental art exhibit may reveal that the program provided new perspectives about a conservation issue or, alternatively, that the material was too obscure and the objectives were not achieved.

One specialized interview technique makes use of photographic documents. Photo interviewing involves taking photographs of participants engaged in an activity, and then using the photographs as interview prompts with participants. Showing a photograph of a farmer planting a native shade tree may stimulate a rich discussion about the effectiveness of a reforestation program. Photographs help participants remember their attitudes and receptivity toward an activity at various points in the program.

Interviews can provide in-depth information, in contrast to written surveys and other techniques that limit feedback. On the other hand, personal interviews can be costly and time-consuming to conduct. Responses can be difficult to analyze, and interviewer or response bias is hard to eliminate.

Focus groups and meetings

Focus groups, public meetings, and advisory committees can provide information for designing new programs and fostering audience support and participation. Focus groups are a useful data collection tool for exploring the general attitudes, motivations, and behaviors of your audience. Focus groups are often used during the planning (formative) stage of a program to receive feedback from a specific target audience about ideas and educational approaches. Educators use focus groups to:

- obtain background information about people's perceptions of a specific topic,
- generate ideas or effective approaches for introducing a new service, product, program, or organization, and
- stimulate new research or interpret previous results from quantitative research.

A focus group consists of an interview with a group of 7–12 individuals, such as urban high school students or community leaders in a rural town, who share some key characteristics (e.g., age, occupation, or interests). A moderator facilitates the focus group meeting using an interview guide. Respondents interact with each other as well as with the interviewer, potentially stimulating new ideas or insights. The session is videotaped for review and analysis. A focus group engaged in a discussion about recreation and other uses of a national park can reveal a range of options for park management planning (Fig. 1.6).

Other group interview techniques involve drawing and mapping exercises. These are most appropriate when evaluating community or individual perceptions of a program with visually oriented cultures or with children. Drawings produced by individuals or a group can facilitate discussion, as well as provide comparison for later drawings. Maps produced by community members are useful tools for monitoring land use and perceptions of land-use change. Community mapping of protected areas can help managers determine zoning and land uses (Eadens et al. 2009). Maps drawn by different groups of people can serve as baseline and comparison data before and after a conservation outreach program is conducted.

Focus groups and other group techniques are socially oriented and allow moderators to probe into a complex issue. This method is inexpensive and provides quick results. Conversely, group methods can be difficult to control and to analyze. They require a trained moderator.

Fig. 1.6 Researcher Browne-Nunez conducts a focus group with Maasai women about their experiences with wildlife around Amboseli National Park, Kenya. (Photo by R. Nunez.)

Observation

Observational techniques provide a useful evaluation tool, especially for assessing behavior. The method involves observing participants before, during, and after a conservation education or outreach program. Some evaluations use behavioral checklists for recording the presence, absence, and frequency of behaviors. Observers must be properly trained to ensure reliable results. If it is impossible to observe the actual program, evaluators can record and analyze audience behaviors from the observation of videos. Photographs can also be used to document changes before and after a program. For example, photographs of a natural area can document a reduction in the amount of trash following a public awareness campaign on littering.

Other forms of systematic observation of behavior involve role-playing or simulation games, in which participants enact "theoretical" situations of interest to the evaluator. Such dramatics can provide insight into the impact of a program, as participants often express attitudes that would be concealed in an interview or survey. Participants in a workshop on conflict negotiation may be asked to role-play a dispute over fisheries issues to test whether new skills were learned.

In general observational techniques are non-threatening to participants and offer an effective way to measure changes in behavior. Keep in mind that the results of observation can be unreliable and trained observers are required.

Content analysis and document review

Content analysis represents an efficient and objective tool for evaluating the text of documents or other materials. To conduct a content analysis, you must first determine which documents to evaluate and define the unit of analysis. For example, you may wish to review all Ugandan Wildlife Authority brochures from 1990 to 2015 for Queen Elizabeth National Park. Your variable of interest might be references to lion conservation messages. After coding the references to lions from each brochure, the evaluator calculates the frequency and type of lion-related information over the years. To evaluate coverage of conservation issues in the mass media, content analysis can be used to quantify the frequency of press releases, blog posts, or twitter feeds on a specific topic, placement within the news, the number of people potentially reached, messages expressed, and the attitude conveyed toward the topic or organization. A content analysis of newspaper coverage of wildfires and prescribed burning in Florida found that the media emphasized the benefits of prescribed fire for preventing wildfires but ignored the benefits of maintaining wildlife habitat or controlling pests. This suggested new topics for an outreach campaign about Florida's fire-adapted ecosystems (Jacobson et al. 2001). A content analysis of the websites of Turkish environmental non-profit organizations revealed that they did not take advantage of social media, only 19 of 50 sites analyzed had social network accounts, and only 10 sites had "like" links. Facilitating public dialogue through websites is crucial for ensuring relevant and current communication, and the analysis was used to make recommendations for improving organizational outreach (Uzunoğlu and Misci 2014).

Case study

A case study is a qualitative evaluation tool that focuses on an in-depth portrayal of one program, institution, or community. The results of a case study provide detailed insight into a particular program and its outcomes. The specific context and impacts are analyzed in detail. Based on the results of a case study, evaluators can make recommendations concerning the methods, tools, audiences, and impacts of a program. A case study of the public outreach program to support the reintroduction of wolves into Yellowstone National Park provided recommendations for modifying the program (Jacobson 1999). The case study also provided examples to other agencies faced with the public outreach challenge of reintroducing carnivores into a region. Similarly, a study of local policymakers' perceptions of climate change risk helped managers develop outreach materials focused on critical local concerns (Carlton and Jacobson 2013). Although the results of a case study cannot be generalized and are dependent on the availability of data, case studies provide in-depth understanding of a situation. Multiple case studies of similar programs might be used to make comparisons or draw broader conclusions.

Portfolios and projects

Portfolios and projects are useful tools for measuring the growth of new knowledge and development of skills in an audience. Portfolios are collections of participants' work that demonstrate increasing capabilities. Portfolios may include journals, reports, displays, illustrations, videos, or other media selected by the participant and evaluator. Scoring guidelines, called rubrics, are often used to evaluate individual projects. Students are graded on factors including their participation in the project, accuracy of information, presence or absence of specific facts or skills, clarity of presentation or visual aids. Group projects are often prescribed as the outcome for cooperative learning assignments in schools. Products might include group presentations or interaction with a community issue, such as the restoration of a city park. These alternatives to traditional testing may be difficult to use in some school settings.

Using multiple evaluation techniques

Using more than one technique for evaluation will strengthen your analysis by capitalizing on the strengths of different methods and minimizing the weaknesses. The use of several methods combines multiple data sources, perspectives, and investigators or participants in data gathering. This provides crosschecks to validate your findings. Accurate program assessments result in more effective education and outreach programs.

1.6 Summary

Effective education and outreach are essential for influencing conservation policy, involving more people in conservation initiatives, improving people's knowledge and behaviors, garnering funds, and sharing scientific advances. The fate of our environment depends on effective communication with a great variety of audiences.

Systematic planning, implementation, and evaluation is the foundation of effective education and outreach programs. This chapter has discussed the PIE guidelines for developing programs. Planning activities begin by identifying education and outreach needs, objectives, and audiences. Possible strategies are selected based on the available resources and constraints of time, money, and staff. The planning process provides information for making decisions about the nature and scope of your actions. Implementation involves pilot testing strategies and monitoring ongoing operations. Evaluations should be conducted both during and after implementation of your program. Formative evaluation occurs during planning and implementation of a program, and provides feedback for design and improvement in the early stages of a program. Summative evaluation is conducted at the end of a program and addresses questions about the program's worth. Program staff, consumers, participants, and funding agencies use information from summative evaluations to answer questions regarding the impacts and continuation of a program.

The evaluation of products and outcomes tells you if your tactics worked. A variety of quantitative and qualitative techniques provide data for making decisions about the fate of the program—if it should be continued, cut, or expanded. Following a systematic approach helps avoid problems such as targeting the wrong audience or using an inappropriate message or medium. Most conservation concerns are urgent. Applying these guidelines as you implement the techniques described in the rest of this book will help ensure your success.

Learning and teaching

Why do we develop conservation education and outreach programs? Because we want people, our audiences, to know more about their environment, care about their environment, and make choices that support conservation. Research shows us that educational programs can help achieve these objectives. Examples abound of people who make the wrong choice because they lack information or fail to act because they just weren't aware of the problem or the solution. Offering effective conservation education programs that increase knowledge and shift attitudes can enable people to understand the need for conservation practices. This chapter offers an introduction to theories about learning and teaching that support effective programs for adults and young people. Since these theories are important to teachers, conservation educators who wish to work with school personnel may find these ideas helpful (Box 2.1). Chapter 3 offers additional theories that can be used in education and outreach programs to motivate people to engage in appropriate conservation behaviors.

2.1 What is learning?

When pressed to identify what conservation educators really want to achieve in educational programs, some might say their goal is for audiences to "understand" the ecology of the area or the implications of conservation issues. To understand means that a learner has a mental model (also called a cognitive map) of a concept that enables them to retrieve information, add new information, draw appropriate connections between related ideas, and use this mental model to solve problems (Kaplan and Kaplan 1982; Pritchard and Woollard 2010). The learning process begins with sensory perception of information. We might see it, read it, hear it, experience it, or smell it. The more we pay attention, the more likely it is that this information will trigger something we already know, activating that memory from long-term storage and moving it into our short-term memory where we can use it, develop it, and expand our knowledge. Once it is no longer active, that information goes into our long-term memory where we store an apparently bottomless pit of experiences.

Retrieval and use of this stored information becomes easier the more frequently we move that information into short-term memory and use it. It takes some degree of work in the form of attention and processing to actually learn from our experiences, to either adequately recall the right mental model or embed new information so that it will be accessible in the future. The more information and experience we have with a concept,

Conservation Education and Outreach Techniques. Second Edition. Susan K. Jacobson, Mallory D. McDuff & Martha C. Monroe © Susan K. Jacobson, Mallory D. McDuff & Martha C. Monroe 2015. Published 2015 by Oxford University Press.

Box 2.1 Overview of learning theories and concepts

Theory or concept	Contribution to education
Piaget's cognitive development	Young children should be engaged in more concrete learning; older children are more capable of increasingly complex and nebulous concepts.
Brain-based learning	Learning opportunities should reinforce neural networks and enable learners to expand mental models.
Experiential learning	Doing and reflecting on the experience helps learners build mental models that can be applied in new situations.
Constructivism	Learners' existing mental models can prevent new information from being adequately assimilated. Questions and discussion can reveal prior knowledge.
Inquiry learning	Questions guide discovery and help learners practice how to learn.
Social cognitive theory	Observing models and behaviors helps youngsters learn. Social influences interact with experiences, expectations, and motivation to create self-efficacy and learning.
Activity theory	Interaction with the social environment creates opportunities for learning and change.
Social learning	Interactions with those who have different experiences or perceptions helps people learn.
Cooperative learning	Group interactions can be designed to engage all learners in gaining content as well as group process and communication skills.
Bloom's taxonomy of the cognitive domain	Thinking skills vary from memorizing information to applying and creating ideas.
Critical thinking	Opportunities to evaluate information for bias, compare conflicting sources, and interpret information build lifelong skills.
Creative thinking	Opportunities to see new connections, solve problems, and generate new ideas build important skills.
Systems thinking	Understanding complex systems requires that learners see connections and relationships at various scales.
Comprehensive model	One model blends how we gain and process information.

the more dense that mental model becomes, and the easier it becomes to use and retrieve our ideas. Experts, for example, have great familiarity and confidence in the mental models that include their expertise, which allows them to reorganize information, seek novel connections, and solve problems. Thus, learning occurs when mental models have been reorganized to accommodate new information.

Thinking is the activity that builds and rebuilds mental structures. It includes processing perceptions and sensory input, retrieving appropriate prior knowledge, reflecting on and comparing both the new evidence and the old concept, altering or accommodating those initial conceptions if needed, and assimilating the new information into a fresh mental model. Long heralded as the goal of a good education, thinking has become a skill that educators aim to improve. Conservation educators who work with schools may wish to develop programs that enhance critical thinking, creative thinking, or systems thinking skills. These techniques are worth using because they ultimately help build understanding and environmental literacy.

Whether in a classroom or on a mountainside, interacting with others and our environment gives us the information and experiences to modify our mental models and learn. Although individuals do the work of learning, both the individuals and the information usually exist in social contexts. Children are in classrooms, and often with siblings at home. Adults can be in community groups or workplace training. We are very good at picking up cues from others, including how they are appreciating, engaging with, or ignoring new information. In addition, the process of explaining what we know to others is an important strategy for strengthening our own mental models. So a good deal of the learning process is affected by our social and cultural environment.

If learning is something that individuals must do, then teaching is the process of creating opportunities that make it possible for learners to gain information and do the hard work of reflecting and altering their mental models. In some environments, and with some learners, educators enhance motivation to learn as well. The more educators know about the learners' interests and prior knowledge, the better they can design a new experience that will attract attention or curiosity, be relevant and meaningful, and be enjoyable. The process of learning should be the same for everyone, yet what we learn is a function of what we already knew, the development of our mental facilities, our motivation, and our environment. Thus there will be differences in understanding between individuals due to varying culture, experience, and age.

This chapter explores these basic ideas in more detail with a focus on the following concepts: (1) learning is a function of mental activity; (2) learning is a function of experience and reflection; and (3) learning is affected by interactions with others and the environment. This chapter provides specific insights into thinking skills, particularly critical, creative, and systems thinking, which contribute additional elements to effective conservation education.

2.2 Learning and mental activity

We exercise the capacity to learn throughout our lives. Information from the world is perceived and synapses between neurons are strengthened or weakened. We perceive

---

Box 2.2 Piaget's stages of cognitive development

- *Sensorimotor stage (infancy)*. Knowledge of the world is limited (but developing) because it is based on physical interactions or experiences. Mobility allows the child to gain experience and develop new cognitive abilities.
- *Preoperational stage (toddler and early childhood)*. Children begin to use symbols, language use matures, and memory and imagination are developed, but thinking is done in a non-logical, non-reversible manner. Egocentric thinking predominates.
- *Concrete operational stage (elementary and early adolescence)*. In this stage cognitive ability is demonstrated through logical and systematic manipulation of symbols related to concrete objects. Children can imagine actions that are reversible.
- *Formal operational stage (adolescence and adulthood)*. In this stage, cognitive ability is demonstrated through the logical use of symbols related to abstract concepts. Only 35% of high-school graduates in industrialized countries reach this stage; many people do not think formally even in adulthood.

Adapted from Huitt and Hummel (2003).

---

different things, and make sense of the same thing differently, based on our prior knowledge and experience. The development of our brains matters, too. Jean Piaget, a Swiss psychologist, noted that as children grow they develop mentally as well as physically. The process of cognitive development begins to override instinctive reflexes even in infants, who develop the ability to use sensory input to understand their world (Box 2.2). Toddlers begin to use language to symbolize physical items, and usually between the ages of 7 and 11 children develop the ability to generalize from concrete experiences, but are less adept in situations they have not experienced before. Beyond the age of 11 children are better able to deal with abstractions, solve problems, and manipulate their mental models to hypothesize about events they have not witnessed. Research suggests that the area of the brain associated with judgment, weighing risks, and considering consequences (i.e., the dorsal lateral prefrontal cortex) is among the last to develop and may not mature until the age of 20 (Davis 2005). In addition, some individuals demonstrate the capacity to learn languages, for example, more easily than others, suggesting that some combination of genetic predisposition or environmental stimuli might affect development of the brain.

Cognitive development theory suggests that young children should be able to learn from concrete objects and experiences they can manipulate and sense. This would suggest that global issues such as climate change and biodiversity, or abstract concepts such as air pollution and energy conservation, may not be well understood by youngsters until they move into the formal operational stage. Conservation education programs should respect the abilities of their audience by making sure programs are "developmentally appropriate," both cognitively and emotionally. Because young children explore a world that is fairly close to home, effective educational programs tend to be limited to concrete concepts found in their neighborhood or schools. As older children expand their territory to include community centers, nearby parks, and more abstract ideas, educational programs can accommodate their interests by focusing on complex, global, or abstract issues (Smith and Sobel 2010).

2.2.1 Brain-based learning

Ideas about learning may have been developed from observations of children, but they have been confirmed by neurological research on brains. The human brain is a complex system of billions of neurons that store memory by generating links between neurons in a neural network. Neurons continue to grow throughout life, though the learning period may be slower and more frustrating for older learners than the young. Neuron growth can be enhanced with good nutrition and supportive environments, that is, less stressful or threatening surroundings (Jensen 2008).

If the goal of an educational event is for learners to gain knowledge, the typical measure of success is the ability to repeat or show what has been learned. This makes memory the key to learning. The more we know about how memory works, the better we can devise educational opportunities to enhance learning.

One form of memory functions below the level of consciousness. It enables us to automatically perform routines out of habit, like getting dressed, responding to children, harvesting food, or going to work. Because these behaviors are not performed with conscious recall, they are difficult to change, though skill development can help modify them.

Within the area of consciousness, memory enables us to store facts and figures by applying effort and also to learn from repeated experiences without any effort at all. It is a powerful tool that allows us to abstract common features from many events and store them collectively. This means that we do not remember every distinct event, but instead form a general impression that is quite serviceable. When learners practice skills, repeat concepts, or write summaries, they are retrieving stored information, reinforcing the neural networks that include this new information, and making it more likely that the proper associations will be made if it is triggered by a cue. Reading about a forest, visiting a forest, drawing a picture of a forest, and listing the plants and animals that live in a forest are different learning activities that employ a range of skills but reinforce the concept of a forest. The more frequently a memory is activated, the more quickly it can be recalled. Educators can assist learners in the recall process by helping them realize the cues that will stimulate the appropriate information (Jensen 2000; Bauer 2005).

We pay attention to our world through both involuntary attention (automatic) and directed attention (requiring effort). Some things attract our attention like a magnet, for example dangerous animals, sharp noises, and quick movement; such stimuli might have affected our survival 10,000 years ago. Directed attention includes those things that we might find interesting but also things that require effort to "pay attention" to, where the effort usually involves ignoring other stimuli that conspire to steal our limited attention. Stress and overstimulation can reduce our capacity for directed attention. Interestingly, a variety of studies have shown that using involuntary attention is a mechanism for restoring directed attention (Kaplan 1978). Gardening, walking in a park, and even seeing trees out an office window can evoke a sense of tranquility which helps recover our capacity for directed attention (Kaplan and Kaplan 1989; Faber Taylor et al. 2001).

Our brains are able to retain information from a variety of sources simultaneously— smells, tastes, emotions, sight, and sounds, as well as context and time. Stimuli that are experienced together become connected by neural links. If one piece of information is triggered, the rest are more likely to be activated. This enables us to learn vast amounts of information and maintain an organizational system so that appropriate information can be retrieved when needed. Emotion can modulate memory, so that interesting, challenging, or relevant information is more easily remembered (Bauer 2005). Educators who ask learners to help identify and then resolve community problems are using the learners' ownership and interest in the problem they choose to increase learning. Similarly, emotional connections to content can motivate learning, which may be one reason why field trips to nature centers and zoos are memorable.

The way we learn new information is also coded into our memories along with the information itself. Reading about fishing regulations, nets, and lures will give people information they can repeat, but may not give them skills they can use. If an educator wants learners to perform skills, the teaching process should include practice with those skills. Pilots use flight simulators and schools practice fire drills so that learners remember how to perform when they need to (Jensen 2000).

Our brains are not foolproof. Memory shifts over time and is susceptible to suggestion. Sometimes we cling to erroneous ideas and perceive only the information that matches our initial concept. This is called confirmation bias; we see what we expect to find, rather than what really is. As an example, when a child heard a tolling church bell from a nature trail, she asked what kind of bird made that sound! Not knowing how developed the area around the nature center was, this child assumed everything was natural and did not even consider the possibility of a nearby church.

Additional time and experience can enhance our understanding of a concept and build familiarity. Even adults learn unfamiliar concepts best by experience or by examples so concrete and real that they mimic experience (Kaplan and Kaplan 1982). Although television, videogames, and motion pictures seem to be a reasonable substitute for being there, listening to and reading stories can be a more effective strategy for preparing people for the world they will experience. Listening and reading enable learners to conjure up their own mental images. Because these learners have done the hard work of creating those mental images, those images may be more readily retrieved than those merely seen in a televised show or online.

Mental models enable us to function in unfamiliar places. Landing at an airport for the first time is not incapacitating because we expect gates to be sequentially numbered, restrooms to be labeled for men and women, and baggage to be retrieved near the exit. We have a mental model of a generic airport (built from experience) that we can employ wherever we land, even if we have no experience at that location. This skill of determining where to go in an unfamiliar place is a type of problem solving—figuring out what to do in a new situation.

Conservation educators can use brain-based research by designing programs that create a comfortable, threat-free atmosphere, allowing learners to obtain real-world experiences, reinforcing new information in multiple ways, providing experiences to restore attention, and enabling learners to practice skills (Caine and Caine 1990; Jensen

2008). Visitors who are anxious about snakes or biting insects, for instance, are not in a position to learn effectively, so consider ways to reduce environmental threats. To accommodate our need to restore directed attention and to give the brain time to reflect on what has been learned, brain-based educators recommend providing a diversity of experiences to engage learners, including those that are more interesting or attractive, such as offering choices (allowing learners to choose a partner, a project, or a place to begin), engagement (providing a physical activity or solving a mystery), and relevance (connecting to the personal and meaningful) (Jensen 1998). Even a walk in the park can give our brains enough of a break to improve cognitive ability (Faber Taylor and Kuo 2009). Thematic learning also makes sense in the context of brain-based learning, since young people learn more efficiently when they can approach the same concept through several different experiences, for example reading a story about a marsh, going on a field trip to a marsh, and conducting an experiment on water filtration (Jensen 2008). A variety of techniques for achieving these goals are described in Chapters 5–7.

2.3 Learning, experience, and reflection

During the late 1800s several educators broke away from the established norms of textbook learning and encouraged students to study the real world. Louis Agassiz, the Swiss scientist noted for expertise in subjects as diverse as fish and glaciers, insisted his graduate students "study nature not books." The Americans Liberty Hyde Bailey, Anna Botsford Comstock, and Wilbur Jackson made significant contributions to elementary science education through the nature study movement (Disinger and Monroe 1994). Children are naturally curious about their world, they reasoned, so by encouraging

Fig. 2.1 Young people enjoy exploring aquatic organisms at the Smithsonian Environmental Research Center on Chesapeake Bay, USA. (Photo by G. Traymar.)

their observations, teachers can use weeds, rocks, or caddisfly larvae to convey concepts about life and earth science (Fig. 2.1). John Dewey, the American philosopher whose work greatly influenced American and British education, was a proponent of learning by doing rather than the commonly practiced rote memorization and authoritarian teaching style. His work and that of others in the progressive education movement, Jean Jacques Rousseau, Maria Montessori, Johann Pestalozzi, Marietta Johnson, and Friedrich Froebel, promoted practical education—industrial training and agricultural education—to make education relevant to living experiences. Schools, Dewey maintained, should reflect society. The work of these educators can be used to justify initiatives such as public participation in scientific research, service-learning, and project-based learning (see Chapter 7) that engage learners in community projects and problem-solving.

Brain research gives educators a firm basis for an explanation of why "hands-on" or experiential learning is effective. Our senses help us gather information as we explore. The "learn by doing" philosophy is firmly embedded in elementary education through field investigations, but begins to fade in secondary school where students are expected to learn from books. This may account for the fact that many secondary students find school less relevant and meaningful (Usher and Kober 2012). By giving older children an opportunity to explore community issues and develop plans for action (see Chapters 4 and 7), schools are realizing important benefits of experiential and practical learning.

Even though experiential learning has an element of doing, the experience alone is not sufficient to build understanding. Understanding requires the mental effort of comprehending what the experience entailed, connecting prior knowledge to new information, and accommodating that new information into the mental model. Dewey called this reflective thinking, and suggested that it is an important part of an educational experience for young people and adults alike. Brain researchers call this reactivation of the memory. Opportunities to write poetry, draw pictures, complete evaluations, design an action plan, and present information to others involve an element of contemplation which enables learners to reflect on what they know.

Of course prior experience affects what we perceive and even how we engage in new experiences. Someone with familiarity approaches a situation in a very different way from a novice, who may not even know how to begin. This distinction led Malcolm Knowles to extend Piaget's concepts of cognitive development and learning in children to adults. Maturity generally brings a different set of priorities for learning, especially a greater sense of self-direction, more experiences to draw upon, and a desire to learn things that can immediately be useful in work or social situations. Knowles suggested that adults need educational experiences that are highly relevant, focused on solving problems, and allow for choice. Interestingly, however, young people respond well to these characteristics too! And age may not be a perfect correlate to expertise, as youngsters can be quite knowledgeable about their favorite dinosaur, video game, or musical instrument. It often matters if learners are required to attend the educational program (i.e., compulsory school versus voluntary non-formal programs). So while there is some wisdom in designing educational programs for young people (pedagogy) differently from those for adults (andragogy), the common variables are critical for all learners who . . .

need to know why they are learning;
need to be in control of how and when to learn;
can use their worldly experiences to support the learning process;
are more ready to learn when learning is contextualized;
are motivated to learn real-life tasks, skills and understandings;
are motivated by acknowledged success.

Pritchard and Woollard (2010, p. 46)

As a result of this understanding of the learning process, educators should (Pritchard and Woollard 2010):

- help learners understand why they are learning and the value of that new understanding;
- provide opportunities for active engagement in the event;
- use learners' previous experiences and perceptions;
- engage learners through dialogue and questions; and
- use real and relevant examples.

2.3.1 Experiential learning cycle

The experiential learning cycle is one strategy that helps educators guide learners through the process of learning. While there are many different versions of learning cycles, they all have two things in common: an experience or active endeavor and a thoughtful, reflective analysis of that experience.

Many versions of the learning cycle have four steps (Fig. 2.2). These steps can be identified in most popular environmental education activities like Project WET's Activity Guide (Project Wet Foundation 2011). Many activities follow the steps in order, which helps educators ensure they include each step. In more complex lessons, however, several experiences may be processed before generalizing and several strategies may be

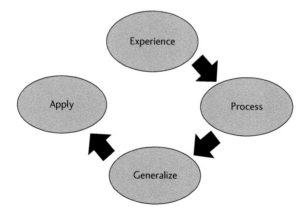

Fig. 2.2 The experiential learning cycle guides educators to use four different approaches in teaching a concept.

used to apply the concept. After introducing the lesson and activating the appropriate memories, the first step is the *experience*, while the following three steps are strategies to help learners reflect on and accommodate the information. Step 2 emphasizes *processing*. Questions about what happened, what data were collected, and what was observed help learners pull the experience into their mental framework. The next step involves *generalizing* the information from the experience. Learners might hypothesize why one group's responses were different from their own. Worksheets and journals are two strategies that help educators guide learners through these two stages by reporting their findings, comparing and contrasting, and making sense of their experiences and feelings. Finally, the fourth step makes the concept more usable and flexible in learners' mental models. Learners are asked to *apply* the concept to a new situation (Braus and Monroe 1994).

Science education in the USA was transformed by the launch of Sputnik in 1957, with greater emphasis on teaching the process of science and inquiry, not just scientific information. In the decades that followed, a five-step learning cycle developed by Bob Karplus at the University of California Berkeley with Myron Atkin at the University of Illinois was adapted by science educators at BSCS (Biological Sciences Curriculum Study) in Colorado and used extensively in their research and educational materials. Today it is known as the 5E Instructional Model (Bybee et al. 2006) and is widely used in science education programs, lesson plans, and curriculum development:

- *Engage.* Learners are introduced to the task and prior knowledge is accessed. Motivating questions and problems are often used to spark curiosity and discussion.
- *Explore.* Learners are directly involved in activities, field observations, data manipulation, or other experiences to create a common base of experience for the current concepts. Questions and interaction with others help them build understanding about the new information.
- *Explain.* An instructor provides information about the concepts through lecture, readings, and discussion. Learners demonstrate their understanding, skills and behaviors. Abstract concepts are introduced and explained.
- *Elaborate.* Instructors challenge and extend understanding. Learners apply concepts in a new situation, testing patterns and ideas and verifying their understanding.
- *Evaluate.* Instructors employ assessment techniques to monitor and quantify learners' progress. Learners assess their own understanding and abilities.

Building a lesson on a common experience helps to erase differences among learners due to socio-economic status, family, culture, or extracurricular activities. Beginning a lesson by asking youngsters how an animal moves or what birds eat would enable the most talkative and those who watch online nature shows to answer with confidence. But because all children do not have the same skills and opportunities, some would be disadvantaged by this approach and less able to contribute. An experiential lesson could have them observe a dog or rabbit move and then duplicate the movement, or simulate birds' beaks with a variety of tools and attempt to "eat" an array of foods. After such an exercise, everyone has ideas to share about how animals move and eat, which will enable them to more actively generalize, elaborate, and apply.

A study in Taipei City, Taiwan used the 5E learning process in seven lessons for elementary students on personal tablet computers, which they used in an after-school science club to study aquatic plants at the school's ecological pool and science laboratory. Students' understanding and identification of aquatic plants increased significantly through this engaging process, despite being administered through personal tablets. One student wrote, "Even though there were many mosquito bites on my legs, I still felt a sense of accomplishment after figuring out the answers through the use of the website and through the observation at the pool" (Liu et al. 2009).

The experiential learning cycle also makes it obvious where educational programs fail to achieve all they should. Some educators are tempted to stop an activity after the "fun" stage and then move on to another. While youngsters may enjoy the game or skit (and having fun is an important motivator in learning), it is unlikely that they will have learned the concept without a structured opportunity to think and reflect on their experience. It is also possible for educators to design exercises that do not have a relevant concept behind them. The ever-popular crossword puzzles and labyrinth mazes are examples of classwork that occupies children and may teach them to spell or draw but will not accomplish an objective about the meaning of those words unless learners experience something other than aligning letters.

The experiential learning cycle also is useful for adults in a learning program. A few questions could remind them of a common experience, or a small group discussion about a case study could serve as an experience to introduce a concept. Process questions would ask a few representatives to describe what happened to them or what their group decided. Generalizing questions would ask them to comment on the underlying constructs. Opportunities to apply that information to their workplace would complete the cycle. When educators neglect to use a learning cycle, they tend to throw a lot of information at the audience. Some of it may stick, but much will be forgotten. It is critical for educators to think about what they want their learners to gain, to identify the main concepts, to design an experience that will enable them to realize those concepts, and to guide them through a process to understand and use these concepts.

Since learners are not identical, and neither is information, any group of learners may contain individuals who thrive with certain types of instruction but not others. It makes sense to provide exposure to a concept in multiple formats to maximize the likelihood that learners will grasp the idea. The concept of learning styles, while intuitively helpful in explaining why some students learn better from reading texts and others from listening to lectures, has not been substantiated despite a large research effort (Pashler et al. 2008). Everyone has a capacity to learn, and effective instructional techniques tend to support all learners.

2.3.2 Constructivism

A relatively new and important concept in education is constructivism, which became popular in the last two decades of the 20th century. This theory acknowledges the role that experience and reflection have in the learning process, but explains that people construct their own understanding from those experiences (Boudourides 2003). Furthermore, some contend that we construct understanding through interactions with people (Pritchard and Woollard 2010). Recognition of the importance of how individuals perceive and assemble their knowledge opens the door to the question of how we know anything. In philosophical circles, much debate revolves around whether science is an objective effort to understand the natural world or is an understanding that is constructed through social negotiation. The middle ground in this turf war suggests "a view of science that acknowledges an external and knowable world, but depends critically on an intellectually demanding struggle to construct heuristically powerful explanations through extended periods of interaction with objects, events, and other people. . . . We believe that human beings are meaning-makers; that the goal of education is to construct shared meanings and that this goal may be facilitated through the active intervention of well-prepared teachers" (Mintzes et al. 2005, p. xviii). This is a useful perspective for conservation educators too.

People have several choices when they are confronted with information or an experience that does not fit their concept or understandings. They can ignore the information that does not fit, or they can actively reconstruct a new understanding that encompasses the new information. Creating new cognitive structures, what Piaget called accommodation, is a personal effort. Teachers or supervisors cannot do it for anyone, mandate it, or prevent it, but they can encourage it by giving learners an opportunity to articulate what they used to think, what they are experiencing, and what they now believe to be true.

Those who choose to ignore the new information present a different problem for educators. When previous mental models do not match the new information, the learner may be holding on to a misconception. Misconceptions (also called naïve theories or misperceptions) are personal understandings that explain observations differently from the accepted theory. It may not be easy to discover exactly what the misconception entails except through discussion and careful listening (Box 2.3). To help someone construct a

---

Box 2.3 Misconceptions about fire ecology can lead to poor communication

The concept of defensible space is often used to encourage residents to reduce nearby vegetation to increase the survivability of their home in case of wildfire. Resource managers often suggest that residents, "Clear 10 m of defensible space to protect the home from fire." However, residents who have experienced wildfire know that burning embers travel well ahead of the fire front and believe that 10 m is not sufficient to prevent their home from burning. They discount the concept of defensible space because it obviously will not work.

The misconception buried in this example has to do with what constitutes protecting a home. The resource manager knows that if vegetation is at least 10 m from the structure, the radiant heat released when those shrubs burn is not likely to ignite the home. The fire will move on to more accessible fuel after the nearby shrubs are incinerated. The residents do not usually think about combustion from radiant heat and instead consider the problem of embers landing nearby. They want to protect their home and nearby shrubs and trees from a wildfire and do not realize that defensible space could protect their home even if a fire burns over it. It is important to engage in a discussion with a resident to clarify the goal of defensible space and how to achieve it (Monroe 2008).

new understanding, the educator must first understand and acknowledge their existing concept and try to show how that belief is not always valid. Then the educator can present a new theory and an example of its explanatory power (Dunwoody 2003).

If the educator comes from a different culture or environment, it may be the educator who holds a misconception. Conversation, explanation, and inquiry may be helpful in sorting out which ideas are useful and which are not. Although most research does not find any cultural differences in the process of building mental models, the process of social interactions and the relative importance of key concepts may vary. Thus, educational programs must be culturally sensitive (Box 2.4).

Five guiding principles of constructivism are helpful for educators of both young people and adults (Brooks and Brooks 1993):

- *Posing problems of emerging relevance to learners.* If learners do not find the topic inherently interesting, an educator must find a way to make it meaningful. Prompting questions, changing perspective, asking for a testable prediction, and offering immediate feedback are some suggested strategies for increasing relevance.
- *Structuring learning around primary concepts.* Constructivist teachers organize their teaching around major themes or essences. If these themes are problems, they engage learners in solving them. By relying on the major theme to connect the lessons, they focus on the whole, the system. It is much easier to break concepts into understandable pieces than to assemble the pieces into a whole system.
- *Seeking and valuing students' points of view.* Understanding learners' perspectives enables educators to challenge learners, reframe questions, and make information meaningful. It takes time to understand and value learners' views, but it is

---

Box 2.4 Several standards used by native educators in Alaska for culturally responsive education that nurture the cultural well-being of youngsters

---

- Culturally knowledgeable students are able to build on the knowledge and skills of the local cultural community as a foundation from which to achieve personal and academic success throughout life.
- Culturally responsive educators incorporate local ways of knowing and teaching in their work.
- A culturally responsive curriculum uses the local language and cultural knowledge as a foundation for the rest of the curriculum.
- A culturally responsive school fosters the on-going participation of Elders in all aspects of the schooling process.
- A culturally responsive school has a high level of involvement of professional staff who are of the same cultural background as the students with whom they are working.
- A culturally supportive community incorporates the practice of local cultural traditions in its everyday affairs.

Source: Alaska Native Knowledge Network (1998).

also key to engaging them and providing appropriate reinforcement. Workshop leaders who ask for participants' expectations should return to the list and confirm they have been addressed. Teachers who receive a confusing homework assignment should ask the student what he or she was trying to convey. Questions like "What do you mean?," "How do you know that?," and "What do you think?" are helpful in building understanding and encouraging learners to take responsibility for their own thinking. The more educators work to understand a learner's viewpoint, the more culturally and developmentally appropriate the lessons will be.

- *Adapting the lesson to address students' suppositions.* Once an educator understands how a learner perceives a situation, he or she should redesign the lesson appropriately. Just as the resource manager uses an explanation to address a misconception, a teacher can fit a learning opportunity to a student's cognitive ability. Misconceptions can be identified in adult audiences through surveys about issues like the sources of water pollution or the causes of global warming.
- *Assessing student learning in the context of teaching.* The act of providing feedback is part of the learning process. A constructivist teacher uses it as an opportunity to continue teaching, not a chance to quell creativity or launch a guessing game for the "right answer." The process of providing non-judgmental feedback often involves, again, asking the learner questions, for example "Why do you think that is the correct answer?"

Constructivism is an opportunity for a skilled educator and learners to engage in the learning process together. It uses discovery and experiential learning to guide the process of building knowledge and making sense of the world. Like most skills, it requires patience and practice to do well. And like many concepts in education, it overlaps with other theories.

2.3.3 Inquiry learning

Inquiry learning is a teaching method that uses and cultivates our natural sense of curiosity. Most commonly used in science education, inquiry learning also fosters an understanding of the scientific process. In inquiry learning, learners actively question, engage in an experience, seek information, and use that information to make sense of the world. Educators who practice inquiry learning emphasize the process of questioning and help students learn to ask questions effectively. Because youngsters do a better job of asking questions when they have learned something about the topic, many inquiry lessons begin with "guided inquiry" where the educator asks questions that lead students toward a discovery. "Pure inquiry" encourages learners to ask their own questions. For some, answering the question is less important than asking, predicting, and figuring out how to test a hypothesis. Educators who use inquiry learning are helping students to fill in gaps and construct their own mental models. It is also helpful that youngsters are typically motivated to seek answers to their own, rather than their teacher's, questions.

Educators who promote use of the inquiry method acknowledge that the world is changing. Simply teaching students information will be limiting, because that information may become obsolete. In an uncertain and changing environment, a better strategy is learning to question, to make sense of the world, to appreciate the inquiry process, and to develop habits that will continue to promote this process of discovery (Matsuoka 2004). Biologists use an inquiry process when setting up an experiment to determine if burrowing owls use dung to attract their food supply—dung beetles. Community planners use the same process when using traffic data and growth projections to determine which roads could include bike lanes. Inquiry learning is simply the procedure an educator can use to model the process that helps us answer questions.

Inquiry is not merely using questions to engage learners in discussion. Likewise, it is not simply allowing learners to ask questions and then answering them! Inquiry learning focuses on using questions and curiosity to guide the learner's efforts to figure out an answer.

"Why do you suppose there is more water in this pond in November than in September?" a naturalist might ask a group. If she responds to their suggestions with "no" or "you are getting close," this is just a questioning technique to motivate the audience to observe and think. It would be guided inquiry if the subsequent conversation went more like: "How could you find out?" When a group member suggests it might have rained a lot in October, the naturalist could distribute rainfall data and ask the group to determine which month had more rainfall. If someone suggests a creek was dammed, a topographic map could be pulled out and the group could compare the existing landforms to the map. If the group needs help, a clue might be, "Instead of thinking about more water entering the pond, consider what might change in the watershed to make more water available on a seasonal basis." An aerial photograph of the watershed might help the learners realize that it is mostly forested, and that between September and November the leaves fall from the trees, removing the trees' ability to pump gallons of water into the air, making more groundwater available to increase the depth of the pond.

Inquiry teaching combines asking questions, hands-on learning, and experiential education. It is structuring a learning opportunity to engage learners in the process of pursuing their questions.

Some critics complain that inquiry learning takes too much time, and takes time away from studying the content that will be on standardized tests. Other critics recognize that learners who are accustomed to learning content and receiving rewards for getting the right answer could be terribly frustrated when a teacher changes the rules of the learning game. Both criticisms are valid and suggest that facilitating inquiry requires that both educators and learners benefit from practice.

Inquiry plays a role in community-based projects that encourage participants to actively collect data, consider multiple perspectives, design a project, and implement it. Conservation educators may find themselves on the receiving end of inquiry learning if they serve as a resource for groups engaged in community problem-solving. If so, students' questions could be answered with more questions that refocus students and encourage their continued exploration. Public participation in scientific research or citizen science programs that engage adults in research projects may also use the inquiry process (see Chapter 4).

2.4 Learning and social interaction

Humans are social organisms. We pay attention to what others are doing and are not likely to seek opportunities to stand out from the crowd; most of us enjoy being part of and blending into a group. We also learn from others. Youngsters watch and mimic older children; even as adults, if we are ever unsure about the proper procedure we quickly check out our colleagues to see what others have decided to do. Albert Bandura expanded on this idea when he formed his general social learning theory (Bandura 1997). He broke from convention by suggesting that reinforcement, such as rewards and punishments, and direct instruction can explain some learning but not all. Even in the absence of any reinforcement or a teacher, people adopt new behaviors by observing others. Bandura demonstrated that children took on new behaviors after watching a film, not just real people, inferring that vicarious learning is possible.

Bandura went on to suggest that the intrinsic satisfaction of achieving or finishing a task is a type of reward that motivates people. He suggested there are four elements of observational learning: paying attention, retaining the information, being able to perform the behavior, and being motivated to do so. This theory was expanded, and in 1986 was renamed social cognitive theory, emphasizing the social influence in the learning process along with the previous experiences, expectations, and motivations that help influence behavior (Bandura 2001). This theory also includes the concept of self-efficacy (a person's confidence in his or her ability to perform a behavior) and outcome expectancy (a person's sense of the outcome of performing a behavior).

Bandura was not the only person to pay attention to the social environment and its influence on learning. Lev Vygotsky, working in Moscow in the early 1900s and a contemporary of Piaget's, also suggested that people are influenced by their social environment or community and that understanding how an individual learns requires that we understand their social and cultural context (Rowe and Wertsch 2002). Since Vygotsky's work was not available outside the Soviet Union until long after his death, it has only recently become widely read. He does not exclude the role of the individual, but suggests that the individual and social elements are "closely interconnected, functionally unified, constantly interacting, and the change and development in one relentlessly influencing the other provides a valid explanation for both social and individual change" (Liu and Matthews 2005, p. 392). This is an important counterweight to the focus on the individual learning in isolation. Vygotsky suggested that cognitive development arises from socially meaningful activity and is influenced by tools and symbols, particularly language, and interrelationships.

Vygotsky is also known for describing the "zone of proximal development" which is helpful in considering communication and mentoring (Rowe and Wertsch 2002). The zone, according to Vygotsky, is the distance between how well an individual solves a problem and how he or she can do so with guidance or collaboration. It is the space between what we know and what remains that is a mystery. It is the area in which we can effectively function with assistance. The translation of this concept into instructional practice supports the application of "scaffolding," where teachers provide support as students learn and explore new concepts and skills. As a scaffold supports the rising structure of a building, teachers help students gain new skills by modeling, providing advice, and helping—at least in the initial phases. As students gain confidence this support system is removed (Ellis and Worthington 1994).

Service-learning and community action projects provide opportunities for conservation managers to become mentors using strategies that could be the basis for exploring this zone, and in time students will expand their competence into this zone, effectively moving it. Finally, Lave and Wenger defined a similar concept, situated learning, as the social process that allows individuals to co-construct knowledge, but emphasizing the importance of a specific context and environment (Pritchard and Woollard 2010). This concept has become the basis of communities of practice, where adults interact to achieve a goal, and has been used to explain social media activity.

2.4.1 Activity theory

Vygtosky's ideas have formed the basis of activity theory (also known as cultural–historical activity theory or CHAT), which is predominately used to help analyze situations and offer explanations for challenges and design suggestions for change (Roth and Lee 2007). By way of example, consider what happened when a teacher and local forest agency staff member introduced advanced middle school students to a serious community problem—the risk of wildfire—and asked if the students might be interested in helping the community reduce their risk. The students were interested and began to learn about the problem by talking to local resource people and paying attention to news reports. Students and adult leaders arranged for a school assembly with the chief of the volunteer fire department and organized a poster contest inviting all students to submit illustrations conveying ways to reduce the risk of wildfire. Students and leaders decided to assist elderly neighbors by raking up leaves and cleaning their yards of brush that might provide fuel for a fire. Students became empowered and were thrilled with the media attention and county awards they received. The experience was powerful; the students gained information and skills, and felt they could make a difference in their community (Monroe and Oxarart 2012).

From the perspective of activity theory, the important components that account for learning are that students had an opportunity to choose to engage and that they began to work on a real issue: reduction of wildfire risk. They were motivated to create community projects that enabled them to work with other students and adults in their community. The products of their effort, such as news reports and awards, were part of community conversations and proudly displayed at their school. Adults in the community suggested additional problems that the students could help solve; students were seen not just as children but as young citizens.

Activity theory often uses the triangle in Fig. 2.3 to explain how individuals learn in the context of social interaction. In this case, starting with the center of each line of the triangle, the students are the subjects who work on wildfire risk reduction (the object) in their local community. The activity that they do (the entire process of working in their community and not merely the poster contest) is bounded by the points on the triangle: the social norms of interaction with adults and forestry staff (rules), the means (rakes, posters, presentations, surveys), and the division of labor (what the leaders do and how

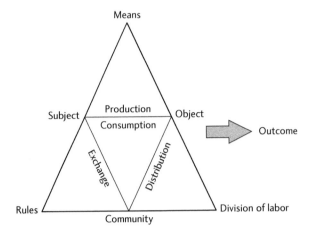

Fig. 2.3 The activity theory triangle describes the system in which human activity occurs and how intervention might effect change.

they interact, what the students do, and what the media do). The outcome over time is reduced risk of wildfire in their region, but exactly how this occurs may not be determined in advance; it is the product of the activity. The new idea for additional ways the students could help reduce risk is one example of an unanticipated consequence made possible by the interacting elements of this model.

If one wanted to advance this learning opportunity, for example, one could make available additional means (video camera), expand the community to other nearby towns, expand the subjects to additional students, and alter the division of labor by changing the actors or the ways they engage. Learning happens because all of these components interact in this particular context. The labels inside the triangle mean that the relationship the students have with their community is an exchange of knowledge and energy; the risk of wildfire (object) is not evenly distributed across the community and students begin by focusing on the greatest risk and need. Neither is awareness about risk reduction evenly distributed; students learn from fire and forestry officials and share their information with the community. Their activity produces outcomes, which benefit the community (adapted from Roth and Lee 2007).

Activity theory has been used to analyze challenges in the workplace; it can enable participants to see explanations for problems and opportunities for change that open possibilities for resolution. In some cases an artifact or means is used to focus attention on the problem, in other cases the rules and divisions of labor are barriers to communication that might reveal how a problem could be solved.

2.4.2 Social learning

Bandura used the term "social learning" to refer to the way people learn in a social context through observation of others and the consequences of their actions. By watching people model a behavior (intentional or otherwise), reproducing the behavior, and comparing the outcome with what was observed, people are motivated to continue, improve, or refrain from this new activity (Bandura 1997). Natural resource managers and educators have expanded on this idea and use the term to mean the process by which people with different perceptions, values, and interests engage with and learn from each other, such that they all gain a new understanding of the issue (Wals and van der Leij 2007). The process can be organized and facilitated, leading some educators to describe the qualities that create opportunities for social learning (Schusler et al. 2003): democratic structure, open communication, diverse participation, multiple sources of knowledge, extended engagement, unrestrained thinking, constructive conflict, and facilitation.

In the context of adults working to resolve natural resource conflicts, workshops and programs designed to facilitate social learning can help participants better understand other people's perspectives, identify a common vision, and form collaborative relationships that can bring about resolution (Schusler et al. 2003; Sutt 2014). When the environment is supportive of meaningful exchange and learning, participants revise their mental model of the issue (Biedenweg and Monroe 2013). Social learning is a key element of successful multi-stakeholder processes that seek to plan projects, resolve conflicts, and enable diverse perspectives to be respected (Allen 2015). It is increasingly used among resource managers who seek to create opportunities for collaborative adaptive management, whether to understand management regulations for a fishery (Sutt 2014), challenges to the water quality of freshwater springs (Monroe et al. 2013), or addressing cormorant management in communities that need the fishery for ecotourism (Schusler et al. 2003).

2.4.3 Cooperative learning

Classroom educators also recognize that learning occurs in a social environment and can manage their classroom to enhance learning with cooperative learning strategies. This involves orchestrating how students work together to identify information or solve a problem by assigning roles and using small group exercises. Not only do individuals enhance their own learning with effective social interaction, but youngsters gain collaborative skills which will be essential for future civic engagement. Solving conservation problems is not something that is usually done by single individuals; it is a group effort. Addressing environmental issues and moving communities toward sustainability require people to work together, and learners can gain these skills in the classroom.

Group tasks also have other educational benefits. Because learners have different strengths, groups that take advantage of members' unique skills may achieve more than an individual could. Research on student achievement that compares three styles of teaching indicates that cooperative learning strategies result in significantly higher achievement and retention than do competitive and individualistic learning strategies. Cooperative learning increases social skills and has been effective in teaching skills for conflict resolution (Johnson et al. 1994).

The period of reflection common to experiential learning cycles can be a good opportunity to promote cooperative learning—asking learners to explain what they saw, helping them to discover what that means, and then justifying their ideas to the group. Many adult educators use small group discussions to engage more people in talking about the topic at the same time. Learning is essentially a social activity; people tend to learn better when they talk through a concept (Pritchard and Woollard 2010).

However, designing an educational program to include the principles of cooperative learning requires more than small group discussions or assigning worksheets to teams. Cooperative learning should include the following essential elements (Johnson et al. 1994):

- *Positive interdependence.* Each member of the group must recognize that their efforts are required and indispensable for group success. This is often accomplished by assigning different roles to learners (timekeeper, note-taker, materials gatherer, questioner, facilitator).
- *Face-to-face positive interaction.* Learners facilitate each others' successes. Trust-building, conflict management, and negotiation strategies can be practiced to help people learn to give each other encouragement and support (Stahl 1994).
- *Individual accountability and personal responsibility.* Groups fail when individuals slough off responsibility or "hitchhike" on the group goodwill. This can be avoided by structuring the cooperative learning task with smaller groups, asking individuals to demonstrate learning, observing the groups at work, and asking each member of the group to explain what they have learned to other groups.
- *Interpersonal and small-group skills.* Success requires that learners master not only the content but also the process of working together. There are several skills inherent in this process: (1) get to know and trust each other, (2) communicate accurately and unambiguously, (3) accept and support each other, and (4) resolve conflicts constructively (Johnson et al. 1994). Young children (ages 5–8) may lack the social skills to succeed at cooperative activities; instead they should practice sharing and taking turns, in preparation for cooperative learning skills that blossom later.
- *Group processing.* Cooperative learning works when groups function well, and this is dependent upon whether groups reflect on what is working and what should change.

Conservation educators can use cooperative or collaborative learning to make learning more fun and effective for groups of adults or young people. It may be challenging if the program is short-term and the educator has limited contact with the learners. If cooperative learning is appropriate for your program, use the following tips to guide you:

- Restructure the lesson to engage groups in a task. Identify roles for each person in the group and provide the skills and resources for them to do their job.
- Clearly explain the objective of the lesson, the task, the roles, and the evaluation procedure.
- Enable the groups to function collaboratively by focusing on the problem and the big picture. This may engage creative and critical thinking skills (see Section 2.5).

Educators can use a variety of methods when designing a cooperative task. Reading alone, then interviewing a partner, and finally sharing information with others is a procedure that can build cooperative skills. A process called "think, pair, share," in which individuals contemplate their response to a question and share their ideas with a neighbor, can

Fig. 2.4 A jigsaw is a cooperative learning activity that engages all learners by making them responsible for teaching something.

be used during lectures to informally take advantage of the social aspect of cooperative learning without the formal process.

A jigsaw is another effective way for learners to review information and share it with others (Fig. 2.4). In this strategy, the group of learners is first divided into equal groups. Each small group is responsible for mastering a different aspect of the information. For example, in a lesson on aquatic insects, group A might identify dragonfly and damselfly nymphs, group B could distinguish stonefly from caddisfly larvae, and group C might work with waterbugs and beetles. When everyone is sure of their information, the learners "jigsaw" into groups comprising one member from each of the original groups. Each person is responsible for sharing their expertise with their two colleagues. This achieves the cooperative learning goals of individual accountability and positive interdependence.

2.5 Focus on thinking skills

2.5.1 Bloom's taxonomy

Educators who wish to enhance learners' ability to think often use Bloom's taxonomy of the cognitive domain. In 1956 Benjamin Bloom led an effort to classify levels of thinking that contributed to learning. One of Bloom's students, Lorin Anderson, coordinated a group of psychologists to update the original hierarchy with terminology that reflects current ideas about learning. The revised version suggests that the first step in cognitive growth is *remembering information*. Questions that test this level of thinking are easy to develop and score, so they are frequently used. They ask for definitions, recall of lists, and recognition of terms.

Understanding is the next step in the hierarchy, the ability to interpret information, describe it in the learner's own words, and go beyond the information to explain what it means or demonstrate its use when asked. Educators assess this level by asking for learners to classify, explain, describe, or translate information. The next level, *applying*, requires that the learner use information in new ways, perhaps to solve problems. Learners may demonstrate, illustrate, or operate to show they can apply information. These first three levels of Bloom's taxonomy are often referred to as "lower-order thinking skills." They are also the thinking processes stressed in the learning cycle which lead toward understanding and mastery.

The three "higher-order thinking skills" are often grouped together because they complement each other in well-designed activities. *Analyzing* is the ability to break down material into separate parts and relationships. *Evaluating* asks that learners select

Box 2.5 Revised Bloom's taxonomy of the cognitive domain

Competence	Activities
Remember	List, define, tell, describe, identify, show, label, collect, examine, memorize
Understand	Summarize, classify, describe, interpret, contrast, distinguish, estimate discuss, extend
Apply	Choose, demonstrate, illustrate, show, solve, modify, operate, use
Analyze	Differentiate, criticize, distinguish, experiment, question, separate, order, connect, classify, arrange, compare, infer
Evaluate	Assess, decide, defend, measure, recommend, convince, judge, support, verify, argue
Create	Assemble, combine, integrate, modify, plan, create, design, compose, formulate

Source: Krathwohl (2002).

or justify a decision. Setting standards or criteria is a key aspect of evaluation. *Creating* is the ability to put information together into new products or points of view. Seeing patterns, applying previous experience to new knowledge, and creating a whole are strategies that reflect these skills.

Standard school assessment tests can encourage teachers to help students master higher-order thinking skills. Box 2.5 suggests some strategies that a conservation educator might use to convey each of these levels of cognition. Educators often use questions to guide learners' thinking, and some of the verbs that trigger each thinking skill are included.

2.5.2 Critical thinking

Logically critiquing complex information, uncovering and understanding bias, and having the motivation to use these skills to shape future actions are ideal traits in learners. Sometimes called decision-making skills, problem-solving skills, or responsible citizenship skills, educators are converging on definitions of critical thinking. There has been some debate over what critical thinking is, how to encourage it, and how to assess it, mostly centered on whether it is dependent upon contextual learning or is an independent skill. The American Philosophical Association gathered input from over 35 specialists in an effort to define critical thinking. They concluded that it is the process of purposeful, self-regulatory judgment that drives problem-solving and decision-making (Facione 1990). A core set of skills can be taught to learners to help promote critical thinking (Facione 1998):

- *Interpretation*: the ability to understand and analyze information.
- *Analysis*: identifying relationships between ideas, main points, assumptions, and bias.
- *Evaluation*: judging the credibility and value of an argument, based on logic and evidence.

- *Inference*: understanding the consequences of an action and being able to decide what to do.
- *Explanation*: communicating one's reasoning process to others.
- *Self-regulation*: monitoring one's own thinking and correcting flaws.

Critical thinking can be taught explicitly by practicing these skills, or can be done in context by using the skills. Of course different situations make it possible to employ different types of thinking. It may be most useful for educators to mimic the real world and provide problems that have missing, uncertain, or extraneous data. The processes of sifting and filtering what is provided and determining how to obtain the additional information that is needed help build important critical thinking skills.

Some standardized tests have been devised to measure these skills. Their use with environment-based education programs indicates that project-based programs contribute to a gain in critical thinking skills among high school students (Ernst and Monroe 2004).

2.5.3 Creative thinking

Creative and critical thinking are both needed to solve problems. They are represented in Bloom's taxonomy (creating and evaluating). Creative thinking helps generate new solutions to problems and also builds learners' confidence.

Creativity is an ability, an attitude, and a process (Harris 1998). It is an ability to imagine something new, often by changing an assumption or rearranging information. Educators believe everyone has the ability to create, but it must be fostered not suppressed. As an attitude, creativity is a willingness to play with possibilities, to try something different, or to experiment. It takes nerve to strike out against the norm and come up with something new. Creative works are often not produced on the first attempt. Creativity usually requires a process of work and patience, trying new strategies, and tweaking to make improvements.

Educators can encourage creativity by designing open-ended assignments and activities that engage learners in generating their own ideas. Several decades ago, the "anti-coloring coloring book" was developed, providing just the background and a sentence to prompt a creative drawing. A caption, "You just found the most bizarre insect in your backyard," with an illustration of a grassy foreground, a picket fence and a big space, invited children to use their imagination rather than coloring inside predetermined lines.

Educators can enhance creative thinking by encouraging peer-to-peer learning interactions. Processes like brainstorming involve a technique that encourages creativity, with prolonged associative thinking involving fluency (number of relevant responses), cognitive flexibility (number of different response categories), and originality (degree of novelty within the population) (DeHaan 2011). Educators can prompt creativity by pushing learners to generate several different answers to every question. They might then realize that not only is there more than one right answer but also that it is useful to think divergently, before going on to use higher-order thinking skills to refine solutions.

The skill of generating new ideas is also called "lateral thinking," a set of strategies that allow people to look at problems in a new way, sometimes using unorthodox methods to break old patterns of seeing (de Bono 2015). The use of specific tools can improve creativity. Tools and techniques include searching for alternatives, challenging traditional thinking patterns, generating provocative statements, reshaping ideas, and increasing peer-to-peer problem solving.

A variation of the think–pair–share strategy mentioned in Section 2.4.3 adds one more element to become think–pair–create–share. In this method, part-way through a class the instructor poses an open-ended problem and gives students 1 minute to reflect on an answer individually before asking them to pair up with a neighbor to reconcile their responses and reframe the problem and their ideas to think of as many solutions as they can before sharing results with the class (DeHaan 2011).

2.5.4 Systems thinking

The world is full of systems. Simple systems, like a refrigerator thermostat, can be understood with a few variables and a direct relationship: when the temperature climbs above a certain point, the cooling system turns on to lower the temperature. Complex systems, like an airport, require the seamless interactions of passenger ticketing, baggage handling, flight scheduling, pilot training, and food preparation not only at one location but at all the places to which those planes are bound. Natural systems, like the planet's climate, involve complex interactions of hydrology, geology, biology, meteorology, and more. As we learn more about seasonal patterns and ocean currents, for example, the better we can model relationships and project how changes in atmospheric gases affect surface temperature, and how temperature affects precipitation, migration, or food production.

Systems thinking refers to mental habits that allow people to recognize relationships in complex systems and use this understanding to make decisions. Viewing problems and their solutions as if they are simple—with one cause and one direct effect—is not realistic or useful. We need to help people see the complex set of relationships and interacting variables that affect most processes. Changes in fishing technology often change menus at urban restaurants as well as target fish populations, ocean floor geology, and populations of predator and prey species. It isn't enough to address one part of the problem, such as the fish population, in isolation. It is more helpful to understand how fishing practices and market forces interact with fish populations.

Because systems thinking is not intuitive, educators must help learners look for relationships, ask questions about connections, and think in terms of system interactions. Our brains, while being magnificently capable of many things, are not very good at compiling data from multiple sources, extending boundaries to intersecting cycles, analyzing, looking for relationships and feedback loops, and predicting how a change will affect the system. But we can train our brains to do just that.

The tools of systems thinking include causal loop diagrams, behavior-over-time graphs, and computer models. Each tool helps people identify the key variables, the relationships between variables, and the results of the system functioning over time.

Recognizing that sustainable communities will require that people understand the system that supports them and the patters of cycles and energy flow, the Center for Ecoliteracy in California, USA, helps educators apply systems thinking in their classroom projects (Capra 2000). They suggest using a project-based approach to identify a local, meaningful, real problem that interests students. By exploring a problem in the context of the local natural and social environment, students will learn from landowners, resource users, resource agencies, government decision-makers, and others (Barlow 2000). These varied perspectives help build connections and deepen the awareness of the problem and consequences, and the specificity of the problem helps ground the understanding of the system in something concrete. The real world may be the best source of complex systems—quite suitable for learners to practice on!

Conservation education can explicitly teach systems thinking skills, and resources are available to help educators to that end. The Association of Fish and Wildlife Agencies offers a manual for teachers that demonstrates how to adapt Project WILD activities to address systems thinking (Ponto and Linder 2011). The Project Learning Tree secondary module, Southeastern Forests and Climate Change, makes systems connections in each of the 14 activities and offers additional exercises on their website (Monroe and Oxarart 2014). Conservation educators can assist in the communication of environmental issues by using a systems framework to identify objects and their relationships. Educators can teach and assess systems thinking (Box 2.6) to develop a citizenry that can effectively tackle environmental issues by enabling them to think about systems and ask questions about connections and unanticipated outcomes.

Box 2.6 Framework for teaching and assessing systems thinking skills

Skill 1	Recognizing interconnections	People can learn to actively seek the relationships between elements in a system, both linear and non-linear.
Skill 2	Identifying feedback	Some relationships form feedback loops that significantly affect the behavior of the system.
Skill 3	Understanding systems at different scales	The ability to conceptualize a system at several scales is essential for inclusion of appropriate variables and interconnections.
Skill 4	Differentiating types of stocks and flows	Stocks and their movement through a system can be affected by various speeds and delay.
Skill 5	Understanding dynamic behavior	Cycles of stability and rapid change characterize complex systems.
Skill 6	Creating simulation models	Experience with simulations help people conceptualize system behavior and create new models.
Skill 7	Incorporating systems thinking into policies	Inferences from systems can be incorporated into a decision-making process, and then applied to make informed decisions about meaningful issues.

Source: Plate and Monroe (2014).

2.6 Integrating learning theories

What makes an effective conservation education program? Effective programs often incorporate several learning theories to increase understanding, for example engaging learners in an experience or activity and helping them process and apply that information to new situations. Learners of all ages tend to be more interested in information that is meaningful and relevant, which is usually easy when teaching environmental themes. Learning also happens in a social context, so it is valuable to have people share experiences, explain the results of an activity to each other, and work in cooperative groups. Because people bring different experiences and skills to an educational program, enabling them to share their understanding helps everyone construct a more similar mental model.

The Danish psychologist and educator Knud Illeris has deftly combined and updated the major theories of learning into one comprehensive model that provides helpful insights for the development of educational programs for young people and adults. He begins by defining learning as those processes that lead to changes in the ability to do something, which includes gaining knowledge, attitudes, and skills.

Illeris (2003) suggests that the activity of learning incorporates two different processes, an external interaction between the learner and his or her social, cultural, and material environment and an internal process of thinking and constructing mental models. Acknowledging both processes combines the brain-based perspective and Piaget's insights with the ideas of those who emphasize social interaction and situated learning. Illeris depicts this perspective as two double-headed arrows that span the continuum between individuals and their environment and within the individual, from learning factual knowledge to addressing attitudes (Fig. 2.5). By including all three elements (environmental interaction, cognitive learning, and emotional learning), Illeris reminds us that learning facts and information happens when there is an interest, desire, or need (emotional states) and an awareness of the ability to use what has been learned.

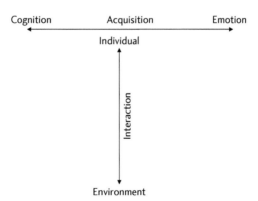

Fig. 2.5 This comprehensive model of learning (Illeris 2003) blends how we gain information with how we process information.

Emotional states affect the degree to which people gain information and so do their interactions with others and the environment.

Illeris continues by describing four types of learning process:

1. *Cumulative learning* occurs when we are introduced to a completely new concept or information that has no relevance to anything else we know. This is more likely to occur in young children or in the case of specialized knowledge, for example a telephone number.
2. *Assimilative learning* is the most common process, where individuals add new information to previous mental structures.
3. *Accommodative learning* occurs when the new information does not fit comfortably and the old mental model must be restructured to accommodate the new information, as when individuals correct a misconception.
4. *Transformative learning* (or expansive learning) occurs when an event is so powerful that restructuring happens in cognitive, emotional, and personality states. This profound change may even be experienced physically as a type of relief.

For most learners and for most conservation educators, assimilation and accommodation, the two processes described by Piaget, are most relevant.

Illeris's model also helps us consider what might be missing when people do not learn effectively or learn incorrect information. Perhaps a problem at home overwhelms their ability to pay attention. Perhaps they worry that a captive snake in a cage in the classroom might escape or they are concerned about walking home from the event in the dark. Perhaps they don't have the time, social support, or interest to explore information that conflicts with what they believe, as can be the case with contentious issues. This latter case, as Illeris explains, involves a pre-understanding of the situation which screens new information. If it conflicts with prior beliefs, it may be ignored or revised to fit, and in both cases no new learning occurs. In the context of climate change, Kahan et al. (2012) and Adger et al. (2013) suggest this is an example of cultural cognition—we screen messages for both content and cultural information with the result being increased polarization instead of more similar perspectives. We control what we learn, consciously and unconsciously, through our social identity and level of interest.

2.7 Summary

For most situations, and particularly with young audiences, creating programs that engage, entice, support, and interest learners will help them focus on new information and learn. Allowing students time to ask questions, reveal prior knowledge, experience new concepts, and reflect on these concepts with others would be ideal. For adult audiences, one important difference is that they are capable of taking responsibility for their own learning. They may choose not to, or they may be interested in gaining new skills and opportunities. Conservation educators need to describe a program to appeal to adult learners by understanding their needs, interests, and motives. The program must include elements that support emotional and social aspects of learning and give learners the opportunity to work with new ideas, compare them with original mental models, and stretch their ideas to accommodate new information. Practicing skills in a comfortable setting and in small groups could be helpful. For situations in which participants resist learning, perhaps due to cultural cognition, additional effort to understand and use the cultural frame that appeals to each group will be necessary.

As we gain new insights about environmental issues and conservation priorities, educational programs are essential for providing information to learners. People need information to make good decisions and understand the world around them. Having information does not always mean that people will use it, but not having information guarantees that they can't use it. The challenge for conservation educators is to understand the audience and create a program that will engage them in altering their mental models to accept new information.

3

Changing conservation behaviors

Conservation education programs can help people understand issues and develop an ethic that will support a host of conservation behaviors. Moving people from "awareness to action" is not a simple task, however. Those educators who are successful probably recognize that the process requires interventions that accomplish several objectives—increase knowledge, build skills, support social norms, and allow people to practice new behaviors. Good conservation education programs can empower learners to take action and build community support for social change. They can help people decide how to improve their quality of life and provide opportunities to build the skills to do so. Chapters 4–12 describe techniques that can help educators and communicators address these broad goals and create successful conservation programs. This chapter looks at how we might design education and outreach programs to influence conservation behavior. We review a number of helpful theories and models that can be used to guide program development (Box 3.1).

3.1 Defining behavior

Although it is easy to talk about "behavior" as a single concept, it means different things to different people. Teachers often define any learning as a change in behavior; behavioral objectives are designed to enhance the measurement of this change. For them behavior could mean the ability to recite the stages of the water cycle. Performing this behavior would indicate that the student knows about the water cycle. The term behavior is broadly used in educational programs that measure cognitive learning in everything from art to zoology. There is often no presumption that these behaviors will directly lead to changes in anything else.

Conservation behaviors are quite different. Some conservation educators design activities to support environmentally responsible behavior in general, while others target a specific behavior. Educational activities to influence general behaviors provide the background knowledge and skills that people need plus the motivation and commitment to make appropriate choices. This is also called environmental literacy (NAAEE 2011). These programs have learning objectives that guide the interaction between the learner and the educator. Behavior in this case means a commitment to environmental stewardship or an environmental ethic. These programs are often seen as an investment in the future; they are quintessential environmental education. While some educators shun controversial issues to avoid the appearance of being one-sided, others thrive on

Conservation Education and Outreach Techniques. Second Edition. Susan K. Jacobson, Mallory D. McDuff & Martha C. Monroe © Susan K. Jacobson, Mallory D. McDuff & Martha C. Monroe 2015. Published 2015 by Oxford University Press.

Box 3.1 Popular theories describing influences on specific and general environmental behaviors

Theories for encouraging specific behavior change

- *Theory of planned behavior.* Target behaviors are determined by intention, which is a product of beliefs and attitudes about the behavior, the opinions of important others, and the perception of control over the behavior and its outcomes.
- *Elaboration likelihood model of persuasion.* Attitudes about a behavior are more likely to remain changed by communication activities that engage people in thinking about the behavior.
- *Diffusion of innovation.* New ideas spread through a community in a predictable manner, accepted first by innovators and last by laggards. The speed of acceptance can be accelerated by using opinion leaders to convey ideas to target audiences.
- *Self-efficacy.* Observation, models, and vicarious experiences can help build a sense that people can take action.
- *Self-determination theory.* Self-efficacy and external incentives can help build competence and autonomy which can evolve into internal motives for behavior change.
- *Flow of behavior change.* Informational and motivational interventions can help move people toward changing or adopting behaviors.

Theories for building environmentally responsible behavior

- *Reasonable person model.* People are motivated to understand the world around them; to learn, discover, and explore at their own pace; and to participate in solving problems. Creating supportive environments to facilitate information participation could lead to increased conservation behavior.
- *Value–belief–norm model.* Behaviors arise from personal values, beliefs about the world, and an individual's sense of appropriate actions.
- *Environmental citizenship behavior model.* Three broad categories of major and minor variables lead to responsible environmental citizenship.

presenting all sides of an issue and helping people sort through the consequences of various options.

Still other educators use psychology, sociology, and marketing principles to focus on a particular action associated with a single conservation issue. They encourage specific changes in target behaviors. Their programs are usually designed for adult audiences and tend to promote socially acceptable behaviors (see Chapter 9). Messages about energy conservation or protecting habitat for endangered species can often be given without generating backlash, but messages that promote the purchase of certain items or suggest lifestyle changes that are not yet a widespread norm can lead to complaints about inappropriate educational practices.

Education to promote an ethic of conservation that leads to environmentally responsible behavior and communication campaigns to change specific behaviors are two avenues that are frequently used to achieve conservation goals (Monroe 2003). Developing a conservation program that uses either strategy will be more successful if planners carefully consider the purpose of the program and the factors that can be strengthened to encourage conservation behaviors. Several theories can help educators design successful programs; they are organized in this chapter in response to typical barriers and goals. For example, conservation educators may believe their audience does not currently engage in a particular behavior because: (1) they do not understand the problem or solution; (2) they are not likely to do something that is not supported by their social group; (3) they don't think they can; or (4) they are not sufficiently motivated to take the time or energy required. The theories that address these barriers are explained first, and then a second set of barriers are tackled that build programs based on the following questions: (5) can environments affect willingness to consider change and (6) how can programs be designed to build support for change?

3.2 Informational needs

The process of changing behavior typically begins with the provision of information. While information is often critical for understanding the need for a behavior, it is rarely the only thing that prevents or motivates the action. Information is necessary but not sufficient. There are several different types of information, some of which some are more motivating than others:

1. *Background knowledge* explains the problem but rarely motivates anyone to act differently. It may help create attitudes about the importance of the action and its likely outcomes, both of which can be helpful.
2. *Normative knowledge* helps publicize that others are already carrying out a new behavior, and is particularly helpful at changing a social norm (Schultz 2002).
3. *Procedural knowledge* describes a step-by-step approach and is often essential (De Young 1988–89). By linking procedural knowledge with examples or models, this information can also help people believe that they, too, can perform the same behavior (Bandura 1997).

The theory of planned behavior combines these three elements into one powerful theory that can be used to explain why people do or do not undertake a specific behavior (Ajzen 1985). The elements of the theory can also suggest ways in which programs can help address gaps in these determinants of behavior.

3.2.1 Theory of planned behavior

While information is what an educator might provide, a belief is what an evaluator would measure. In the theory of planned behavior, beliefs form the foundation of attitudes. Attitudes are the combination of knowledge (cognitive component) and a positive or negative evaluation (affective component). A combination of three types of attitudes forms intention, and intention is the predecessor of behavior. Beliefs about the consequences of the behavior and the degree to which one cares about those consequences are one type of attitude. The second is a function of the importance we place on doing what "important others" would approve of. The third element, perceived control, is the sense that we can conduct the behavior (Fig. 3.1). In this theory, intention is based on:

1. The attitude an individual holds toward the behavior. There is usually more than one relevant belief about the behavior; this element is the sum of all those beliefs. In studies of the behavior of boaters near manatees (*Trichechus manatus*), for instance, attitudes about boat speed, manatee injury, and manatee population status were suggested as influences on behavior (Aipanjiguly et al. 2003).
2. The perception of social pressure to conduct the behavior. This measures attitudes like: if I believe my father would think well of the people who do this, I am more likely to do it. It is often confused with a more general sense of a cultural norm, which is described in Section 3.3.
3. The perception that one has the ability to conduct the behavior. This attitude is closely related to self-efficacy, which is described in Section 3.4. If a hunter believes he won't shoot anything, he has low perceived control.

A fourth factor is also relevant in some circumstances—actual control. Sometimes it does not matter whether someone believes they should recycle, the fact that there are no recycling facilities within 50 miles would prevent them from acting on their intention. Indeed, in some areas it is dangerous to walk or ride a bike, and in other areas the lack of resources may force people to enter conservation areas for wood or food, for example. Actual control may be a barrier to behavior that overrides intention. It can also influence perceived control.

Specificity is an important dimension of this theory. The attitudes people have about general things—such as wildlife or endangered animals—may not be predictive of the attitudes they have about a particular bear in their neighborhood. Consequently, educational programs involving nature study may not affect how people address specific environmental issues.

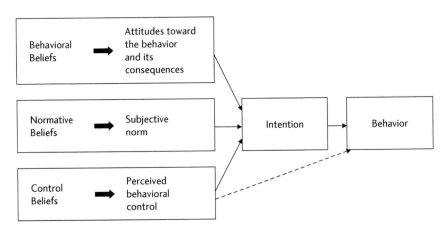

Fig. 3.1 The *Theory of Planned Behavior* suggests that three factors contribute to the intention to conduct a conservation behavior (from Ajzen 2002).

Researchers use the theory of planned behavior to help understand the strength of the factors that lead toward intention and behavior. A study in Vermont, USA, measured preferences and attitudes about hunting and other types of outdoor recreation in a mailed survey to hunters, wildlife watchers, and outdoor visitors (Daigle et al. 2002). Each group perceived they would receive a variety of benefits from their recreational pursuits, and held different perceptions about the value of each behavior. The results support the theory of planned behavior in that respondents preferred activities that they believe are supported by important others, that they believe are feasible, and that they believe would lead to favorable outcomes. The differences between the groups might be due to political orientation and worldview, as well as their experiences. Educators would want to develop different messages and materials to most effectively motivate each group. Another study of environmental interpretive programs in Galapagos National Park explored well-designed and implemented programs that provide information and experience with local flora and fauna as well as the need for financial contributions for conservation management. The 61 adult participants in the week-long boat tour were highly satisfied with the program and increased their knowledge, attitudes toward the park, and intentions to contribute money to conservation. Some of the measured intentions suggest that more general pro-conservation behaviors were positively affected as well (Powell and Ham 2008).

Most behaviors are a function of the interaction of knowledge, attitudes, social pressure, and perceived control. Unfortunately, different behaviors and contexts change the relative importance of these variables. In cases where the behavior is conducted in public, for example, social pressure may be greater than when the behavior is conducted in private. Understanding the motives of the audience helps educators and communicators develop a program that will be more likely to reduce barriers and support motives to change.

3.2.2 Elaboration likelihood model of persuasion

Information aimed at affecting beliefs and attitudes can be presented in many different ways. Many messages are ignored, but some gain our attention. Marketers conduct research to understand the characteristics of messages that increase our attention, become memorable, affect attitudes, and lead to action. The elaboration likelihood model of persuasion (Petty and Cacioppo 1981) suggests that there are two different routes of persuasion that could lead to a change in behavior (Fig. 3.2). One provides information that engages people in thinking about the circumstance, which changes attitudes and ultimately influences behavior. The other changes attitudes by association or reference, not by thoughtful reflection on information.

Long-lasting and durable changes in attitude are usually the result of thoughtful consideration and cognitive information processing, called elaboration. The elaboration route to persuasion involves mental effort, prompted by the message. Communicators are more likely to engage the elaboration route if they use strong arguments, credible sources, relevant topics, clear messages, few distractions, and favorable comparisons (Petty and Priester 1994). The receiver of the message actively considers whether this information is sufficiently interesting to think about and if the argument has merit.

Not everyone reacts in the same way to a message—some people find religious arguments persuasive while others rely on legal information when considering an issue such as hunting. For whatever reason, if they think about the message they have engaged the elaboration route.

The alternative or peripheral route may generate a short-term change in behavior (for example, brand switching) through less relevant cues and motivators. Especially when people are not inclined to engage in the mental effort needed to elaborate on an issue, their attitudes may be influenced by messages that make them feel good or that trigger agreement. Many advertisements for luxury items use status as a motivator, which has little to do with the quality of the item. Similarly, propaganda techniques like "Four out of five doctors agree . . ." could be effective with people who are momentarily cognitively lazy. If the alternative route generates a change in behavior, people may find themselves seeking information to justify their action and then thinking about it later. When people eventually learn more about the product or behavior, or when moods change, the reasons for agreeing with the message may change to more durable support or the behavior may disappear.

Many social marketing messages and public service announcements strive toward elaboration by using humor to attract attention and then adding vivid, concrete

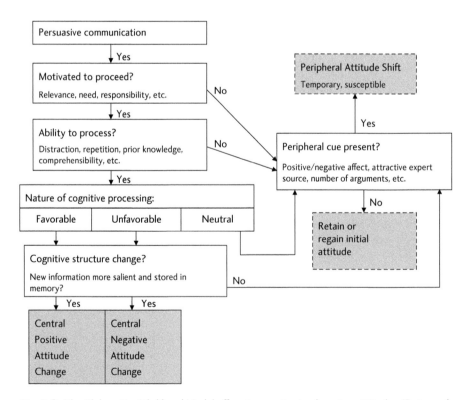

Fig. 3.2 The *Elaboration Likelihood Model* offers two routes to changing attitudes (Petty and Priester 1994).

examples that make information personally relevant. They provide clear information that is easy to remember and act on, and emphasize what is lost by not acting instead of what is gained by acting (Chapter 9). Knowing what people care about can certainly increase the possibility that a communicator can encourage elaboration. For those people who are too busy to elaborate, communicators can use messages that appeal to a sense of responsibility or pride—"Leave the world a better place," or "Keep our community beautiful."

3.3 Influence of social groups

People are social organisms. We pay close attention to what others around us are doing and tend to avoid situations where we do not blend in. According to the theory of planned behavior, the degree to which we perceive that others would approve or disapprove of a certain behavior influences our intention to act. We also pay attention to our peer group or social circle, even to the point of waiting for a de facto leader to try something first.

Everett Rogers described this process in his book *Diffusion of innovations* (Rogers 1995). The theory of diffusion of innovation combines the process people use as they decide to try something new and the influence of their social group on that decision.

3.3.1 Diffusion of innovation

The theory of diffusion of innovation suggests that new ideas and changes move through social groups in a community in a predictable manner (Rogers 1995). Within each social group, opinion leaders help set the norm. These respected people may have an official role, like a rabbi or mayor, or may be any other informed and well-networked individuals. If the opinion leaders adopt a new behavior, others are likely to pay attention. Within each community, however, there are people who will adopt a new behavior sooner than others, though the characteristics that identify the rate of adoption might vary a little with the innovation. For example, among member of the US House of Representatives, age was one factor that determined their use of Twitter (younger members were more likely to use it) but was not a significant variable in predicting who followed their Tweets (Williams and Gulati 2010). Those with well-funded campaigns, as with other types of innovations, were able to take risks and try new things. It often takes the involvement of early adopters to launch an innovation in a community. Because the categories of adopters have certain general characteristics, a communication campaign can be developed that speaks to each category (Box 3.2). When opinion leaders are among those who understand the innovation and believe in its benefits, their testimony and leadership could help diffuse the new idea more quickly.

Diffusion theory can make it easy to see which forms of education and communication should be used to raise awareness among early adopters and the early majority. News articles, television stories, social media, and other mass media techniques can reach large number of people with basic information. But when it comes to actually doing something, like voting, planting native flowers, or donating to a wildlife refuge, it is the personal contact we have with friends, neighbors, opinion leaders, and educators

Box 3.2 Innovations will be accepted by different categories in a community at different times

Category of adopter	Percentage of the community	Characteristics
Innovator	2.5% of a group	Venturesome, risk takers, cosmopolitan set of relationships. Communicate with other innovators, even if they live in other cities.
Early adopter	13.5% of a group	Respected member of the local community. Often a leader; others look to early adopters for advice and information.
Early majority	34% of a group	Deliberate members of the community. Interact with peers, but usually not the leaders. Interconnected with networks.
Late majority	34% of a group	Skeptical members of society. Not likely to change until the majority have already done so. They respond to peer pressure.
Laggard	16% of a group	The last group to adopt an innovation. May be unable to take risks due to limited resources. Traditional norms and resistance to change keep them isolated.

Source: Rogers (1995).

that makes the difference. The techniques of demonstrations, workshops, meetings, and events where individuals interact with each other can help give people the information they need to make a commitment and launch a new behavior. This two-step model, using mass media to reach community leaders and then working with those leaders to influence the public is simplistic, but it has helped educators realize that different techniques have different strengths and can be used strategically at different times (Rogers 1995). Even studies with social media appear to follow the same patterns—the online community shares information that people perceive to be either generic or more personally meaningful and adopts in patterns that depend on perceived attributes and benefits (Avery et al. 2010; Chang 2010). In order to promote the equitable distribution of the benefits of an innovation, Rogers suggested that educators target the opinion leaders who are well-respected by the late adopters and laggards, thus speeding their acceptance (Dearing 2005).

The suggested techniques for achieving diffusion through personal communication from peers and leaders may be effective because they rely on the social aspect of learning and may even develop a critical mass of people who are launching a new community-accepted social norm for that behavior. Finding the right group of people and orchestrating the appropriate educational program for them requires skill in matching audiences, needs, and opportunities. The norms, or standards of behavior, that a community agrees to follow help establish new patterns of behavior because people who want to be accepted by the community will probably conform to the accepted norms.

Certain aspects of a change make it easy or difficult to spread through a community, for example, the degree to which it can be observed, the importance of the benefits, and the extent to which it conflicts with current culture (Rogers 1995). Conservation educators can overcome these barriers by advertising the benefits of conservation behaviors that may be less observable, providing feedback about the early successes, establishing demonstrations so others can see an example, and obtaining testimonials from community leaders so people recognize social approval (see Chapter 9). Rogers' work has been applied to agriculture, health, and environmental innovations. An analysis of the diffusion of concepts of sustainable development in over 5800 courses in 19 schools that are part of Cardiff University, for example, suggested that some schools have incorporated selected elements of sustainable development better than others. A dozen different barriers were suggested that prevent the incorporation of sustainability, from lack of awareness and confusion to lack of support or a belief that it is irrelevant. This analysis revealed where schools might improve their attention to sustainable development and where a coordinator might focus examples and explanations to fill in gaps (Lozano 2010).

As another example, chefs could serve as potential opinion leaders who might encourage greater consumption of local food. An analysis of the characteristics of chefs and restaurants that had adopted local foods and those who had not in Ohio, USA, suggested key variables that might encourage greater adoption (Inwood et al. 2009). The taste of the food was one of the most important criteria for purchase, regardless of whether the restaurant was a high- or low-volume facility with high or low prices. Restaurants that used local food rely on signs, waiting staff, and cooking classes to share information about the origin of the items on their menu. The lack of an efficient food distribution network was a perceived limitation across the respondents, though there was a bias in favor of direct relationships with farmers and other local providers and an opportunity to use the local chamber of commerce as a networking tool.

3.4 Self-efficacy

Self-efficacy is the belief that one has the capability to exert control over one's life (Bandura 1997). It is a broad concept that explains why some people rise above adversity or approach challenges with resolve while others fail to act. Procedural information certainly plays a role in whether we think we can do something, but so too does our awareness of examples of others who have attempted a change and the existence of an appropriate opportunity. Bandura suggests that self-efficacy can be enhanced through three types of strategies. The most effective strategy is to personally master a new skill, which can be promoted by educational programs that engage learners in practice, project-based education, or issue investigation. A second strategy is vicarious learning—watching others succeed or fail. In the third strategy persuasion can be used to convince people that they have the ability to succeed (Bandura 1997). Persuasive materials may be more effective, however, if they use examples and models of success, blurring the second and third strategies. Feedback about how well people are doing with a new behavior can also serve to continue to motivate those who have started and communicate a changing norm, making it more likely that those who are participating will continue and others will join the new movement.

Hopefulness, or its converse, helplessness, may be closely linked to efficacy (Snyder et al. 2001). Both suggest that knowing what to do and how to do it are essential for people to rise to new challenges, and those without this knowledge may even come to believe there is no hope.

Programs can be developed to build efficacy and hope. For teachers attending a workshop on climate change, obtaining information and answers to their questions is one important step, but so too is providing activities that are easy to use with tips on how to teach them, ideas about where students might have difficulty, and imagery about how others have used this information. Giving participants time to plan or, better, to lead an activity during the workshop, also builds self-confidence. Even online training courses can be designed to build efficacy with videos of other teachers using new materials, chat rooms where participants can share ideas, and exercises where participants try something new and report on their experience (McConnell and Monroe 2012).

3.5 Motivation

There are times when people know they should do something, know how to do it, and may even know others who do it, but they lack the motivation to actually do it. It may be that specific barriers are too large to overcome, for example a public transport system that does not reach their neighborhood. Or it may be that they perceive barriers to be bigger than they really are. In these cases incentives may be effectively used to entice people into trying an appropriate behavior. Of course external incentives are not usually sustainable. If the behavior itself becomes perceived as easier, more enjoyable, or worthwhile, however, internal motivators could help continue it. A number of theories speak to this process.

3.5.1 Self-determination theory

We all know people who are curious, inspired, and active learners. While they are probably the norm for human development in any culture, others are more apathetic and listless. Ryan and Deci (2000) suggest that personality traits and situations can facilitate or undermine motivation. They base their theory on three basic needs that we all have—for competence, relatedness, and autonomy—and the importance of intrinsic motivation (the tendency to seek opportunities and learn) in achieving these needs. In general, when the environment provides feedback or rewards to those who attempt challenges, people increase their competence and intrinsic motivation if they simultaneously believe they can and want to do something (i.e., self-efficacy and self-determination). There is a fine balance between extrinsic reward and intrinsic motivation, however. A huge payoff or penalty can undermine someone's own desire to act. If people only obey hunting regulations when the ranger is present (an extrinsic punishment) the agency has to keep staff on patrol every day. Clearly, it is important to reinforce intrinsic motivation in the context of conservation behaviors.

If intrinsic motivation is the goal, one might assume that people must choose the action. Of course that is ideal, but not necessary. Researchers have explored the conditions that increase autonomy and efficacy when tasks are assigned. They suggest that helping learners consciously value the goal of the behavior, making that goal personally important, selecting from choices, and engaging in opportunities to make decisions may help people gain autonomy and enhance intrinsic motivation (Fig. 3.3). In addition, knowing that significant others care about the action (i.e., a subjective norm) helps reinforce feelings of relatedness, one key to intrinsic motivation (Ryan and Deci 2000).

This suggests there are benefits to engaging groups of peers or families in new behaviors where people can encourage and support each other. Successful practice sessions and feedback help build efficacy. De Young (2000) suggests that small external incentives could be used to launch a new behavior, as long as follow-up information helps people consciously realize that the benefits of participating and making a difference are actually satisfying. Another key to building efficacy and autonomy is achieving success. This may be more likely when people experience a "small win"—a successful outcome for a small problem (Weick 1984). Although we might wish to tackle large problems they are, by definition, difficult. Large problems can easily overwhelm the most dedicated activists, whereas breaking down a large problem into smaller, attainable, and realistic tasks may lead to concrete and measurable change in a reasonable period of time.

3.5.2 Flow of behavior change model

Scott Geller (2002) suggests that a combination of incentives and information about consequences (such as rewards) can move people through a process of changing their

Amotivation	Extrinsic Motivation	Intrinsic Motivation
Non-regulation: Non-intentional, non-valuing, incompetence, and lack of control prevent action	**External Regulation:** Compliance based on external rewards and punishment **Introjected Regulation:** Self-control and internal rewards and punishment motivate action **Identified Regulation:** Personal importance and conscious valuing encourage action **Integrated Regulation:** Actions are blended with personal values and needs	**Intrinsic Regulation:** Interest enjoyment and inherent satisfaction maintain action

Fig. 3.3 The *Self-determination Theory* (Ryan and Deci 2000) offers an explanation for motivation.

environmental habits (Fig. 3.4). People may begin the process in any of the four quadrants. They may not know that they are doing environmentally destructive things (Quadrant 1), but can be made aware of appropriate and inappropriate action by being informed through specific instructional intervention with feedback. Motivational interventions may be needed to prompt appropriate behavior (Quadrant 2), along with supportive intervention like feedback and reassurance. After an individual decides to adopt the behavior and practices it successfully, it may become an unconscious habit (Quadrant 4). Designing campaigns with different interventions for people in each quadrant may help to move them efficiently to more responsible behavior.

3.5.3 Needs and benefits as motives

One way of understanding why people behave as they do is to explore the motives that underlie their behavior. Usually a variety of reasons provide the motivation. For example, hunters often say they like to spend time in the woods, test their skills in nature, relax, or be with friends as motives for hunting.

Some motives are based on needs. Maslow's hierarchy of needs (Maslow 1954) suggests that people are motivated by five different levels of need. Basic needs such as food, shelter, and safety must be satisfied before higher-level needs like belonging, love, self-esteem, and self-actualization.

Other motives are based on perceived benefits. In the field of outdoor activities, several theories explain why people choose certain forms of recreation (Driver et al. 1991). One perspective (Box 3.3) suggests that people obtain eight broad psychological benefits from leisure activities.

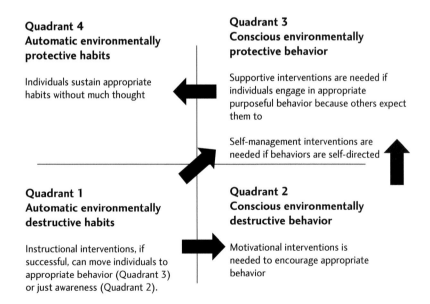

Fig. 3.4 The *Flow of Behavior Change Model* (Geller 2002) suggests that information and incentives can help people form pro-environmental habits.

Box 3.3 Psychological benefits of leisure

- Self-expression—the need to use one's talents to express oneself
- Companionship—the need to sustain relationships
- Power—the need to be in control
- Compensation—the need to experience something new
- Security—the need to make a safe commitment
- Service—the need to be of assistance
- Intellectual aestheticism—the need for intellectual stimulation
- Solitude—the need to be alone

From Tinsley (1984).

The Recreation Experience Preference scales allow researchers to quantify benefits that people fulfill through recreation. According to this expectancy-value theory of motivation, people expect that certain behaviors will lead to desired events (i.e., if I drive to this trailhead, I can go for a hike) and that those events will lead to valued psychological outcomes (i.e., if I go on this hike I will enjoy seeing wildlife and being with my family). Researchers have identified at least 19 different motivations that tend to drive recreation behavior (Box 3.4). Of course different types of people have different motivations. By understanding the population of users and what they wish to achieve, managers can provide a more appropriate suite of opportunities.

These internal motives tend to be successful as drivers of behavior because they lead to satisfaction or benefits. Birdwatchers may be satisfied with their outing if their experience matched their expectations for pleasant weather, interesting group interactions, the number of birds seen, or seeing one favorite bird. People who recycle report that

Box 3.4 Recreation experiences involve a variety of perceived preferences

Enjoy nature	Escape physical stressors
Physical fitness	Outdoor learning
Reduce tension	Share similar values
Independence	Family relations
Introspection	Be with considerate people
Achievement/stimulation	Physical rest
Teach/lead others	Risk taking
Risk reduction	Meet new people
Agreeable weather	Creativity
Nostalgia	

Source: Driver et al. (1991).

their satisfactions include participation in something that benefits the community and conserving resources (De Young 1988–89).

3.6 Conservation program development to influence behavior

By recognizing some of the reasons why people may not adopt environmental behaviors, it becomes easier to think about how conservation educators might encourage people to act appropriately. Educators might excel at providing information, but these theories suggest that this not likely to be enough to motivate and sustain a new behavior. Understanding the social system in which groups operate, considering what could motivate a change in actions, and building self-efficacy are key to developing programs that can change behavior. Social marketing campaigns (see Chapter 9) use demonstrations of how others have accomplished the new action, provide feedback on how well the community is doing as they make the transition, and use prompts or incentives to help remind people and motivate change. There are a few other considerations that conservation educators might contemplate.

3.7 Supportive environments are key

People tend to be most comfortable in environments where their needs are met. Environmental psychologists Steve and Rachel Kaplan suggest that people will be most reasonable when their environment enables them to meet their needs for information. In this case they define an "environment" as the immediate surroundings, in which the required information may or may not be easy to obtain. We can address such problems by developing helpful navigational aids for confusing buildings as well as engaging platforms that help people know how to interact, such as a workshop agenda, users' manuals, or a camp curriculum. An environment could also mean the workplace norms that encourage or deter experimentation, volunteerism, or shared governance. Thinking of all these environments, it is easy to see how confusing information, a lack of information, or too much information could allow people to disengage or become agitated and even belligerent. If we want people to be open to change, curious about learning more, and interested in new ideas, we need to create an environment that supports their informational needs in three dimensions. These three factors make up the reasonable person model.

3.7.1 The reasonable person model

The reasonable person model (Kaplan and Kaplan 2009; Kaplan and Basu 2015) was derived from a consideration of human evolution, cognition, and motivation. Because people are motivated to understand the world around them, one factor to support reasonableness in people is creating opportunities to help them build their mental model or better understand a topic. People need information that makes sense, that links to what they already know, and that provides new information in a manner and at a pace that allows them to learn. Many of the experiential learning strategies in Chapters 5–7 are successful because they are designed to allow learners to experience, discover, share, and build their own mental models. Supportive environments are those that encourage and facilitate learning. The importance of thinking and learning is not unique to this theory, of course. The elaboration likelihood model (Petty and Priester 1994), designed to explain why only some advertisements change attitude and affect behavior, suggests that the most stable change in attitude comes from helping people think about it. The more time they spend elaborating, for example considering, ruminating, comparing, or remembering, the more likely the message will affect their attitudes. The work of thinking is similar to the work of building a mental model.

People are also motivated to participate. They enjoy feeling needed and that they can make a difference. This includes a range of opportunities, from merely being heard and respected to being engaged in a large project. Here it is essential to offer strategies and opportunities by which people can reasonably participate. Many conservation actions are made possible through the efforts of groups. While each individual's effort may not be onerous, together they add up to something meaningful, and knowing that is powerful. Reinforcing the value of each contribution and helping people realize their accomplishments are two important ways that conservation educators can help participants recognize the many ways they are making a difference (Jacobson et al. 2012). Working together also enhances social capital—the glue that enables groups to work together and solve problems (Keeley 2007). Conservation programs that are designed to engage groups of people and help them increase levels of trust, usually by using forms of social learning, are enhancing the group's ability to cooperate in the future (Allen 2015).

Finally, people need to be effective. This factor suggests that educators can create environments that enable people to be effective at building their mental model and at making a difference. An effective environment for learning might involve periodic breaks, tasty snacks, opportunities to be outdoors, and something fun. Effective participation may require building skills, practicing with support, and using examples or success stories from other communities. Knowing that other towns have successfully deterred bears from becoming a nuisance helps others believe change is possible. That sense of hope, along with the skills to make a difference, motivates people to dig in and try. Without such information, one might never start. Reducing helplessness may be the key to motivating people toward environmentally responsible behavior.

These elements, of course, interact, and successful conservation education programs are often a blend of all three (Fig. 3.5). Community members found it easy to learn about a controversial wood-to-energy facility when they attended a forum and could ask questions of a panel of experts (Monroe et al. 2009). A facilitator kept the conversation friendly, made sure everyone had a chance to speak or write down their question, and limited the experts to short presentations to give more time for discussion. When people ask a question, they pay more attention to the answer and revise their own mental model accordingly. Participants were given a chance to complete a survey about their opinions, which was summarized and shared with city decision-makers. It was an easy way for people to register their ideas. An evaluation of the process suggested that what participants appreciated most were the credible speakers, the opportunity to ask questions of experts, an opportunity to learn about the issue, an unbiased facilitator, and an opportunity to share ideas with community leaders.

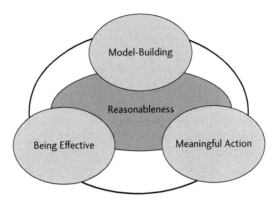

Fig. 3.5 The *Reasonable Person Model* includes three interacting elements.

In secondary education the reasonable person model suggests a strategy for meeting the sometimes competing goals of academic achievement and teaching lifelong skills like critical thinking (Kumler 2009). Service-learning and community action projects, discussed in Chapter 7, give young people an opportunity to make a meaningful contribution to their community. The pursuit of these types of projects enable students to gain knowledge to build mental models and confidence. Place-based education (Sobel 2005) similarly suggests that local projects empower students and lead to academic achievement and the acquisition of life skills. This combination of local place and active projects enables youngsters to learn, be effective, and make a difference, and in doing so they may be more likely to improve their test scores and enjoy attending school (Lieberman and Hoody 1998).

The challenge for conservation educators is to create opportunities where people can be empowered with information and have the opportunity to participate in solving a problem. Too often sponsoring agencies define the problem and the solution, only using public participation when complications arise. Where prescribed burning is part of a forest management program, prescribed burning permits are carefully managed and controlled; burns on large properties are planned well in advance and implemented only when weather conditions are appropriate. One would think there is little opportunity to engage the public in planning a burn. However, forest managers were able to work with a group of hunters who did not want certain areas burned during the deer season. Their new approach considered the hunting season and the location of deer stands as additional variables to be used when planning burns.

Real participation in protecting the environment can be a powerful motivator. These programs may also be successful because they build community, overcome helplessness, and engage people in exploring and understanding their world.

3.8 Designing programs to support change

A variety of theories and models provide insights into the components that educators may want to include in a program to move people toward new behaviors, and how these components could be sequenced to be most effective. As educators explore these ideas, however, they may generate important questions for which there are no good research-based answers. In such cases paying attention to the assumptions that underpin a program, evaluating for impact, and reflecting on what was and was not successful will enable conservation educators to increase their effectiveness. Perhaps this is the educator's version of adaptive management, a strategy of resource management that relies upon small experiments, monitoring, and learning before launching large-scale ecosystem change.

3.8.1 The value–belief–norm model

The ideas of Paul Stern (2000) about the precursors of environmental behavior suggest that people are motivated to undertake responsible environmental actions from a personal sense of obligation or a norm, which is based on their beliefs about the environment in general, specific problems or threats to the environment, and their ability to reduce those threats (Fig. 3.6). These beliefs are influenced by the values people hold, which can be a unique mix of three different value types: egoistic, altruistic, and biospheric. Each value is a sort of predisposition that makes certain beliefs and attitudes more likely. A nurse, social worker, or teacher may have a stronger altruistic value, which makes them more likely to believe they can relieve suffering, empower individuals, and improve society by helping others. An environmentalist would build on their biospheric value to hold beliefs about the role of people concerning the planet, the severity of ecosystem threats, and the promise of actions to reduce those threats. These beliefs influence the personal norms someone lives by, which in turn influence actions. Researchers often use values and value orientations to predict beliefs, attitudes, and behaviors (Decker et al. 2001). This model also suggests what an educator might do to encourage action: remind people of their concern for the environment, the adverse consequences of inaction, and their responsibility to do something.

Environmental beliefs and behaviors may also stem from egoistic values, since helping the environment can provide clean air or recreational opportunities that benefit oneself, and from altruistic values, since helping the environment helps guarantee a

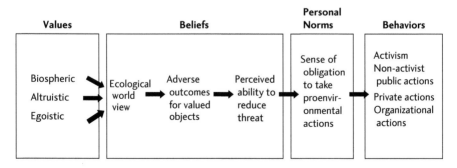

Fig. 3.6 The *Value–Belief–Norm Model* suggests variables that account for changes in conservation behavior (Stern 2000).

future for children (De Young 2000; Kaplan 2000). This complicates matters for educators designing a program to promote values that will enhance environmental behavior; however, it can also simplify matters, because behind most environmental behaviors are many good reasons people use to justify their actions. We need not be limited in our belief that environmental action must stem from caring about the environment. Indeed, it can also come from caring about clean water for personal consumption, about engaging in community activities, and about caring for future generations.

Because values are the foundation on which beliefs and norms rest, some educators stress the need for programs that strengthen and support biospheric values among young children. Positive experiences in nature, especially with those who cherish the natural world, may help establish caring and concern about the environment that will be part of their future decisions (Chawla 1998, 1999). People who work in conservation often look back to formative childhood experiences and outdoor play spaces, or even books and other media, to explain their career path. These life experiences do not explain the whole story, however, since siblings are often exposed to the same adventures yet make very different employment choices. We do not yet know what else nurtures and cultivates environmental concern, nor at what age values may be shaped by experiences. In a study of 10-year-olds, a combination of four factors—childhood experiences in nature, perceived family values toward nature, natural areas near their home, and knowledge of the environment—were found to contribute to children's connection to nature, which helped predict their interest in participating in nature-based activities in conjunction with family values toward nature and previous experience (Cheng and Monroe 2012). Another analysis of survey data from American adults about their childhood experiences suggests that adventures in wild areas, such as hunting, fishing, hiking, and camping, particularly before the age of 11, help form attitudes and shape perspectives about conservation (Wells and Lekies 2006). Personal responsibility is a variable closely associated with the belief that one is obligated to adopt an environmental behavior, and might be cultivated with such early experiences of nature (Kaiser and Shimoda 1999).

3.8.2 Environmental citizenship behavior model

Curriculum developers may find it helpful to use the environmental citizenship behavior model developed by Hungerford and Volk (1990) to explain how educators might aim to build the skills needed to help people act to protect the environment. This model uses three broad categories of elements (Fig. 3.7):

1. Entry-level variables are a prerequisite to environmental interest and knowledge. They include environmental sensitivity—an empathetic perspective toward the environment.
2. Ownership variables help personalize environmental issues—in-depth knowledge of environmental issues and their consequences and a personal investment built out of prior experience or knowledge.
3. Empowerment variables give people a sense that their actions can help resolve a problem. They must perceive that they have the skill and knowledge to act effectively, as well as the belief that they can and should act.

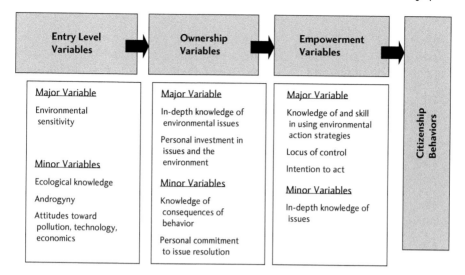

Fig. 3.7 The *Environmental Citizenship Behavior Model* identifies determinants of behavior that can be addressed in educational settings (Hungerford and Volk 1990).

These variables can be addressed through age-appropriate educational programs that increase environmental sensitivity and knowledge, engage people in direct experiences, and practice skills to improve proficiency in taking action. Direct experiences could involve a backpacking trip to build a personal relationship with nature or data collection activities to explore a local issue in great depth. An issue investigation and analysis process could involve exploring how electrical power is produced in the community from economic, social justice, and environmental perspectives, and understanding how different stakeholders perceive local needs. A variety of other environment-based projects are also available that achieve similar goals (NEETF 2000; see also Chapter 7). Programs that use this format report that young people can become so engaged in community actions that their parents and other community members learn to anticipate that they will be able to take the lead on identifying problems and raising awareness (Volk and Cheak 2003).

3.9 Summary

These popular theories and models help to explain human behavior. They are commonly used to support a variety of conservation education and communication techniques, from social marketing to community education, and often in combination (Kollmus and Agyeman 2002).

Some conservation education programs still reflect the exuberant but naïve approach of telling participants how to "save the world." Few people enjoy that sort of dictatorial treatment, and some react against it in ways that undermine the original message (Brehm and Brehm 1981). A few theories borrowed from the social sciences will help conservation educators think more strategically about their conservation messages and activities.

A program can use several of these theories to introduce the benefits of conservation behaviors, provide examples, build peer pressure for change, empower individuals to gain skills, and create supportive environments for people to learn and work together. A better understanding of what people think, what motivates their behavior, how they perceive the change, and who else in their world cares, can provide educators with ideas and resources to build a conservation education program that leads to appropriate conservation behavior.

Conservation education in schools

Conservation education in schools takes many forms—from schools that use supplemental materials provided by wildlife agencies to schools that focus on the environment throughout the entire curriculum. Within a school, conservation education can range from a 1-day field trip to an organic farm to campus greening initiatives that construct sustainable buildings on college campuses.

In New South Wales, Australia, the Department of Education and Training supports the development of "landscapes"—features on school grounds such as wildlife corridors that promote learning in the local environment. Through the Memphis City Schools Nutrition Services in Tennessee, USA, students help to plant and harvest produce such as spinach, peppers, and tomatoes to serve in the cafeteria. Working with a farm educator, students use the garden to study mathematics, science, and language arts in this city-wide program that addresses nutrition and childhood obesity.

Richard Louv's bestselling books *Last Child in the Woods* and *The Nature Principle* document a growing disconnect between nature and young people, as well as the substantive benefits of nature for childhood development (Louv 2005, 2011). Several state and national governments, for example in the Netherlands, New South Wales in Australia, and California and Pennsylvania in the USA, have taken a lead in developing environmental education policies and practices in schools that promote the exposure of young people to the outdoors.

However, environmental education often remains marginalized within the formal school setting, especially with the increased emphasis on standardized testing in many school systems. There is no consistency in how environmental education is administered worldwide. In some countries environmental education is housed within the ministry or department of the environment, while in others the ministry of education oversees its programming. Many countries have no formal policy or supporting institution for conservation education.

In this situation, non-governmental organizations (NGOs) and agencies can provide informal, though less coordinated, support. For example, international initiatives like the Asia-Pacific EE Network have supported professional development for teachers in environmental education. State-level professional organizations in the USA, like the Environmental Education Alliance of Georgia, also provide training and conferences for both teachers and non-formal educators who work for organizations such as nature centers and wildlife agencies.

Conservation Education and Outreach Techniques. Second Edition. Susan K. Jacobson, Mallory D. McDuff & Martha C. Monroe © Susan K. Jacobson, Mallory D. McDuff & Martha C. Monroe 2015. Published 2015 by Oxford University Press.

The plethora of approaches to conservation education in schools highlights the importance of both understanding, and using the school environment in a community to maximize benefits for students and teachers. Conservation education in schools can be a powerful approach for students, teachers, administrators, conservation organizations, and community members. This chapter highlights techniques that range from communicating with schools to supporting academic standards (Box 4.1). Case studies are used to illustrate a sample of successful strategies for practicing conservation education in schools.

This chapter targets conservation educators aiming to work with schools, but also teachers or school administrators who wish to enhance their curriculum through conservation education. We use the term non-formal educators to refer to conservation educators from organizations such as agencies, parks, and NGOs, while formal educators are teachers in a classroom setting. For those readers who want to develop conservation education programs in schools we also suggest reviewing Chapter 1 for general tips on developing goals, selecting strategies, developing and pilot testing materials, implementing, and evaluating your program. Chapter 2 provides details on matching conservation education programs with appropriate learning theories.

Box 4.1 A variety of techniques and approaches can help integrate conservation education into schools

Technique	Purpose
Communicating with schools	Focuses first on understanding the school environment and then choosing appropriate communication strategies for teachers, parents, administrators, students, and education agencies
Acting as a resource for schools	Identifies strategies for meeting the needs of school systems, for example serving as a judge at a science fair, developing an outdoor lab, and providing professional development for teachers
Supporting academic standards	Focuses on correlating conservation education programs with academic standards to increase the use of conservation education resources and improve student achievement
Integrating conservation education into legislation and educational policy	Strives for systematic inclusion of conservation education into government funding, training for teachers, educational standards, and legislation

A sample of approaches to conservation education in schools

- *Environment-based education*: uses the environment as a context for learning and focuses on academic achievement.
- *Education for sustainability*: integrates the study of social, economic, and environmental systems to enable learners to take responsibility for creating a more sustainable future.

4.1 Communicating with schools

If the last time you entered a classroom was as a student yourself, the classroom environment can seem like a foreign country. The first step in planning your communication with schools is to take the time to understand the school environment by talking with educators. As many teachers will admit, the language of schools—from preschools to universities—includes specialized terms such as standards, learning outcomes, and assessments. But teachers and conservation educators share a common interest in one word: education. This connection makes conservation education in schools not only viable, but also valuable to all partners.

4.1.1 Planning

Like learning a new language, understanding the classroom environment requires learning the basics like the structure of the administrative system as well as complexities like the pressures of standardized testing. Begin by talking with and listening to teachers, students, and community members, exploring the websites and Facebook pages of school systems, and volunteering in schools. Consider again the analogy of planning a visit to another country. Savvy travelers talk to friends who have visited that country to learn about customs and study a phrasebook to master simple greetings before arriving in a new environment. In schools this understanding about factors such as time, administrative interests, academic standards, testing, the backgrounds of students and the local community, and environmental issues will promote effective communication about conservation education programming.

Time

A reality of most school systems is time constraints. Find out how schools structure their day for various grade levels and subjects. In most primary schools teachers are with their students for the entire day, which provides flexibility in terms of field experiences and outdoor activities. In upper grades teachers usually specialize in one subject, taught in blocks of time, often ranging from 50 to 90 minutes. In the USA, middle schools often operate through "team teaching" where teams consist of mathematics, science, language arts, and social studies teachers. This can allow integration of conservation education across the curriculum as teams of teachers meet to plan their curriculum and discuss student needs. The subjects of music, art, and physical education are often rotated between classrooms throughout the week. This rotation could provide a place for conservation education activities within art, for example, for multiple classrooms during a single week.

Administrative interests and structure

Whether you are a conservation educator with a wildlife agency or a teacher you will need the support of administrators such as the principal and curriculum coordinator. If you can identify the interests of administrators in a school system, you can dovetail the strengths of conservation education to match administrative priorities. The research that reveals achievement gains shown by schools using the environment as a context for learning can appeal to administrators (Lieberman 2013). Addressing administrative interests through conservation education can lead to greater cooperation, increased funding, materials for outdoor projects, release time for teachers to attend workshops, and the subsequent sustainability of your efforts.

Explore the following questions: Who makes curricular decisions at the individual school level? Can teachers plan their own projects with or without approval from their supervisors? How influential and active are groups such as the parent–teacher association? What kind of support does the school system receive from the national ministry or department of education? The answers to these questions place you in a better position to communicate with administrators. In fact, your planning may reveal that a colleague or neighbor has a connection to a key administrator to facilitate your first communications.

Academic standards

Schools are required to follow national, regional, or state academic standards, and most national or state departments of education post their academic standards on their websites. Standards define the knowledge and skills students are expected to learn in a subject for each grade level. Learning standards describe educational objectives or learning outcomes specifying "what" must be learned. Curriculum and instruction describes "how" the standards will be taught, which is often left to individual schools or teachers. In the USA, the majority of states have adopted the Common Core State Standards for two subject areas: English language arts and mathematics, with other subjects being governed by state standards.

A review of the academic standards will reveal what information is taught and which subjects could be enhanced by conservation education. The standards will also show if conservation education is a part of the academic course of study, either as a separate course such as environmental science or infused throughout the curriculum. But the standards won't specify *how* students acquire the skills, a context that conservation education can address. (Section 4.3 provides specific guidelines for correlating conservation education with educational standards.)

By reviewing the academic standards, and even spending time in a classroom if possible, you can get a feel for what content teachers emphasize and why. Many kindergarten classes, for example, spend more time on reading than on mathematics and science. The rationale for this is that reading forms a foundation for learning other subjects. If your conservation education program addresses gaps in the curriculum or supports a priority area, you will have an easier time gaining support.

Testing and accountability

Many school systems give their students a hot breakfast on the morning of a test to enhance their performance on standardized tests. The outcomes of these tests are often linked to school funding and student advancement. Arm yourself with knowledge about how and when these tests occur before you propose conservation education activities in a school. Is there a national test and when do students take it? What is the pass rate in your area? Do schools use alternative assessments like portfolios? Do standardized tests

Fig. 4.1 College students in the EcoTeam program facilitate conservation education lessons that correlate to science standards for third-grade students. (Photo by J. Bowers.)

include knowledge about the environment and conservation? The standardized tests in Kenya, for example, include environmental content. This gives a good opportunity for conservation educators to assist teachers in preparing students for the exam, through field experiences and hands-on activities that reinforce these concepts.

In contrast, many US states do not test science in primary grades. The EcoTeam program in the USA provides a series of hands-on environmental education lessons correlated with science standards for third-grade primary students. With the pressures of testing in other subjects, many teachers do not have the time to emphasize science in their classes, so they have been eager for college students with the EcoTeam program to provide this science instruction (Fig. 4.1).

Background and developmental levels of students

Building support for conservation education in schools requires knowing your target audience—the students. Remember to research variables such as languages, cultural norms, racial and ethnic background, special needs, knowledge, attitudes, and skills of students in relation to the local community. A conservation education program that only emphasizes conservation of elephants may not find an appropriate audience in a rural region of Central Africa where elephants routinely destroy subsistence crops. An emphasis on ecosystem processes might be more successful in this context.

As you consider the background of students, match your conservation education goals to their developmental level (see Chapter 2). Some conservation educators have done more harm than good by introducing complex concepts like global warming to 5-year-old children. With young children (aged 8 and younger), for example, focus on sensory awareness and positive outdoor experiences rather than more complex concepts of habitat loss or sea-level rise that can invoke a sense of powerlessness and fear.

Techniques like games, hands-on activities, nature awareness, and the arts are perfect for this younger age group. Older students in middle and secondary school can address critical and more complex topics like climate change. For these students you can use role-plays, for example, to explore the conflicting interests of stakeholders in an environmental issue like hydraulic fracturing. Issue investigation and citizen science are techniques that also work well with older groups.

Local environmental and community issues

Understanding the needs of the community will help link your conservation education program to the local environment. Think about what knowledge and skills students need to explore issues such as the management of community forests, restoration of wildlife habitat, creation of community gardens, or monitoring water quality. A conservation education program might involve students investigating local environmental issues or conducting a community mapping exercise (see Chapter 7).

As you assess environmental needs, also look at the dynamics of the local community. Do local businesses and organizations support schools? Could you partner with existing groups working in the schools? If you already work in a school as a teacher, you have an inside view of what issues matter to your students and your community.

4.1.2 Implementation

Your communications with schools, whether with teachers, parents, or administrators, should focus on matching the needs of a school with your resources and skills. Once school administrators or other teachers realize that you have an interest in addressing existing needs, from organizing field trips to judging science fairs, they may be more likely to try new or innovative programs. Communication often begins with a personal connection, for example a teacher or parent you already know. If administrators see that teachers are excited about a new possibility (and willing to help coordinate the efforts) they are more likely to get on board.

Start by assessing the school's current support for conservation education and what resources they need. Is there adequate money for field trips? In the USA, one North Carolina district needs approximately $300 to cover the cost of paying bus drivers and transporting 80 second-grade students and their teachers 60 miles away for a day-long field trip to a national forest. A school in this district will typically ask students to contribute $4 each, which covers these expenses. As an agency or organization you could raise those funds as a one-time donation, showcasing your program and building support for future collaboration.

Invite a teacher or group of teachers for a quick walk around the school grounds to assess physical needs. Does the school have any space for outdoor activities? Is there a garden, a nature study area, or a stream for studying water quality? Do they have teaching materials related to conservation? Have teachers participated in any professional development opportunities connected to conservation education? Often, you may find a few teachers within a school system who are enthusiastic about conservation education. Communication with these leaders can help promote your efforts. Also, ask teachers to identify their most involved parents, or those who may be interested in volunteering or supporting your project.

You may be working in a school district where basic needs have a priority over outdoor spaces. As a conservation educator you can help address needs for supplies, whiteboards, books, paper, or even iPads for wildlife monitoring research. Does the school have information about the available conservation education resources? Compile a list of nearby environmental education centers that offer free field trips for students or contacts for guest speakers from conservation agencies. Members of the school-based Wildlife Clubs of Kenya, for example, receive reduced entrance fees to any national park in Kenya. Many clubs work in partnership with conservation agencies to help raise funds for transport to the parks.

Remember that teachers do not sit in front of a computer or by the phone during the day. Instead, they are interacting with students during school hours. Most schools do not have voicemail for individual teachers, and teachers cannot stop their lesson to answer a phone call from an enthusiastic conservation educator. Ask teachers to tell you the best method to communicate with them. Many teachers prefer an e-mail message, while others respond better to a text or a phone message offering a number where they can reach you after school. During individual meetings with teachers or administrators, take notes and summarize what you have heard. Keep meetings focused and brief to respect the time constraints.

In addition to communicating with individual teachers, find out how teachers communicate with each other. Do most teachers attend regular faculty meetings? Do they attend regional education conferences? As you begin to communicate with teachers, assess the substance of their communications. How can your resources help address the stresses felt by teachers, such as the pressures of high-stakes testing? Are they motivated by specific topics? How can you build on these interests? Do not be discouraged if there are only a few teachers who are open to a new conservation education program. Start small with those who are interested, and others will come to you as they see the benefits involved in the initiative.

Communications will identify key players—teachers, students, parents, administrators, community members, agencies, and organizations—who can help you in the next steps of programming conservation education. Even if you are planning a small-scale program, a steering committee can generate feedback on your ideas and delegate responsibilities. Invite a group of stakeholders to an initial steering committee meeting to identify ways you can serve as a resource and to generate support for conservation education in the schools.

Another important aspect of communications with a steering committee is identifying potential barriers, for example lack of planning time or administrative support, and strategies for overcoming those barriers (Box 4.2). With any meeting, come prepared with an agenda or list of topics to address. Be sure to write down ideas on a flipchart or a shared online document so everyone can see that you have captured their suggestions. Lastly, remember to send all committee members an electronic copy of the minutes of the meeting.

Box 4.2 Overcoming barriers in the schools: comments from teachers and suggestions for conservation educators

---

Structural barriers

"The school year isn't long enough to cover the academic standards and prepare for testing, and also address conservation education."

If conservation education activities and programs help teachers address academic standards, they will be more likely to integrate them into teaching.

"My class periods are too short, and there's no time to plan."

Administrative duties often consume teachers' planning periods. Consider several alternatives: cover information in small steps over several months; find funding for a substitute so teachers can attend workshops with conservation agencies; or restructure a school day through team teaching and occasional double periods.

"I don't have relevant materials for teaching about the environment."

Help teachers identify and adapt resources. Use local materials from environmental organizations and natural resource agencies. Provide opportunities for training and support from outside agencies.

Support barriers

"My principal doesn't support this kind of education."

Consider offering a workshop for administrators to learn about experiential methods for teaching and improvements in test scores from schools using environment-based education. Use research documents with real data on student improvements to support your case.

"My colleagues aren't supportive."

Sometimes just talking with colleagues about their concerns can build understanding. Invite teachers in your school to participate in a sample activity based on their needs or interests. Find one or two other teachers who share an interest in conservation education and pilot test an activity or program.

Perceptual barriers

"I don't know enough about this subject and this kind of teaching."

Do your part to provide resources that can help bridge knowledge gaps, such as conservation workshops, local experts, books, and articles. Provide training in experiential methods of teaching and learning.

"Parents and community members might not approve."

Emphasize the role of conservation education in building responsible citizenship skills.

Adapted from Pennock, M.T., Bardwell, L.V., and Britt, P. (1994). *Approaching Environmental Issues in the Classroom*. EE Toolbox—Workshop Resource Manual. Kendall Hunt Publishing, Dubuque, IA and Adams, T.R. (2013) Overcoming barriers to teaching action-based environmental education: a multiple case study of teachers in the public school classroom. Masters Theses and Specialist Projects. Paper 1230 (<http://digitalcommons.wku.edu/theses/1230/>)

4.1.3 Evaluation

Effective communication with any audience involves active listening. If people *feel* heard they are more likely to hear what *you* have to say. Good communication involves paraphrasing and summarizing what you have heard. Assess if you are using these strategies, even in email correspondence, to help evaluate the effectiveness of your communications with schools.

While you can evaluate the consistency and effectiveness of your own communications, ask teachers and other stakeholders to give feedback on the communications. At the end of the first steering committee meeting, facilitate a discussion on what has worked well in terms of communications and what needs improvement. Ask individual teachers and administrators for this same information.

4.2 Acting as a resource for schools

Communication lays the groundwork for your role as a resource for schools through conservation education programming. In turn, students, teachers, and parents can help achieve conservation goals in the larger community. Your role may start small, for example serving as a judge at a science fair or providing materials for an Earth Day celebration. Starting small promotes successful experiences and establishes a good rapport with schools.

4.2.1 Planning

Your initial meetings with teachers, administrators, or a steering committee should have helped identify strategies for meeting the needs of your school or school system. Now the goal of planning is to prioritize these strategies and decide which role to implement first. Start with a small task that has a high chance of success, and then plan subsequent activities or programs to build the profile of conservation education. For example, a coastal education agency might start by bringing a hands-on display on estuaries into a few classrooms and then invite teachers for an afternoon field visit, with meals and materials provided. Subsequently, work with teachers to design grade-appropriate field trips that correlate to the academic standards.

4.2.2 Implementation

The following ideas give some examples of the resources needed by many school systems. Remember that with more extensive projects, developing outdoor labs or resource materials for example, you will need to follow the systematic steps of program design outlined in Chapter 1.

Serving as a judge at fairs, exhibits, and celebrations

An age-old tradition in many schools is the annual science fair, and schools usually need outside judges from the community. Providing this resource to schools allows you to spend a few hours with teachers, students, and administrators. The projects will also give you an insight into possible environmental issues on the minds of the students.

Many schools have contests involving environmental projects for Earth Day, so consider helping with these events or providing an information booth at the school.

Creating scholarships and awards

Most professional organizations for conservation educators are eager to attract teachers to their conferences. Yet many schools do not provide funding for teachers to attend these conferences or pay for substitutes. Providing scholarships to teachers so they can attend conferences and network with conservation educators serves both schools and conservation education. Professional organizations for environmental educators often receive grants to offer scholarships so teachers can attend their annual conferences. Offering scholarships to pre-service teachers also provides a resource, and a hook for future partnerships with schools.

Another resource for schools are awards that promote environmentally responsible projects or actions. The Auckland Regional Council in New Zealand sponsors the Enviroschools campaign to encourage schools to incorporate best environmental practices into their school communities. Wildlife Clubs of Kenya sponsors a national art and essay competition for schoolchildren, with a theme related to a critical environmental issue, for example marine conservation or forests. Chapter 5 and 9 include additional details on organizing environmental contests and incentive systems.

Providing resources and field experiences

Students and teachers may lack specific resources to study environmental concepts in their community. A review of the curriculum framework can provide ideas for existing materials that could enhance the content teachers need to cover. Existing resources often provide the required information but teachers lack the time to find these materials. Alternatively they may have materials that are not relevant for their geographic region, so adapting resources to fit a local context can address a need. If you are creating new resources consider hosting an afternoon workshop to get input from teachers into the design and focus of materials. Educators are more likely to use materials if they have helped to develop them.

When selecting or developing materials, use established guidelines to help identify quality materials. The North American Association of Environmental Education (NAAEE) involved more than 1000 practitioners in the development and review of the *Environmental Education Materials: Guidelines for Excellence* (NAAEE 2009a). This publication identifies six key characteristics of quality environmental education materials, with accompanying indicators to help educators evaluate materials (Box 4.3). The National Project for Excellence in Environmental Education spearheaded the publication of a number of other guidelines, including: *Guidelines for the Preparation and Professional Development of Environmental Educators* (NAAEE 2010a), *Nonformal Environmental Education Programs: Guidelines for Excellence* (NAAEE 2009b), and *Early Childhood Environmental Education Programs: Guidelines for Excellence* (NAAEE 2010b).

Another strategy for providing resources is to create a network that links teachers to conservation educators. In the USA, the Wisconsin Green Schools Network is an association of schools and statewide agencies that promotes environmental education

Box 4.3 Characteristics and indicators of quality materials for environmental education

Key characteristic 1: fairness and accuracy

Environmental education materials should be fair and accurate in describing environmental problems, issues, and conditions, and in reflecting the diversity of perspectives on them.

Indicators: factual accuracy, balanced presentation of differing viewpoints and theories, openness to inquiry, reflection of diversity

Key characteristic 2: depth

Environmental education materials should foster awareness of the natural and built environment, an understanding of environmental concepts, conditions, and issues, and an awareness of the feelings, values, attitudes, and perceptions at the heart of environmental issues, as appropriate for different developmental levels.

Indicators: awareness, focus on concepts, concepts in context, attention to different scales

Key characteristic 3: emphasis on skills building

Environmental education materials should build lifelong skills that enable learners to prevent and address environmental issues.

Indicators: critical and creative thinking, applying skills to issues, action skills

Key characteristic 4: action orientation

Environmental education materials should promote a civic responsibility, encouraging learners to use their knowledge, personal skills, and assessment of environmental issues as a basis for environmental problem solving and action.

Indicators: sense of personal stake and responsibility, self-efficacy

Key characteristic 5: instructional soundness

Environmental education materials should rely on instructional techniques that create an effective learning environment.

Indicators: learner-centered instruction, different ways of learning, connection to learners' everyday lives, expanded learning environment, interdisciplinary, goals and objectives, appropriateness for specific learning settings, assessment

Key characteristic 6: usability

Environmental education materials should be well designed and easy to use.

Indicators: clarity and logic, easy to use, long-lived, adaptable, accompanied by instruction and support, make substantiated claims, fit with national, state, or local requirements

Adapted from NAAEE (2009a). *Environmental Education Materials: Guidelines for Excellence.* National Project for Excellence in Environmental Education. Retrieved May 21, 2014 from: <http://eelinked.naaee.net/n/guidelines/posts/environmental-education-materials-guidelines-for-excellence>

in the state. In some cases, schools may need access to experts such as extension agents, wildlife officers, or even health officials to address an environmental health issue, like high asthma rates caused by air pollution.

Lastly, nature centers and parks can provide a destination for field trips (Chapters 5 and 12), as well as pre- and post-visit lesson plans with supporting activities. Correlating these materials with the national or state academic standards again increases the likelihood of their use and effectiveness.

Providing professional development

Lack of training in environmental education is a barrier that has been identified in repeated studies about environmental education in schools (Ham and Sewing 1987/88; Monroe and Cappaert 1994; McKeown-Ice 2000; Adams 2013). Many teachers perceive that they lack the experience and knowledge to teach about the environment. In other cases, teachers share a common misconception that conservation education connects only to the natural sciences. Agencies and organizations can provide teachers with well-organized workshops that include ready-to-use materials suitable for the classroom. The inclusion of a wealth of resources, quality facilitation, efficient use of time, incentives, and even good food at these workshops will encourage teachers to spread the word about your work.

The US state of Wisconsin mandates that new teachers complete training in environmental education to receive their certification in elementary education, secondary science, social studies, and agriculture. The Centre for Environmental Education in India organizes workshops to promote resilience of local communities in the face of climate change. The USDA Forest Service and the US Fish and Wildlife Service are among the agencies to sponsor workshops on curricula such as Project WILD, Project Learning Tree, and Project WILD Aquatic. Teachers attending these workshops receive teaching materials as well as credits for continuing education. In many cases, state agencies have also correlated these national curricula to the academic standards to promote use of the lessons in the classroom.

When marketing a workshop for teachers, emphasize how the content will help educators do their job. One popular workshop session, for example, involves showing teachers how to design a "literacy bed" using a school garden (Box 4.4). This workshop session helps teachers learn to integrate props from children's literature into an existing or new garden bed at a school. For the children's book *Growing Vegetable Soup* by Lois Ehlert (1987), conservation educators painted garden tools the same color as tools pictured in the book (Fig. 4.2). With any book that focuses on food, students could paint the cover of the book on a piece of plywood, plant crops from the book, and conduct research on the plot and characters!

Developing an outdoor lab

At Isaac Dickson Elementary School in Asheville, North Carolina, USA, a partnership with the USDA Forest Service, an environmental NGO called Quality Forward, the state department of natural resources, and the garden program MAGIC, resulted in the reestablishment of a nature trail by the school. This previously abandoned trail on

Box 4.4 A lesson plan to help teachers use "literacy beds" to integrate literature and conservation education

---

Objectives

By the end of the lesson, students will be able to:

- create and integrate props from the plot of a children's book into a garden bed,
- plant produce described in a children's book in their school garden,
- work in cooperative groups to depict the book in their school garden.

Participants

Students in a classroom.

Materials

- Children's literature that integrates gardening or environmental themes.
- Recycled props to depict the plot of the book—a gardening hat, old buckets, stuffed animals, and gardening tools.
- Ply board, paint, and paintbrushes.
- Seeds or seedlings of produce featured in the book.
- An existing garden bed or a new bed.

Procedure

1. This activity creates a garden bed based on the information in a specific piece of children's literature, for example Beatrix Potter's *The Tale of Peter Rabbit* or Dr. Seuss' *The Lorax*. Begin by reviewing the suggestions for books in Step 4 and engage your students in choosing the book they want to use for the project. Explain to the students that the class is going to "grow" their book by creating a garden bed based on the plants, characters, and plot line of the book.
2. Tell the students that they are going to include as many as possible of the props that figure prominently in the book. Since you are using a garden, the class will also grow as many of the plants mentioned in the book as possible. If the book includes vegetables that do not grow together at the same time, such as peas and corn, improvise by using a laminated drawing or a piece of plywood painted like a corn stalk! Color a picture of the book's cover on plywood, so everyone in the schools can see the connection between the book and the garden bed. Divide students into cooperative groups to accomplish the necessary tasks for this activity.
3. If you do not have gardening experience, model the learning process for your students by inviting a grandparent, local farmer, or extension specialist. Local nurseries will often donate seedlings. Use your imagination to integrate art, mathematics, history, literature, nutrition, and literacy into this conservation education project. Invite parents, school administrators, and the local media to an official "reading" of the story by the students.
4. Below you will find a few suggestions of books and activities that correspond to a literacy bed:

Box 4.4 *Continued*

- *The Lorax* by Dr. Seuss—consider planting a "thneed" garden, reminding students that thneeds are things you don't need! Plant seeds and transplants in old buckets or shoes. Integrate a lesson on recycling into this activity. You could also build a strange tree that could be a Truffala Tree for a lesson on extinction.
- *Growing Vegetable Soup* by Lois Ehlert—use bright paint to color props like old shovels, rakes, a hoe, watering can, soup pot, ladle, and spading fork. The book includes numerous vegetables to plant.
- *Scarecrow* by Cynthia Rylant—this book is appropriate for children or even adults. Props can include scarecrows, owls, rabbits, and worms. Have students research these characters for the project. Write stories from the perspective of the scarecrow.
- Other suggestions: *The Ugly Vegetables, The Carrot Seed, Sunflower Sal . . .* or any book you find that will work!

Evaluation

Have students assess how effective they have been at working in groups on this project by engaging them in discussion several times during the project. How well are they working together? What have been their successes? What have been their challenges and areas for improvement? Take pictures of the garden bed before and after the project for concrete assessment of the project's outcomes and achievement of lesson objectives.

Adapted from Jackson, E. (2005). *Literacy Beds.* Unpublished document from the Appalachian Sustainable Agriculture Project, Asheville, NC.

Fig. 4.2 A workshop on "literacy beds" used the book *Growing Vegetable Soup* to display images from the book in the school garden. (Photo by S. Wagner Booth.)

the outskirts of the urban school grounds became the focus of a partnership that involved 500 hours of work from parent and other adult volunteers to bushwhack, mulch, and dig to restore the trail. The project included the development of curriculum resources and trail guides. Classes regularly use the trail to study wildlife habitats. Since the reestablishment of the trail, the project has expanded to include an archaeological study by students of an African-American community that previously resided on the site.

Helping schools develop an outdoor lab, a schoolyard ecosystem, a school garden, or an outdoor site for monitoring wildlife or water quality can be one of the most direct ways to increase the positive outdoor experiences of young people (Fig. 4.3). The involvement of a wide range of partners expands the level of publicity and community involvement and thus increases the sustainability of the project. Outdoor learning labs also provide a perfect context for infusing conservation education into the curriculum, as students can use the natural site for writing a journal, observing wildlife, restoring habitat, and graphing seasonal changes. A partnership between the Los Angeles County Fire Department, local businesses, concerned citizens, and the Chaparral Middle School in California, USA created a plant nursery for drought-tolerant species that could be grown locally. Thousands of trees were planted as a result of this project, and the entire school is now involved with the nursery (Project WILD 2007).

Fig. 4.3 Outdoor learning labs can engage students in direct experiences with the environment. (Photo by the Appalachian Sustainable Agriculture Project.)

4.2.3 Evaluation

The needs of school systems change over time, so the impacts and effectiveness of new resources in schools resulting from conservation education must be regularly evaluated. Evaluation will ensure that you replicate success, not failure. Most donors or foundations want to see evidence of the effectiveness and impacts of funded programs. Identifying your questions and tools for evaluation before starting a project will help focus your efforts and clarify your project to others (see Chapter 1).

The necessary evaluation tools will depend on the specific type of conservation education resources provided to a school. If the resource is as simple as providing scholarship money for teachers to attend a conservation education conference, compare the number of teachers attending the conference before and after funding became available. A few months after the conference, ask the participating teachers how they have used the information obtained at the conference in their classrooms. If their testimonies are positive, use them to attract more funding and applicants. For serving as a judge at a science fair, informal observation and discussions will indicate whether your participation has been a positive addition to the event.

Evaluation of more involved resources will demand multiple evaluation tools. If a project involved building an outdoor lab, for example, you can measure the knowledge of students about their schoolyard ecosystem before and after incorporating the lab into classroom activities. Students can also take photographs of a natural area before and after a conservation project to document environmental changes over time.

If a steering committee was involved, use interviews and feedback sheets to gather systematic feedback from them about the effectiveness of the projects. This same feedback from students, through interviews, observation, and even short surveys, can prove valuable not only in improving programs but also in gathering anecdotal evidence of impacts to include in funding reports. Student portfolios provide additional concrete evidence of the effects of conservation education. Lastly, if the resources significantly affect delivery of content in the classroom, consider before and after tests of knowledge and skills.

One strategy for planning your evaluation is to meet your steering committee during the planning stages of your program and brainstorm evaluation questions. The Wildlife Clubs of Kenya, for example, conducted workshops on evaluation throughout the country and asked staff and teachers to brainstorm questions they most wanted an evaluation to address (McDuff 2001). The teachers and staff members also identified sources of evidence for the questions and indicators of success (Box 4.5).

Some other questions that can drive the evaluation of outcomes in environmental education include (Bennett 1988/89; Russ 2014):

- What learning gains, if any, occurred as a result of the program?
- What instructional techniques contributed to the results of the program?
- What aspects of the learning environment contributed to the results of the program?
- What impact did the program have on the environment?
- What impact did the program have on other people in the school and community?
- Are the goals and objectives of the program appropriate?
- Were there unanticipated outcomes of the program?

Box 4.5 Example of evaluation questions developed by teachers with the Wildlife Clubs of Kenya

Evaluation question	Sources of evidence	Indicators (signs of success)
How effective is the implementation of your activities?	Photographs Artwork Surveys Interviews Letters of appreciation	Variety of activities conducted Number of members/ renewal of membership Active involvement of students Gender balance among members Innovative conservation projects Accurate record keeping and minutes Submission of articles to *Komba*, the Wildlife Clubs of Kenya magazine

4.3 Supporting academic standards

Student assessment and testing are linked to academic standards to provide a measure of accountability. Thus, a teacher is expected to cover the material in the academic standards, evaluated by student achievement on tests based on these standards. In most school systems the academic standards include measurable objectives or benchmarks that students must achieve: "The students will be able to explain the process of decomposition." The teacher often has the flexibility to choose the activities and materials for teaching the concept of decomposition to achieve the objectives. Academic standards are also linked to professional development for teachers, student progress, and school funding. Conservation education activities can provide the context for building skills that lead to achievement of academic standards.

4.3.1 Planning

Reviewing academic standards

The structure of academic standards varies depending on the country or state. All academic standards, however, include what students should know or be able to do by the end of a specific grade. The organization of academic standards is typically by grade level and subject. Each subject or content area has broad goals with more specific benchmarks as objectives.

Knowledge and skills build upon each other, so students in primary grades may be expected to describe what plants need to grow (soil, water, sun, and air), while older students should be able to explain the process of photosynthesis. In some regions or states, for example California and Pennsylvania in the USA and New South Wales in Australia, the academic standards include specific objectives for the environment. In California, the state developed its own environmental principles and concepts, as a part of an education and environment initiative. This framework combines one or more science or history/social studies standards with one or more environmental principles, which then tie to a "California connection" story that presents a relevant environmental topic in the state (Lieberman 2013).

In a different structure, Pennsylvania includes "Environment and ecology" as a content area in its academic standards. These standards can be found on the Pennsylvania Department of Education website (Pennsylvania Department of Education 2014), where the standards for subjects such as arts and humanities, civics and government, and mathematics can also be retrieved. The academic standards for environment and ecology include the following content areas, with numbers for reference:

- 4.1 Ecology
- 4.2 Watersheds and wetlands
- 4.3 Natural resources
- 4.4 Agriculture and society
- 4.5 Humans and the environment

Each content area includes objectives for the specific grade level, so students build on their knowledge and skills in subsequent grades. Academic standard 4.2.7, for example, corresponds to "Watersheds and wetlands" for the seventh grade with goals and specific objectives. (Standard 4.2.4 would correspond to a fourth-grade benchmark on watersheds and wetlands.) By the end of the seventh grade students should be able to:

- Explain how water enters, moves through and leaves a watershed.
- Explain the concept of stream order.
- Describe factors that affect the flow and water quality within a watershed.

Note that these standards focus on the science content related to watersheds, yet the last objective opens the door for examining the positive and negative impacts of human behavior on watersheds. Conservation education programs developed by the Brandywine Valley Association in Pennsylvania explore this content by providing outdoor lessons to schools within walking distance of the school. As the oldest watershed association in the United States, the Brandywine Valley Association developed its outdoor lessons to correlate to the state standards (Kenny et al. 2003). This program also trains teachers through peer-teaching to conduct outdoor activities, making it easier for them to cover the standards on their own school grounds.

The environmental education policy for New South Wales, Australia, requires schools to integrate environmental education to support other content (e.g., English and mathematics), as well as use special events and school community projects to enhance student learning. The Australian government also provides a sustainability curriculum framework as a guide for incorporating sustainability into teaching and learning within the school system (Commonwealth of Australia 2014).

Unfortunately, environmental education is not a priority area of content for the academic standards in most states or countries. Many dedicated groups, however, are working to integrate environmental education into legislation, educational policy, and capacity-building for teachers and non-formal educators who deliver programs to schools. Because the environment relates to both natural and social systems, connecting conservation education programs to traditional standards is not difficult. And because the environment is locally relevant, such programming creates engaged learning among students. In Section 4.3.2 we present examples of how to correlate lessons when environmental knowledge and skills are embedded in other standards, such as those for language arts, science, and healthy living.

Two strategies for addressing academic standards: infusion and insertion

The Department of Education in Queensland, Australia recognizes environmental education for sustainability as a "cross-curriculum" area of learning, integrated into other content areas (Department of Education, Training, and Employment, Queensland 2014). To that end, the outdoor and environmental education centers in Queensland have correlated all the activities in their programs with the academic curriculum, team building, and leadership objectives. Their programs highlight biodiversity and education for sustainability. By matching their outdoor education programs with academic standards, the centers increase the probability that teachers can take the time to integrate experiential learning in unique environments such as forests, estuaries, and freshwater habitats into their teaching.

This strategy of *infusion* is one used by many conservation educators to integrate conservation education into an already crowded curriculum. Infusion incorporates conservation education content or process into established courses (Monroe and Cappaert 1994). Subject areas including science, social studies, art, mathematics, and music can be used for infusion. Some advantages of infusion are that conservation education does not have to compete with other subjects, and teachers do not need a new textbook as they often can use supplementary resources (Box 4.6).

When you infuse conservation education into the curriculum, you must address the current academic standards and the conservation material that you want to infuse. Some conservation education programs work with an existing program to determine the overlap between their conservation objectives and the objectives in the academic standards. Other programs use the standards as a starting point for designing new conservation education programming for specific grade levels.

As opposed to infusion, *insertion* involves creating a separate conservation education course or a specific theme focused on conservation topics. For example, students in high school may be required to take an environmental science course, or teachers might explore a 2-week theme in social studies on environmental issues. An individual course allows teachers to build on specific concepts throughout the course, but this strategy also requires more in-depth knowledge and training of selected teachers. As both

Box 4.6 Benefits and barriers of infusion and insertion

Infusion—conservation education throughout the curriculum

Benefits:
- Needs fewer resources
- Does not compete with other subjects or times in the curriculum
- Encourages learning and problem-solving across the curriculum
- Reinforces and builds upon key environmental concepts

Barriers:
- Requires extensive teacher training and effort
- Relies on the efforts of motivated teachers to succeed
- Can dilute the environmental message to fit course objectives
- Evaluating success can be challenging

Insertion—creating a separate conservation education course

Benefits:
- Easier to implement and evaluate as a single subject
- Allows teachers to present concepts in greater depth that build throughout the course
- Places a priority on the subject

Barriers:
- Requires trained teachers with in-depth environmental knowledge
- Takes time from standard topics in curriculum
- May imply that environment is not an interdisciplinary subject
- Can limit the number of students exposed unless it is required content

Adapted from Braus, J.A. and Wood, D. (1993). *Environmental Education in the Schools: Creating a Program that Works*. Peace Corps Information Collection and Exchange, Washington, DC.

infusion and insertion have advantages and disadvantages—and require training—the ideal situation involves using both strategies within a school system whenever possible. With both infusion and insertion, however, conservation education must connect to academic standards.

An example of both insertion and infusion is the residential Conserve School in Wisconsin, USA, a semester-long program that offers full scholarships to high school students across the country. This school uses the outdoors as a context for learning traditional academic content (e.g., mathematics) but also emphasizes environmental studies as a discipline for the semester. One planning strategy to link a conservation education program to academic standards is to sponsor a workshop that involves teachers, administrators, and subject matter experts to develop resources that match the curriculum framework or to correlate existing materials. Consider which teachers and other stakeholders would be most interested in such an endeavor, plan a time that is convenient for them, and find support for incentives such as a stipend for participation. Draft lessons developed in the workshop can be reviewed by other teachers and experts, pilot tested, and revised (see Chapter 1).

4.3.2 Implementation

An online learning center in New Zealand, Te Kete Ipurangi, presents an eight-step process for using the New Zealand curriculum framework to develop environmental education programs in schools (Box 4.7). Four options for connecting environmental education to the academic standards are available: (1) develop programs in the context of achievement aims and objectives in one curriculum area, (2) develop programs with cross-curricular themes from two or more curriculum areas, (3) use an action-oriented approach developing knowledge, attitudes, and skills for taking action on an environmental issue, or (4) develop an environmental studies course (Te Kete Ipurangi 2003).

Box 4.7 Outline of a process for planning environmental education programs within the New Zealand curriculum framework

---

Step 1: Identify the needs of students

Ask the following questions to identify student needs:
- What are the natural and built environments in which students live, work, and play?
- What environmental issues do students encounter in their daily lives?
- What attitudes, knowledge, and skills will students need in order to become involved with other conservation issues?

Step 2: Review current programs

Ascertain which of the following aims of environmental education are found in current teaching and learning programs:
- Awareness and sensitivity to the environment.
- Knowledge and understanding of the environment and the impact of people.
- Attitudes and values that reflect feelings of concern for the environment.
- Skills in identifying, investigating, and problem-solving with environmental issues.
- A sense of responsibility through participation in addressing environmental issues.

Step 3: Identify opportunities

Identify new opportunities for the inclusion of environmental education within the New Zealand curriculum.

Step 4: Identify links

Identify possible links between school programs and initiatives undertaken by regional and local councils and community agencies.

Step 5: Decide how environmental education will be managed

There are four basic ways to structure the environmental education program within the framework of the New Zealand curriculum:
- Develop a program in one curriculum area.
- Develop a program based on cross-curricular themes, for example languages and mathematics.

Box 4.7 *Continued*

- Use an action-oriented approach to help students develop attitudes, knowledge, skills, and values to take environmental action.
- Develop an environmental studies course to enable students to make an extended study of environmental issues.

Step 6: Develop programs

Effective learning requires teachers who can achieve the aims of environmental education by:

- Planning programs based on the aims of the national curriculum statements.
- Using a variety of teaching and learning approaches: inquiry-based learning, games and simulations, case studies, community-based learning, experiential learning, education outside the classroom, investigation of local environmental issues, and evaluation and action in environmental problem-solving.
- Providing opportunities for students to use their new knowledge, attitudes, values, and skills.
- Creating and maintaining a supportive learning environment for students.
- Assessing both cognitive and affective learning in environmental education.

Step 7: Select appropriate resources

Consider the following criteria for resources to support teaching and learning: appropriate content, skill development, language level, student interest, date, bicultural perspectives (Maori and non-Maori), multicultural perspectives, gender perspectives, and balance.

Step 8: Plan how to conduct evaluation

Adapted from Te Kete Ipurangi (2003). Planning environmental education programs within the New Zealand curriculum framework. Retrieved May 20, 2014 from <http://efs.tki.org.nz/curriculum-resources-and-tools/environmental-education-guidelines>.

Connecting to content or process

Remember, if you have an existing conservation education program look for standards or objectives in the curriculum that your program already addresses or that students could achieve with greater success through hands-on experience. When developing a new program, consider which objectives best fit your resources and skills. The next example shows several learning objectives and the corresponding conservation education activities developed by teachers in a fifth-grade "water works" unit at Jackson Elementary School in California, USA (Lieberman 2013):

- English/language arts:
  - Learning objective: use electronic media to gather information.
  - Conservation education activity: students use the Internet to gather information and discuss the pros and cons of water conservation, and create a graphic organizer for a writing assignment.

- Mathematics:
  - Learning objective: make plots to display a data set of measurements.
  - Conservation education activity: Students plot the data from their survey of campus-wide water use and create histograms and bar graphs to show their individual data.
- Science:
  - Learning objective: locate community-based sources of water and describe ways to conserve it.
  - Conservation education activity: students identify their reservoir on a local map and identify two ways that they could conserve water.

Environmental education students at Warren Wilson College, North Carolina, USA, use gardens to teach ecological concepts, and they wanted to develop a 1-day field experience with classes from a local elementary school. Through prior communications with teachers, they learned of the need for a spring field trip that corresponded to the study of plants in first grade. They analyzed the first-grade standards and brainstormed potential activities for their site and resources. The academic standards for science included the following essential standard and clarifying objectives:

- North Carolina essential standard:
  - Science 1.L.2 Summarize the needs of living organisms for energy and growth.
- Clarifying objectives:
  - Summarize the basic needs of a variety of plants (including air, water, nutrients, and light) for energy and growth.
  - Summarize the basic needs of a variety of different animals for energy and growth.

The students then met with the lead teachers to discuss ideas and share the results of their brainstorming. After this meeting, the college students developed a field experience entitled "How does your garden grow?" which correlated to several objectives in science, language arts, and healthy living. The first-grade students then took a 10-minute bus ride to a large organic garden on campus to rotate through four stations of hands-on lessons where they dug in the soil, transplanted tomato plants, read stories about what plants need to grow, and talked about the garden as a growing system, just like their bodies (Fig. 4.4). This 1-day project did not require a workshop with teachers or meetings with a steering committee. The teachers left with a packet of four lesson plans complete with all correlations, as well as a post-field-trip lesson and instructions for transplanting the tomato plants, which each student took home.

Conservation education activities can also address process objectives, such as critical thinking, creative thinking, problem-solving, cooperative learning, and value clarification. Process skills are becoming increasingly important in educational policy, with a focus in schools on leadership, citizenship, and community development. An emphasis on the role of conservation education in promoting process objectives also helps with connecting your program to overall educational goals. For example, students can explore a local environmental issue from the perspective of different stakeholders or attend a local hearing, analyze editorials, and choose to participate in a conservation campaign (Monroe and Cappaert 1994; Monroe and Krasny 2013).

Fig. 4.4 Checklists in hands, students explore soil during a field experience designed to correlate with the academic standards. (Photo by R. Griffin.)

In some schools, administrators are charged with developing programs that enhance the ability of students to communicate with diverse groups of people within both school and the community. By their nature, many conservation education activities emphasize group dynamics and communication skills. While conservation education is certainly no panacea for all societal issues, bringing diverse students together to analyze shared environmental issues uses the process skills necessary for building healthy human and natural communities.

Helping teachers address academic standards through new or existing resources

Conservation educators typically have a toolbox of existing activities or lesson plans that have not been correlated to academic standards. In this scenario, figure out what concepts or skills students would learn if a teacher followed the exact instructions for the activity. Find that concept or skill in the academic standards, and include the correlation in your lesson plan. Do not focus on the many possible ways in which teachers could modify or enhance the activity. Just correlate the activity as written to what the students will understand as a result of the lesson. Your lesson plan should list these correlations for easy reference for teachers. Typically, this section of a lesson or activity plan follows the overall lesson objectives.

A second typical scenario is that conservation educators must develop new activities or resources to help teachers address standards. As already mentioned, you should become familiar with the standards and use them to explore the concepts you wish to convey. Choose a few standards to focus on, and develop activities or lessons that use environmental content to introduce and reinforce the standards. Use one of the experiential learning cycles to develop opportunities to experience, reflect, and apply the new information (see Chapter 2).

4.3.3 Evaluation

Upon completion, have other teachers review the correlations between your materials and the academic standards, and revise them as needed. Give teachers or administrators who review your materials a free copy of the resources as a thank-you. Pilot testing of materials will be likely to reveal necessary changes that may affect the correlations. During implementation one direct measure of the effectiveness of the material is whether or not teachers use the program. If not, investigate the reasons why, and revise it to address the problems.

The advantage of developing programs that support academic standards is that the quantitative measurements can provide data for evaluating the effectiveness of the program. In Florida, USA, a study showed that environmental education lessons designed to correlate to the state standards improved student achievement, based on performance on a post-survey modeled after the state achievement test (Wilson and Monroe 2005). The students' writing scores significantly improved after using a set of lessons focused on biodiversity. These lessons engaged 132 ninth and tenth grade students in practicing writing techniques while learning about biodiversity, exotic species, and endangered habitats. (Wilson and Monroe 2005).

4.4 Integrating conservation education into legislation and educational policy

Comprehensive conservation education in schools will require the systematic inclusion of environmental concepts in educational standards, capacity-building for teachers and non-formal educators, funding, materials development, and legislative support for increasing the environmental literacy of students. A nationwide survey in the USA found that 95% of adults supported environmental education in schools (Coyle 2005).

Despite this public support, the consistency of the environmental content taught in schools varies by grade level and school system. Given the pressures of time and accountability in schools, institutionalizing environmental education and supporting these efforts through training and funding remains paramount. Many countries and states have made great strides in using a legislative agenda and educational policy to promote conservation education in schools. This section provides a case study from the No Child Left Inside movement in the USA that highlights the successes and challenges of this approach.

4.4.1 Planning

The publication of Richard Louv's (2005) *Last Child in the Woods* galvanized teachers, psychologists, nutritionists, parents, and environmental educators with its research-based argument supporting the need to connect young people with the outdoors. In his book, Louv synthesized decades of peer-reviewed studies about the critical role of nature in the cognitive, social, physical, and emotional development of children. He also documented the decreased exposure of children to the outdoors and the impacts of what he calls "nature-deficit disorder."

Concurrent with this publication, US educators observed the impacts of federal legislation entitled "No Child Left Behind" that linked school funding to student performance on standardized testing. Many environmental educators felt that the increased emphasis on testing correlated with decreased time spent on outdoor learning. This confluence led to the creation of a coalition called, No Child Left Inside to support environmental education in the schools.

4.4.2 Implementation

The implementation of this national campaign began with the creation of an alliance that could advocate for federal legislation to fund environmental education. Coordinated by the Chesapeake Bay Foundation, the No Child Left Inside coalition involves more than 2000 organizational members, including the Alaska Botanical Gardens, the Sierra Club, the National Wildlife Federation, and the Arkansas Coalition for Obesity Prevention. The members span a diverse range of interests, from organizations that focus on public health to those that promote wildlife conservation (No Child Left Inside 2014).

The overall goal of the campaign is to amend the Elementary and Secondary Education Act of 2001, known as No Child Left Behind, to provide support for environmental literacy plans in public education. On a practical level, this advocacy work has included providing tools and tactics for members to lobby their legislators in support of this federal legislation. To that end, the website includes talking points for contacting members of Congress, sample letters to the editor about the role of environmental education, and links to the Facebook page and Twitter feed of the No Child Left Inside coalition.

One component of the legislation is to provide additional funds for environmental education to states that develop environmental literacy plans. Thus a step in the implementation was the development of guidelines for states to create such plans. As described in the No Child Left Inside Act, an environmental literacy plan includes content standards for environmental literacy, a description of how graduation requirements will ensure environmental literacy, plans for professional development for teachers in environmental education, a description of how to assess environmental literacy, and an implementation plan (No Child Left Inside 2014).

In 2011, Maryland became the first state to require that its high school graduates should be environmentally literate with the development of state environmental literacy standards. Of 48 states surveyed, 14 states have completed environmental literacy plans that have been adopted by departments of education, 11 states have completed plans that have not yet been adopted, and 23 states are in the process of writing their plans. In short, this national legislative effort has translated into state and local planning efforts, providing a blueprint for both planning and action (No Child Left Inside 2014).

4.4.3 Evaluation

The penultimate measure of the success of the proposed legislation is the passage of laws that support environmental education. On Earth Day, April 22, 2009, the federal bill No Child Left Inside was introduced in the House of Representatives and the Senate, after an unsuccessful attempt in 2008. In an effort to revive the legislation, a second bill

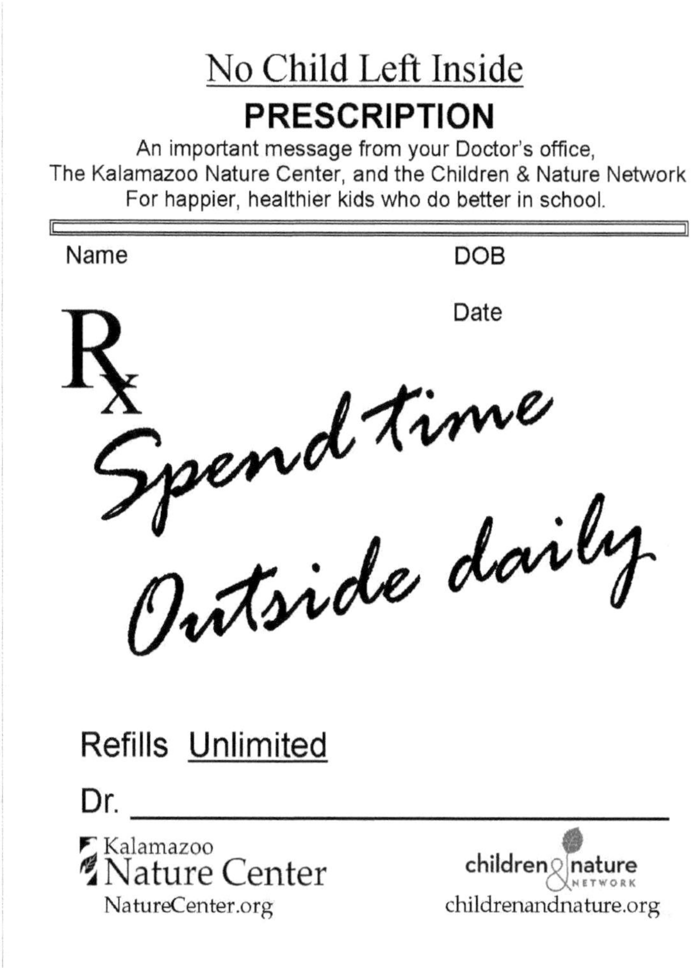

No Child Left Inside

PRESCRIPTION

An important message from your Doctor's office,
The Kalamazoo Nature Center, and the Children & Nature Network
For happier, healthier kids who do better in school.

Name   DOB

R̲x   Date

*Spend time
Outside daily*

Refills Unlimited

Dr. _____

Kalamazoo
Nature Center
NatureCenter.org

children & nature
NETWORK
childrenandnature.org

Fig. 4.5 The No Child Left Inside campaign includes materials such as "prescriptions" for children to spend more time outside.

was reintroduced on July 16, 2013 with bipartisan support, and the bill was referred to committee. The No Child Left Inside bill was reintroduced again in 2015.

In tight economic times, bills calling for increased support for education are meeting obstacles at many steps in the process. Yet one unanticipated outcome of the No Child Left Inside movement was building momentum at the state level for developing plans that link the achievement gains of students with learning in the outdoors. In addition, connecting environmental education with health and well-being created new allies and impacts within public health, a critical partnership given that one-third of US children are at risk for obesity (Fig. 4.5). Indeed many states—California, Maryland, Indiana, and Nevada, for example—passed a "Children's Outdoor Bill of Rights" to highlight the right of young people to participate in outdoor play. Whether or not this specific national bill passes, the alliances formed during lobbying for legislation created a network of organizations that will act on educational policy in the years ahead.

4.5 A sample of approaches to conservation education in schools

The type of conservation education program you plan and implement will depend on a variety of factors, including the characteristics and needs of the school system. Historically, different labels, from place-based education to project-based learning, have characterized specific approaches to conservation education in schools. The case studies in the next sections present two approaches for conservation education with schools: environment-based education and education for sustainability. Chapter 7 explores additional techniques for connecting classrooms with conservation.

4.6 Environment-based education

Environment-based education describes instructional programs in schools that use local environments as the context for integrating subjects, and as a source for real-world learning experiences (NEETF 2000; Ernst 2009). Environment-based education includes three goals for students: (1) academic achievement, (2) understanding of the interactions between nature and human social systems, and (3) preparation to become engaged members of society with skills to resolve environmental challenges (Lieberman 2013). Driven by increased testing and accountability in the school system, environment-based education uses the environment to promote measurable gains in student learning.

Environment-based education includes approaches such as place-based education, environmental service-learning, and issue investigation (Chapter 7). With its emphasis on interdisciplinary learning, development of action skills, and student-directed learning, it differs from other environmental education programs that include a one-time field trip, supplemental use of resource materials, or a sole focus on ecological awareness and knowledge (Enrst 2009).

Research has demonstrated that schools using environment-based education not only show improvements in student achievement but also increases in student motivation, higher-order thinking skills, and a decrease in discipline problems (NEETF 2000, Ernst and Monroe 2004; Lieberman 2013). Some barriers to environment-based education include lack of training for teachers, while a significant influence on its implementation is evidence of positive outcomes for educators (Ernst 2009).

Environment-based education serves as one model for teachers, administrators, parents, and non-formal educators interested in integrating environmental education into schools. Environment-based education can start with one study unit, one classroom, one team of teachers, or an entire school. In one classroom at Kruse Elementary School in Texas, USA, teacher Libby Rhoden instructs a class of 19 first graders, mostly Latino children, who live within five square miles of a refinery. In contrast to other teachers at her school, Rhoden bases her lessons on experiences children have in their local environment. When the students go on a nature walk, they write about their observations. The students build math skills by observing and then tallying behaviors of birds near the classroom. While Rhoden's students reflect the same abilities as students in other classrooms, her students consistently perform higher than all other first graders in reading, language, and mathematics (NEEFT 2000; Coyle 2010).

Indeed, proponents view environment-based education as an avenue to achieve needed educational reforms. In practice, the differences between environmental education and environment-based education become blurred, but a focus on student achievement remains the defining characteristic of environment-based education.

4.6.1 Planning

A group of education agencies from 12 US states coined the term EIC, which stands for "environment as an integrating context for learning." This group, State Education and Environment Roundtable, or SEER, conducted an assessment to survey the impacts on student learning of using the environment in the K–12 curricula (Lieberman and Hoody 1998; Lieberman 2013).

The programs use a form of environment-based education with the following six characteristics: (1) interdisciplinary integration of subject matter, (2) collaborative instruction, (3) community-based investigations with service-learning opportunities, (4) combinations of independent and cooperative learning, (5) learner-centered and constructivist approaches, and (6) natural and community surroundings as a local context for learning (Lieberman 2013).

The planning steps for EIC schools apply to any environment-based education program and include the following:

- Build a team with like-minded teachers and designate one or two people to be in charge of communications.
- Allow ample time for planning before implementation.
- Seek guidance and support from the administration from the beginning.
- Create a network of support—businesses, parents, nature centers, zoos, museums, resource management agencies, university faculty, and city officials.
- Invest significant time, because integrating the curriculum can be a slow process.
- Start small: for example, begin with one teaching team and a 1-month study unit.
- Build gradually by adding team members and study units.
- Plan to evaluate your progress, review your programs, and seek suggestions for improvement.
- Stay patient as experience shows that 3–4 years are needed to build a stable program (Lieberman and Hoody 1998).

4.6.2 Implementation

The "environments" used in environment-based learning can range from a small green space by an asphalt parking lot to 80 acres of woodlands surrounding the school. Third-grade students and teachers at Seven Generations Charter School in Pennsylvania,

USA, worked with parents, volunteers, business owners, and a native plant specialist to restore the riparian zone along a creek that runs from a mountainside and past the school. This environmental service-learning project was a component of a unit called "Interdependence on South Mountain." In the Riverwatch program at Glenwood Springs High School in Colorado, USA, students' participation at a community meeting sparked their interest in applying for a Great Outdoors Colorado grant to develop a riverside park. This group became the first high school application to receive funding, and students worked with city officials on the development of the park (Lieberman and Hoody 1998; Lieberman 2013).

Some schools begin environment-based education with classroom experiences and later expand to the outdoors, as in the endangered species program at Waldo Middle School in Oregon, USA. Teams of teachers responsible for science, geography, mathematics, language arts, and computer literacy coordinate a curriculum that uses endangered species as a focal point. Students gather information on endangered species through library and online research, interviews with biologists, and correspondence with conservation organizations. They then write a species recovery plan and conduct a public presentation with wildlife experts in the audience. Several years after implementation, the school expanded the program to include outdoor field visits (Lieberman and Hoody 1998).

Implementation of environment-based education typically involves teams of teachers working together to facilitate learning across different subjects. Teams from primary schools often include several teachers from one grade level, while secondary schools draw teachers from multiple disciplines. Usually these teams incorporate other stakeholders, such as non-formal educators, conservation experts, students, and parents. One obvious constraint of implementing this approach is time. At some schools, teachers use their planning period for team meetings, reducing the time available for grading and paperwork. The importance of finding a core of dedicated members on the teaching team, and providing training, is critical to the sustainability of environment-based education.

4.6.3 Evaluation

The first qualitative assessment reported on 40 schools in the USA using EIC through interviews with more than 400 students and 250 teachers and principals, as well as comparisons of standardized test scores (Lieberman and Hoody 1998; Lieberman 2013). The findings reported in "Closing the achievement gap: Using the environment as an integrating context for learning" (Lieberman and Hoody 1998) revealed benefits to EIC programs, including reduced discipline problems, improved achievement on standardized tests, and increased motivation for learning. A more rigorous study compared eight EIC schools with a control group of eight traditional schools and found that students in the EIC schools scored significantly higher on achievement tests than students in traditional schools (SEER 2000).

Evaluation research involving 11 environment-based programs in high schools in Florida, USA, showed a positive relationship between environment-based education and students' critical thinking skills, a disposition toward critical thinking, and achievement motivation (Athman and Monroe 2004; Ernst and Monroe 2004). This study involved 586 high school students in a pre-test/post-test non-equivalent comparison group design (ninth grade) and a post-test only non-equivalent comparison group design (twelfth grade). These results corroborate findings from the EIC schools and provide evidence for the role of environment-based education in educational reform efforts.

4.7 Education for sustainability

Many educators view education for sustainability as the future of environmental education (Elder 2003). The goal of sustainable development lies at the heart of education for sustainability, which brings together diverse fields such as systems thinking (Chapter 3), nature study, economics, and civics. The integration of social and economic systems with environmental systems is central to this approach, which is also called education for sustainable development. Indeed, the UN Decade of Education for Sustainable Development, from 2005 to 2014 propelled the growth of this educational movement worldwide.

Education for sustainability challenges students to find and evaluate solutions to the human influence on social and natural systems. In contrast to traditional environmental education, education for sustainability examines the connections between conservation, human rights, poverty, development, and the political process (Henderson and Tilbury 2004). By its nature, education for sustainability requires integration across disciplines. In addition, environmental justice remains an important aspect of education for sustainability, given the disproportionate impact of environmental mismanagement on people of color and the poor (Monroe and Krasny 2013). As an example of these connections, an 18-lesson high school unit on using wood for renewable energy involves students in lessons about environmental justice, economics, biology, and public opinion (Ireland et al. 2010).

Many countries and states with school policies for environmental education have used concepts from education for sustainability as a framework for teaching and learning. The organization Global Learning correlated curricula on sustainability with the New Jersey state standards (Elder 2003). The Mekong River Education for Sustainability project promotes increased awareness and sustainable choices for students living on the banks of the Mekong River in Thailand, Cambodia, and Vietnam. In this initiative, students conduct projects in their local communities and share outcomes with students living in other countries who share the river as a resource (Projects International 2002).

There are unlimited ways in which schools can address education for sustainability, from energy conservation to campus divestment from fossil fuels. One strategy in higher education focuses on campus greening initiatives, which contend that colleges and universities must model principles and practices of sustainability to society. The University of British Columbia was the first university in Canada to adopt a sustainable development policy and a campus sustainability office. Its climate action plan commits the university to reduce greenhouse gas emissions by 67% before 2020 and 100% by 2050, compared with 2007 levels. Their website for campus sustainability features dashboards that allow users to view variables such as energy use of specific buildings in real time, so a student dorm could monitor its own energy consumption on a daily basis. The site also measures the amount of resources conserved, from paper to water, by the sustainability initiatives (University of British Columbia Campus Sustainability 2014).

For administrators in particular, sustainability can be attractive due to economic incentives. The National Wildlife Federation's campus ecology program calculated the annual revenues and savings of campus greening and conservation initiatives among 23 US campuses. The revenues and savings included more than $9 million from energy conservation at SUNY-Buffalo, New York and $235,000 from new toilet and water fixtures at Columbia University, New York. The program also publishes resources and establishes networks to help college campuses implement climate action plans (National Wildlife Federation 2014). Finally, campus sustainability can follow the momentum of global conservation movements, like the decision by Stanford University to divest its $18 billion endowment of stock in coal-mining companies.

4.7.1 Planning

One model for education for sustainability is the whole-school approach, which integrates the theme of sustainability into all facets of the school environment, including curriculum, pedagogy, facilities management, and school governance (Henderson and Tilbury 2004). This approach is found in primary and secondary schools throughout Europe, South Africa, Australia, China, and New Zealand. Three examples of such programs are discussed here: Enviroschools in New Zealand, the Green School Project in China, and Eco-Schools in South Africa. Box 4.8 compares the planning, implementation, and evaluation of these programs.

Initiated in the 1990s, the Enviroschools program is managed by the Enviroschools Foundation, an independent trust with regional councils. This program offers two choices for schools: an award program or a 3-year program, with extensive support materials.

The Green School Project, initiated by China's Ministry of Education, centers on the international standards for environmental management, called ISO 14,000, first developed by the International Organization for Standardization. Managed by the Center for Environmental Education and Communications, this program builds knowledge and skills in the management of school grounds and the larger environment. Schools follow a series of steps in order to apply for Green School awards, received by 15,000 schools (Henderson and Tilbury 2004).

The Eco-Schools program, managed by the Foundation for Environmental Education (FEE), involves schools in 28 countries including South Africa. Schools work through seven steps to achieve Green Flag certification. The initial steps in this program begin with the curriculum rather than environmental projects in the schools.

The planning for all three programs involves developing action plans for the school. A committee of diverse stakeholders oversees the planned steps toward integrating sustainability into the school. For any whole-school program, partners such as the department of conservation, ministry of education, community groups, universities, and business are key to the planning process. Partnerships in education for sustainability

Box 4.8 A comparison of three approaches to education for sustainability

	Enviroschools, New Zealand	Green School Project, China	FEE Eco-Schools, South Africa
School focus	Kindergarten, primary and secondary schools	Kindergarten, primary, middle, vocational, and special needs schools	Kindergarten, primary, and secondary schools
Funding and management	Managed by Enviroschools Foundations (funded by government and charitable contributions). Implementation supported by regional councils	Coordinated by the Center for Educational Education and Communications and local networks. Funded by the State Environmental Protection Administration of China (SEPA)	Managed by Wildlife and Environment Society of South Africa in collaboration with South Africa Department of Education. Funded largely by corporate sponsor
Framework	Connected to the New Zealand curriculum framework and linked to activities of the ministry of education's environmental education guidelines	A government framework based on the concept of ISO 14,000 and the European Eco-Schools. Connected to the National Action Program for Environmental Publicity and Education	Links to action detailed in the Millennium Declaration, signed at the 2002 World Summit on Sustainable Development. Correlated to the revised national curriculum statements in South Africa
Focus and principles for planning	Partnerships through existing environmental education initiatives that integrate five principles: 1. sustainability 2. environmental education 3. respect for diversity of people and cultures 4. student participation and Maori perspectives 5. knowledge to enrich the learning process	Encourages schools to use its educational resources to support the environment and integrate environmental education into the curriculum	Focuses on curriculum-based action for a healthy environment. Schools choose three focus areas from the following themes: school calendar, environmental information and community knowledge, schools grounds and fieldwork, resource management, health safety, action projects and contests, adventures and cultural activities

Box 4.8 *Continued*

	Enviroschools, New Zealand	Green School Project, China	FEE Eco-Schools, South Africa
Stages of implementation	1. Develop an Envirogroup, school policy, and partnerships 2. Create a whole-school vision map 3. Focus on five themes in classroom learning and action. 4. Reflect through documenting and sharing lessons learned	1. Establish a Green School committee 2. Focus on environmental management of resources 3. Integrate environmental education into the curriculum 4. Provide in-service training for teachers 5. Ensure participation from the entire school in environmental protection 6. Consider lifestyle choices 7. Participate in campus greening 8. Establish an eco-club for students	1. Create a working group 2. Audit the school environment 3. Choose three focus areas 4. Draft an environmental policy 5. Develop and implement lesson plans linked to sustainability 6. Take action involving the school and community 7 Develop a portfolio and review progress
Evaluation	Through questionnaires and reflection workshop	Not yet conducted	Not yet conducted
Achievements	Documented environmental achievements in greening campus and reducing waste, water, and energy usage Integrate environmental education into science, language, social studies, technology, PE, and well-being. Students involved in planning and evaluation	Gave 15,000 Green School awards at different levels	Focused initial round of awards to Green Flag schools for special environmental days, recycling programs, and a native plants garden

Adapted from Henderson, K. and Tilbury, D. (2004). *Whole-school Approaches to Sustainability: an International Review of Sustainable School Programs*. Report prepared by the Australian Research Institute in Education for Sustainability (ARIES) for the Department of the Environment and Heritage, Australian Government.

provide technical and financial support, connect the program to government policies, relate the program to community needs, and avoid duplication of effort (Henderson and Tilbury 2004).

4.7.2 Implementation

A review of the whole-school approach across different countries revealed factors that define sustainable schools. These include (Henderson and Tilbury 2004):

- School leadership and administration that values participatory decision-making with sustainability at the core of school planning.
- Integration of education for sustainability across the curriculum.
- Professional development for teachers, program partners, and facilities management staff.
- Greening of the school grounds.
- A decrease in resource consumption and an increase in environmental quality at the school.
- Participatory learning approaches that promote critical thinking and intercultural understandings.
- A focus on reflection and evaluation to guide future decisions, as well as encouragement of research to improve teaching practices.

The steps for implementation depend on the specific program (see Box 4.8). For the Enviroschools program, schools form partnerships with the community, develop a vision map for the school, integrate sustainability into student learning and action, and reflect by documenting and sharing the lessons learned and outcomes (Enviroschools Foundation 2014).

4.7.3 Evaluation

Some whole-school programs like the Enviroschools in New Zealand have conducted evaluations which include a questionnaire for schools and a 2-day reflection meeting with teachers, funders, and community groups to gather qualitative feedback. In terms of environmental impacts, schools participating in the Eco-Schools program in Ireland reported a 50% reduction in waste during a 5-week waste monitoring survey in the schools. Documented environmental achievements in the New Zealand program include greening campuses and reducing waste, water, and energy usage. Educational outcomes include the integration of education for sustainability into the subjects of science, language, social studies, technology, physical education, and well-being (Henderson and Tilbury 2004).

Many whole-school sustainability programs, however, are characterized by a lack of evaluation. However there are successes that appear to correlate with effective programs, including: connection with national government priorities; access to experts in education for sustainability; secure funding; professional development for teachers and partners; linking with established sustainability efforts; and partnerships that include a diversity of stakeholders (Henderson and Tilbury 2004).

4.8 Summary

Conservation education in schools will only succeed when benefits accrue to all partners. When conservation education helps teachers and administrators do their jobs more effectively this approach becomes more practical. Taking the time to understand the realities of school systems, using effective communications, serving as a resource to schools, and developing programs that support academic standards will provide the building blocks to effective conservation education in schools. The documented impacts of these efforts provide evidence to use when lobbying for conservation education in legislation and educational policy.

Some of the most successful conservation education programs in schools have found strategies to meet educational requirements by involving students in local conservation needs. Education in schools should include learning about local places, but too often academic demands preclude the chance to study the natural world outside the classroom. When conservation education links academic demands to the study of natural and social systems and their interactions everyone benefits.

There are a variety of approaches to choose from for implementing conservation education within schools, from environment-based education to education for sustainability, as well as other techniques in this book such as service-learning and project-based learning (Chapter 5). To evaluate any conservation education initiative, feedback must be gathered from all stakeholders and improvements made for the benefit of the students and the local environment.

Making conservation come alive

Remember how a powerful story told by parents, grandparents, or friends makes family history come alive? By immersing listeners in the rich details of their past, storytellers create a sense of ownership and excitement about local history. We all know stories that we continue to tell to others because of the inspirational pull of the tale.

Like a good story, the techniques in this chapter bring conservation education to life, infusing energy and excitement into environmental conservation (Box 5.1). These techniques celebrate the wonder of nature, immerse learners in different perspectives, and use the outdoors as a context for discovery. These educational strategies reveal the beauty and complexity of the environment around us. Each technique presented in this chapter engages the audience in learning, whether through a simple environmental game or an extensive field studies course. The educational techniques also rely on the experiential learning cycle (Chapter 2), using reflection to enhance learning.

Techniques like hands-on activities foster discovery of the natural world. Storytelling, games, case studies, and role-plays promote understanding of the interests and positions of multiple players in conservation issues. Conservation educators may find they can use these techniques to build on each other; for example, the characters in a case study might inspire you to create a role-play for your participants and some games also have a compelling story as their introduction.

This chapter features contests that provide incentives for conservation by recognizing artistic expression or sustainable transportation choices. We also include the nuts and bolts for organizing field trips—an exploration of a nearby urban park or a semester-long field studies course. Lastly, the chapter provides tips for using backcountry skills to promote awareness and low-impact travel in nature. Such field experiences give real meaning to conservation, discovered not in a magazine or a YouTube clip, but in the outdoors.

5.1 Hands-on activities

Hands-on activities in conservation give learners first-hand experience of exploring a new phenomenon or concept in the natural world: students dissect the parts of a flower before learning about the concept of pollination; adults explore the shoreline of the ocean, collecting shells to document species of aquatic life. Hands-on activities involve learners working with and manipulating materials to solve a problem or explore a concept (Haury and Rillero 1994).

Conservation Education and Outreach Techniques. Second Edition. Susan K. Jacobson, Mallory D. McDuff & Martha C. Monroe © Susan K. Jacobson, Mallory D. McDuff & Martha C. Monroe 2015. Published 2015 by Oxford University Press.

Box 5.1 Many techniques bring conservation to life by engaging learners in direct experience

Technique	Purpose
Hands-on activities	Involve learners working with and manipulating materials to explore a concept or solve a problem
Storytelling	Transmits knowledge through an oral tradition and allows the audience to experience the emotions and environment of characters in the story
Games	Demonstrate and teach environmental concepts through fun but structured play, involving elements such as challenge, collaboration, movement, and quiet concentration
Case study	Uses narratives about individuals and communities facing environmental dilemmas to engage participants in studying the characters, identifying lessons learned, and proposing potential solutions
Role-playing	Assigns learners to specific roles in a scenario to "act out" the situation and gain new perspectives, self-awareness, and often communication and problem-solving skills
Contests	Provide incentives for environmental action or involvement to raise public awareness of an environmental issue, resource, or organization
Field trips	Provide first-hand experience for participants with a physical site and resources in a community
Backcountry skills	Promote a connection to the earth by increasing awareness and skills for self-reliance and low-impact living in the outdoors

Children learn about their environment through exploration and play. Not surprisingly, research shows that young children learn most effectively through these direct interactions with their environment rather than passive learning activities (Riskowski et al. 2009). Hands-on activities build on our innate, natural processes for learning.

Schools in the low-income East Feliciana parish in Louisiana, USA, adopted a hands-on mathematics and science program called Project Connect with activities that included identifying aquatic organisms and exploring the local pine forest ecosystem. Two years after the expansion of Project Connect, the number of students passing the science portion of the state standardized tests increased by 13% in a year (Null 2002). Hands-on activities typically use inquiry and constructivist theories of learning (see Chapter 2). Learners construct new understandings by combining previous knowledge with new discoveries (Pritchard 2014). For this technique, we explore strategies for conducting three types of hands-on activities: outdoor hands-on activities, experiments, and manipulative exercises and collections.

5.1.1 Planning

Planning will connect the hands-on activity to the attitudes, knowledge, and skills you are exploring with your learners. Ask yourself a few questions when you consider hands-on activities in conservation education—What information, concepts, or skills do you want to teach? How long will the activity take? What is the context for this new concept?

Hands-on activities reflect the experiential learning cycle described in Chapter 2, as learners typically first explore a new concept, materials, or the environment with minimal guidance from the facilitator. For example, the Minnesota Department of Natural Resources Nongame Wildlife Program developed hands-on activities to facilitate learning about the state bird, the common loon (*Gavia immer*). The initial stages of one activity allow students to compare the bones of a loon with those of a goose and record their observations. After the hands-on exploration, the facilitator takes a more active role, introducing conservation concepts, and then learners apply their new knowledge to a new situation or problem.

One Project WILD (2007) activity, Owl Pellets, gives students in a classroom the chance to explore the contents of an owl pellet, the regurgitated, indigestible parts of an owl's prey. The facilitator gives an owl pellet to students in pairs or teams and asks them to use a toothpick and their hands to examine and dissect the owl pellet. Students quickly find bones and bone fragments from the owl's prey. Their findings lead to rich discussions of predator–prey relationships, and students then use the bones to identify the species of prey, including voles, mice, and even skunks (Fig. 5.1).

Hands-on activities usually require more organization, creativity, and logistical support than traditional instruction, but they often generate more enthusiasm in learners.

Fig. 5.1 Students explore the contents of an owl pellet in this hands-on activity that explores predator–prey relationships. (Photo by S. Cross.)

Before implementing an activity the following simple steps should be considered (WGBH Educational Foundations 2000):

- Try each activity yourself, so you know what to expect with your learners.
- Collect all materials, and have extra materials on hand in case participants need to try the activity a second time.
- Prior to the activity, divide all materials into the correct amounts for each group. Cooperative groups provide more opportunities for participants to interact with materials, and groups are easier for the facilitator to manage. Consider the number of participants you want in each group. Many conservation education programs keep their materials for hands-on activities in boxes, so they can grab the "lesson box" with all the materials before the activity.
- Think about local organizations or businesses that might donate materials for your program or school.
- If you work with participants on a long-term basis, build some excitement about the upcoming activity by displaying a picture or object related to the hands-on activity.
- Practice giving clear instructions for the activity in multiple ways, for example verbally and in writing. Before participants begin exploring, remind them to make a prediction about what they think will happen during the activity.
- Consider the location for the activity. Is this an indoor lab experiment or a nature walk with outdoor exploration?
- Integrate critical reflection into the activity, so participants can process the experience and transfer learning to new contexts.

5.1.2 Implementation

Outdoor hands-on activities

Many hands-on activities involve learning in the outdoors—from identifying wildlife from its tracks to journaling while following a nature trail. If you are an educator used to working indoors, implementing hands-on activities outdoors without boundaries can seem daunting. If you are a conservation outreach specialist used to working with small groups of adults, the prospect of taking 30 youngsters to explore a marsh may feel overwhelming. But a few guidelines for implementing hands-on activities outdoors can address most concerns—the following are adapted from Grant and Littlejohn (2001):

- *Have clear expectations.* With both children and adults discuss behavioral expectations before you conduct hands-on activities in the outdoors. Such an atmosphere, similar to a group contract, ensures greater willingness to follow the guidelines. Make a list of behaviors and keep them positive, such as "Use quiet voices" instead of "Don't make a noise."
- *Plan the logistics*
  - Have a clear signal for getting everyone's attention, for example a birdcall or three handclaps.

- Discuss where you will gather once you are outside. When using trails, establish clear meeting places at trail heads.
- Explain that if participants get separated, they should sit in one place and wait for someone to find them.
- Decide who will lead the group.
- Use a variety of group sizes, from pairs to large groups, throughout the hands-on activity.
- Give specific assignments to focus attention.
- Discuss safety and any hazards. Bring a first-aid kit.
- Be prepared for any kind of weather by bringing rain gear, coats, and water bottles.
- Reflect with participants and then evaluate at the end of the hands-on activity. Discuss what went well, what did not, and changes for future activities.

- *Practice and model activities.* Clear instructions for the hands-on activity will help focus your learners when outdoors. Practice gathering together with your signal before venturing outdoors. When possible, model your assignments by becoming an active participant yourself.
- *Be flexible.* When teaching outdoors, natural distractions will divert participants' attention. Be flexible when these compelling distractions occur and try to create natural transitions. Sometimes a bird flying overhead will give the perfect stimulus for the next discussion. Use these teachable moments!
- *Communicate strategically.* Be prepared to face noise, wind, sun, and other distractions you cannot control. Keep the following in mind:
  - Keep the sun in your eyes, rather than your learners' eyes.
  - Stand so the wind is to your back, which will push the sound of your voice toward the participants.
  - As you talk, try to reduce the distance between you and your participants. This may mean kneeling down when talking to younger participants.
  - If you are on a narrow trail, have participants form a single- or double-file line, depending on the width of the trail. When you stop, either choose a wide spot to gather the group, or walk to the middle of the line and ask those closest to kneel.
- *Carry props.* Carry a prop bag with natural artifacts to redirect learners' attention. You can also use hand lenses to get a closer look at the natural world or bring photographs of native wildlife that you may not glimpse on the trail.

Experiments

Hands-on activities also include lab or field experiments that allow learners to handle, manipulate, or observe a scientific process related to conservation. For example, members of the Wildlife Clubs in the Central African Republic worked with ecologists to compare the germination and growth rates of seeds collected from elephant dung with seeds collected on the ground. This simple experiment exposed the critical role of the elephant dung in promoting the growth of plants in the forest ecosystem.

As a warm-up activity, ask your participants to write the safety rules for the experiment on the board or a poster. Safety is a critical factor during any experiment. You are responsible for ensuring that all participants follow the safety rules. For both lab and field experiments, consider the following ideas to ensure both a fun and educational experiment:

- *Participant-designed experiments.* Split the group into small teams and ask each team to design an experiment to test one variable. For example, if you are testing for factors that affect the rate of erosion, have the participants identify all the factors that could influence erosion, such as slope, water flow rates, and soil type. Each group can then isolate one factor and test one at a time.
- *Lab stations.* If you want to explore several different concepts, set up numerous stations around the room. Give participants written directions and have them circulate to each station.
- *Silent/interactive lab.* Have participants work silently in the lab or in pairs and then give them time to interact and share results.

Manipulative exercises and collections

Science classes are known for the use of objects for manipulation and collections, for example models of chemical structures or leaf collections. Similarly, conservation educators can use such hands-on activities to explore ecological concepts with young people and adults: you could bring in an unfamiliar object, such as an aquatic sponge, and get participants to explore the object and guess its origin. Have learners create models of ecological concepts, for example a model of their watershed. Another option is to ask participants to collect different seashells and identify the marine species for each shell. The possibilities for using objects and collections are only limited by your imagination!

5.1.3 Evaluation

Your own observations will be a powerful evaluation tool as you assess the effectiveness of the hands-on activities. An observation checklist is a tool for documenting student engagement and learning from the hands-on activity. Your checklist might include a rating of a number of factors including level of participation, engagement, on-task behaviors, clarifying questions, contribution to discussion, consistency with behavioral expectations, and connections made between hands-on observation and ecological concepts.

You can collect your own evaluation data comparing traditional lecture teaching with hands-on activities. Try teaching one of your classes or groups of participants with more traditional teaching while another learns the same concepts through hands-on activities. Give each group the same pre- and post-tests and compare results. You can enlist the help of evaluators in the education departments of your local college or university to review your methodology and evaluation instruments.

One zoo education program in Florida used evaluation as a tool for assessing the efficacy of hands-on activities for pre-schoolers. The Tots program challenges the traditional approach to zoo education of simply exposing children to animals to promote learning. This educational program involves hands-on activities such as direct inter-action with the animals, as well as the involvement of parents or guardians in all activ-ities. An evaluation that used observation and interviews showed that the Tots program was effective at promoting knowledge about animals and environmental awareness among the children (Pringle et al. 2003). Another evaluation of a hands-on environ-mental education program called Earthkeepers in Cyprus gathered quantitative data from questionnaires and surveys and qualitative data from interviews. The evaluation involved 491 students from fourth to seventh grades from nine different schools over a 2-year period. Results revealed gains in ecological understanding, changes in environ-mental attitudes and knowledge, as well as changes in behavior of participants (Manoli et al. 2014).

5.2 Storytelling

"Stories form a link between our imagination and our surroundings," write storytell-ers Caduto and Bruchac (1997). Indeed, for most cultures oral traditions and stories transmit local knowledge and wisdom about the environment, our relationship to the earth, and our relationship with each other. Stories allow us to become the characters and experience their emotions and environments.

Why is storytelling so effective at transmitting information—from the latest gossip at work to the medicinal uses of local plant species? Storytelling is effective because it is (Armstrong 1992):

- Simple: no one needs training to tell a story.
- Timeless: storytelling has been and will be around forever.
- Empowering: stories give people information, so they can better live their lives or perform their jobs.
- Appealing: everyone, from the very old to very young, likes to hear a good story.
- Effective: it is an excellent strategy for passing along traditions.
- Rewarding: including someone in a story recognizes that person as a presence in the community or audience.
- Fun: think about how often you have heard the request, "Tell me again the story about. . . . "

For centuries, families have used stories to promote cultural and behavioral norms. Likewise, storytelling can teach vital conservation lessons and inspire environmental action. To preserve environmental stories, organizations like the Wildlife Clubs of Kenya, (WCK) have collected traditional stories in print. Ibrahim Ali, former direc-tor of the WCK, remembered sitting by the fire as a child listening to stories at the end of each day with his grandmother and grandfather, sisters, brothers, and cousins. WCK staff coordinated the creation of *Trees, Myths, and Medicines* (WCK 1997), a book of stories, myths, and artwork related to trees in Kenya as told by Kenyan stu-dents (Box 5.2, Fig. 5.2). Such compilations of stories are a rich resource for envir-onmental educators who want to use storytelling as a technique for conservation education.

Box 5.2 *The People of Coco* by Zeenat Parpia

Wildlife Clubs of Kenya collected stories and artwork from Kenyan students about the trees and forests in their community. This story, entitled *The People of Coco*, was written by Zeenat Parpia, when she was a 16-year-old student at Star of the Sea High School on the coast in Mombasa (WCK 1997):

> "Oh God of hunger please help us, the people of Coco. It's over a month now since famine struck our village. Our herds have died and our land has become barren. We are now on the verge of losing our people," prayed the chief of Coco. The effects of the famine were evident. He was so skinny and fragile that one could see the bones protruding out of his skin. Suddenly a monkey-faced structure fell from the sky. Terrified, the chief ran home to take refuge.
>
> Next day, the cock doodled very early and the chief went to pray before the sun rose. But on reaching the place where he had been worshipping the day before, a surprise awaited him. There before him stood a miraculous and giant tree. Since then the coconut has grown naturally and has solved the problem of the people of Coco. The coconut in fact received its botanical name—*Cocos nucifera*—from the people to whom it was given.

Trees, Myths, and Medicines. Jacaranda Designs, Nairobi, Kenya. Used with copyright permission granted from the Wildlife Clubs of Kenya and their publisher, Jacaranda Designs Ltd. PO Box 76691-00508 Nairobi, Kenya (info@jacaranda-africa.com).

5.2.1 Planning

Think about the specific objectives of your storytelling and the interests of your audience as you choose stories to fit your program's theme. Do you want to inspire awe at the power and beauty of nature? Is your objective to instill an environmental ethic? Do you want your listeners to laugh and have fun? Are you looking for a calm evening story at the end of a day of activities?

Rich resources exist for storytelling about the environment, including a large body of both fiction and non-fiction books on the theme of natural resources. A diverse range of books can inspire storytelling from tales such as *Kenju's Forest* (Monmoto 1991) to *The Giving Tree* (Silverstein 1964). Books like *Keepers of the Earth*, *Keepers of the Night*, and *Keepers of the Animals* (Caduto and Bruchac 1989, 1994, 1997) focus on Native American stories about the environment, with corresponding activities. Books can also present the facts about topics such as climate disruption in an age-appropriate way; examples include *The Magic School Bus and the Climate Challenge* (Cole and Degen 2010).

You can draw on the cultural traditions and local stories in your area. Folklore about native plants and animals, for example, can inspire learning about local species. *The Folklore of Birds* by Edward Armstrong (2012) presents a collection of British stories about birds. Another source for storytelling is the life stories of naturalists or environmental heroes. For example, several children's books feature the lives of well-known environmentalists like Rachel Carson and Wangari Maathai. Joseph Cornell (2015)

Nazmina Panju

Shil Shanghavi

Jatinder Panesar

Preeti S. Shah

Fig. 5.2 Artwork by Kenyan students from the coastal region of Kenya illustrates the importance of the coconut tree, as told in the story "The People of Coco" (WCK 1997). *Trees, Myths, and Medicines*. Jacaranda Designs, Nairobi, Kenya.

Used with copyright permission granted from the Wildlife Clubs of Kenya and their publisher, Jacaranda Designs Ltd, PO Box 76691-00508 Nairobi, Kenya. info@jacaranda-africa.com.

recommends studying the biographies and stories of your own heroes and telling their story in your own words.

In addition, you can develop stories that describe the actions and lives of well-known local environmentalists. The EcoTeam, an environmental education curriculum for third-grade students in the USA, includes one lesson about local citizens who have made a difference to the environment. These stories show students that every person in the community has a role to play as an environmental citizen. Environmental magazines and websites often feature environmental heroes too. The magazine *Yes! A Journal of Positive Futures* highlights modern environmental success stories across the globe.

When telling a story about an environmental role model, select props to portray the historical times and unique traits of your character. Depict the dress of the character with simple props like a hat or tie. Memorize passages from their written or spoken words and learn the plot lines of key events in his or her story (Cornell 2015). Avoid memorizing the entire text and instead learn the key points while you "become" the character for the audience. Listen to recordings of other storytellers to hone your skills.

If you are telling a story from a written text, read the story aloud to yourself several times before you tell it from memory or even read it to an audience. One technique you can use to help plan your stories is a bag of items that represent mnemonic devices—with each item representing a key plot line in a story (Caduto and Bruchac 1997).

Another storytelling strategy for both children and adults is guided visualization, which can help your listeners become more aware of their environment. Guided visualization involves describing a scene so listeners can imagine that environment. Used in meditation, guided visualization begins with the listeners sitting or lying down with their eyes closed as you begin to tell them about a scene. Ask the audience to describe, write, or draw the images, sounds, or smells they imagine.

As you practice your stories, think about the traits of good storytellers that you have heard in the past. What made them special and why do you remember their faces, voices, and stories? One key to planning a good story about conservation is to choose stories and characters that give you real joy. If you find joy in the story you are telling, your audience will also experience the energy in your voice and the movements of your body (Cornell 2015).

5.2.2 Implementation

A few tips will help you involve your listeners in your story and have fun while you are telling your tale. Remember that part of becoming a good storyteller is finding a style that suits you. Enjoy experimenting with the power of stories to evoke attitudes and actions about the environment.

Tips for successful storytelling

The following tips for storytelling are adapted from Caduto and Bruchac (1997) and Cornell (2015):

- Have your listeners sit in a circle, if possible, so everyone can make eye contact.
- Incorporate responses from the audience to involve your listeners and help with pacing of the story (e.g., when you say "Ho" they respond with "Hey!").
- Teach any chanting or hand movements before the story begins.
- Memorize the beginning and ending of your stories to increase your confidence.
- Try to feel the quality and mood of each story before you begin.
- Describe the setting with specific details so listeners can "see" it in their minds.
- Maintain eye contact with your audience.
- Use your hands to express emotions and actions.
- Establish and preserve the timeline of your story by using key phrases such as "then," "next," "finally," and "but at the same time. . . . "
- Alter your rhythm and speech to maintain interest in your stories, and vary your voice to suit different characters.
- Use humor to relax the audience and keep them open to your message.
- Adapt your stories to different age groups. Adults focus on verbal messages while children are more visual and physical.
- Remember to share the joy of your stories with the audience.

As you model effective storytelling, engage your students or participants in telling their own stories. Ask learners to write and tell their own fictitious environmental stories or ecological autobiographies that describe their connection to the natural world. Telling these tales can empower learners, in the role of storyteller, to teach others. Older students or senior citizens can practice their storytelling with younger audiences.

5.2.3 Evaluation

Assess the effectiveness of this technique before you start to tell stories to your actual audience. Start by practicing your story in front of a few people to get feedback. Ask them specific questions—When were they most involved in the story? What points were most and least interesting? What could you do to improve your stories?

After you have adjusted your storytelling based on the feedback, you may want to record your storytelling session and listen to yourself. Listen for places when you speak too quickly or slowly. Do you enunciate clearly throughout the tale? Put yourself in the place of a listener and evaluate your storytelling.

When you tell your stories with a "real" audience, try to observe the places in the narrative arc when the audience seems most engaged. Are there points where your listeners seem to drift? Did any external factors, weather, lighting, or outside noises for example, help or hinder your delivery? Try telling your stories to different age groups and audiences to adjust your delivery and increase your confidence. Lastly, ask yourself if you truly became your characters and lived the lessons they shared!

5.3 Games

Games are a powerful technique for demonstrating and teaching ecological concepts to both children and adults (Project WILD 2007). Games can energize a teaching environment, immerse learners in the material, promote collaboration with other players, and encourage students to learn from their mistakes (Teed 2004). Just as important, games are fun! Through games, a generation that can memorize 100 video-game characters with all their traits and history can also learn the names and interactions of 100 wildlife species and their habitats. Games provide a useful strategy for introducing or reinforcing concepts taught through other conservation education techniques. Because games often use movement and action, these techniques can appeal to learners of all ages (Fig. 5.3).

Many conservation education games build on those played by children of all cultures and times, such as freeze tag or hide and seek. The fast-paced game Quick Frozen Critters allows participants to simulate the actions of predators and prey as they find food or avoid capture (Project WILD 2007). Others, like environmental board games, use logic and memory to teach environmental concepts.

Environmental games for adults are often adaptations of childhood games, books, and game shows. Charades, bingo, Monopoly, Trivial Pursuit, and even Jeopardy have been adapted for environmental topics. Bingo can be adapted to any topic by making bingo cards that have environmental categories. Renditions of Monopoly include National Parks Monopoly, Astronomy Monopoly, and Wild Animalopoly, where

Fig. 5.3 Games that involve movement and fun can engage learners of all ages. (Photo by J. Overholt.)

players are animal caretakers who learn animal facts and trade for land, food, water, clean air, and habitat. Online games are also available: Clim'way that allows players to help a larger community reach specific climate goals, and Astro-Venture from NASA that challenges players to design a habitable planet (Basu 2010).

Conservation educators working with adults may encounter administrators who have difficulty appreciating the value of "games" as an instructional tool. Referring to games as "activities" in your agenda for a workshop or training can avoid this misperception. Whether you work as a teacher in a primary school or as a conservation educator with a forestry agency, games inject a dose of fun into learning.

5.3.1 Planning

Full value contract

Before playing active games, you should establish rules with your participants to ensure a safe, fun experience. One strategy is to establish agreements or a group contract, sometimes called a "full value contract." If you are facilitating a group for a short period of time you can introduce three simple agreements for a full value contract: play safe, play fair, and play hard.

Talk with your participants and have them give examples of what it means to "play safe." Even children as young as 4 years can explain the meaning of "playing safe." If time permits, represent the agreements on a flag or stickers and have each person sign their name to show their commitment. Ask the group if they want to add any other agreements. You can accomplish a full value contract in 10 minutes or less.

If you have more time the group can develop its own contract, with examples like "be respectful to others," "be safe with words and actions," "listen to others," and "give 100% effort" (Frank 2013). Since everyone agrees to follow the full value contract, the facilitator can call a time-out in the game if players violate the contract. If you are playing quiet, sedate games such as board games it is still a good idea to establish group norms before playing. With these expectations, participants young and old assume the responsibility for a fair and respectful game.

Content and location

The content of your game will depend on the ecological concepts you want to explore with your participants. Follow these steps when planning your games (Teed 2004):

- Define objectives. What do you want the participants to learn?
- Decide the type of game you want and the storyline. Do you want an active game or an indoor activity? Do you want to use an established game, for example a trivia game or relay race, as a foundation? Will participants play in teams or alone?
- Divide your objectives into challenges. You may choose to have multiple levels of challenges so participants progress to more difficult tasks during the game.
- Design rewards, if appropriate. Link incentives to learning or applying the material.
- Create the game, with the required props or cards.
- Test the game. Ask players to try the game and give you feedback on the duration of play, clarity of instructions, and engagement of players.
- Play the game!

Conservation agencies and educational organizations publish numerous resources with environmental and outdoor games such as Project WILD (2007), Project WILD Aquatic (Project WILD 2013), and Go Out and Play! (Hammond 2013). The activity guide Project WILD Aquatic, for example, includes games that connect to STEM (science, technology, engineering, and mathematics) learning. There are also books with games you can adapt for environmental themes, for example *Everyone Wins!: Cooperative Games and Activities* (Luvmour and Luvmour 2007) and *Best New Games* (LeFevre 2012).

One game, Hooks and Ladders, simulates a salmon run, while another, Migration Headache, demonstrates limiting factors affecting populations of migrating birds (Project WILD 2013). A challenge in facilitating games is to ensure that players identify with their role while maintaining a link to the concepts. You can accomplish this connection by planning a focused discussion of the activity that reinforces the concepts. The discussion you have at the end of a game should establish that the game is a "model" that does not represent all the real-world complexities (see Chapter 2) (Project WILD 2007).

Games are perfect for outdoor locations like fields. However, you can play most active games indoors as well. Before you begin a game in an outside area, walk the field and look for any items, such as broken glass, that could cause injury to players. You may need to create boundaries and can use sticks, ropes, or cones to mark the space.

5.3.2 Implementation

Looking at examples of games will give you ideas for the breadth of concepts that it is possible to demonstrate using these activities. From carrying capacity to population growth, games model and reinforce concepts that are important for conservation education. Challenge your participants to create their own games as teaching and learning tools with unique adaptations to the ecology of your area.

Environmental board game: Monopo-tree

Modeled on the board game Monopoly, in Monopo-tree players toss a dice and move their game piece around the board to collect "property." Instead of collecting houses and apartments, however, players collect tree species representing different layers of the forest. Players also must answer questions related to forest ecology to advance in the game. The level of detail and strategy make this game perfect for adult learners. In fact, college students developed Monopo-tree for a forest biology class. You could adapt the game for your local forest ecosystems or enlist adult learners in creating the board game as a learning experience.

Camera

Divide the participants into pairs, and instruct one player to take the role of photographer while the other plays the role of a camera. The photographer leads the camera, with her eyes shut, to find a striking picture. When the photographer wants to take a picture, he points the lens of the camera (his partner's eyes) and presses the shutter button (by tapping the shoulder) to open the lens. The camera's "eyes" stay open only for three to five seconds, until the photographer taps the shoulder again to close the lens. This simple activity often has a powerful effect, with people remembering their pictures for years. Partners should switch roles so each can experience being the camera. When adapted for different ages, both adults and children enjoy this game. Participants should sketch their "photograph" after taking the "picture" (Cornell 2015).

Stalking the shoe

Choose one person in the group to be "it" and instruct her to sit in the middle of the circle with a blindfold over her eyes. Have everyone else take off their shoes and place one of their shoes around her. The rest of the group members are the "stalkers," who start about 30 paces from the blindfolded person. The stalkers must advance as quietly as possible and try to reclaim their shoe without alerting the person in the middle. Instruct the stalkers to pretend they are walking through a wooded path and must walk with complete calm and quiet. You can place branches or leaves on the ground to increase the difficulty.

When the blindfolded person hears a stalker, she points in that direction. If she points to someone, that person must freeze. The stalker who is frozen must return to the outside of the circle to begin again. (A referee can help observe and ensure fairness.) Those who succeed in getting their shoe have a chance to be in the middle of the circle.

5.3.3 Evaluation

Before you try a new game for the first time, practice the directions for the game with a colleague or friends. Ask for feedback on the clarity and flow of your instructions. When you are playing a game with participants, observe the activity with the following questions in mind: Are all players involved? Are players making the connection between the game and the concepts? Are they listening and understanding the instructions?

Each game should include some form of debriefing to evaluate the immediate impact of the activity, just as described in nature awareness activities (see Chapter 12). Debriefing uses questions to allow reflection by participants after the activity. During a workshop, for example, one teacher playing the camera game said the activity allowed her to slow down and observe the natural world for the first time in months. Such comments made during an effective debrief reveal rich qualitative data for evaluation.

Structure the reflection or debriefing around three types of questions: What?, So what?, and Now what? Start by asking questions that allow participants to talk about what happened during the experience ("What did you just experience?"). Then ask questions that allow the group to reflect on "What does that mean?" Lastly, engage the group in identifying applications of the activity to their lives—"Now what can you do with this knowledge?"

Debriefing can last just a few minutes or expand into a longer discussion. This method of debriefing follows the experiential learning cycle described in Chapter 2. Debriefing also provides an opportunity to check the participants' understanding of the ecological concepts explored in the game. With practice, games become a practical tool to teach and energize!

5.4 Case studies

Learners in an introductory environmental studies course at Oberlin College, Ohio, USA, read about ecological, legislative, and economic issues associated with land development and subsequent wetland loss. The class presents the perspectives of four different stakeholder groups on expanding the airport and then writes a report giving recommendations to the mayor. At Framingham State University, Massachusetts, USA, students review published data on the effect of lethal control of coyotes in their state. Teams analyze the data and predict how changes at one trophic level affect populations and communities at other trophic levels (Case Studies in Science 2003).

These examples of case studies immerse learners in real-life problems, allowing them to develop decision-making skills about conservation issues. Disciplines such as medicine and business have traditionally used case studies to teach the applied skills of decision-making and problem-solving. Case studies present dilemmas, with a background of people, institutions, and problems to engage learners with the characters and circumstances of the story (Stanley and Waterman 2002; National Center for Case Study Teaching in Science 2014). Although case studies are a type of story, they are usually factual, interactive, open-ended, and encourage participants to learn from the experiences and ideas of others. Case studies sometimes involve role-playing, a technique presented in the Section 5.5.

With a case study, learners typically collaborate to identify issues, locate resources, pose pertinent questions, and support their conclusions. The goal of case studies is to teach students *how* to think about conservation rather than memorizing the content of conservation issues. As such, critical thinking skills (Chapter 2) are at the heart of case studies as a teaching technique.

5.4.1 Planning

When planning, decide whether to write your own case study or if you should use an existing one or published documents, such as newspaper articles, magazines, or journals. Choose which teaching format to use with your case study. Your choice will depend on what skills you want learners to gain and the time needed to prepare your case study.

Using existing case studies

Resources like the National Center for Case Study Teaching in Science (2014) provide environmental case studies with teaching notes that you can adapt for your own teaching objectives and local environmental conflicts. Box 5.3 presents an example of a case study entitled "Goodbye honey buckets" that analyzes environmental health issues of native Alaskans.

Box 5.3 Goodbye honey buckets

The case study "Goodbye honey buckets" follows specific steps as participants analyze environmental health issues among native Alaskan residents.

1. Introduce the case

Give the case to participants and ask a volunteer to read the case aloud while others read along silently:

> More than 20,000 rural Native residents live in Alaska in communities without running water and where homes and offices use plastic buckets for toilets—called "honey buckets." The waste from these toilets is often spilled in the process of hauling it to disposal sites and these spillages have led to the outbreak of epidemic diseases such as hepatitis A.
>
> US Congress, Office of Technology Assessment, *An Alaskan Challenge: Native Village Sanitation,*
> OTA-ENV–591 (Washington, DC: US Government Printing Office, May 1994)

Even today, there are still <u>villages without a municipal sewage system</u>. John Kepaaq is a member of the <u>tribal council</u> in Icy Valley, and he is concerned about the type of sewer system being considered, since outside developers often do not realize the <u>problems of construction in the Arctic</u>. Icy Valley is a village of 200 people who live with <u>permafrost</u>, darkness, and long cold winters. John wants to ensure that the sewage system is appropriate for cold temperatures and safe for <u>the tundra environment</u>.

2. Recognize the issues

Ask participants to read the case again by themselves and note key words or phrases that are important to understanding the case (the underlined parts in the above passage).

3. Identify major themes

Ask this general question: What is the case about? You will probably get a diversity of answers. Post five to seven responses on flipchart paper on a board, which might

Box 5.3 *Continued*

include: tundra ecology, health issues in rural Alaska, arctic climate, multicultural perspectives, sewage treatment, groundwater and permafrost, and Alaskan geology.

4. Pose specific questions

Ask participants to use a chart, listing *what they know* and *what they need to know*. This strategy is a productive way to generate questions. For this case, allow 10–15 minutes in small or large groups. Ask each group to identify three to five key questions they feel are essential for understanding the case.

Some sample responses to a know/need to know analysis could be:

- *Know*: Alaska is cold and sparsely populated. There is oil in northern Alaska. Sewage treatment systems are common in the "lower 48." There are several different sewage treatment systems—city sewers, outhouses, septic tanks.
- *Need to know*: How do honey buckets work? What is the environmental impact of the current system? Why is there no municipal sewage treatment system in the village? How does the tribal council work? What is a tundra? What are the seasons like in Alaska? What is the soil chemistry and composition? What is the effect of permafrost on sewage treatment? What are the major limiting factors due to tundra climate and soils? What are the feasible sewage treatment plants? How will climate change affect these options?

5. Obtain additional resources

Assist learners to obtain additional resources to help them answer their questions. Resources could include: textbooks, library materials, computer simulations, journal articles, interviews with tribal elders, relevant maps, climate data on the tundra, interviews with local experts, and websites.

6. Define problems

As participants learn more about a case, they can better define problems and frame questions for investigation. Examples of defined problems for this case include: comparisons of climatic conditions in different biomes; effects of temperature on decomposition; role of microbes in decomposition.

7. Design and conduct scientific investigations

Students might locate or generate datasets, conduct additional interviews, or perform lab and field experiments.

8. Produce materials to support conclusions

Ask participants to identify different ways to present their conclusions: examples include a public presentation on the problems and solutions to Arctic waste treatment; an evaluation of existing sewage treatment facilities in the Arctic; a marketing report on the effectiveness of composting toilets in Icy Valley.

Adapted from McNeil, L. (2001). Goodbye honey buckets. Retrieved May 24, 2014 from <http://serc.carleton.edu/introgeo/icbl/strategy1.html>.

From this same online resource as "Goodbye honey buckets," "The river dammed" explores the removal of the Lower Snake River dams in the USA. Students must decide the vote of their federal representative as she weighs the perspectives of stakeholders who represent farmers, local tribes, sports fishermen, and government agencies. The "Exotics" presents students with the ecological, political, social, and economic factors surrounding exotic species, and the role of resource management in natural resource policy. Other case studies include titles, such as "But it's just a bottle of water" and "Global climate change: impacts and remediation."

The basis of a case study can be as simple as an article in the local newspaper, which students use to analyze the issues, interests, and consequences for action. Other existing material includes novels, television shows, magazine articles, cartoons, and advertisements. College teachers have used Michael Crichton's novel *State of Fear* as the basis for a case study on global warming (Herreid 2007). The topics illustrated in Gary Larson's *Far Side* cartoons provide simple but rich material for an ecological case study. Ask students in groups to explore an environmental issue like the loss of biodiversity depicted in such a cartoon by asking "What is the issue presented?," "What do you currently know about this issue?," "Who are the stakeholders involved?," and "What are potential approaches or solutions to this issue?" Some educators collect a series of articles on one topic, for example sea-level rise, and ask students to analyze the issue through a series of questions about the actors, their values, the conflict, and the options (National Center for Case Study Teaching in Science 2014).

When you consider an existing case study, ask yourself the following questions (Stanley and Waterman 2002):

- What are the learning objectives I want to address with this case?
- How easily can I modify the case study?
- How difficult or complex are the issues in this case study?
- Will my participants care about these issues?
- What product will I ask my participants to produce?
- Is the case too short or too long for the time I have?
- What other resources will be available for this case?

Writing your own case study

While more time-consuming than using an existing case study, the advantage of writing your own is that you can tailor the case to meet specific objectives. You can choose from three types of case studies:

- *Decision or dilemma cases* present a central character who must make a decision or solve a problem. The case study begins with an introduction to the problem and the character, as well as a background section. An additional section includes recent developments in the situation and appendices of documents, tables, and letters. An example might be the head of the environment ministry in Colombia deciding whether to allow logging in a national forest reserve.

- *Issue cases* teach students to analyze issues. There is no central character or pivotal decision to make. Rather, the case study asks the students to work out what is happening in the case. Students might analyze several descriptions of an oil spill along the US Gulf Coast or in the Mediterranean, for example.
- *Case histories* are completed stories that illustrate conservation issues in action. This type of case study is often less exciting than decision or issue cases, but case histories allow students to analyze historical events, like the recovery of bird populations after clear-felling of *Eucalyptus* forests in Australia.

Planning assignments or outcomes from case studies

Outcomes of the case study will flow from your objectives. Before you decide how to teach the case study, think about the desired outcomes (Teaching and Learning with Technology 2003):

- For learning content, ask questions that require learners to pull information from background documents.
- To explore multiple perspectives, stage debates, online discussions, trials, or discussions.
- For critical thinking and analysis, ask for opinion papers, recommendations, or statements of the problem.
- To synthesize concepts, require participants to write a proposal or create a multimedia presentation.

5.4.2 Implementation

The following formats are commonly used to present case studies (adapted from Herreid 2007):

- *Discussion* involves presenting learners with a decision or issue case. Typically, law and business schools use this format, with the facilitator asking questions and students identifying issues, problems, solutions, and consequences.
- *Debate* is useful when an issue involves two opposing views: "Globalization is a threat or a benefit to the environment." Both teams prepare written briefs of the issue and come prepared to argue either side. One side presents for 5 minutes, and the other side presents for the next 5 minutes. Then a 5-minute rebuttal follows on each position. Lastly, each side presents a 3-minute summary.
- *A public hearing* is used by many regulatory and public agencies. The format allows the expression of a variety of opinions. Structure the public hearing format with a panel that listens to presentations by different groups role-playing specific positions. For example, participants could be involved in deciding the protected status of an endangered species in their country.
- *A trial* uses two opposing sides, their attorneys, witnesses, and opportunities for cross-examination; such a case could be opponents versus supporters of a wind farm that may produce clean energy but also harm birds or bats. To ensure involvement from all students, ask students to prepare position papers in support of each side, as well as reaction papers to the trial.

- *Problem-based learning* is a method used by many medical schools. A teacher works with a small team of four to five students and presents a written account of a patient. The students identify what they understand about the symptoms and additional information they need before formulating a diagnosis. Modify this format to involve an ecological scenario, such as the health of an ecosystem.
- *Scientific research team* mimics the scientific method where learners pose questions, make hypotheses and predictions, test those predictions through experimentation, and draw conclusions. Student research projects are often based on actual studies; an example could be collecting samples from several bodies of water to assess water quality. Learners write a research paper on their results and peer-review the papers of other teams.
- *Team-based learning* involves organizing a group into teams of four to seven students and dividing the content for a course or workshop into learning units. For each learning unit, participants read individual assignments that cover the basic facts of the unit. Each student takes a short test covering the essential points of the reading. The teams of students immediately take the same test together. Then the teams discuss their answers with each other and the teacher, who clarifies points from the test and reading. Lastly, the student teams apply the facts to analyze a specific problem or case.

Note that several of these formats, for example the public hearing and trial, involve role-play of characters in the case study.

5.4.3 Evaluation

When evaluating your use of case studies, assess the skills you want participants to learn from their engagement with the case. Some skills that learners may acquire during case studies include (Stanley and Waterman 2002):

- participating in group work
- identifying issues
- developing questions
- locating resources
- conducting research and investigations
- producing materials such as blogs and websites
- making presentations, negotiating, and debating

Case studies present many opportunities to assess learning outcomes, through tools like peer evaluations of a debate and self-evaluations. You also may use assessment forms that allow students to rate their own work experience with peers and your teaching (Stanley and Waterman 2002). Use the following questions as a guide for evaluating the effectiveness of your case study (Stanley and Waterman 2002):

- How effective was the case study as a learning tool with students?
- What were the stumbling blocks in the case study for students?
- Did student discussion address the objectives of the case?
- Were students able to locate additional resource materials?

- How useful were supporting materials and background information?
- Was adequate time given to the case study?
- How well did the case study fit with other components of the course or workshop?

5.5 Role-play

As children, we first experience the perspectives of others by pretending. Through imaginative play, children become mothers, fathers, babies, dogs, or even monsters! Children negotiate resources like toys, space, and power in their imaginary games. Adults often use role-plays to test systems such as a mock emergency in a community. Role-playing as a technique in conservation education builds real-world skills and understanding of different perspectives by assigning roles to learners in a scenario. Role-playing can range from young children imitating the movements of a deer to adults conducting a mock environmental summit on climate disruption.

5.5.1 Planning

Role-play is a useful technique to choose if your learning objectives involve self-awareness, teamwork, initiative, communication, empathy, and problem-solving (Blatner 2009). In addition, students are often more motivated to seek solutions to complex issues when role-playing than with traditional assignments like writing a research paper. Two other techniques in this chapter, games (Section 5.3) and case studies (Section 5.4), may involve role-playing by participants as well.

The objectives of the role-play

As with other techniques, first define the objectives of the role-playing exercise (Teed 2003):

- What topics do you want the role-play to include?
- What awareness or skills do you want the participants to gain?
- Do you want to use or adapt an existing role-play or write your own?
- How much time is there for the role-play?
- What outcomes (e.g., presentations, reports, research) do you expect from participants?
- Do you want students to role-play separately or as a group?

If your primary aim is to increase sensory awareness, create simple role-plays that allow participants to imagine the sensations of other life forms. Ask participants to choose a plant, tree, or animal and pretend to be that organism. As you plan these sensory role-plays, begin with simple images like the life cycle of a tree, starting with the seed in the ground, growing into an adult tree, rotting and falling, and then becoming part of the soil (Cornell 2015). You can use role-plays to visualize concepts such as the food chain by asking learners to role-play different organisms in the food chain. Draw from the natural settings around you—a nearby creek or an urban park—as a source of inspiration for choosing the "characters" in your role-plays.

If you want participants to explore how to solve an environmental problem, planning the role-play will be more involved. As a facilitator, provide the setting and characters for the participants, but allow them to decide the dialogue and direction taken by the role-play. Try asking the learners to conduct research in order to make informed decisions in their role.

Types of role-plays

You can plan either individual or group role-plays. In an individual role-play, learners take on a character assigned to them. Instruct the characters to present their issue in a format of a letter to the editor or a blog post. Provide learners with some background information, as well as sources for additional research.

Interactive or group role-plays ask participants to prepare for specific roles and engage with other characters on the environmental issue—through a debate, negotiation, town meeting, or summit. Participants usually role-play different stakeholders, such as landowners, politicians, developers, and scientists, who are affected by the same conservation issue. One role-play introduces students to environmental justice by studying historic Warren County, North Carolina, USA, where African-American community members fought the siting of a landfill for disposal of the toxic chemical polychlorinated biphenyl (PCB) in 1978. After students have researched the case, which propelled the environmental justice movement in the USA, they take on roles, including the media, the Environmental Protection Agency, community members, polluters, and scientists, among others (The Exchange Project 2007). Allow participants to plan their arguments and come up with some recommendations as part of the exercise. The amount of preparation and research depends on the time available and the complexity of the issue.

Conservation education facilities like the Pullenvale Nature Center near Brisbane, Australia, use role-plays to bring environmental history to life for its visitors. For example, fifth-graders recite the following poem:

> Travel the path of time unknown
> A destiny awaits you but not on your own
> Your strength is the group a bonding of trust
> Seize now this challenge before time turns to dust.

And then with a snap of their fingers, the students become bush kids in the 1890s who solve an environmental mystery. Facilitated by staff with drama skills, the students use props and their imagination to interact with characters who have devised an evil plan to capture birds and sell them to a museum. The students identify evidence, make inferences, draw conclusions, and develop an action plan to save the birds. Students wear costumes and use quill pens and ink while creating the strategic steps in their plan.

Before immersing themselves in the role-play, the students read a fictional story about how bush kids stopped a plan to dam a creek, and thus saved a habitat for wildlife. The story reflects the habitat surrounding the nature center. When the fifth-graders arrive at the center, the staff members assume character roles to encourage students to work together to address issues involving native wildlife.

Sources for role-plays

Reading existing role-plays can give you ideas for writing your own, or you may find published role-plays that fit your learning objectives. One excellent source of environmental role-plays for adults is the Program on Negotiation at Harvard Law School (PON 2014). These negotiations build from single-issue, two-party negotiations to multi-issue, multiparty negotiations with a focus on conflict resolution. For example, "Bradford development" involves a negotiation between a mayor and a land developer on an open space fund for developers. More complex role-plays, for example "Lake Wasota fishing rights," involve multiple interests, from native peoples to scientists, and ask participants to interpret complex environmental documents and data. Similarly, "Mediation role play: flooding," involves a role-play with seven stakeholder groups that explores how cities can adapt to climate change.

If you write your own role-play decide on a setting for the characters affected by an environmental problem. Provide background information about the problem and the characters, and define the goals of each character. Data and maps can be used to aid understanding. Decide what background information will be provided to all characters and what will be given only to individual players. Differing access to information in the role-play illustrates that peoples' perspective often depends on the information they have about an issue. This also adds the element of surprise and simulates the real world of nuance and power.

5.5.2 Implementation

When beginning any role-play, promote a safe and supportive environment so participants feel comfortable getting into their character. Introduce the role-play by providing characters with all the background information and goals. Articulate your expectations for the participants, including any research or reading they must accomplish before the role-play.

If you are conducting an interactive role-play, assign the roles and put participants in groups. There may be different groups role-playing the same scenario at the same time. This situation provides rich material for discussion, as each group may arrive at different conclusions. All the students playing the same character can meet for 10 minutes before the role-play begins to discuss any questions they have about their character.

Discuss the challenges of playing a character with very different views from those of the participants before the role-play begins. Encourage everyone to assume the role of actors, getting into the feel and emotions of their character. Additional research you require before the role-play can also enhance implementation, as you can ask participants to interview people similar to their character. For example, the role-play "Model United Nations" asks participants to talk to the embassy of the country they represent for advice on the role of the United Nations (Teed 2003).

Before the role-play begins set any ground rules, such as time limitations. As facilitator for an interactive role-play, observe each group and make notes about the process and interactions between characters to use during the discussion. The job of the facilitator is to provide enough structure to achieve the learning objectives but allow the participants leeway to dialogue as they learn.

If you have any adult participants who may resist the idea of role-playing, describe the activity as a scenario or simulation, and maintain a professional attitude yourself. Role-plays like the negotiation simulations from the Program on Negotiation at Harvard Law School stem from a vast body of research. Sharing such information with adult learners can increase their investment in the activity.

5.5.3 Evaluation

Before attempting a role-play you have written ask a colleague to read it and give you feedback on clarity. If possible, test the role-play before implementing it with a larger group. Practice giving instructions, even if you are conducting a simple role-play depicting the parts of a tree, for example.

One of the most important elements of a role-play is the reflection at the end. During this discussion, learners should describe what happened in their groups, the interactions and motivations of characters, their conclusions, and what they learned from the activity. Often, participants will be amazed to learn the motivation of another character from pertinent background information revealed during the discussion. They can write a reflective essay about the process and products of the role-play and post it online. To assess learners' involvement, evaluate how they worked to promote the goals and perspective of their characters.

As you evaluate the effectiveness of the role-play, ask yourself if the role-play helped to achieve your stated objectives. Consider indicators of an effective role-play. Were there any stumbling blocks in the role-play? Did the learners understand the background information? Did they conduct the required background research? Did participants get "into" their characters? Did all characters interact with each other? Did learners gain a new appreciation for different perspectives? Were there any unintended outcomes from the role-play? What would you do to improve it in the future?

5.6 Contests

Avoid driving your car during the "Strive not to drive" campaign and enter your name in a draw for a free bike! Race your adventure team down the Green River and win cash and prizes. Write a winning essay about the value of wildlife for the African Wildlife Foundation and get a free trip to Nairobi National Park.

Contests and competitions can raise public awareness and knowledge about your environmental issue and the mission of your organization. Contests are a fun strategy for involving people in an environmental cause with concrete incentives for participation. You can use contests in collaboration with other conservation education techniques to increase public awareness and involvement. For example:

- Each year, Kinabalu National Park in Malaysia, hosts a race up a mountain, the Mount Kinabalu International Climb-a-thon. Local media promote and cover the event, which increases awareness of the park and conservation activities.
- The World Population Film and Video festival conducts an international video competition for college and high school students. This competition awards critical

thought and expression through video of resource consumption, the environment, and population growth.

• Another contest, the G-8 Summit Sea Turtle Naming Contest, gives students in grades K–5 the chance to name sea turtles fitted with satellite transmitters and follow the movements of the sea turtles on a website.

As you research other environmental contests, pay close attention to the sponsorship of the contests. Many large corporations sponsor environmental competitions to promote a green image. International Paper Company, for example, gives a $10,000 award for environmental educators who teach their students an understanding of the relationship between economic growth and environmental protection. Discuss with your partners or a steering committee the types of sponsorship you want for the contest.

5.6.1 Planning

Think about the target audience and outcome for your contest. Do you want to target schoolchildren or adults? Do you intend to sponsor an art, video, essay, photography, speech, or music contest? Or do you want to organize a sports event like a bike race, a triathlon, or an adventure race? Would your organization prefer to sponsor a contest aimed at increasing environmentally responsible behaviors, for example reducing energy use in the home or reliance on automobiles?

Decide on the scale of your contest—will you advertise on a local, regional, national, or international scale? Look for successful models of other organizations that have sponsored similar events. When you have decided on the scope and scale of your contest, begin to identify partners and promote the competition.

Identify partners and create a timeline

Your partnerships with other organizations, from schools to the media, are key to a successful contest. Meet with local organizations that will help attract participants and promote the contest (e.g., schools, corporations, youth clubs, newspapers, and sports teams). Ask groups connected with your target audience if the contest appeals to them. What could you change to maximize participation? If you are working with students, enlist them in planning the logistics of the contest.

Meet with partners who could provide external funding for prizes and logistics. Coordinate recognition for donors, for example names on T-shirts or websites. Once you find one donor, others are often more willing to contribute. Send letters to partners explaining the contest and offering to visit schools and facilitate integration of the contest into the curriculum. Work with partners to identify the site, equipment, and any required permits for your competition.

If your competition needs volunteers, for example judges for a photography contest or timekeepers for a race, use your partners to recruit and train them. As you select judges, ensure they reflect the diversity in your community. With the help of partners, create a realistic timeline. Consider how much time people need to prepare for the contest, publicize it, recruit participants, and receive sponsorships. Co-sponsoring an event can be the start of a long-term partnership (see Chapter 8).

Promote the contest

Submit news releases and public service announcements to media contacts and post on a Facebook page and Twitter feed. Ask other environmental organizations for the names of helpful reporters at local newspaper, radio, and TV stations and invite the media to cover the event itself. Enlist the help of volunteers or students with graphic design experience to create flyers for the contest, and ensure that your partners post links to the contest on their websites or Facebook pages. Circulate announcements of the contest well in advance of the deadline for submission or application. For art and essay competitions, begin advertising at least 4 months in advance. Remember to use the media to engage people in the competition and announce the winners.

5.6.2 Implementation

Contact your volunteers or judges to remind them prior to the contest. If your contest does not involve on-site judging and you are collecting entries, distribute copies of the entries to each judge. Ensure that participants know what to do in case of inclement weather if your competition involves the outdoors. Many competitions hold their races come rain or shine.

Distribute the awards for a contest to at least the top three winners, and give certificates to all participants. If possible, send thank-you notes to all participants to promote participation in future contests. Write thank-you notes to all partners, and send them a copy of any media coverage, for example photos of the winners, to celebrate a successful contest!

The range of contests and competitions is as broad as the different objectives of conservation groups. The following examples reflect that diversity and can provide ideas for your own contests:

- The Stockholm International Water Institute awards the Stockholm Junior Water Prize recognizing a young person involved in water–environment issues on a regional, national, or international level.
- The United Nations Environment Programme hosts an international children's painting competition on the environment annually for children aged 6–15. The contest asks participants to paint a picture of a healthier, cleaner, environmentally friendly world.
- The river conservation group, Riverlink, hosts a triathlon along the French Broad River, USA.
- The Dublin Nature Center in Ireland coordinates an art contest, culminating in the production of a calendar used in a fund-raising campaign.
- The River of Words contest, awards prizes and recognition to young people who create visual art and poetry depicting rivers in their communities.

5.6.3 Evaluation

The day after your contest, meet with your planning committee to discuss its successes and limitations. What worked well? What would you do differently in the future? Did you receive an adequate number of entries? Was the media coverage sufficient? Review your objectives for the contest and implement strategies for measuring your success.

Ask partners to identify the strengths and weaknesses of the contest. What recommendations for improvement would they give? For competitions, a three-question survey can be given to all competitors at the end: (1) What did you like most about the event? (2) What did you like least about the event? (3) What recommendations would you make to improve the event? Participants can complete the short survey while standing in line for donated food and drinks!

If one of your objectives is to increase membership of your organization, see how many people joined after the competition. Membership applications can include a question asking how the new member heard about the organization. For larger organizations, the information in your advertisements can include a phone number or email address unique to the media piece, so you can measure the number of inquiries about your organization from the advertisements for the contest.

5.7 Field trips

Field trips can involve a variety of locations and participants: senior citizens taking a tour of their local nature center, pre-school children taking a bus journey to hear an environmental storyteller at the local library, or politicians touring a toxic site cleaned up after pressure from community members.

Field trips provide first-hand experience with physical sites and resources in a local or distant landscape and community. Whether you arrange a field trip for your own learners or design one to attract participants, field trips take advantage of the physical environment to enhance learning about conservation.

Field trips can range from a 10-minute visit to investigate the biodiversity of a back-yard or schoolyard (Russell 2001) to a semester-long environmental field studies course exploring the ecosystems of another country (Fig. 5.4). There are even virtual field trips such as those offered by LEARNZ, an online education program in New Zealand that offers 16 virtual field trips for schools. Field trips provide opportunities for giving out information, receiving public input, and providing first-hand experience with on-site sensory activities (see Chapter 12). Field trips often occur in particular settings such as zoos, museums, and parks.

With adults, field trips are often used in environmental planning processes to allow people to see a site for a proposed development or park. Field trips are a particularly useful tool when:

- diverse stakeholders are involved in issues that connect to a specific place;
- community members require information best explained on-site;
- educators or planners need engagement with key stakeholders; and
- the public needs knowledge about a local issue.

No matter what the duration or scale, effective field trips include trip selection, logistics planning, pre-visit and post-visit activities, and evaluation. The Ridgefield National

Fig. 5.4 A field trip helps students explore the ecology of the Costa Rican cloud forest (Photo by S. Jacobson).

Wildlife Refuge in New Jersey, USA, for example, previews field trips on its website, which includes pre-visit activities, field maps to study before the visit, and on-site activities. The field trips include "Refuge habitats," "Birds of the refuge," and "Refuge cultural history." The pre-site planning page also includes a description of basic ecological concepts that visitors should know before their field trip.

5.7.1 Planning

One certainty about learning in the field is that you should expect the unexpected. Changes in the weather, the interactions of participants, budget, transport, access to the field site, and administrative support can affect your field experience in both positive and negative ways (Crimmel 2003). Detailed planning together with contingency plans can help reduce the possibility that the unexpected will ruin the trip. Try to identify the most critical elements of the field trip or those most likely to change (like the weather) and develop back-up plans. Thorough planning using the following step-by-step process can help you anticipate the challenges of taking learners into novel environments (adapted from Camp Silos 2002):

Trip selection

- Identify the objectives, rationale, and evaluation plan for the field trip.
- Select the site to visit. Always contact the site to arrange the date and time. Obtain any pre-visit materials.
- Visit the field site to acquaint yourself with the area. Some field sites have apps that you can download to familiarize yourself with the place. Get ideas for pre-visit

activities that connect with your curriculum or your organization's goals. If working with students, the field trip and its pre-visit activities should correlate with academic standards (see Chapter 4).

Logistics

- Get approval for the trip from the appropriate supervisor of both your institution and the location (e.g., the director of organization or the departmental chairperson at school).
- Arrange transportation and any funding required to cover costs.
- Make arrangements for lunch and other meals as needed. Think about how to keep food cool in hot weather and provide extra water.
- Develop a schedule for the day. Select times to suit the largest number of participants (after-hours for full-time workers, school times for student groups, daytime for retirees or parents with small children).
- Publicize the field trip and agenda with local media. Place posters at stores and libraries. Let participants know what to bring, what to wear, and what to expect.
- Arrange for special equipment, for example a video camera, iPads, or journals.
- Prepare nametags for participants, chaperones, and visitors. If participants will be divided into small groups, make that designation on the nametag through a colored label or sticker.
- Collect money for admission fees and pay the field trip site.
- Write a letter of permission for parents, if you are taking children, including the following information: date and location of the field trip and transportation arrangements; the educational purpose of the field trip; provision for students with special needs; cost and scholarships if available; lunch or other meal arrangements; money needed; schedule; materials or equipment such as wet weather gear; information if the child needs prescribed medicine to be administered; emergency contact information; and parent/guardian signature. School systems will usually have a standard permission form for field trips.
- Request the required chaperones by sending a letter to parents or including a request in a school or organizational newsletter.
- Take copies of permission slips, extra food and water, and a first-aid kit.
- Leave a plan with a supervisor that includes the transportation route, contact names with phone numbers, and the location of the nearest hospital.

Preparing participants for the field trip

Discuss the connection of the trip to the current unit of study or the goals of your organization. Introduce any pre-visit activities to familiarize participants with vocabulary, concepts, or issues covered in the field trip. You can provide a visual introduction to the site by exploring the website or showing the site via Google Earth. The virtual field trips provided by many environmental centers facilitate research and discussion while planning the actual field trip.

Think of strategies for introducing observation skills to participants; for example you could ask them to describe an ordinary object like a pencil or paintbrush to their peers. Brainstorm open-ended questions to gather information during field trips, and ask participants to come prepared to record their responses in a journal. Consider assigning groups of participants in the role of "researchers" to explore a specific aspect of the trip and report to the others. Remember to ask the group to brainstorm expectations of behavior on the field trip as well. Finally, review the schedule for the field trip with participants (Camp Silos 2002).

Monterey Bay Aquarium in California, USA, includes a planning section on its website for youth leaders, elderhostel leaders, homeschoolers, and teachers preparing a field trip. Since its inception in 1984, more than two million students have participated in its educational programs, and many teachers start their planning at the aquarium website. Monterey Bay Aquarium field trips include facilitated and self-guided programs, with developmentally appropriate programs for different ages with choices including "Discovery Lab," "Ocean Explorers," and a self-guided program. Each field trip topic is tied to the California science standards. The field trips are available in both English and Spanish. The online registration form allows leaders to list their top 10 choices for dates and their top choices for field trip programs.

5.7.2 Implementation

The field trip itself is the time to watch participants directly engage in the landscape around them—from watching sea turtles return to their nesting sites to viewing a proposed green space in an urban community. The field trip immerses participants in the experience, a critical part of the experiential learning cycle (see Chapter 2). One such field trip, a "toxic tour" in the Roxbury neighborhood in Massachusetts, USA, shows tourists, environmental educators, students, politicians, and citizens reclaimed and cleaned hazardous waste sites in this low-income community outside the city of Boston. Residents in these communities deal with environmental injustices ranging from lead contamination in buildings, dumping in vacant lots, and toxic substances in the air and groundwater.

More than a thousand diesel vehicles are housed in the 14 bus and truck depots within a 1-mile radius of Roxbury. The low indoor and outdoor air quality in Roxbury has resulted in the state's highest rate of hospitalization from asthma, more than five times the Massachusetts average. A non-profit organization called ACE (Alternatives for Community and Environment) developed this "toxic tour," featuring a walk that highlights polluting businesses, some of which have been closed due to the efforts of ACE.

Young interns with ACE lead this field trip with detailed maps showing the toxic sites in their neighborhood and stories about successful community efforts to mitigate these sites. The tour also stops by the Environmental Protection Agency air monitoring station now established in the area, which shows that levels of particulate matter are 20% higher there than at the Harvard School for Public Health only 1 mile away. Several of the interns who lead tours have planned careers in environmental law, prompted by their experiences with the field trips.

Helpful hints

During field trips, remember to take the following steps:

- Ensure that all participants have nametags and are aware of any considerations concerning safety and behavior on the trip.
- Divide the group into smaller groups or partners.
- Use a speaking style that engages the entire group; for example, if you are leading a group along a trail, stop in a place wide enough for the group to gather, and move toward the middle before you start talking (see Chapter 12).

Give specific activities to the participants; these could include sketching pages in a journal based on their observations, following a mystery with clues, writing postcards to themselves at the end of the field trip, recording answers to prepared questions in field notebooks, and recording resources seen with a video or digital camera (Camp Silos 2002).

Ask participants open-ended questions as they make observations, such as:

- How are these objects or resources different from each other?
- Describe observations, including the setting and the object.
- Describe your favorite scene from the field trip.
- Pretend you are an archaeologist in the future observing this scene. What would you be able to conclude about this culture and the ecology of the area?

Many successful field trips rely on the importance of place-based education, where learning is rooted in local places. Community members in the Central African Republic, for example, had questions about the researchers working with an international conservation organization. Who were these outsiders living in the rainforest with the elephants? Conservation educators developed partnerships with the researchers through weekly field trips for the wildlife clubs to the research camps. The elephant ecologist taught the youngsters in the wildlife clubs to compile research data by observing elephants and identifying individual elephants by the shape and markings on their ears. In post-trip evaluations, the wildlife club members reported that they understood much more about the elephants, which they often regarded as a pest species. The assessments also revealed that the students gained more positive perceptions of wildlife research and conservation.

Field studies courses

A field studies course is an extensive field trip in which facilitator and students live in the field for an extended period of time. Some field courses are of a short duration, such as the 2-week international field experiences that are part of the study abroad courses at Warren Wilson College in North Carolina, USA. Students spend a semester in academic study preparing for the field and then travel to experience diverse cultural and natural resources in destinations including Ireland, Brazil, and China.

The United Kingdom and several European countries have a long history of field studies courses. Scotland has the Aigas Experience offering field studies at the Aigas

House in Inverness in the Highlands of Scotland and abroad. The Field Studies Council has a network of 17 field centers in England and courses overseas. The Barcelona Field Studies Center in Spain offers courses in geography, biology, and environmental studies covering topics including coastal processes and management, ecosystems, hazard management, river processes and management, rural depopulation, sustainable development, tourist impact and management, urban management, and volcanic landforms and landscapes. These courses provide hands-on study of academic content in the field, rather than only in a traditional classroom.

5.7.3 Evaluation

Post-visit activities and evaluation are critical to the success of any field experience. This aspect of the field trip allows for reflection and application of learning in the experiential learning cycle.

Post-trip activities

Facilitating or providing post-trip activities makes the field experience more than just a fun trip, as these activities provide a context for and extend learning. The following guidelines give examples of post-trip activities (Camp Silos 2002):

- Share observations and reactions from participants about the field trip.
- Create a webpage, shared journal, or blog about the field trip.
- Share assignments or journal entries completed on the field trip.
- Link field trip observations and activities to the curriculum or the goals of the organization through reflections and discussions.
- Send thank-you notes to facilitators, chaperones, and donors and include special information gathered during the field trip.
- Create a news report about the field trip and submit it to the local newspaper or organizational newsletter.
- Present a public multimedia presentation about the field trip.
- Document lessons learned by participants about the field trip.

Assessment activities

You can use multiple methods to evaluate the effectiveness of your field trip. Pre- and post-tests are one method for assessing gains in knowledge and attitudes as a result of the field trip. Staff with the Wildlife Clubs of Kenya asked students to draw and list the species and habitats they thought they would see in Nairobi National Park before a field trip to the park. The students completed a similar drawing after the field trip. The drawings revealed that a significant number of students increased their knowledge about the park as a result of the field trip.

Interestingly, field trips to the national parks were an impetus for the creation of the Wildlife Clubs in Kenya more than 40 years ago. Students in local Kenyan schools told a Peace Corps volunteer that Kenyan students never got to see the wildlife in their national parks, while tourists were the primary visitors to the parks. The students negotiated with the Kenyan government to allow all members of Wildlife Clubs free access to the national parks, prompting many clubs to raise money for field trips to the parks.

As the facilitator or leader for a field trip, use the following questions as a guide for documenting your own observations about the field trip. Learners could even edit their own video footage to address specific evaluation questions. Involve your participants, volunteers, and administrators in these questions during a reflection about the trip (Camp Silos 2002):

- Did the participants meet the learning objectives?
- What aspects of the field trip provided the most educational value to participants?
- Was there adequate time?
- Was there adequate staff supervision?
- What would improve a visit to this site in the future?
- What points could be emphasized next time?
- What problems arose that should be addressed in the future?

Use the photos or videos you took during the field trip as a prompt for feedback during the debriefing session. Collecting information for evaluation from a variety of stakeholders involved in the trip will give you valuable data for improving the quality of the experience.

5.8 Backcountry skills

The increase in urban living worldwide has resulted in a decrease in our direct connection to the outdoors. For many people food comes from grocery stores and fast food restaurants rather than gardens and farms. At the same time, outdoor recreation is expanding, but people who enjoy the outdoors often lack adequate backcountry skills and ethics, which can result in human injury and harm to protected areas.

Backcountry skills teach a connection to the earth by increasing awareness and skills for self-reliance and low-impact living in the outdoors. You do not need a large tract of wilderness to teach the skills of nature observation, wild edibles, shelter building, and animal tracking.

Some skills, for example identifying edible plants, can be introduced in an urban area—watch as participants change their perspective of dandelions from pesky weeds to tasty snacks. Backcountry skills can connect us to our ancestors, as well as some indigenous people today who use these same skills in their daily lives.

5.8.1 Planning

Planning to teach backcountry skills involves assessing the needs and knowledge of your participants and identifying local resources, such as people and places. Even if you are not an expert in animal tracking or plant identification, field guides and local experts can provide an ideal starting point for your lessons. Remember that the focus of backcountry skills is discovering the natural world and strategies for reducing human impacts on it. As an educator you can build your skills along with those of your participants.

Content

During planning, you can choose to focus on sensory awareness activities or specific backcountry skills, ranging from making a fire to building a shelter. Many workshops and extended teaching sessions begin with sensory awareness and progress to concrete skills. Alternatively you may choose to teach a backcountry skill to meet a group process goal, for example building teamwork among participants. Creating a shelter like a debris hut can enhance group skills among participants along with backcountry skills.

Tom Brown's field guides (Brown 1983a,b) provide rich resources for planning lessons or workshops on backcountry skills. Known as "the tracker," Brown was raised in the United States under the guidance of Stalking Wolf, an Apache Indian. Brown's wilderness school, books, and educational philosophy draw heavily on Native American tales and knowledge. His books include field guides to wilderness survival, nature observation and tracking, city and suburban survival, wild edible and medicinal plants, and nature and survival for children (Brown 1984, 1985). While the guides include North American species, the techniques and educational focus can apply to any geographic area.

Another useful source for content is the Leave No Trace Center for Outdoor Ethics, an organization that conducts workshops across the globe in the seven principles of Leave No Trace (Box 5.4). This non-profit organization with an emphasis on backcountry skills has trained 4600 master educators worldwide, who in turn educate others in responsible outdoor recreation (Fig. 5.5). Alice Cohen, a former wilderness ranger and current educator with the USDA Forest Service, facilitates these Leave No Trace workshops for adults. "Too often recreationists have a desire to go to 'wilderness' areas when they don't have the skills or knowledge to rough it," she explains. "Often they really just want recommendations and skills to camp outdoors." Training courses like the Leave No Trace workshops help minimize the impacts on public lands.

Box 5.4 The Leave No Trace principles

The Leave No Trace principles reflect the importance of backcountry skills and outdoor ethics

1. Plan ahead and prepare

- Know the regulations and special concerns for the area you will visit.
- Prepare for extreme weather, hazards, and emergencies.
- Schedule your trip to avoid times of high use.
- Visit in small groups. Split larger parties into groups of four to six.
- Repackage food to minimize waste.
- Use a map and compass, or perhaps GPS to eliminate the use of marking paint, rock cairns, or flagging.

Box 5.4 *Continued*

2. Travel and camp on durable surfaces

- Durable surfaces include established trails and campsites, rock, gravel, dry grasses, or snow.
- Protect riparian areas by camping at least 200 ft from lakes and streams.
- Good campsites are found, not made. Altering a site is not necessary.

In popular areas:

- Concentrate use on existing trails and campsites.
- Walk single file in the middle of the trail, even when wet or muddy.
- Keep campsites small. Focus activity in areas where vegetation is absent.

In pristine areas:

- Disperse use to prevent the creation of campsites and trails.
- Avoid places where impacts are just beginning.

3. Dispose of waste properly

- Pack it in, pack it out. Inspect your campsite and rest areas for trash or spilled foods. Pack out all trash, leftover food, and litter.
- Deposit solid human waste in catholes dug 6–8 in deep at least 200 ft from water, camp, and trails. Cover and disguise the cathole when finished.
- Pack out toilet paper and hygiene products.
- To wash yourself or your dishes, carry water 200 ft away from streams or lakes and use small amounts of biodegradable soap. Scatter strained dishwater.

4. Leave what you find

- Preserve the past: examine, but do not touch, cultural or historic structures and artifacts.
- Leave rocks, plants, and other natural objects as you found them.
- Avoid introducing or transporting non-native species.
- Do not build structures, furniture, or dig trenches.

5. Minimize impacts of campfire

- Campfires can have lasting impacts in the backcountry and can start wildfires. Use a lightweight stove for cooking and enjoy a candle lantern for light.
- Where fires are permitted, use established fire rings, fire pans, or mound fires.
- Keep fires small. Only use sticks from the ground that can be broken by hand.
- Burn all wood and coals to ash, put out campfires completely, then scatter cool ashes.

6. Respect wildlife

- Observe wildlife from a distance. Do not follow or approach it.
- Never feed animals. Feeding wildlife damages the health of animals, alters natural behaviors, and exposes them to predators and other dangers.

Box 5.4 *Continued*

- Protect wildlife and your food by storing rations and trash securely.
- Control pets at all times, or leave them at home.
- Avoid wildlife during sensitive times: mating, nesting, raising young, or winter.

7. Be considerate of other visitors

- Respect other visitors and protect the quality of their experience.
- Be courteous. Yield to other users on the trail.
- Step to the downhill side of the trail when encountering pack stock.
- Take breaks and camp away from trails and other visitors.
- Let nature's sounds prevail. Avoid loud voices and noises.

Used with permission from the Leave No Trace Center for Outdoor Ethics (2014). For more information about Leave No Trace, visit <https://lnt.org/>.

Fig. 5.5 Participants in a Leave No Trace workshop prepare to naturalize a fire ring on public lands. (Photo by A. Cohen)

Location

The location for teaching backcountry skills depends on local resources and object-ives. Even the most urban localities have potential as teaching sites. You can teach a skill like orienteering using a map and compass in any location, from a city block to a rural farm. In urban areas such as Ann Arbor, Michigan, USA, weekend orienteering clubs offer adults the chance to participate in a recreational activity that promotes a backcountry skill.

If you have the time and access to wildlands, such settings give a real-life context for teaching. Instructors from Outward Bound, an international outdoor education organization, take participants on wilderness courses ranging from 4 days to 3 months. During these courses in locations as diverse as Alaska, Scotland, and Chile, partici-pants learn skills like rock climbing, kayaking, and orienteering, along with reliance on their group for navigation. At the end of the course, they participate in a "solo" experience, where they spend at least one night alone in the backcountry. Another inter-national organization with an emphasis on backcountry skills is the National Outdoor Leadership School (NOLS), with schools in countries as diverse as Kenya and the USA. These organizations tailor programs to specific audiences, including at-risk youth, high school and college students, teachers, corporate leaders, and other adults.

5.8.2 Implementation

You may decide to focus your content and location simply on building an awareness of the natural world. One resource for starting such activities is a tool called the "Tourist test," published by Kamana Naturalist Training Program (Young 2010). Naturalist Jon Young showed 125 public school students slides and sound tracks of plants and animals in their neighborhood, and the majority of students could not identify the flora and fauna. To counter this lack of knowledge, he created a curriculum guide appropriate for rural, urban, suburban, or backcountry settings. The objective is for participants to go from being "tourists" in their own neighborhoods to "natives" with an intimate connec-tion to the natural world around them.

One activity involves instructing learners to find a "secret spot," a place in their back-yard, their community, or a local park that they could visit on a regular basis. Ideally, they must visit the secret spot frequently through different seasons. Participants record obser-vations regarding specific questions about their secret spot, for example "Is there water in the area? How big is the area? Do you feel safe in this place?" (Young 2010). Students then create maps of their secret spot and sketch the topography, hydrology, soils and rocks, hazards, inspirations, trees, mammals, and plants they can see from the spot. Each subsequent map increases students' awareness of their place in the natural world.

5.8.3 Evaluation

When you design a lesson, allow someone with local knowledge of your area to give you feedback before implementation. After teaching a backcountry skill, include some follow-up activities so learners can practice using their skills in their daily lives. For example, you may have them keep a journal about edible plants they see in their neighborhood or schoolyard. Also, have your participants give you feedback on which aspects of the lessons were most informative. What improvements could you make? Facilitators of the Leave No Trace workshops use peer evaluations of teaching presentations given by participants on specific backcountry skills. Such evaluation tools involve the learners in evaluating specific aspects of the instruction.

If you are working with students, you can also involve their teachers in observing how often school-age participants use the knowledge and skills from your lessons. During a backcountry skills workshop at Warren Wilson College, North Carolina, USA, environmental education students designed lessons on edible plants and animal tracking for local fourth-grade students. On the college campus, the fourth-graders collected dandelions for a salad and pine needles to make a tea. One month later, teachers observed that the fourth-graders still snacked on dandelions and wild onions collected from their own playground! (The teachers also enforced a rule that students had to wash the wild edible plants before eating them.)

Another important evaluation tool is pre- and post-lesson assessments to measure achievement gains in knowledge and skills. You can use both qualitative and quantitative measures, ranging from journal entries, maps, and written tests. The program 3-D Life Adventures used pre- and post-expedition surveys to measure the effectiveness of its 21-day Appalachia to Atlanta expedition that explored both ecological and cultural diversity with high school students. The staff worked with local college professors to design the surveys that measure changes in both knowledge and attitudes. The survey results revealed a significant increase in environmental and cultural knowledge among participants, as well as more positive environmental and cultural values at the end of the program.

5.9 Summary

Making conservation come alive can mean discovering the natural world around us through a neighborhood scavenger hunt or understanding the interests of an industry group by researching their perspective for a role-play. Many of the techniques in this chapter emphasize the experiential approach to conservation education, such as hands-on activities, field trips, and backcountry skills. The aim of these techniques is to immerse participants in exploration of the outdoors or an environmental concept. Other techniques bring conservation alive through a minds-on approach, using storytelling, games, case studies, role-playing, and contests. Most of the techniques in this chapter involve an element of fun.

Planning these techniques involves both research and logistics, for example selecting the site of an outdoor hands-on activity or researching appropriate case studies for a group of learners. This chapter contains many helpful hints for implementing the techniques, including tips for engaging an audience in your storytelling to encouraging participants to identify with a character in a role-play. Lastly, evaluation allows you to measure impacts and collect feedback for improvement. And every technique—from storytelling to contests—engages the audience in learning through direct experience.

6
Using the arts for conservation

The failure of people to engage in sustainable land use or consumption patterns may be partially due to our focus on technology and the dissemination of scientific information. Conservation education and outreach ideally promote interdisciplinary understanding of the natural and built environment through the sciences, arts, and humanities. Yet teaching materials often emphasize a science-based understanding of topics, while other ways of knowing are overlooked (Turner and Freedman 2004). This technocentric approach often fails to engage people in reflecting upon their values or personal behaviors. While science may be viewed as a creative process of discovery, the arts serve as another mode for acquiring and interpreting knowledge about the world. Different perspectives help people realize that we are all engaged in the search for understanding the world around us. Interdisciplinary programs help learners appreciate and engage in the wonders science reveals to the artist, and the philosophical and historical context that the arts and humanities provide for science (Rous 2000).

Environmental art includes a range of practices that describe or celebrate nature, as well as ecological or politically motivated work that addresses environmental issues. Environmental art programs are often experiential as well as interdisciplinary. Exploration, observation, reading, writing, environmental monitoring, and problem-solving activities embedded in environmental art projects can help make topics relevant to learners. Art can help students examine people's impacts on the environment. Incorporating art into the classroom can engage students who may not otherwise excel in academic settings or reveal students' hidden talents (Ford Foundation 2005).

Researchers have found that using multiple ways to teach, for example drawing or drama, in addition to written activities, enhances long-term memory. Brain-based learning theory suggests that educators use multiple modalities—such as the arts—to enhance learning (Weiss 2001). Within formal education, in the National Curriculum for England and Wales environmental education is a cross-curricular theme. Activities like art, music, poetry, and creative writing offer opportunities to address students' attitudes, beliefs, and emotions (Gurevitz 2000). At the university level, a joint field trip with art and biology students produced both art products and new ecological understanding. Focusing on the theme of climate change processes, students explored coastal ecosystems and created abstract collages using found objects. Test scores showed increased knowledge about climate change risks after their art-making and interaction (Jacobson et al. 2013) (Fig. 6.1).

Conservation Education and Outreach Techniques. Second Edition. Susan K. Jacobson, Mallory D. McDuff & Martha C. Monroe © Susan K. Jacobson, Mallory D. McDuff & Martha C. Monroe 2015. Published 2015 by Oxford University Press.

Fig. 6.1 Students explore coastal climate change issues through an interdisciplinary art experience. (Photo by S. Jacobson.)

Most conservation issues are relevant to personal values and ethics, as well as science and economics. Conservation educators have used the arts to inform public opinion. In Tasmania, the photographs of Peter Dombrovskis brought the Tasmanian wilderness to the public's attention. The Tasmanian Wilderness Society printed a poster of his photograph of the Franklin River that became the symbol for a campaign to prevent the construction of a dam on the wild river (Grant 2001; Curtis 2003a). Environmental artist Eve Mosher designed participatory art work, called *HighWaterLine*, in neighborhoods in New York City and Miami, USA, and Bristol, UK. Local artists attract the public to collaborate on drawing the high-water lines through their neighborhoods that are at high risk of flood damage due to sea-level rise. In 2014, the Bristol effort engaged the community in mapping the line along the rivers Avon and Frome, highlighting the vulnerability that the region faces from the impacts of climate change on the waterways. Videos of the activities on Vimeo and YouTube, as well as photographs, oral histories and blogs, helped carry the message to the greater community. In Miami, an architecture competition was held to redesign a home to make it more climate resistant, and a series of sound portraits was created by artist Patricia Hernandez (http://www.high waterline.org/miami).

Literature, painting, photography, film, theater, music, and dance, offer a way to make an emotional connection to people. Art can transcend beliefs and cultures.

Using the visual and performing arts can help conservation educators reach new audiences. Art can provoke reactions that typical education and outreach methods do not. Art has the potential to inform audiences or participants about conservation topics in a new way. It can stimulate new dialogues and catalyze new perspectives.

Artist Paulus Berensohn, a ceramicist, focuses on reaching people emotionally:

> We're constantly being touched . . . by nature, and it's only our imaginations that can help us know that. That's how I would save the planet. I would start with the senses and imagination. Now that may sound naïve and impossible, but it can start in kindergarten . . . I've been interested in environmental problems for a long time, and I just don't see economics solving it or politics solving it, because they're all bandages, and it seems to me that if we are going to have a new connection to the environment it will have to happen in individual hearts and souls. The artist can help us fall in love with the earth again.
>
> Berensohn (2002)

6.1 Emotion, art, and learning

When emotional input is added to learning experiences it makes them more memorable and exciting. The brain deems the information more important and enhances memories of the event (see Chapter 2). Presenting facts alone is less likely to result in long-term changes in feelings and behaviors: good teaching engages feelings (Weiss 2001; Cable and Ernst 2003). Because we do not completely understand our emotional system, however, we do not fully incorporate emotion into environmental curricula in schools or environmental outreach programs (Sylwester 2010).

Greater understanding of the psychobiology of emotion should eventually enable educators to apply this knowledge in and out of the classroom. Emotion is often a more powerful determinant of our behavior than our brain's logical/rational processes (Sylwester 2010). Purchasing a lottery ticket (when the chance of winning is slim) or wearing an unflattering style because it is fashionable provide daily evidence that rational thought does not rule our behavior. Emotions allow us to respond quickly to incoming information by avoiding conscious deliberation. This leads to both irrational fears and foolish behaviors, but also to immediate and appropriate action.

Our brainstem and limbic system, along with the cerebral cortex, regulate our emotions. The limbic system is the brain's main regulator of emotion and helps process our memories. The limbic system is powerful enough to override both rational thought and innate brainstem response patterns. Memories formed during a specific emotional state are easily recalled during a similar emotional state later on (Thayer 1989). For example, during an argument people can remember similar previous arguments. Educational techniques like simulations and role-playing activities (see Chapters 5 and 11) enhance learning because they provide emotional prompts that tie memories to the kinds of emotional contexts in which they will later be used in the real world.

Our emotional system is modulated by molecules that travel throughout our body and brain. Some of these molecules respond to the arts! For example, music as well as positive social contact can elevate levels of endorphins and dopamine, creating a feeling of pleasure (Levinthal 1988; NME 2013). By engaging multiple senses or by emphasizing social interaction, the arts can provide emotional pleasure and support to participants. The arts also seem to be important to the development and maintenance of the systems that initiate and conclude cognitive activity (Sylwester 2010).

Religious and political leaders throughout history have used the arts—from frescoed church ceilings to political theme songs—to reinforce beliefs and promote certain behaviors. Research into the emotional and health benefits of the arts is attracting increasing interest and use of the arts in medical practice has taken many forms. Art therapy engages the patient in dance and movement, music and sound, and painting, or other visual arts to promote physical or psychological healing. Artists create art for patients, patients become artists themselves, or patients co-create with artists. Therapists have found that incorporating movement, sound, art, and journal writing into their therapeutic relationships has helped patients identify and be in touch with feelings, explore unconscious material, gain insight, and solve problems (Rogers et al. 2012). The arts have also enhanced the practice of medicine. Physicians at medical centers have introduced daily doses of poetry as part of medical students' training and writing and reading poems has helped medical students better understand a sick patient's feelings and their own relationship to disease and healing (Grace 2004).

Research carried out in the behavioral sciences has shown that images of nature and some types of music can reduce stress and hold attention in positive ways across cultures and different personalities. Paintings, views out of a window, and photographs of nature can decrease stress in patients in healthcare settings. Post-operative heart patients randomly assigned to rooms with a nature scene of still water surrounded by trees had a more rapid recovery than patients who viewed abstract rectilinear forms or no art at all (Friedrich 1999).

Conservation problems require creative solutions, so it makes sense to access multiple fields of knowledge and many ways of knowing the world in order to take care of it.

6.2 Visual arts for the protection of natural areas

The visual arts—painting, sculpture, photography, and other media—can inspire environmental protection, help with fundraising, influence political activities, stimulate a new perspective, or improve classroom instruction. Although participation in an arts event may not directly stimulate changes in environmental behaviors, it can make people more open to information or engage their positive feelings in support of an organization or a cause like the protection of a natural area.

When geologist Ferdinand Hayden made plans to explore the Yellowstone area in the western USA with his US Geological and Geographical Survey team in 1871, he recognized the value of having artists accompany him. Hayden always tried to employ artists to enhance his scientific observations and reports and understood the popular appeal and scientific value of photographs and paintings. For him, photographs and illustrations of the American West were as important as scientific specimens in studying the region and presenting it to the public for their understanding and comprehension (Hassrick 2002).

Fig. 6.2 Wood engraving, *Rock Pinnacles Above Tower Falls*, by Thomas Moran; printed in *Scribner's Monthly* in May 1871. (Courtesy of the Huntington Library, San Marino, CA, USA.)

Hayden used Thomas Moran's wood engravings to illustrate his first published account of the exploration of Yellowstone that was printed in a popular magazine, *Scribner's Monthly*, and to illustrate his government report. Moran's images stirred great interest, and helped advocate for the Yellowstone area to be set aside as a national park (Fig. 6.2). Moran's watercolor paintings as well as photographs taken by his traveling companion, William Henry Jackson, proved remarkably effective props for Hayden and others who used them to persuade Congress to take the historic step of establishing the world's first national park.

Moran's paintings and Jackson's photographs "Did a work which no other agency could do and doubtless convinced everyone who saw them that the regions where such wonders existed should be preserved to the people forever," wrote Corps of Engineers Captain Chittenden. Jackson wrote that the watercolors and photographs made during the exploration "Were the most important exhibits brought before the [Congressional] Committee." The "wonderful coloring" of Moran's sketches, he wrote, made all the difference (National Park Service n.d.). Moran created a monumental painting, over 3 meters long, of the Grand Canyon of the Yellowstone. His intent was to "satisfy the myth of a bigger, newer America," and to enlighten the nation about the magnificence of the region, as well as entertain them (Hassrick 2002). Congress purchased the canvas for the US Capitol building, and it was the first landscape painting to hang there.

> **Box 6.1** Tips for taking good photographs to promote conservation
>
> 1. Get close and fill the picture frame with your subject.
> 2. Balance the composition; follow the rule of thirds by dividing your frame into three parts horizontally and vertically, like a tic-tac-toe board. Place the subject or landscape elements where these lines intersect.
> 3. Be selective; crop out extra elements that are distracting.
> 4. Focus on your subject.
> 5. Capture interesting light, such as during dawn, dusk, or storms; use side and back lighting to create special effects.
> 6. Use a tripod for long-distance shots to ensure your camera is still.
> 7. Put people in your pictures. People like looking at other people.
> 8. Photograph animals doing something—eating, yawning, running—not just sitting there.
> 9. Have your image tell a story.

Artists continue to be influential in promoting conservation and exposing the unique beauty of wildlands. Conservation organizations can often solicit paintings or photographs from professional artists to use in conservation campaigns, to accompany news releases, or to illustrate websites or interpretive kiosks. Regardless of the source, obtaining high-quality images is one key to success when using the arts to help achieve conservation objectives. Box 6.1 provides some tips for taking or selecting effective photographs.

Sometimes amateur pictures capture the uniqueness of a place and can stir the imagination. The Nature Conservancy launched a project, Photovoice, in the Tibetan hamlet of China's northwest Yunnan province. Although most residents could not read or write, with cameras in their hands 223 people from 64 villages took more than 50,000 photos. The effort gave local communities a voice in such issues as unsustainable tourism and rapid development. Their photographs spoke volumes about their rich cultural heritage, the landscape's stunning diversity, and the hardships they endure.

The story of how powerful photographs contributed to the debate about protection of a remote Alaskan refuge illustrates the capacity visual images have for stirring people's emotions. The photographic exhibit and book, *The Arctic National Wildlife Refuge: Seasons of Life and Land*, by Subhankar Banerjee helped stir concern for Alaska's Arctic National Wildlife Refuge, a place few people ever venture. Controversy over drilling for oil and gas has surrounded the 8 million hectare refuge for decades. Proponents of oil development often describe the refuge as a wasteland. Defenders of the pristine ecosystem call it "America's Serengeti," for its vast caribou herds and other wildlife. Policy-makers and environmental groups used Banerjee's stunning pictures to counteract the claims of some oil developers that the refuge is a "flat, white nothingness."

6.2.1 Planning

Banerjee became interested in the Arctic Refuge after visiting other parts of Alaska and reading a US Fish and Wildlife Service report about wildlife in the refuge. "I was stunned by the biodiversity of the refuge, and how little had been documented photographically. I was inspired by what I read, and dreamed of doing a year-round exploration and documentation of the refuge," Banerjee explains in his book. "I thought, my God, it is the most debated public land in the US. Every magazine, every newspaper, every TV station has done multiple stories on the place, and yet, believe it or not, while there had been pockets of studies by biologists and botanists, it had not been visually documented in a way that was comprehensive and included all four seasons. I realized I had a tremendous opportunity," said Banerjee (Sischy 2003).

The refuge is the calving ground for a herd of 120,000 caribou that migrate there each year. They join 36 species of land mammals, nine marine mammals, and 180 bird species, including migrants from six continents coming to nest. Magnificent displays of wildflowers carpet the refuge each summer. Banerjee found the landscape filled with life, even in the subzero winter temperatures when he photographed polar bears near their dens.

Banerjee spent several months carefully planning the development and publication of his photographs and book. His lofty goal and seriousness of purpose impressed the publisher, Mountaineers Books, during their first meeting. Banerjee described his objective for the publication of his book: "I want to see official, permanent wilderness designation for the coastal plain of the Arctic National Wildlife Refuge." He brought with him an exquisite, though incomplete, collection of images. He also had commitments from a number of well-known environmental writers and biologists, such as Peter Matthiessen and George Schaller, to provide authoritative essays to accompany his photographs.

Among his supporters was the Blue Earth Alliance, a non-profit organization dedicated to supporting photographic documentary projects that educate the public about endangered environments, threatened species, and current social issues. Banerjee credits the organization for providing him with advice about shooting the photographs, managing a project of this magnitude, writing grant proposals, and hosting a photo exhibit of his work.

As political interest in oil exploration and development increased, Banerjee raised funds to return to the Arctic to complete his photographic project. Dozens of organizations and individuals supported and contributed to his work. His association with the Blue Earth Alliance made fundraising easier. Supporters could now give tax-deductible donations to his project. Ultimately the project raised over US$200,000.

6.2.2 Implementation

Banerjee's book and photographic exhibits provide a visual document of reasons for preserving the Arctic Refuge in its pristine state. Proposed oil exploration and development may threaten the delicate ecosystem and the subsistence livelihoods of indigenous people, adding to other threats such as global warming. Banerjee spent 14 months in the field to investigate the year-round story of the landscape and the indigenous cultures, the Gwich'in Athabascan Indians and Inupiat Eskimos, who depend upon it.

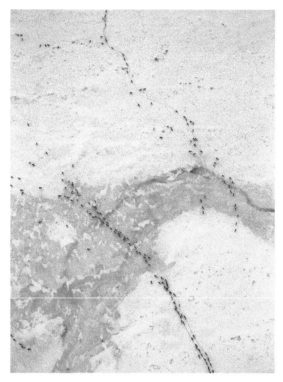

Fig. 6.3 Photographs by Banerjee, such as this aerial view of the Porcupine caribou herd in the Arctic National Wildlife Refuge, were used to sway congressional support for protection of the refuge. (Photo by S. Banerjee.)

During this time, Banerjee, with an Inupiat guide, traversed more than 4000 miles by kayak, raft, snowmobile, and on foot through this harsh, yet stunning, refuge. He understood why the Gwich'in people call this coastal plain "The sacred place where life begins."

Word of Banerjee's photography spread, and the Alaska Wilderness League asked him to bring some of his images to Washington, DC, to support the campaign to prevent oil drilling in the refuge (Fig. 6.3). His photographs were enlarged into mounted pictures, over a meter long, and were used by members of the House and Senate at press conferences and debates over energy policy. During Senate debate on the administration's plan for drilling in the Arctic refuge, a senator held up one of Banerjee's photos and referred to the area's beauty in her arguments to ban oil and gas exploration in the refuge. She urged her colleagues to visit Banerjee's photo exhibit on display at the nearby Smithsonian Institution to see the refuge's pristine wilderness for themselves.

6.2.3 Evaluation

Victory, at least in that particular battle, was won by Banerjee and other supporters of the Arctic Refuge, as the measure was defeated in the Senate. The foreword to Banerjee's book was written by Jimmy Carter, former US president and winner of the Nobel Peace Prize. Carter wrote, "It will be a grand triumph for America if we can preserve the Arctic Refuge in its pure untrammeled state. To leave this extraordinary land alone would be the greatest gift we could pass on to future generations."

Banerjee's book and exhibits provide a good example of how the arts can help inspire concern for the natural world. "I don't look at myself as an activist," says Banerjee. "I'm an artist bringing information to the public. What I hope to bring back to people is the land itself, and to raise awareness of its importance. The debate about this issue is not an informed debate, and I want the public to know the truth" (Griggs 2004). Conservationists are still fighting for the protection of this pristine wilderness, employing the arts as well as politics. In early 2015, Bannerjee's epic photographs of migrating caribou joined images of migrating monarch butterflies by Fernando Palma Rodriguez and other contemporary artists for a major exhibition, Rights of Nature: Art and Ecology in the Americas, at the Nottingham Contemporary gallery in the UK. The museum press release stated: "The artists in this exhibition reflect on our current environmental crisis—economic, political and cultural, as well as ecological. . . ."

6.3 Art exhibits

Organizations like the San Isabel Land Protection Trust in Colorado, USA, rely on an annual art sale to help provide funds to accomplish their goal of protecting ranch and forest lands. With proceeds from the sale of regional oil paintings, watercolors, pastels, woodblock prints, and bronzes, the trust purchased conservation easements to protect scenic beauty and wildlife habitat. The art exhibit brings together artists, donors, local businesses, landowners, and others at an enjoyable social function and many are involved in the organization of the exhibit.

Art exhibits have the capacity to provide more than fundraising and social benefits. They can also engage the audience in contemplating new perspectives and ideas for viewing the environment (Fig. 6.4). An art project on the theme of global climate mounted by the organization 350.org used social media to gather crowds in six continents to form large-scale images related to climate change threats. The resulting designs formed by human bodies included a wildfire image in Australia and a blue flash flood in Mexico City. These were captured on satellite imagery and shared with viewers across the world on Twitter and Facebook (Fallon 2010). A more traditional art show provided a way for forestry extension faculty at Oregon State University, USA, to communicate with new audiences about forest management (Withrow-Robinson et al. 2002). Extension agents were accustomed to talking with traditional clientele such as forest landowners, but had little experience with an urbanized public, people who were becoming more involved in natural resource policy debates in the northwest USA. To reach this audience, extension foresters decided to use a traveling art exhibit to engage the public in a discourse about forestry: "The idea behind this exhibit is to stimulate visitors with provocative images to get them thinking and talking about values, forests, and forestry issues," said project team leader, Withrow-Robinson.

Fig. 6.4 Artist Ilene Sunshine transforms discarded plastic bags and other salvaged objects to explore the relationship between people and nature, shown at her exhibition at the Maison Patrimoniale de Barthete, Boussan, France. (Photo by S. Jacobson.)

6.3.1 Planning

The main educational objectives of the forestry art exhibit were: (1) to increase viewers' awareness of the complexity of forest issues and stimulate a dialogue about them; (2) to reach new audiences; and (3) to learn about the public's understanding of forestry and promote the university extension program. The extension team developed a template for the content of the exhibit. They selected ten issues to illustrate the scope and complexity of regional forestry concerns—the topics included wildlife habitat, aesthetic beauty, harvesting methods, jobs, forest health, recreational use, water resources, fire management, conflict resolution, and urban sprawl.

In addition to topical content, Withrow-Robinson and his team wanted to include images that represented different regions of the state and different ecological zones. They also selected a diversity of artistic media, including painting, photography, ceramic sculpture, Native American carvings, quilts, and furniture. Six venues around the state were selected for the traveling exhibit. Locations were based in part on having an extension agent who could serve as a local coordinator. The local coordinators searched for locations with potentially many public visitors and each site needed to be secure so the art was safe from theft or vandalism. The sites also required well-lit rooms, appropriate wall space, and room for three-dimensional exhibits.

Planning for the art show began 18 months ahead of time in order to book exhibit halls and contact artists to make arrangements. When the art show was first developed, the team perused art galleries and regional art books to try to identify artists from whom they could solicit work. By the third year of organizing the art exhibit, the Oregon Council of Arts had joined the collaboration and contacted local artists' guilds with solicitations for work that would address the forestry theme and content areas

Box 6.2 Guidelines to artists submitting works to the Seeing the Forest traveling exhibit

---

Submission guidelines

- *Exhibit content.* Artwork relating to all aspects of forests and forestry will be considered for Seeing the Forest. However, the central theme we wish to explore is how Oregonians, by their actions as consumers, are linked to and have an impact on forests and forestry [additional information was provided in a prospectus]. Work that relates to the central theme will be given preference in the selection process. We will also select artwork supporting a secondary theme and so will still consider artwork relating to a broad range of forest topics. The secondary topic is to illustrate the complexity of forestry issues, and diversity of individual values and cultural perspectives. To accompany the artwork, the exhibit will include artists' statements, supporting text, brochures, a questionnaire, corkboards for visitors' comments, and a publicity poster.
- *Selection process.* Seeing the Forest is an educational art exhibit. We will select artwork of the highest artistic quality that allows us to fulfill our educational goal by illustrating the themes of the show. We hope to include artwork in a broad range of media, and seek representation from various regions around Oregon. Ultimately, we wish to produce a traveling show that engages and appeals to a diverse public audience. Artistic approaches may include abstract, conceptual, expressionistic, fantasy, representational, portraits, and still life, among others. A jury made up of extension faculty and members of university art departments will select the art.
- *Submission.* There is no entry fee. Both two- and three-dimensional artwork in a range of media will be accepted. Please remember that each art piece should be easily transportable, available for sale, and available for touring for the entire 7-month show. To submit work, send images to the Seeing the Forest project.

  Please include your name and title of each work with the entry form and your contact information and facts about the artwork represented in a brief written statement for each piece of art submitted (125 word limit). Explain how the piece relates to this year's central or secondary show themes. These statements will be available to the jury during the selection process to help in interpreting art under consideration, and some may also be used when selected work is displayed in the exhibit.

  The deadline for slide and statement submission is 3 months prior to the show.

  Artists whose work is selected for the show will be notified by 2 months prior to show.

Additional submission restrictions

- All work must be prepared for display. Two-dimensional work must be framed and under Plexiglas (not glass). Frame clips are not allowed. Flat pieces must be framed and wired for both wall hanging and free hanging from a rail and wire system. For wall-hanging preparation, insert a ring on each side and string wire between them. Free-hanging preparation must ensure pieces hang straight from a rail and wire system. Fabric art must arrive ready for display (i.e., with a metal, wood, or plastic dowel rod for hanging support).
- Artwork is limited to 20 kg or less.

Box 6.2 *Continued*

Agreements

If your art is selected, you must:

- Send your artwork to Seeing the Forest at your expense. Deadline for delivery in Corvallis is [2 weeks prior to show]. Specific details on location will accompany your letter of acceptance.
- Pack your art piece in a sturdy, reusable container. Containers are required even for hand-delivered artwork. (At the end of the tour, your art will be shipped back to you at your expense unless other arrangements are made.)
- State a valid price, reflecting the current market value for your artwork.
- Handle any sales transactions directly with the purchaser, and be responsible for any gallery fees. (Oregon State University Extension Forestry does not charge a commission, but some of the venues where we will be exhibiting do. Commissions range from 0 to 35%.)
- Keep the art piece in the exhibit for the entire 6 months.

Courtesy Withrow-Robinson, Oregon State University Extension Service, Corvallis, OR, USA.

(Box 6.2). Artists submitted slides or photographs of their work. A selection committee made up of team members and art department faculty reviewed the materials. They rated and selected artists' work based on its congruence with the program's educational themes—the link between consumption and management of forests and the illustration of a diversity of forestry issues. The selection committee also judged the work based on its relevance to a general audience, effectiveness of the artistic image, technical quality, use or depiction of recycled materials, and diversity of subject matter and geographic origin. "We provided the selection committee with a scoring sheet to rank each art piece," said Withrow-Robinson. "We received several hundred entries. Of course, one challenge is that the artists didn't necessarily depict the entire range of issues we wanted to explore with the public. We worked with what we got."

6.3.2 Implementation

The art show was produced by the efforts of the central leadership team, local coordinators, and a host of volunteers from the arts and forestry communities. About a dozen forestry extension agents around the state helped to find sites for the show. These local coordinators communicated with local papers to promote the show and handled other logistical details of the local show. In order to reach a general audience with little awareness of forestry issues, the exhibit was displayed in public spaces, such as libraries, community centers, and government buildings, in addition to art galleries.

Scheduling was handled centrally. Moving an art exhibit is a major task. It involves carefully packing the artwork, loading, traveling, unloading, hanging, and then tearing down and hanging again at the next site. A transition time of a couple of days was allotted to complete these tasks between each 1-month show. The team had restricted the size and weight of the art in order to make a traveling exhibit feasible. The team also recognized the importance of involving artists in the set-up and hanging of each show. "We're foresters by training," explains Withrow-Robinson. "We always needed artists to help lay out the artwork in each exhibit space, based on light, space, proximity of other pieces, and a host of artistic concerns."

Extension agents promoted each show using various media and an attractive poster was distributed to media outlets and posted on public buildings and meeting places around towns. News releases (see Chapter 10) were sent to the local media ahead of the exhibit.

More than 65,000 people visited Seeing the Forest in six Oregon communities (Fig. 6.5). The show used several methods to communicate with the audience. The obvious communication was through the 53 pieces of art—the visual communication from the artist to the viewer. Most artists also supplied a short written statement to accompany their image. For example, artist Stev Ominski contributed an acrylic painting of a tree stump and sawyer in a forest. He called it *Predator*. Beneath the painting was his artist's statement: "This piece was painted as a personal 'crying out in disbelief' at the loss of a grove of Douglas fir I used to enjoy visiting. The fact that the trees were privately owned and ready for harvest did little to dampen the fire of my feeling of outrage. One visit, a forest; the next, gone! Admittedly, I was fascinated by the process I had missed . . ." (Withrow-Robinson et al 2002).

The extension team produced a brochure that was available at the exhibit sites. It explained the goals of the show and key points for consideration. This information was also displayed on text panels scattered throughout the exhibit. "We realized some people wouldn't bother looking at the brochure," said Withrow-Robinson. "So we produced

Fig. 6.5 Visitors to the art exhibit Seeing the Forest were exposed to images showing the complexities of forest management. (Photo by V. Simon-Brown.)

the text panels on poster board to make sure the purpose of the exhibit was clear and the viewers' experience more informed."

The team also provided ways for the audience to communicate with them, with each other, and with the artists. The public could meet and discuss the show with the team and the artists at a reception hosted at each site when the exhibit opened. Comment cards were available to viewers to post at the exhibit for everyone to read. This program occurred before the advent of social media, but now organizations can set up Twitter and Instagram accounts and other social media tools to enable viewers to share comments from their cellphones, or to allow a larger audience to view exhibits remotely.

6.3.3 Evaluation

Comment cards allowed participants to share feedback with other viewers. Researchers also provided a six-question survey inside each exhibit brochure asking viewers for their anonymous feedback (Box 6.3). A box was placed at the exit of the show for viewers to leave their completed surveys.

The extension team received many informal comments at the exhibits. Comments pasted on the corkboards for other viewers to read were often emotional, and sometimes polarizing. For example, one response to *Predator* complained that it was ". . . inflammatory and ill-conceived . . . " while another thought it was "fabulous." Other notes were more constructive: "I think people are too harsh. Our forests are really valuable, and it's important that we do care. They are a renewable resource, but it takes a long time to grow one tree. It's important that we don't get careless."

Box 6.3 Viewer questionnaire used in evaluation of the Seeing the Forest exhibit

---

1. Did Seeing the Forest succeed in illustrating the diversity of forest issues in Oregon?
   Yes   No

2. Which issues did you see illustrated?
   Harvest methods   Conflict resolution   Wildlife habitat
   Aesthetic beauty   Recreation   Water resources
   Jobs   Forest health   Fire control

3. I think Seeing the Forest increased my understanding of the complexity of forestry issues.
   Strongly agree   Agree   Disagree   Strongly disagree

4. Where do you live? [list of regions provided]
5. Which art image did you like the best? Why?
6. Which art image did you find the most intriguing or thought-provoking? Why?

Source: Withrow-Robinson et al. (2002).

Overall, the extension team was impressed with the thoughtful dialogue that was generated in this informal setting. The written survey included in the exhibit brochure was completed by 365 visitors. The extension team compiled statistics on the responses to the multiple-choice questions. They found that 85% of respondents thought the art show successfully illustrated the diversity of forest issues in Oregon and 77% agreed that viewing the show increased their understanding of the complexity of forest issues. The team performed a content analysis on the open-ended questions to identify recurring themes in preferences and provocations by specific art pieces. Because the respondents were self-selected, bias was a problem in interpreting the results. Yet there were a wide range of responses, from positive to negative, displaying the gamut of attitudes about forest management and the art in the show. Visitors were aware of forest issues and were able to identify them in the images. Both the quantitative and the qualitative data indicated that forest issues, such as aesthetic beauty, harvest methods, wildlife habitat, forest health, and conflict resolution, were the easiest issues for people to recognize in the artwork.

The team was satisfied that they had done a good job of selecting artwork for the show that represented a diversity of issues. They had reached new, non-forestry audiences across the state by using art as an alternative educational approach. Project leader Withrow-Robinson felt the show had moved their forestry extension program forward to engage individuals and communities in a dialogue about natural resource issues. It cost several thousand US dollars to produce a traveling show, not including the salary costs of the teams. "It was a very rewarding experience," said Withrow-Robinson. "After three years of producing the show, the only way we could keep doing it would be to hire a coordinator dedicated to the program. We're experimenting with other art forms now, such as theatre. There's a lot that can be done!"

6.4 Hands-on arts programs

Some art groups have embraced environmental protection as a meaningful artistic subject. Japanese artist Tadashi Tonoshiki and 100 residents of Niinohama, Japan, collected litter that had washed up on the beach, some from as far away as Taiwan and Siberia. The artist's "ecological action art" stimulated participation in a beach cleanup by people who may not otherwise have become involved. In a similar manner, the Gyre Project, a collaboration between scientists, artists, museums, and filmmakers, hosted an exhibition at the Anchorage Museum in Alaska, USA, to draw attention to the plastic trash that collects in the world's oceans and washes ashore even in pristine places like Alaska. The gyres are currents that keep the trash circulating in loops. Trash used in the museum exhibits, which included a display of transformed plastic sandals, *Thongs*, by artist John Dahlsen, came from the northern Pacific gyre. Artist Susan Middleton presented a collage of plastic trash removed from the stomachs of dead albatrosses. In a video that accompanied the museum exhibition, a voice comments: "Marine debris is a global tragedy. You have to touch a person's soul in order to change a person's behavior" (Sierra Club 2013).

Artistic creation has been used in therapies to help patients identify feelings, gain insight, and solve problems (Rogers 1993). In a similar way, art can be used as an educational tool to help participants explore new landscapes and examine feelings and concerns they have for the environment. The opportunity to produce arts and crafts can attract non-traditional visitors to a site, entertain traditional audiences, and reveal new perspectives. An innovative example is a program developed by The Nature Conservancy that combined art with lessons about urban ecology.

6.4.1 Planning

The Nature Conservancy, in partnership with the New York Foundation for the Arts (NYFA), created a community art and urban environment project entitled Wild New York: Creating a Field Guide for Urban Environments. The project aimed to increase awareness of urban ecology through a hands-on artistic experience (The Nature Conservancy and NYFA 2004).

The idea stemmed from collaboration between The Nature Conservancy and the NYFA to develop a community environmental art project that could creatively illustrate people's interactions with their environment. Project leaders Molly Northrup and Chris Slevin determined the objectives, audience, and budget for the project. The format was a series of four field trips to different parks around New York City. Naturalists and an artist guide would accompany participants, explain ecological phenomena, and introduce a new art project at each site. A final meeting would allow participants to piece together their art creations into a "guidebook."

The audience was initially recruited from among the many dedicated birdwatchers/naturalists in New York City. The Nature Conservancy works closely with various organizations that coordinate public lectures and bird/nature walks for their members throughout the year. Working with this group of regular birders and constituents involved in the NYFA, the project proposed to create a multidisciplinary activity illustrating the importance of open spaces for wildlife and people in New York City. By creating art from their experience in nature, participants could address urban environmental issues in a creative way that would capture the attention of people who might otherwise be unconcerned. Those people who were already engaged in the issues could see them illustrated in a new way. It also would be an opportunity for the birders to create a document that arises from their wildlife observations and passion for nature.

Some issues that would be addressed on the field trips included:

- New York City as part of a major migration corridor for birds,
- urban encroachment on many important natural areas, for example wetlands in Jamaica Bay,
- historical and natural changes in parks and natural areas in the city, including invasive species,
- biodiversity in New York City,
- people's role in maintaining and supporting open space and natural areas, and
- the use of art to educate and engage New Yorkers about their natural environment.

Participants would create a field guide of their observations while taking nature walks in areas around New York City. The field guide would be loosely designed and structured by the NYFA artist, and then assembled and created by the participants. There would be three 2-hour nature walks led by naturalists and the artist. A final afternoon would be devoted to assembling the books and discussing the results. Ten to fifteen participants would be accepted into the program.

The program schedule was as follows.

- March: staff interviewed and selected a NYFA artist to serve as the instructor (five artists applied for the short-term position) and worked out logistics—dates, materials, and guidelines.
- April: staff sent program invitations to potential participants with details and a schedule. Due to the small budget, The Nature Conservancy limited advertisement of the program to their website, email, and flyers mailed to people who had participated in birdwalks offered in the past. Northrup was surprised by the response: "Interestingly, none of our regular birders joined us," she said. "It was a new group of participants: younger, some with artistic interests, and a couple of teachers. I think this was partly due to offering the program on the weekend, as well as the content." The NYFA also advertised to their trustees; none attended, although a number expressed interest. Fifteen participants were accepted on a first-come, first-served basis. Participants were required to reserve space in advance, and were encouraged to attend all four sessions if possible.
- May–June: program began. The 2-hour nature walks took place on three Saturdays. On the fourth Saturday participants assembled their field guides and discussed their experience.

As part of the planning process, the staff calculated that the program would require a budget of several thousand dollars. Expenses included: artist ($1200), materials ($1200), transportation ($400 van rental for distant field trip site), and mailing/marketing ($400 for copies and postage).

6.4.2 Implementation

Artist Maddalena Polletta and two New York City naturalists led the series of guided walks through some of the city's parks and wildlife areas. On each walk the naturalists discussed the general ecology of the area, and Polletta introduced participants to simple art techniques for capturing images from the natural world. Each session involved a hands-on activity designed for new artists and those with little or no art-making experience (Fig. 6.6). Over the course of the project, participants created simple, hand-made field guides documenting their experiences observing bird life and diverse natural habitats and creating an artistic record of their field observations.

The project was free of charge, and all art materials were provided to participants. Each participant was asked to fill out a survey before and after the series of walks to provide formal feedback on the impact of the project. Some typical walk schedules follow.

Fig. 6.6 Participants in The Nature Conservancy program in New York create their own artistic guides to urban environments. (Photo by The Nature Conservancy.)

Session 1 Site: Central Park, Manhattan

Activity: leaf and flower prints. Participants explored a pond and meadow in Central Park, looking for examples of native species used in landscaping. The naturalists discussed non-native, invasive plants and the problems they cause. During the walk, participants collected samples of such plants. At the end of the walk, Polletta demonstrated a simple printmaking technique to create leaf or flower prints from the invasive plants.

Session 2 Site: Inwood Hill Park, Manhattan

Activity: sunprints (cyanotypes). Inwood Hill Park contains the last area of natural forest in Manhattan. In this woodland site, participants searched for the typical oak and hickory trees that characterize this forest and provide habitat for birds. They collected leaves, grasses, branches, and other specimens to use in creating sunprints (cyanotypes), a photographic process that creates silhouettes of objects by using natural sunlight on treated paper. (The cyanotype paper was obtained from an art supply store, but directions for making your own paper are available in photography books and websites.)

Session 3 Site: Jamaica Bay Wildlife Refuge, Brooklyn

Activity: watercolors. The diverse habitats of Jamaica Bay offered an inspiring landscape for creating watercolor paintings. The refuge, which includes a salt marsh, upland field and woods, fresh and brackish water ponds, and an open expanse of bay and islands, is renowned as a prime birding spot where thousands of water, land, and shorebirds stop during migration. Using reference materials and personal observations, Polletta instructed the group in techniques for creating drawings and watercolor paintings of the birds and the landscapes they inhabit.

Session 4 Site: New York Foundation for the Arts, Manhattan

Activity: creating and assembling the field guide portfolio. During the last session, Polletta led an indoor workshop on bookbinding. Using techniques for creating handmade books, participants learned yet another art form. They each assembled a handmade portfolio, incorporating the various pieces of artwork created during the guided walks. The portfolio serves as a vivid record of each participant's relationship to and experiences in nature throughout the program.

6.4.3 Evaluation

Project leaders conducted a written before-and-after survey to assess changes in participants' awareness and their perceptions of their experiences. At the beginning of the first session and the end of the last session they asked participants to complete a short survey to provide feedback on the impact of the program.

Most participants had a fair amount of experience of visiting natural areas prior to registering for the program. In contrast, most of the participants reported "not a lot" of artistic experience before the program.

When asked what they hoped to gain from the program, participants wanted to increase their knowledge of both the natural and the art world. Some examples of participants' expectations were to:

- "Become more familiar with plants and birds, and learn new art techniques in a natural setting."
- "Have a memorable experience, a little more knowledge, closeness with nature, some satisfaction in executing the craft elements."

In the survey at the end of the project all participants rated their experience most highly. All responded that they learned from both the guided walks and from the art activities. They reported that they would be more likely to do more art projects in the future, and that they would be more likely to visit natural areas more often.

The enthusiasm for the course is apparent in the responses to the questions: "Did the activities and the guided walks change your experience of visiting natural environments in any way?" and "If so how?":

- "The walks with Sean made what would otherwise seem like not very wildlife-filled walks seem to be teeming with a variety of species. He demonstrated the value of close attention. So did Maddalena's instruction to always be noticing and drawing details."
- "Absolutely. I pay more attention to trees, the leaves, the birds and have more of an interest in learning about them."

The program also had other impacts. It introduced The Nature Conservancy to new audiences that had not been attending the traditional conservation lecture programs and nature walks. The participants tended to be younger and have an interest in art first, with a secondary curiosity about or appreciation for nature. It encouraged an artist and environmental educator to call Northrop and propose a new art and nature program for children to be conducted by The Nature Conservancy in partnership with another organization. The Nature Conservancy also helped promote a lecture series, Human/Nature: Art and the Environment. After further disseminating information about their art activities, Northrop received numerous requests, mostly from teachers, for copies of their program guide.

6.5 Environmental literature

For a long time writers have been raising concern for the environment. Science writers have contributed to public understanding of the connections between people and a healthy environment. In the USA in the early 1960s, Rachel Carson's book, *Silent Spring*, awakened people to the dangers of chemical pollution from toxic pesticides. She warned of impacts to the food chain and the threat of springtime without the songs of birds. Legislation to protect the environment followed her publication. Internationally, thousands of scientists have contributed to the publication of the Millennium Assessment Report and subsequent documents on topics such as environmental sustainability and human well-being (The Millennium Development Goals Report 2012). Articles produced by scientists with the Intergovernmental Panel on Climate Change have provided ample evidence to encourage policy-makers to take action to protect the global environment (IPCC 2014).

While these international reports provide stark facts to increase awareness, other types of environmental writing arouse emotions and enhance people's appreciation for the diversity and beauty of nature. Naturalist writers often combine these approaches and provide a rich source of literature to explore people's relationship with nature. Reading journals and stories of naturalists' experiences can provide new perspectives and build awareness of different ways of being in the world. Environmental writers provide unique learning experiences, from demonstrating the value of uninhibited inquiry to developing an appreciation for observation skills (Matthews and Bennett 2002). In classroom settings, courses on nature writers have helped participants examine their sense of place or provided training in history or language arts. One such class in the USA might read the works of authors mentioned in Box 6.4. Every region has writings and stories that stimulate reflection about the environment.

Writers have also inspired people to examine more closely the natural world and our relationship to it. Well-known poems, such as William Blake's (1789) "Auguries of Innocence," provide simple metaphors to help people view the world:

> To see a world in a grain of sand
> And a heaven in a wild flower
> Hold infinity in the palm of your hand,
> And eternity in an hour. . . .

Some poetry helps readers reflect on the relationship between the environment and their spiritual or emotional well-being. It reminds us of the solace nature offers. Wendell Berry's (1985) poem "The Peace of Wild Things" captures this introspection:

> When despair for the world grows in me
> and I wake in the night at the least sound

Box 6.4 Environmental literature and writing programs

Environmental literature and writing programs explore books, poetry, or journals to enhance participants' environmental awareness. A list of US books might include the following:

Abbey, Edward (1968). *Desert Solitaire: Season in the Wilderness*

Berry, Wendell (2002). *The Art of the Commonplace: The Agrarian Essays of Wendell Berry*

Dillard, Annie (1988). *Pilgrim at Tinker Creek*

Dungy, C. (ed.) (2009). *Black Nature: Four Centuries of African-American Nature Poetry*

Ehrlich, Gretel (1985). *The Solace of Open Spaces*

Leopold, Aldo (1966). *A Sand County Almanac*

Lindbergh, Anne (1978). *Gift from the Sea*

Maclean, N. (1983). *A River Runs Through It*

Muir, John (1911). *My First Summer in the Sierra*

Snyder, Gary (1974). *Turtle Island*

Thoreau, Henry (1854). *Walden*

> in fear of what my life and my children's lives may be,
> I go and lie down where the wood drake
> rests in his beauty on the water, and the great heron feeds.
> I come into the peace of wild things
> who do not tax their lives with forethought
> of grief. I come into the presence of still water.
> And I feel above me the day-blind stars
> waiting with their light. For a time
> I rest in the grace of the world, and am free.

An international non-profit organization, River of Words, combines the use of poetry and art with observation-based nature exploration to interest young people in their local watersheds. The River of Words conducts training workshops for teachers, park naturalists, community groups, and resource agencies to use this multidisciplinary, hands-on approach. The program targets children's literacy, critical thinking skills, and creativity. River of Words sponsors the largest annual international poetry and art contest on the theme of watersheds for students aged 5–19 throughout the world. From tens of thousands of entries, a hundred winners are published in an anthology and on the organization's website (<http://www.riverofwords.org>). A classic winning entry is a poem by an 11-year-old who, after studying a spider's web, transformed his observation into a poem: "Dawn's reflection / honeycomb of light / bound by diamonds / caught overnight" (Pardee 2005). Both reading and writing about the environment promote reflection about our place in the world. Teachers may use environmental prose or poetry to stimulate students of any age to examine other perspectives about the environment or as examples for creating their own stories and exploring their personal experiences. To be effective, environmental writing assignments should be planned in advance and integrated with related activities. The following questions should be considered when developing a writing project (Lindemann and Anderson 2001; Brew 2003):

1. What is the purpose of the writing assignment—to prepare for a discussion, reveal attitudes, reinforce a skill, or encourage reflection?
2. When should learners complete the assignment—after a specific experience, at intervals during the experience, at the end of the experience?
3. Can you provide a relevant example to help guide the assignment?
4. How should learners complete the assignment—on their own, with a partner, in groups?
5. Who is the audience for what is written—the learners themselves, the class, a publication, the instructor?
6. What will be the response to what the learners have written—a discussion, written comments, a grade?

Once these questions have been answered an instructor can provide a detailed description of the assignment for the learners to follow. Clear communication between teacher and students will help ensure that the writing is integrated with other environmental activities to promote reflection and learning. The following section on keeping a journal provides a model for planning, implementing, and evaluating a writing project.

6.6 Keeping an environmental journal

Environmental journaling usually involves a combination of careful description and personal thoughts and feelings. In describing an object, scene, or phenomenon, journaling can provoke the writer to delve deeper into the scientific basis of nature and stimulate a greater ecological understanding. At the same time, journaling can help people reflect on their thoughts, feelings, and impressions of the environment. Whether it is the smell of a walk in the woods or the sight of a polluted wetland, positive and negative responses can be examined and shared. Through writing and reflecting, journaling can help people discover why something is important to them. Sometimes it can reveal deeper meanings in a childhood memory and reconnect people with a place.

Writing a daily journal is often prescribed to keep writers' prose loose and fluent. As with a physical activity, practice keeps a writer in shape. Journaling is used in the classroom to help learners overcome any fear of writing they may have and to provide a chance to practice skills they are acquiring. Environmental writing projects are a wonderful opportunity to infuse environmental education across the curriculum.

6.6.1 Planning

Many guides to journaling suggest key steps to make the process successful. If keeping a journal is a school assignment, teachers often specify the type of writing instrument to use, from notebook paper to online submissions. In a class, time is often divided between the outdoors, for inspiration, and inside, where thoughts can be shared and work critiqued. Outside of a structured class, whatever materials feel comfortable may be used, whether it is jotting with a pencil in a decorative book or typing on a laptop computer. The physician–poet Dr. William Carlos Williams wrote some of his famous poems on blank prescription forms.

As an educational technique, journal keeping involves more than telling learners to look at the world and write what they see and think. Few students can produce beautifully worded details and insights without facilitation and practice. To stimulate ideas, successful examples of writing from current or prior classes can be shared with participants. Another approach is to read and analyze examples from published environmental writers, non-fiction and fiction, prose and poetry. Teachers also may use structured writing assignments to help students observe and think in new ways about the world around them.

People keeping a journal outside of a structured class find it helpful to establish a set time to write in their journal—when waking in the morning, during lunch break, or before bed. Ten to 15 minutes a day is a minimum recommendation if a writing habit is to be maintained. Entries can be just a few phrases or a few pages. The important thing is to write for the recommended amount of time. Many authors recommend writing freely, without correction or revision and without worrying about spelling, vocabulary, or punctuation. They encourage journal keepers to write in whatever idiom or voice feels comfortable.

As part of a structured class it is useful to provide students with a suggested word count to set a minimum goal for their writing requirement. Rous (2000) suggests 700 words a week for upper-level school students. Writing workshops or weeklong courses for adults encourage daily entries. Participants may post their entries to class blogs for feedback and discussion.

6.6.2 Implementation

The content of the journal may capture an arresting sight or a significant moment. Journals are different from diaries. A diary is a record of things that occurred, such as "had a picnic lunch with Blema and Perry." A journal reflects on the event and gives a sense of why it was meaningful and can provide a record of the rich details of daily experience. By jotting down reactions and ideas about the environment and the people or wildlife sharing a place with them, writers may come to a deeper understanding of their relationships.

A variety of exercises can assist learners as they explore ideas for journal keeping. Journals offer a good opportunity to practice writing literal or impressionistic descriptions—short, medium, and long—of people, places, and things. A popular exercise for nature writing is to describe a natural scene, whether a still pine forest or a stormy ocean. With enough detail, these descriptions can form word pictures, which are common in nature writing. Writers can use words to describe a scene in the same way that artists use paint and canvas. Word pictures help the reader visualize the world the writer is creating.

A conventional approach to painting a word picture of a landscape is to begin with the foreground, move to the midground, and then conclude with the background (Murray 1995). This basic technique mimics how artists might draw a landscape, or how your eye might traverse the setting. Murray suggests looking for texture, color, lines,

Box 6.5 Painting a word picture

Henry David Thoreau's journal entry on November 1, 1855, paints a word picture through his description of a wading bird on the Musketaquid River (Thoreau 1906):

> As I pushed up the river past Hildreth's, I saw the blue heron (probably of last Monday) arise from the shore and disappear with heavily-flapping wings around a bend ahead; the greatest of the bitterns (Ardeoe) with heavily-undulating wings, low over the water. Seen against the woods, just disappearing, with a great slate colored expanse of wing. Suited to the shadows of the stream, a tempered blue as of the sky and dark water commingled. This is the aspect under which the Musketaquid might be represented at this season: a long smooth lake, reflecting the bare willows and button-bushes, the stubble, and the wool grass on its tussock, a muskrat cabin or two, conspicuous on its margin, and a bittern disappearing on undulating wing around a bend.

shadowing, and movement in the same way an artist would. Determine what makes the scene unique, as well as what makes it familiar. Observing and carefully describing a favorite outdoor scene helps the writer understand it in a way that a passive visit does not. If it is not possible to go outdoors, looking out a window or choosing a photograph or painting of a landscape, plant, or animal can provide a useful topic for painting a word picture (Box 6.5).

Journal-keeping activities provide an opportunity for learners to record their observations and sensory experiences, and probe their reactions to readings and landscapes (Brew 2003). Rous (2000) suggests several topics for use with upper school students. She gets students to write about their favorite place. Students are encouraged to close their eyes and think about a place where they enjoy spending time, or where they go for refuge. Then students imagine their feelings as if they were currently in that place. What sounds, tastes, smells, sights, and textures do they associate with the place? Students then write a description (in class or at home) of the favorite place with sufficient detail for readers to be able to place themselves in the scene and appreciate it along with the writer. Rous has the students read their descriptions in class. Discussion centers on the range of places, and what "favorite" places have in common. This provides the opportunity to share the importance of nature in students' lives and to analyze good writing techniques.

To help students become more aware of what their senses perceive and ways to describe these sensations, Rous has her students write "sensory monologues." Students are asked to sit quietly and describe, rather than name, every sound that occurs (e.g., "the increasing then fading buzz of a hummingbird as it flies by," not "a bird passes"). In another exercise aimed at describing sensation, a bag of objects is passed around, and students have to describe the texture, rather than naming the object. In a similar exercise, students are blindfolded. Then containers of various foods to taste or aromas to smell are passed around for the students to describe.

For a semester-long course, keeping a journal about a specific piece of land over the duration of several months or longer offers learners the opportunity to develop a sense of place and facilitates a feeling of stewardship toward the land. Thoreau's (1854) *Walden*, describing his life at Walden Pond, set a standard for writers to share insights about their natural surroundings with a broad audience. Students should choose a site that is easy to access regularly. It can be a small plot, which enhances detailed observation, or a larger area that provides more variety.

A number of different journal styles can serve as a model for a journal-keeping class or private exercise. Examples range from scientific observation, to a literary approach, or an eclectic style that combines prose with visual graphics.

A "day book" style records daily and seasonal observations of the plants, animals, weather, and natural phenomena of a particular place. Over time, it can reveal patterns in nature, such as the monthly cycles of the moon or the annual returns of migratory birds. Students are encouraged to notice small things, like the order in which flowers bloom or how insect numbers increase. Students can also set up monitoring projects and check changes in water quality in a lake or stream with simple equipment or note changes in bird species in a yard.

This approach can be expanded into a collection of exploratory field notes. Charles Darwin's *The Voyage of the Beagle*, about the expedition which led to his theory of evolution, exemplifies this style. Darwin's diary combines detailed scientific observation with personal reflection and discovery. The descriptions of travel in land foreign to him and his boundless enthusiasm help make the prose engaging.

A final approach might combine verbal observations with sketches and other visual mementos of the land. Field journals may juxtapose vivid written descriptions, scientific field observations, or poetry with drawings, maps, photos, designs, or even cartoons (Fig. 6.7). This type of journal can inspire a learner with new insight for understanding the land and may help spark creativity.

6.6.3 Evaluation

In the classroom, specific assignments and the use of styles can be evaluated based on criteria of appropriate language and writing skills. In the semester-long journal class

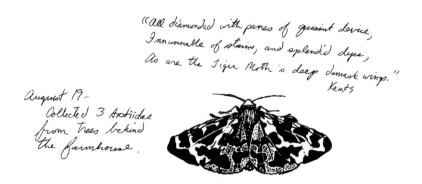

Fig. 6.7 Field journals may combine written descriptions with sketches, poetry, and other personal expressions (Illustration by S. Jacobson).

taught by Rous (2000), students hand in their journals once a week for comments and feedback from the teacher. Rous records her comments on a separate paper, not writing directly on the student's journal to respect the personal nature of the assignment. Rous uses her comments to open a dialogue with the student about their special place. She asks specific questions about the events recorded about the site, and notes which parts of their writing she found interesting, enjoyable, surprising, or unclear.

If the class agrees to this ahead of time, students can swap journals and read and comment on each other's entries when posted online through a discussion or individual site. Sharing journals in class gives students new examples of writing ideas and styles. Rous encourages self-evaluation. Half-way through the semester, she asks the students to write in their journals what they have learned so far about themselves, their places, and journal keeping, and gets them to set goals for the remainder of the semester. She asks them to consider what approaches have worked, what new approaches they would like to try, and what else they want to know about the place. At the end of the course, students write a final entry to critique whether they have accomplished their stated goals and what they have learned.

Rous grades the journals midway through the semester as a progress report and again at the end of the semester. She bases her grades on the consistency and quality of effort. Criteria include full entries completed weekly, entries demonstrating in-depth observation and reflection, and efforts to try a variety of journal-keeping approaches.

Students also give an oral presentation about their site at the end of the course. Their presentations include (Rous 2000):

- reflections from the self-evaluation of the journal-keeping process,
- excerpts from their journals,
- information they have collected from documents or interviews about soils, plants, animals, and history,
- environmental problems associated with their site and possible solutions, and
- visual representations using photos, drawings, maps, or videos of their land.

From samples of student journals and their reflections in their final entries, Rous has found ample evidence of how affection for a piece of land starts and grows through the journal-keeping process.

6.7 Environmental theater

Dramatic performances appeal to people's emotions and use the traditional technique of a story to engage an audience. They can also incorporate music and dance into the performance to appeal to a broad range of people.

The theater group Human Nature has produced two musical comedies to help audiences examine the relationship between humans and nature. They designed their first play, *Queen Salmon*, to address the demise of king salmon in their Pacific Northwest watershed, where habitat has been destroyed by shortsighted forestry, fishing, and planning policies. The play became a rallying point for their local community and instigated the formation of the Mattole Watershed Alliance, charged with changing logging standards and sport fishing regulations. David Simpson, the playwright, said *Queen Salmon* was supposed to entertain, yet at the same time he notes, "The dramatic form is a great vehicle for presenting the many conflicts and points of view of people in our community interacting with the natural resources. Theater can create a scenario to show people how they can live and work and even laugh together" (Jacobson 2009).

A theater performance was used in Oregon to introduce high school students to the complexity of natural resource issues. The play *Saving Eden Creek* allows audiences to view—through the safe environment of storytelling—fictional characters espousing a variety of land ethics. Loggers, environmental activists, developers, homeowners, and a threatened squirrel are represented. Students can either read or act the script, and afterwards audience members and actors can join in a conversation about the differing perspectives presented (Creighton et al. 2004). In experiencing such a performance, people come to a better understanding of their own values, beliefs, and actions in relation to a complexity of environmental issues.

6.7.1 Planning

Staging a performance is a major undertaking. Environmental educators may enlist the help of a local drama club or may engage an entire community. The goal of the performance, the time, budget, and expertise available, and the intended audience will dictate the scope of the program. A dramatic performance entitled *The Plague and the Moonflower* was composed in the UK by Richard Harvey and Ralph Steadman. It was staged in Armidale, Australia, to raise awareness about environmental degradation and the need for people to behave in more sustainable ways (Curtis 2003b). The pageant combined music, drama, and poetry to portray a story of the destruction and protection of nature.

The planning for staging *The Plague and the Moonflower* in the small community of Armidale took over a year and involved 170 performers and crew. The Armidale Symphony Orchestra, the Armidale Musical Society Choir, a folk band, and two dance groups (which included dancers from local high schools) participated in the event. The involvement of so many groups and individuals facilitated advertising of the performance throughout the community by using the networks of the many organizations.

6.7.2 Implementation

Careful planning and community participation resulted in a well-attended event. Two performances played to a total of 1000 people.

The Plague and the Moonflower additionally incorporated other art forms into the event to enhance the audience's experience. At the beginning of the performance, the audience was confronted with images of people's discarded rubbish. They walked through a foyer with litter and plastic lining the walls and part of the floor. For contrast, an art exhibit celebrating the beauty of the natural environment was on display next to the foyer. During the performance, images and photographs of the environment were projected above the orchestra. The performance itself included a variety of musical styles, dances, and drama. Collectively, the work extolled the beauty of nature, reflected on the impacts of industrial society, and raised the hope of living in a sustainable manner in the future.

A portion of the proceeds from ticket sales was donated to the Armidale Tree Group to fund their woodland education center. The education center would later be the site for displaying the concert's art exhibition. Additional art contributions were made by school groups that, with help from the local office of Greening Australia, created illustrations of native flowering plants to depict native biodiversity (Curtis 2003b).

6.7.3 Evaluation

Assessment of environmental performances must consider audience numbers, their satisfaction, and potential shifts in attitudes or increased knowledge. Curtis (2003b) conducted in-depth interviews with participants and members of the audience at varying times after the performance. He asked why they came to the performance, which performances they saw, what was most memorable for them, what messages they gleaned from the event, how they felt immediately after the performance and at the time of the interview, whether they would attend again, what effects the event had on their beliefs or behaviors, and how they would improve the production.

Results indicated that audience members were strongly moved by the performance and identified with the environmental message of the work. Although the numbers interviewed did not allow extrapolation to the larger audience, the results provided evidence that the drama seemed to engender a strong feeling for the environment and appreciation of their community. The event expanded the audience for environmental awareness. Many audience members were regular concertgoers, not people necessarily attracted to environmental content. The musicians and choir members reported being exhilarated by the performance. As a result of performing the work, participants refined their opinions about environmental issues (Curtis 2003b).

The goals of the performance were to increase respect and appreciation for the natural world and engender disapproval of environmental degradation. Many interviewees mentioned being inspired and uplifted by the performance. Specific behavioral changes were not advocated by the play, so it was not possible to measure direct impacts on subsequent activities of audience members. Some respondents mentioned, however, that they were reminded to re-examine how their consumerism and waste was affecting their environment.

Many communities are divided by economic and philosophical differences. Families may find participating in theatrical activities less controversial and more appealing than joining an environmental group. In this way, theatre can help bridge social or intergenerational divisions and bring people together to work on environmental problems.

6.8 Music and the environment

Music can play a role in conservation education because of its ability to attract the attention of an audience and to foster a positive attitude toward the environment (Morgan 2001; Ramsey 2002). Music can connect people with nature. An event organized by the Archie's Creek Afforestation Group in Gippsland, Australia, used music to attract their target audience: teenagers. The musical event was attended by hundreds of young volunteers who planted corridors of trees on farmlands to the accompaniment of loud dance music. In this way, music was able to attract a large audience, and create a fun, social event to provide a lot of hard labor for the land (Curtis 2003b).

Educators can introduce music through multimedia presentations, musical performances streamed from the Internet, and by enjoying natural sounds in the outdoors. Music can be used to explore issues associated with the preservation or destruction of the environment. People can learn through melodies and lyrics (Turner and Freedman 2004). As music producer Darryl Cherney said, "Music is sugar-coating for the truth pill. It reaches the heart, and usually the heart is more open to new ideas than the mind" (Jacobson 2009).

Music can invoke emotional responses. Children have a natural affinity for music and rhythm, suggesting it could be a powerful technique when incorporated into educational programming about the environment. Educators have successfully engaged students with a musical experience and piggybacked the learning of an environmental topic on this hook. Researchers embedded learning objectives within a musical activity that youngsters were already physically and often emotionally invested in, and found they were more likely to remember the content of the lesson (Lenton 2002). A group of Canadian teachers and musicians created a CD entitled *Passengers*, with songs about environmental stewardship. The lyrics were written to encompass the elementary environmental science curriculum. This integration of science themes with music allowed students to have fun singing while rehearsing the learner outcomes specified in their curriculum. Teachers were happy to check off their program requirements and students derived additional benefits from a community singing experience, such as boosted self-esteem, increased confidence, and social connection with others (Lenton 2002).

In his book *The Disciplined Mind*, Gardner (1999), the author of the theory of multiple intelligences, suggests that teachers should incorporate more integrated skill sets, including musical and kinesthetic intelligences, into learning activities. Using complementary intelligences in conservation education would foster environmental literacy for a greater variety of participants. The emotional benefits would help learners internalize lifestyle approaches to lessen their impact on the earth (Lenton 2002).

A number of different techniques exist for integrating music into a classroom or outreach program. Many popular singers have recorded songs that describe environmental problems, such as singer Billy Joel's "Downeaster Alexa." His lyrics describe the declining fishery in northeast USA and its impact on the life of a commercial fisherman. The song is the hook that engages students' interest in an aquatic resources education activity.

A huge variety of songs can be easily downloaded from the Internet, and the audience can listen for key words or can follow along with a lyric sheet. Teachers may ask students to act out particular parts of a song. For example, in a song that explores the natural history of a marine mammal, children can listen for the word "whale" and then act out a whale spouting by shooting their arms up with a whooshing sound. Children listen with focused attention for their next cue. The audience can accompany the music with physical actions and sound effects. After the song, a variety of language arts exercises can reinforce the concepts from the song. The emotional and creative activity of listening to, singing, or acting/reacting to the song helps stimulate the audience to learn (Lenton 2002).

Participants can write additional lyrics to songs, or can be encouraged to write their own songs or music to explore environmental topics and better reflect on their own understanding and feelings about the issues (Orleans 2004). Students can make a spoken-word recording of a poem or song they have composed with a simple percussion background. More musical students can collaborate to create a school ecology song for World Environment Day or some other celebration. Local musicians may be willing to participate in these activities and add their talent to songs that celebrate everything from biodiversity to recycling and watershed protection.

6.8.1 Singing a conservation message

The Bahamas National Trust launched a campaign to protect the several thousand remaining Bahamas parrots that survive on two islands in the Bahamas. A primary goal was to establish a national park to protect the Caribbean pine forest on Abaco Island where the parrots nest. The campaign had many facets, from a human-size parrot mascot named Quincy that visited schools to the use of songs to attract a wider audience and to carry the conservation message out into the community.

6.8.2 Planning

During the early months of the Bahama Parrot campaign, coordinators Monique Clarke Sweeting and Lynn Gape and the Bahama Parrot Conservation Committee met with a number of local musicians. Musicians were invited to lend support to the program by donating their time and talents. Several songs were produced, including a children's song for use in schools and a rap song and music video for broadcast on radio and television for a broader audience.

Clarke worked with the ministry of education to plan visits to schools throughout the targeted islands. They designed a parrot costume of their mascot, Quincy, for the coordinator to wear for school visits. Funding to record musicians singing the rap song and to develop the music video was obtained through donations from a regional bank, other businesses, and the Audubon Society.

6.8.3 Implementation

The project coordinators visited over 60 primary schools reaching more than 26,000 students on the four target islands—New Providence, Grand Bahama, Abaco, and Great Inagua. The lyrics to the parrot song were displayed in each school. Children were asked to read the words out loud. The song's first few verses were played, and the children were invited to join in singing the parrot song. The coordinators encouraged the children to sing louder with the challenge that students at the previous school visited had sung with more enthusiasm. Once students could sing the words, they were invited to clap and do a "parrot dance" as well as sing. Quincy danced to the song with the students and teachers, much to their amusement. By singing the tune several times over, the information about the parrot was easily remembered by the children through an enjoyable format. During the presentation, Quincy also gave parrot badges to students who answered questions correctly at the end. This reward kept the students attentive and provided a tangible reminder of the experience.

Box 6.6 The Bahama parrot campaign

A campaign to protect the Bahama parrot included the creation and production of several songs. The rap song "Quincy Rap," excerpted below was written by Bahamas National Trust project coordinators Lynn Gape and Monique Sweeting and recorded by a well-known Bahamian rapper.

> . . . Quincy needs protection
> Give it from your heart
> The Bahama parrot, Quincy needs a park
> Quincy needs protection
> Give it from your heart
> Our national bird, we all know
> Pink and pretty flamingo
> Bahamians tell me have you heard
> The squawks of our emerald green bird
> Bright and beautiful watch 'em fly
> Junkanoo Parade up in the sky
> Bahama parrot I tell you so
> Been here from long long time ago
> Bahamas! Help our parrots please
> Don't cut down our pine forest trees
> Bahama parrots help them to survive
> We must we must keep them alive . . .

Project coordinators Sweeting and Gape additionally wrote the lyrics for a rap song about the Bahama parrot (Box 6.6). Rap is a popular form of music in the Bahamas and provided a vehicle for including a lot of information about the parrots in an enjoyable, entertaining manner. Local rappers TMC rallied to the cause, providing music and talent for a recording. An inaugural version of this song was produced by Tecnol Studios and was used in local clubs. The song was re-recorded by Tony (the Obeah Man) McKay—a well-known musician and recording artist. He recorded the "Quincy Rap" and additionally agreed to donate some of the royalties to the conservation of the Bahama parrot.

The full lyrics skillfully included many pertinent facts about the Bahama parrot, including its plumage, habitat requirements, uniqueness, status, and the threats it is facing. The song also prompted the audience with a specific message about the solution to the conservation of the parrots—the establishment of a national park on Abaco Island.

The Bahamas National Trust provided the rap song to radio stations in New Providence and Grand Bahama. It also was used in the production of a music video. With sponsorship from local businesses, a professional production company filmed the music video over a 5-day period and included many scenes with McKay, Bahamian school children, and some captive Bahama parrots. Copies of the video were sent to schools, and the video appeared as a filler on local television channels as well as a feature on several Bahamian TV-magazine shows and in theaters.

6.8.4 Evaluation

The role of music was not evaluated as a separate technique within the overall outreach campaign to save the parrots. However, the coordinators found the songs and music to be tremendously popular among every group they worked with. The campaign resulted in almost a thousand school children writing to the minister of agriculture to encourage the establishment of the Abaco National Park for the protection of the Bahama parrots. The legislation was approved a year later and a new park encompassing 8200 hectares of Caribbean pine forest was established for the Bahama parrot.

6.9 Summary

The arts—including painting, photography, film, literature, theater, and music—offer an emotional connection to people. Using art for conservation can help attract new audiences, increase understanding, introduce new perspectives, and create a dialogue among diverse people. The arts can be used to inspire people to take action. Visual arts have helped direct public attention to the loss of wilderness and the beauty of nature or its destruction.

Planning art activities requires reaching out to artists and the art community, audiences with which scientists and educators may seldom interact. Implementing programs involving the arts may take a cast of one, dozens, or hundreds. Although participating in an art event or singing songs may not directly stimulate changes in environmental behaviors, it can make participants more open to information or engage their positive feelings in support of a cause or organization. Conservation problems require creative solutions. It makes sense to access multiple ways of knowing and caring about the world in order to take care of it.

Connecting classes and communities with conservation

Ultimately, success in conservation education and outreach will be measured by the biodiversity and ecosystems services that are conserved worldwide, yet success hinges on our ability to link conservation with the quality of life of individuals, groups, and communities. This chapter highlights techniques that can help conservation educators use real issues in a community to achieve conservation goals. A study of future needs and trends in environmental education research revealed the importance of community learning and action and the intersection of learning within diverse social–ecological communities (Ardoin et al. 2013).

To that end, techniques such as service-learning, issue investigation, and project-based learning involve school-based audiences in diverse initiatives including protecting native species, promoting healthy foods in neighborhoods, and increasing resilience to climate change Other techniques in conservation education, for example public participation in scientific research and mapping, can target adults as well as students. Public participation in scientific research has resulted in concrete environmental and social changes, such as safe drinking water for a community in Kentucky, as well as sustained monitoring projects like the Christmas Bird Counts which have assessed bird populations worldwide since 1900. Local communities from Botswana to Bolivia have used mapping techniques to identify gender differences in access and use of natural resources. All these techniques engage young people and adults while enhancing learning and conservation in the community.

The five techniques in this chapter share many similar characteristics and often overlap (Box 7.1). Students immersed in project-based learning could focus on a service-learning project. Fitting existing conservation education programs into neat descriptive categories can be difficult because some programs reflect several techniques described in this chapter. The global initiative GREEN (Global Rivers Environmental Education Network) developed as one of the earliest examples of an action-oriented program in which students monitor the water quality in their local watershed (Stapp et al. 1996). Recognizing the intended characteristics and goals of your conservation education program is more important than making your program reflect a single technique.

Although similar, these techniques differ in their historical roots and vary in their degrees of community participation and goals (Box 7.2). The thread that holds the techniques in this chapter together is the capacity to change attitudes, increase knowledge

Conservation Education and Outreach Techniques. Second Edition. Susan K. Jacobson, Mallory D. McDuff & Martha C. Monroe © Susan K. Jacobson, Mallory D. McDuff & Martha C. Monroe 2015. Published 2015 by Oxford University Press.

Box 7.1 Techniques to help conservation educators use real issues to connect schools and communities to conservation

Technique	Purpose
Service-learning	Applies academic learning to community needs by involving learners in planning, service, reflection, and celebration of environmental action
Issue investigation	Involves students in defining, investigating, and analyzing an environmental issue and developing an action plan
Project-based learning	Uses projects as an organizing framework to engage learners in addressing a real-world question, problem, or challenge and presenting their findings in groups
Public participation in scientific research	Uses the general public, teachers, or students in any or all of the steps of a scientific research project, most typically in data collection
Mapping	Allows individuals or groups to create visual representations of resources, community, and regions. Can document either (1) knowledge and perceptions or (2) scientific data

Box 7.2 Historical roots and goals of the techniques in this chapter

Technique	What are the historical roots?	What are the primary goals?	Who usually instigates?
Service-learning	Experiential education, community service	Impact on community needs and student learning	Teacher, community group, students
Issue investigation	Problem-solving skills and goals for environmental education	Student learning	Teacher
Project-based learning	Experiential education, neuroscience and psychology, constructivism	Student learning	Teacher, students
Public participation in scientific research	Citizen science, action research, community-based research	Collaborative research and scientific literacy	Researchers
Mapping	Participatory research methods	Data collection	Researchers, facilitators

and skills, and affect social–ecological systems. With these strategies, conservation education *can* make a difference in people's lives and their environments.

7.1 Service-learning

Service-learning is a form of experiential education in which learning occurs through action and reflection as students apply what they are learning in the classroom to community needs (Eyler and Giles 1999). A key characteristic of service-learning is the integration of academic material, community-based service, and critical reflection (Bringle and Clayton 2012). In contrast to a volunteer program or a service requirement for graduation, service-learning connects objectives for both service *and* learning.

For example, at Warren Wilson College, North Carolina, USA, students taking a course on housing and homelessness examined the intersection of sustainable and affordable housing through a service project with INSULATE, a program that reduces carbon emissions by weatherizing homes of low-income families who then benefit financially from the improvements in energy efficiency. In another course on religion and environmental justice, students engaged in weekly service trips to a community garden called The Lord's Acre, which brings diverse congregations together to practice sustainable agriculture and supply a local food bank with organic produce. In both courses students participated in systematic reflection using written prompts, small-group discussion, and verbal feedback with the community partner.

The essential elements of service-learning include (Clayton 2013):

- integration of goals for both learning and service,
- goals for academic learning supplemented with civic learning and personal growth,
- an organized, structured process,
- reciprocal collaboration among students, teachers/staff, and community members,
- assessment of a wide range of outcomes, and
- a duration and intensity sufficient to produce meaningful learning and service.

Service-learning presents a win–win opportunity for conservation education organizations, students, teachers, schools, and communities (Fig. 7.1). Many pressing community needs reflect environmental problems like environmental injustice, habitat degradation, and climate change. The majority of conservation groups and community-based organizations lack adequate staff or resources to address all their priorities. Service-learning can help meet these needs while enhancing student learning, community engagement, and personal growth. Effective service-learning includes five steps based on the experiential learning cycle (see Chapter 2): investigation, planning, action, reflection, and demonstration of outcomes (Kaye 2010; LearnToGive 2014).

7.1.1 Planning

Identifying the benefits and constraints (e.g., funding, transportation, connection to academic standards, and time) of service-learning is an important piece of planning. The benefits of service-learning are unique to each of the partners involved. Through service-learning, students experience the hands-on application of classroom learning

Fig. 7.1 Service-learning projects, such as trail work with community parks, can provide mutual benefits for conservation organizations, students, teachers, schools, and communities. (Photo by the Service Program Office at Warren Wilson College, Asheville, NC, USA.)

and networking with conservation staff, while schools benefit from access to community resources and increased engagement from students (Cairn 2003; Clayton et al. 2013). Conservation organizations and agencies can gain service from volunteers, positive publicity in the community, and access to the resources of schools and universities.

A service-learning project begins with a community investigation followed by preparation and planning. The details of each step differ slightly for staff members within a conservation organization and for teachers initiating the planning process. This section addresses strategies for service-learning from the perspective of both schools and conservation groups.

Conducting a community needs assessment will help identify feasible projects in the local area. As students are members of their community, they have a unique vantage point from which to assess local environmental needs. With support from teachers or conservation educators, students can conduct observations and interview local residents for their input on issues including household waste, wildlife, transportation, water quality, air quality, green spaces, food security, and natural disasters. Students can consider issues of feasibility, environmental benefit, educational value, available resources, and connection to academic content (Dobbins and Pittman 2001; Kaye 2010).

For conservation organizations, a needs assessment can explore ways that students could help address organizational and community needs, such as the development of a volunteer guide program that has been pushed down the "to do" list for years at a local nature center. Staff can help identify activities that have been neglected due to lack of human resources or time, and brainstorm roles in which students can participate.

This stage also includes identifying potential partners for service-learning. Partners to schools can include organizations or individuals that can provide financial, educational, or technical support. For example, in Mississippi, USA, four local schools worked on a service-learning project to provide more green spaces and play areas at school sites. Their partners included the Mississippi Department of Forestry, Mississippi Project Learning Tree (PLT), the Federal Bureau of Land Management, the Jaycees (a professional group), the parent teacher organization, a garden club, the Plant-a-Tree Foundation, and a hardware store (Dobbins and Pitman 2001). Like the Mississippi project, schools can partner with conservation groups, governmental agencies, departments of natural resources, service clubs, television networks and radio shows, businesses, neighborhood associations, youth groups, and educational organizations in their area.

After identifying a potential project for schools to take part in, dialogue with potential partners is critical. Send an email or contact possible partners with an outline of the proposed goals and what type of collaboration you are seeking. Ask to schedule a meeting to discuss the possibility of a partnership. The organizing teacher and several students should attend the initial meeting. If students and teachers are brainstorming a project with a partner, consider asking the representative to visit the classroom and present his or her ideas for projects. For students, this stage also includes creating an inventory of the interests, skills and talents of peers and partners, as well as baseline data to use in evaluation (Kaye 2010). As a conservation agency or non-profit organization, your first contact with a school may be an interested teacher or students. Think about any individual contacts who could help get your foot in the door. Brainstorm how the service-learning project could benefit the teacher and students as they cover the required academic standards.

Be sure to define goals and objectives that involve both learning and service, with a clear connection between the two. Then develop critical reflection tied to objectives in areas such as academic content, civic engagement, and personal growth, three of the key priorities in service-learning (Ash and Clayton 2009).

As an educator, communicate these objectives to your partners so they can give the students feedback during evaluation. One challenge is that service-learning projects which start with good intentions can become mere volunteer programs without these defined objectives. Conservation professionals working with schools should set clear and realistic expectations for students engaged in service-learning. Be specific about the number of hours expected. Research shows that service-learning programs which involve students for a total of at least 30 hours have an increased impact on students' learning (Cairn 2003). If possible, develop monthly or yearly projects to involve classrooms over time and build a sustainable service-learning program.

Advance planning of logistics increases success and helps overcome the inherent challenges of the service-learning experience. Establish a timeline for the project—who will do what and when? Students can plan major milestones and tasks for the service-learning project in collaboration with partners. Identify specific roles and outcomes and put them in writing so expectations are clear. Gain support from any decision-makers in the participating organization or school by getting them involved early in the project. Presentations by students are often effective methods for harnessing support.

Develop a list of potential sponsors that could donate time, money, or publicity to the cause. Next, research ways to advertise the service-learning project, for example through news releases, public service announcements, posters, or a mayor's proclamation. Spread the positive news about your plan and you may find other institutions that want to support you. Lastly, develop a budget and raise any funding necessary for the service-learning experience (Dobbins and Pittman 2001). For example, in the USA Project Learning Tree's GreenWorks! provides funding for environmental education projects that combine service-learning with community action and trees.

As a conservation agency you may be responsible for planning the training of students. Consider who will supervise the students, how you will ensure their safety, and the methods for communicating standards of dress, behavior, and confidentiality (Cairn 2003).

7.1.2 Implementation

As you engage in action and implement the service-learning project, adjust the timeline as needed and ensure you document the process by keeping a journal, taking pictures, maintaining a blog, and recording reactions from students, partners, and community members. Also seek media coverage by inviting government officials like the mayor or city council members to the project, or asking environmental experts to speak to your group. If you are organizing an on-going project, like a stream restoration, take pictures of the location before the project and invite the local media to a celebration at its completion.

Working with students and schools may present new challenges for conservation organizations. Remember that teachers spend most of their day in the classroom and have little time to communicate about the project, so be persistent as you establish a relationship with teachers and the principal. Determine the best way to communicate with teachers, whether through email, phone calls, or texts. Emphasize to teachers how the service-learning project can help students, since that is the first priority for the school (Cairn 2003). (See Chapter 4 for more tips on collaborating with schools.) If your conservation organization is working with young people for the first time, remember that treating them with respect is a major step toward earning their respect. When giving students responsibility in service-learning projects, ask for their creative input early, give them space to make decisions, and document their responsibilities (DesMarais et al. 2000).

One organization, Campus Compact (2014), provides resources to colleges and universities that implement service-learning. Their website includes program models, databases, grants and fellowships, training resources, and service-learning syllabi. One example is "Neighborhoods and watersheds," a senior capstone course that involved students in a real-life proposal to develop a resource center at a community-supported farm. During the course, students worked in teams to determine the costs and feasibility of the center, develop a long-term vision, conduct a survey of residents and businesses, design environmental education tours, prepare an exhibit, and initiate a neighborhood fair. They also presented proposals for watershed protection and conservation to business partners and city representatives. The assignments for reflection included individual reflection in journals, group reflection in a team activity log, and class discussions.

Critical reflection generates learning (identifying questions, confronting bias and assumptions, contrasting theory with practice), deepens learning (inviting alternative perspectives, asking "why"), and documents learning (producing concrete evidence of new understanding) (Ash and Clayton 2009). One effective model for critical reflection is the DEAL (describe, examine, articulate learning) model, which presents specific reflection questions in three stages (Ash and Clayton 2009) (Box 7.3). Some options for reflection include small group discussion, blogs, wikis, presentations, learning logs, theatre, essays, and research papers, among many others. Service-learning scholar Patti Clayton advises educators to design reflection prompts using Bloom's taxonomy (see Chapter 2) to help students examine their service-learning experience in a way that connects directly to learning objectives.

The scope of a service-learning project can range from students participating in a 1-day community clean-up to students planning their own environmental service-learning project in the community. The six models of service-learning reflect the diversity of approaches to integrating service into a curriculum (Box 7.4).

Box 7.3 The DEAL model for critical reflection—sample reflection for academic learning

---

Describe a service-learning experience (objectively and in detail)

When did the experience take place? Where did it take place? Who else was there? Who wasn't there? What did I do? What did others do? What actions did I/we take? Who didn't speak or act?

Examine that experience (academic learning)

What academic material is relevant to this experience? How did the material emerge in the experience? What academic skills did I use/should I have used? In what ways is my understanding of the material or skills the same or different? What are reasons for that difference, such as my assumptions, bias, lack of information?

Articulate learning

- "I learned that . . . " (express an important learning, not just a statement of fact)
- "I learned this when . . . " (connect the learning to a specific activity).
- "This learning matters because . . . " (consider how the learning has value to this situation, other organizations, the community, professional goals, etc.)
- "In light of this learning . . . " (set accessible goals; consider inherent benefits and challenges)

Adapted from Clayton, P.H. (2014). *DEAL Model for Critical Reflection*. Retrieved May 28, 2014 from <http://curricularengagement.com/handouts>.

Box 7.4 Service-learning projects vary in scope and scale

---

1. *"Pure" service-learning.* These courses and projects send students into the community to serve without connecting the course to a specific academic discipline. The intellectual core of the course is service to communities.
2. *Discipline-based service-learning.* Students have a presence in the community and reflect on their experience using specific course content as a foundation for analysis.
3. *Problem-based service-learning.* Students work with community members or a community organization to understand a specific community need. Students work as "consultants" in the community.
4. *Capstone courses.* Capstone courses require students to use knowledge gained throughout their studies in a discipline and combine it with service in the community. These courses establish professional contacts and synthesize knowledge and skills in the real-world context.
5. *Service internships.* Students work as many as 10–20 hours a week in the community with on-going reflection. Unlike traditional internships, the service internship reflects a mutual benefit between the student and the organization or community.
6. *Community-based action research.* Students work closely with teachers or faculty members to learn research methods while exploring and promoting solutions to community issues.

Adapted from Heffernan, K. (2001). *Fundamentals of Service-Learning Course Construction.* Campus Compact, Providence, RI.

7.1.3 Evaluation

For on-going service-learning in particular, evaluation is a process of collecting data to demonstrate outcomes and impacts on students, faculty, communities, institutions, and the environment, as well as to determine directions for improvement (Clayton et al. 2013). To quantify the impacts on student learning, a meta-analysis of 11 quasi-experimental studies, with a cumulative student sample size of 2129 undergraduate students, found that service-learning had a positive impact on cognitive learning outcomes (Warren 2012).

An evaluation of three national service-learning initiatives in the USA compared the impacts of service-learning on middle school and high school participants with a comparison group (Melchoir and Ballis 2002). The evaluations of Serve-America, Learn and Serve Program, and Active Citizenship Today (ACT) programs all used the same design of pre- and post-program surveys, content analysis of school records, interviews, and observations. All three programs increased students' confidence in their ability to identify issues, organize and take action, work in groups, and commit to service-learning in the future (Melchoir and Ballis 2002).

Follow-up surveys of 72% ($n = 764$) of the 1052 students (both participants and comparison group) in the Learn and Serve evaluation revealed that one-time involvement in service-learning did not result in long-term impacts on attitudes and behaviors. Yet students who continued to participate in service-learning projects the year after the program showed significant impacts on measures such as service-leadership, educational aspirations, school engagement, and reduced alcohol use (Melchoir and Ballis 2002). These findings support the need for on-going service-learning programs rather than one-time participation in service. However, one study assessing the impact of short-term (3 hour) service-learning in environmental science courses at the university level showed positive gains in student attitudes and learning in comparison with a control group of classes without service-learning (Cawthorn et al. 2011). Thus well-designed service-learning projects—even short-term ones—hold promise for conservation education.

One strategy for organizing your evaluation is a matrix that addresses: (1) What will we look for? (2) What will we measure? (3) What methods will we use to measure? (4) What are our information sources? (Gelmon 2003). For example, the matrix in Box 7.5 reflects an evaluation of the benefit of service-learning to students in a Portland State University project in Washington, USA. The evaluation matrix included survey data collection methods, focus group interviews, and reflective journals for the evaluation of students' commitment to community service and personal and professional development. Students can also help develop evaluation tools and collect data from different stakeholder groups for an evaluation.

If the original objectives of the project included an improvement in the local environment, document any changes through tools such as pre- and post-biological surveys

---

Box 7.5 Sample matrix for evaluating the impacts of service-learning on students

What will we look for? (concepts)	What will we measure? (indicators)	How will it be measured? (methods)	Who will provide the information? (sources)
Commitment to community service	Attitude toward involvement. Level of participation over time. Plans for future service	Survey, focus group interviews, reflective journal with prompts	Students, community partners, faculty service-learning coordinator
Personal and professional development	Knowledge of content/subject matter. Communication skills. Self-confidence. Leadership activities. Impacts on environment and organization	Interviews, observations, focus groups, reflective journal with prompts	Students, faculty, service-learning coordinator

Adapted from Gelmon, S. (2003). How do we know that our work makes a difference? Assessment strategies for service-learning and civic engagement. In: Campus Compact (eds), *Introduction to Service-Learning Toolkit: Readings and Resources for Faculty*, 2nd edition (pp. 231–240). Campus Compact, Providence, RI.

and photographs. If community members were involved in the service, use interviews or surveys to solicit their input. If the service-learning project aimed to change local environmental behaviors, such as the number of households involved in backyard composting or urban recycling, again, use pre- and post-project tallies to show evidence of an impact.

As a formative and summative evaluation method for your service-learning program, consider the use of a published self-assessment tool to help document success and identify areas for improvement. The website of the National Service-Learning Clearinghouse includes tools for conducting a quick assessment, in-depth analysis, and action plan for your service-learning initiative (National Youth Leadership Council, 2015). The data from evaluation will help you improve the efficacy of service-learning for the benefit of students, the community, and the local environment.

7.2 Issue investigation

Conservation issues are rarely one-sided scenarios with simple solutions. Typically, issues such as global warming, waste management, pollution, habitat degradation, environmental racism, and biodiversity conservation involve multiple stakeholders with diverse perspectives. Learning how to address these challenges involves the ability to define, investigate, and analyze environmental issues and possible actions, as well as communicate with people who have values that conflict with your own.

The structured technique of issue investigation has primarily been used with middle school, high school, and college students to build knowledge and skills to resolve complex environmental issues (Ramsey et al. 1981; Ramsey and Hungerford 1989; Monroe and Krasny 2013). The original framework for issue investigation was developed into a curriculum guide, *Investigating and Evaluating Environmental Issues and Actions: Skills Development Program* (Hungerford et al. 2003).

Students participating in an issue investigation begin by analyzing given environmental issues and their own environmental beliefs and values. They then identify local environmental issues, develop research questions, and conduct background research. After developing data collection tools, students collect and interpret data and develop strategies for environmental action. Students using issue investigation develop strategies and skills for action, but do not always implement these actions.

Fourth- and fifth-grade students on the island of Molokai in Hawaii, USA, were researching solid waste management issues in their local area when the local waste dump announced a significant increase in fees for waste pick-up and disposal (Winther 2001). The fee increase represented a financial burden for these Native Hawaiian families, and the students began investigating the issue of a bottle bill to reduce solid waste in their neighborhoods. A bottle bill is a law that aims to encourage recycling by requiring a refundable deposit on drinks sold in cans and bottles.

The students conducted background research and discovered the legislature had recently defeated a bottle bill. They spoke with state legislators and then developed their own research questions and a survey for community members. Their results from the survey revealed that the majority of residents supported a bottle bill. The students then presented their results to the state legislators, who reintroduced the bill and heard testimony from three of the students (Winther 2001). Ultimately, a bottle bill was passed in Molokai.

7.2.1 Planning

The first step in planning an issue investigation involves collecting articles, background research, and resources about relevant environmental issues. Before their own original investigations of the local environment, students should build a set of skills and practice these skills using examples and scenarios. Relevant examples can be found in newspaper and magazine articles and on websites, together with your own knowledge of past environmental problems and issues.

A problem is any situation in which something valuable is at risk. An issue arises when two or more parties or "players" disagree about the solution to the problem (Winther 2001). To prepare students to identify the players in an issue and the values that shape their positions and beliefs, consider the following values that may influence a person's choices about environmental solutions (Hungerford et al. 2003):

- ecological—the maintenance of natural biological systems
- religious—the use of belief systems based on faith
- social—shared human empathy, feelings, and status
- egocentric—a focus on self-centered needs and fulfillments
- legal—national, state, or local laws
- economic—the use and exchange of money, materials, and services
- ethical/moral—present and future human responsibilities, rights, and wrongs, ethical standards.

Given an environmental issue, such as logging in a protected area in Uganda, students would analyze the players and their positions, their belief statements, and underlying values. One stakeholder, or interested party, in this issue is the logging company whose position is that loggers should be able to harvest trees in the protected area. Their belief statement would be that timber has economic importance for both the companies and the local communities, so the underlying value is economic.

7.2.2 Implementation

The initial steps in implementing issue investigation are called "issue analysis," as these skills set the stage for the students' own investigations of local issues. Students should practice identifying and analyzing an issue by naming the players, their positions, beliefs, and values in the scenarios developed during planning. These scenarios become case studies for analysis by the students. Case studies (see Chapter 5) for issue investigation have also been developed for teachers and tested in classrooms. One such case study uses fishery issues and human impacts along the southeastern Gulf Coast and Florida Peninsula, USA (Culen et al. 2000).

Ensure that students also analyze their own beliefs and values about specific environmental issues, such as population control, food security, or hunting. A careful look at their own beliefs and values will enhance students' ability to perceive the values of others in real environmental issues. Next, have students brainstorm local environmental issues they are interested in investigating. Use your collected resources, such as newspaper articles, YouTube videos, and websites, as material for students to read when developing their lists of issues. Students can conduct the issue analysis individually or in cooperative groups. Practice comparing the perspectives of different information sources, perhaps by reviewing articles on various webpages or newspaper articles written with conflicting political slants.

When students have identified an environmental issue, work with them to develop research questions. For example, what are the beliefs and values about the lack of public transportation in the province? What is the extent and location of illegal dumping sites in their county? Research questions should be open-ended, indicate a population or geographic area, specify the variables for measurement and any relationship between the variables, and involve a relevant environmental issue (Hungerford et al. 2003). The research questions will then direct the populations or area for sampling and the sampling method. Students may combine surveying a geographic area, such as the location of illegal dumping sites, with a questionnaire on the knowledge and attitudes of government officials and residents.

Developing data collection instruments involves consultations with the teacher or facilitator and a review of existing surveys and questionnaires for models. After collecting data, students should summarize their results and present the information in the form of graphs or summary tables. From these analyses, students can draw conclusions and make final recommendations.

The data collected by students and their interpretations of the findings are used to inform their action plans. To begin, have students study environmental actions taken by both individuals and groups in local, regional, national, and global contexts. Four methods of taking action include (Hungerford et al. 2003):

1. Persuasion: used when an individual or a group of people tries to convince others that a certain action is correct.
2. Consumer action: involves buying or not buying something based on your philosophy.
3. Political action: refers to any action that brings pressure on political or government agencies or individuals. Political action can mean supporting political candidates or influencing officials through letters, petitions, emails, and phone calls.
4. Environmental action: involves responsible physical action taken with respect to the environment.

You should also discuss legal action with students, although this method requires adult involvement.

Next, help students develop an action plan and decide if they will execute the action and, if so, whether on a local, regional, or national scale. One impressive example of a student action was a group of fourth-graders informing state officials about public support for reintroduction of the timber wolf in central Wisconsin, USA (Winther 2001). An important point is that students implement these action plans of their own volition, rather than the influence of a teacher or conservation educator. When teaching students about complex issues with multiple stakeholders, it's important for educators to avoid biasing students in one direction (Monroe and Krasny 2013). Again, students must develop their own action plan but are not required to implement the action strategies.

Some questions to guide students as they consider environmental action include (Hungerford et al. 2003):

- Is there enough evidence to pursue action?
- Are there legal, social, economic, or environmental consequences of this action?
- Do my personal values support this action?
- Do I understand the beliefs and values of other stakeholders about this issue?
- Do I know the procedures necessary to take this action?
- Do I have the skills and resources for this action?

Finally, ask students to present their findings and recommendations to the class and, if possible, to a larger group, such as parents or the city council.

7.2.3 Evaluation

Each component of issue investigation should include performance objectives, which form the basis for evaluating the progress of students. For example, students may analyze issues presented by identifying players, positions, beliefs, and values. An assessment could ask students to apply those skills to a new issue, such as a recent newspaper article about a local environmental issue. This formative evaluation measures the progress of students while they learn the content. The summative evaluation, on the other hand, assesses the original issue investigation and action plan implemented by the students. A portfolio is an effective tool for assessment; it consists of a collection of student work throughout the issue investigation, which corresponds to the instructional objectives (Hungerford et al. 2003). Students can document their portfolio on a website or blog, or present it in a simple binder.

To monitor the progress of students, use a task checklist as a formative assessment tool (Box 7.6). Another useful evaluation tool is a contract between students and the facilitator that documents the criteria for evaluating the students' work, including the quality of the research question, the techniques used, the quality of data collected, the accuracy of the conclusions and inferences, the accuracy and organization of final report, and the quality of presentation (Hungerford et al. 2003).

In addition to evaluating individual students, you should assess the overall effectiveness of your instruction. Did the students accomplish the objectives? Do the instructions need modification? How motivated were the students? You can use reflective journals during the issue investigation for both the students and instructor to collect data.

Researchers have also used quasi-experimental designs to assess the impact of issue investigation and action training on variables influencing environmental behavior (e.g., Ramsey et al. 1981; Ramsey and Hungerford 1989; Ramsey 1993). For example, a study using a modified pre-test/post-test design revealed that eighth-grade students who participated in the training showed significantly greater knowledge about resolving environmental issues and stronger beliefs about their ability to affect the outcomes

Box 7.6 Task checklist for formative assessment of issue investigation

Investigation task	Due date	Teacher's review
1. Selection of research topic	——	——
2. Search for secondary sources	——	——
3. Research question	——	——
4. Letters for information	——	——
5. Interview questions/format	——	——
6. Data collection plan	——	——
7. Instrument development	——	——
8. Data collection completed	——	——
9. Charts, tables, graphs	——	——
10. Conclusions, inferences, and recommendations	——	——
11. Action plan	——	——
12. Final report	——	——

Adapted from Hungerford, H.R. et al. (2003). *Investigating and Evaluating Environmental Issues and Actions: Skills Development Program.* Stipes Publishing, Champaign, IL.

of such issues (Ramsey 1993). A similar study of seventh-grade students revealed that issue investigation and action training promoted responsible environmental behaviors (Ramsey and Hungerford 1989).

7.3 Project-based learning

Humans learn best when they perceive a *need* to learn (Newell 2003). In our jobs, families, and communities, we learn best when a task, situation, or project demands or attracts our intellectual and physical involvement. For example, a new homeowner learns to maintain a garden using xeriscaping techniques. Similarly, wildfires that threaten a neighborhood encourage residents to learn how to clear underbrush around their homes to prevent future damage or promote prescribed burning in natural areas.

Project-based learning draws on this innate ability of humans to learn when immersed in a real-life task of interest (Fig. 7.2). Project-based learning is an instructional technique that involves students working for an extended period of time on a project that investigates a complex question or problem of meaning to them (Bender 2012). The projects often emerge from a real-life context, addressing issues faced by students, the school, or the community. For example, students in one school in Seattle, Washington, USA, engaged in a project focused on the following driving question: What are the barriers to good nutrition? Their research identified access to nutritious foods as a major barrier, which led to a project focused on local food deserts, i.e., neighborhoods that lack fresh and affordable food. This project involved the use of Google Maps, field trips

Fig. 7.2 Project-based learning immerses participants in addressing a problem or question without a known solution. (Photo by the US National Park Service.)

to surrounding neighborhoods, interviews with residents, and a final public presentation with recommendations (Kraus and Boss 2013).

Project-based learning involves eight key features (Bender 2012; Larner and Mergendollar 2012):

1. *Significant content.* The project is focused on knowledge and skills derived from academic standards but also connected to the lives of the students and their interests.
2. *A need to know.* The engagement of students begins with an "anchor" that hooks their interest and presents background information and can involve a field trip, guest speaker, video, or initial research.
3. *A driving question.* An open-ended question captures the essence of the project and provides purpose and challenge. Some examples include: How can we create more green spaces at school? Is healthy food a right? What wildlife live near our school?
4. *Student voice and choice.* Students should have some input into the tasks and tools used, the products created, or the process.
5. *Development of collaborative skills.* During the project, students have the chance to practice problem-solving, collaboration, communication, and critical thinking.
6. *In-depth inquiry.* Within the driving question, students generate additional questions that shape the direction of the project.
7. *Feedback and revision.* Critique and revision by peers, the teacher, and even other adult mentors is built into the process through rubrics.
8. *Public audience.* The authentic products created are shared in a presentation to a public audience.

The terms "project-based learning" and "problem-based learning" are sometimes used interchangeably because both techniques immerse learners in concrete issues to build content knowledge and problem-solving skills. However, problem-based learning more frequently uses scenarios and role-plays in prescribed problems, such as those used in medical schools (Markham et al. 2003). These scenarios reflect the case study approach that is also used in law and business schools (see Chapter 5).

Project-based learning, as a student-centered approach, shifts the role of teacher to that of resource provider and facilitator. At Minnesota New Country School, USA, teachers are called "advisors," and classrooms are set up like offices with workstations. Early in the history of this charter school, a group of students visited a local nature center near the school to get ideas for projects in environmental studies and biology. The students found several deformed frogs on the grounds of the nature center, which became the basis for an ongoing class project. Upon returning to school, they put the information on the school webpage. They worked with the Minnesota Department of Natural Resources staff and university researchers to secure funding for environmental research, which continued with school collaboration for 6 years. Students at this school may have three or four projects under way at one time (Newell 2003).

Most schoolchildren have experienced the ubiquitous science fair project or poster display. Project-based learning, however, is *not* this type of add-on to the curriculum, but an organizing framework for learning. Project-based learning has its roots in John Dewey's experiential education (see Chapter 2), as well as research in neuroscience and psychology that reveals how learners construct their own knowledge through past experiences, culture, and community (Markham et al. 2003). The project question or issue creates the need to know that drives learning.

Studies have shown that students engaged in project-based learning show a deeper knowledge of the academic content, increased motivation, and improved problem-solving skills compared with traditional instruction (Bender 2012). For conservation educators collaborating with schools, project-based learning presents a technique for engaging students in relevant projects that affect their daily lives and the environment. For teachers, project-based learning is a way to excite students about environmental issues of interest to them. While project-based learning often focuses on schools, adults also are more effective learners when they are engaged in real-life projects.

7.3.1 Planning

At Avalon Charter School in Minnesota, USA, a student met several content standards in biology through a project restoring her backyard to its native habitat. She wrote a project proposal that included the tasks and activities, resources needed, and assessment rubric. She researched prairie habitats and then planted native plants and flowers (Newell 2003). At Monteverde Friends School in Costa Rica, a teacher involved children as young as first and second grade in project-based learning. She used the local cloud forest as a context for projects that taught skills ranging from mathematics to literacy.

Each individual educator may use a slightly different sequence of steps for planning project-based learning, but these guidelines from the *Project-based Learning Handbook*

(Markham et al. 2003) provide a foundation for planning. Remember to involve the learners in these planning steps:

- Summarize the theme or main ideas for the project.
- Identify the academic standards students will learn from the project.
- Identify key skills students will gain from the project.
- Craft the "driving question"—the essential question or problem statement for the project.
- Plan the assessment by defining the products and artifacts of the project and stating the criteria for exemplary performance. You should define products for the beginning, midpoint, and end of the project.
- "Map" the project. Look at one major outcome for the project and analyze the tasks needed to produce a high-quality product. What do students need to know and be able to do to complete the tasks successfully? How and when will they gain that knowledge and those skills? Draw a storyboard or a map of the project, with activities, resources, and timelines.
- Consider any modifications needed for special-needs students.
- Meet with other students, teachers, and resource people to refine the project design.

The planning process for New Country School involves a project proposal form completed by students and signed by parents and the teacher (Newell 2003). The proposal requires them to identify the title of the project, the topic of investigation, three questions they would like to answer, the importance of the project to the community or world, an outline of the project, a timeline of tasks, three different types of resources, and the educational standards that will be addressed. The students must review the proposal with a friend, parent, and teacher, and then the project planning team.

7.3.2 Implementation

Implementing project-based learning is when the fun begins, as students acquire knowledge and skills through real-world interactions, rather than traditional lectures and memorization. As with project management for a job, project-based learning for students requires time- and task-management tools as organizational aids, and technology can aid in these tasks. Learners should be provided with a project checklist or online weekly planning sheets to enhance efficiency and record progress (Box 7.7).

At the beginning of each week, ask students to complete a weekly planning sheet that documents what products and investigations the student will work on. The sheet also includes space for reflection at the end of the week (What did I learn this week from the project?). For the entire project, the students should have their own copy of an implementation sheet to document the focus on their project, necessary tasks and due dates, resources needed, and how they will demonstrate learning (What? How? Who?, and Where?).

Decide on methods for students to organize the data they collect from research, such as a project research log with citations, the names of people interviewed, websites, and descriptions of information gained from each secondary and primary source. These

Box 7.7 Sample weekly planning sheet and project milestone sheet for project-based learning

Implementation tools

Student weekly planning sheet:

Project:_____   Student:_____   Date:_____

This week I will work on the following products:

1. _____ Begin by myself

Continue with _____

Complete with _____

2. _____ Begin by myself

Continue with _____

Complete with _____

This week I will conduct the following investigations:

1. _____ Begin by myself

Continue with _____

Complete with _____

2. _____ Begin by myself

Continue with _____

Complete with _____

Reflections at the end of the week: What did I learn?

Project milestones

Project: _____   Student:_____   Date:_____

Milestone	Due date	Completed
☐		
☐		
☐		

Adapted with permission from Markham, T., Larmer, J., and Ravitz, J. (2003). *Project-Based Learning Handbook*, 2nd edition. Buck Institute for Education, Novato, CA.

tools can be simple research journals or an online worksheet for recording data. The key to implementation is to manage the collected information in an efficient manner. Helping students organize their data using spreadsheets and project webpages will aid them in the process (Markham et al. 2003).

In addition to research logs, you may decide to use learning logs and time logs during implementation. In a learning log, students document their specific goals or tasks, what they accomplished, their next steps, concerns or problems, and major concepts they have learned. A time log is simply a documentation of how much time students spent on the project and on which tasks. Students can also create products such as websites or blogs, a journal of volunteer work, a demonstration, or a model as a result of their investigations during implementation. For example, at Mountlake Terrace High School in Washington, USA, teams of students in a high school geometry class used project-based learning to design a state-of-the art energy-efficient high school for the year 2050. The students made architectural drawings and a model, created a budget, wrote a report and presented their work to architects who "judged" the projects.

Presenting the products, findings, and reflections is an important component of project-based learning. Before the presentation, students should outline what they expect the audience to learn from the presentation, their responsibilities during the presentation, a plan for preparing for the presentation, what *they* expect to learn from giving the presentation, and what technology or visual aids they need (Markham et al. 2003).

7.3.3 Evaluation

Working with students to create assessment rubrics turns evaluation into a participatory process rather than a top-down grading process. Since the criteria for evaluation are transparent, assessment becomes less about teachers judging students and more about

---

Box 7.8 An evaluation rubric for project-based learning

The following is an evaluation rubric for project-based learning to assess presentations by K–2 students in elementary school. The Buck Institute for Education publishes sample rubrics on its website for other components of project-based learning for all grade levels.

Presentation rubric for project-based learning

I plan a beginning, middle, and end

1. Still learning	2. Sometimes	3. Almost always
☺	☺ ☺	☺ ☺ ☺

I use pictures, drawings, and props

1. Still learning	2. Sometimes	3. Almost always
☺	☺ ☺	☺ ☺ ☺

I look at my audience

1. Still learning	2. Sometimes	3. Almost always
☺	☺ ☺	☺ ☺ ☺

I speak loudly and clearly

1. Still learning	2. Sometimes	3. Almost always
☺	☺ ☺	☺ ☺ ☺

I answer questions from the audience

1. Still learning	2. Sometimes	3. Almost always
☺	☺ ☺	☺ ☺ ☺

Used with permission from Buck Institute for Education (2013). Rubrics. Retrieved June 21, 2014 from <http://bie.org/objects/cat/rubrics>.

accountability and improvement. The skills you want to document in an evaluation rubric will depend on the mission and goals of your organization or school, as well as the educational standards.

At the Minnesota New Country School the evaluation rubric covers three key areas: basic project skills (documentation of time and learning, tasks, project assessment, project quality, resources, ownership, and task completion); critical thinking skills (comprehension, competency, and context); and life performance skills (a set of skills ranging from mediation to organization) (Newell 2003). The rubric documents criteria for each competency. At this school, an assessment team sits with the student to quiz them at the completion of the project and evaluate the project using the rubric.

Other skills that can be documented in evaluation rubrics include: accessing information, selecting information, processing information, composing a presentation, making a presentation, individual task management, individual time management, group task and time management, and group process (Markham et al. 2003). The assessments by teachers, facilitators, or even students often include rubrics to evaluate different components of the project (Box 7.8).

7.4 Public participation in scientific research

In her book of essays, *The Incidental Steward: Reflections on Citizen Science*, writer Akiko Busch (2013) describes searching for vernal pools and pulling up water chestnuts in the Hudson River in New York, USA, as she collaborates with scientists in conservation research. She contrasts the more solitary discoveries of early naturalists like Henry Thoreau with the collective reporting by local community members of migrations such as the snowy owl on eBird, an online site hosted by Cornell Lab of Ornithology and the National Audubon Society.

Increasingly, sustainable conservation initiatives are tied to public participation in both environmental decision-making and scientific research. Examples of public engagement in decision-making and management include the Land Care movement in Australia and New Zealand, community forums, collaborative adaptive management, and even the community garden movement (Monroe and Krasny 2013).

In scientific research, public participation can range from a 1-day shorebird monitoring project in Washington State, USA, to a community-based water monitoring program in the Philippines spanning several years. Depending on the research methods, community members can record data from their backyards on a cellphone app or walk a transect in a national forest with an avian ecologist (Fig. 7.3). Given the urgency in the field of conservation, public participation in research provides a unique opportunity to use technology, integrate local knowledge, and identify strategies for crowdsourcing the critical work that is necessary.

Public participation in scientific research (PPSR) is defined as an intentional research collaboration between members of the public and scientists, whose work aims to generate new science-based knowledge (Shirk et al. 2012). This term serves as an umbrella for a variety of techniques that include citizen science, community-based research, community-based participatory research, community-based monitoring, and volunteer

Fig. 7.3 Public participation in scientific research involves data collection by community members, which requires appropriate training in methods and protocols. (Photo by M. Hutten.)

monitoring. While similar, many of these techniques arose from different disciplines: citizen science has its origins in ecology and ornithology with an emphasis on data collection and monitoring. Examples of citizen science include the Monarch Larva Monitoring Project in Minnesota, USA, where fifth-grade students have collected data on a land trust close to their school for more than a decade, or Beach Watch, a shore-line monitoring project conducted by the Monterey Bay National Marine Sanctuary in California, USA (Landgraf 2013).

In contrast, community-based research stems from action research and Paulo Freire's (1970) popular education movement, with a focus on linking knowledge to community action (Strand et al. 2003a; Hacker 2013). One example of community-based research includes the Yellowstone to Yukon Conservation Initiative, or Y2Y, a transnational endeavor between scientists and communities with the goal of creating a connected corridor from Yellowstone National Park in the USA to the Yukon in Canada (Krajnc 2002). With its emphasis on public involvement, citizen science shares common characteristics with community-based research, but in community-based research, members of the public are typically involved in more steps of the research process.

In the context of conservation, each of these types of research shares an interest in three categories of outcomes: (1) *science*, such as knowledge/observations, data networks, and peer-reviewed publications; (2) *social–ecological systems*, including conservation actions, improved relationships between communities and agencies, and strengthened community groups, and (3) *individuals*, including access to information, renewed sense of place, or new skills (Shirk et al. 2012). Some of the challenges of engaging the public in research for conservation include negotiating interests in these varied outcomes, recruiting and retaining volunteers, validating data, and resolving cultural differences between community members and scientists.

7.4.1 Planning

The degree and quality of participation in the research process often distinguishes the type of participatory research and the outcomes. The degree of participation includes the question "Who participates and in what?" The quality of participation focuses on the question "Whose interests are being served and to what end?" (Shirk et al. 2012). In the planning stages it is critical to consider these questions, which will shape the responsibilities and relationship between the various stakeholders in the project.

In light of these questions, three models describe a range of public participation in scientific research (Shirk et al. 2012):

- *Contributory:* scientists ask members of the public to collect and contribute data, such as many citizen science projects.
- *Collaborative:* members of the public assist scientists in developing a study and collecting and analyzing data with common goals, including some collaborative monitoring projects.
- *Co-creative:* members of the public develop a study and address a question with input from scientists, like community-based research.

Once you have determined the model for public participation, consider the following questions in the design of your research project (Prysby and Super 2006):

- What is your research question and who is involved in identifying the question?
- What is the intended audience? Identify potential partners, such as researchers, schools and universities, clubs, landowners, and funding organization. Have you worked to establish meaningful relationships within local communities? (Read more about creating partnerships in Chapter 8.)
- Will the results be used for decision-making?
- What are the safety concerns? Think about potential risks and any safety training your staff or participants may need, such as first-aid. Consider your liabilities and procedures for dealing with any injuries.
- Is this project feasible with volunteers/citizen scientists? Identify ways to support and acknowledge your participants, and ensure they receive adequate training. If you are working with students, distribute permission forms for the parents or guardians to sign. As participants gain more experience, give them additional responsibilities.
- What is the funding for the project? Identify sources of funding, and keep track of all income and in-kind donations to use as matching funds in grant proposals.
- What are the protocols for your research? Check the scientific literature to follow protocols if they exist for your type of research question.
- Who will collect the data? Who is going to enter, validate, and analyze the data? Involve community members in the development of protocols and go over data sheets and database entry in your training. Consider making online or mobile data entry available to your participants. Online systems are used by programs such as the Evolution Megalab project to study the distribution of banded snails in Europe (Silvertown et al. 2013) and the Cornell Lab of Ornithology to monitor

bird populations. Methods to ensure quality of data, such as pre-testing of proto-cols and data sheets, online training, and data entry by teams, are important in the development of the research project.

• Will your project have a strong education component? Decide on educational products for your project, such as class visits, news articles, websites, blogs, and public lectures. If you are working with students, collaborate with local teachers to design projects that take into consideration both academic standards and logistical factors, such as transportation. Think about issues of accessibility and any special needs of your participants in the project design. Develop pre- and post-visit lessons for students, or pay teachers to help you design these lessons. Try to incorporate opportunities for community members to test hypotheses during their field visits.

• What is the time frame of the project? How will you promote the sustainability of your research project? Help maintain the longevity of your project by document-ing all your decisions, and identifying strategies for keeping members of the public involved over time.

• What will you do with the data once you have them? Determine how you will pub-licize your results, such as news media, public meetings, a newsletter, or website. (See Chapter 10 for tips.)

The sample lesson plan in Box 7.9 highlights steps in a citizen science project at the Great Smoky Mountains National Park, USA (see Fig. 7.4).

Box 7.9 A citizen science lesson plan on terrestrial invertebrates

This citizen science lesson plan engages students in the All Taxa Biodiversity Inventory, a research project in the Great Smoky Mountains National Park. The lesson uses the "5Es" (engage, explore, explain, elaborate, evaluate) to organize the instruction.

Overview

Students engage in the scientific practices of collecting and analyzing biological inven-tory data. Since 1998, scientists working in the Great Smoky Mountains National Park have been involved in an effort to identify all forms of life within the park. More than 900 species have been found that are new to science, and 80% of these are inver-tebrates. The Terrestrial Invertebrate Study is a citizen science project that allows stu-dents to get involved—in the park, their school ground, or another site.

Learning objectives

Students will be able to:

1. Identify and categorize a variety of terrestrial invertebrates to the taxonomic level of order or class.

2. Describe the role of invertebrates in food webs and their interdependence with plants, birds, and other taxonomic groups.

3. Interpret citizen science data and make comparisons to address questions related to habitat needs and environmental change

Box 7.9 *Continued*

Time required/location:
- two 45-minute class periods, indoors
- one 45-minute class periods outdoors

Materials

- Computer with internet access, computer projector, data sheets (one per group), clipboards (one per group), magnifying glasses (one per group), tweezers (one per student), jars or bug boxes (several per student).
- Terrestrial invertebrate data sheet (one per group) (available at: <http://www.handsontheland.org/monitoring/projects/inverts/insctdata.pdf>).
- Leaf litter sifter for collecting invertebrates (optional, instructions at <http://www.handsontheland.org/monitoring/projects/inverts/shaker_box_instructions.pdf>).

Conducting the activity

Engage

Play the biodiversity podcast video at <http://www.electronicfieldtrip.org/smokies/10modules.html> which defines biodiversity and describes how geographic, geological, and atmospheric features contribute to biodiversity. It also introduces invertebrate diversity in the forest litter and the value of biological monitoring.

Explore

1. Select a study plot on or near your school property. Divide students into groups and provide each group with collection equipment. You can use hula hoops as borders for students to survey organisms found in the leaf litter within each hoop. Use a leaf litter sifter to collect them or rely on a visual search for invertebrates.
2. Ask students to work together to identify invertebrates to the level of taxonomic order or class, and count the number of individuals in each group. Use the picture guide to soil invertebrates and data sheet available through the Hands on the Land terrestrial invertebrates site. Release all insects back to the study site after identification.
3. If you want to define your own study site you can enter the data into the Hands on the Land database. Data entry also includes soil temperature, air temperature, soil pH, cloud cover, precipitation, and percent canopy cover. Explore the concept of citizen scientists with students, describing the importance of citizen scientists who partner with researchers to collect and analyze data, which helps track change over time in species diversity and density.

Explain

Use the terrestrial invertebrate citizen science dataset online to address questions of your choice. You can use data submitted by others or your own data if you have submitted them. For example, you can look under "Reports, graphs, and maps" and select "Comparing order difference by date." You could compare the relative abundance of

Box 7.9 *Continued*

various taxonomic orders of invertebrates found in a single sample, or results for up to four samples at a single site. Model how to ask questions and use the data to answer them: for example, you could ask: "Did they find more gastropods or more coleopterans in their samples?" Use the graphs to pose questions and answer as a class.

Elaborate

After going through examples, ask students to work in pairs to post questions of their own and query the citizen science database to seek answers. Some options include: Are more insects found in the spring or summer? Are different species found at lower elevations than higher ones? Students can use the website to create graphs and charts that illustrate the answers to their questions. Or they can compare invertebrates associated with environmental variables like temperature and pH.

Evaluate

Pose a question of your own for students to answer using the database. Ask students to explain the importance of diverse forms of life living in soil and to describe the interdependence of animals in the leaf litter.

Ask each student to select a terrestrial invertebrate and research its life history, adaptations, importance in the food web, and other features. As a class, use this information to discuss the role of invertebrates in food webs and ecosystem functions.

Adapted from: Sachs, S. (2013) Terrestrial Invertebrates. In Trautmann, N.M., Fee, J., Tomasek, T.M., and Bergey, N.R. (eds), *Citizen Science: 15 Lessons that Bring Biology to Life 6–12*, pp. 77–83. NSTA Press, Arlington, VA.

Fig. 7.4 Citizen scientists from the local mushroom club record the distribution of species in the Great Smoky Mountains National Park, USA. (Photo by Great Smoky Mountains Institute at Tremont.)

7.4.2 Implementation

For educators, an exciting aspect of implementation is watching the collaboration and learning that occurs between participants such as students, teachers, researchers, and other community members. The steps in implementation depend on the model of public participation: to that end, this section presents illustrations of both *citizen science* and *community-based research* as examples of implementation.

Some of the earliest examples of citizen research in the USA include the Christmas Bird Count that began in 1900 and wildlife monitoring programs such as the Bird Banding Program, that started in 1920. Citizen science in conservation can serve a range of uses including monitoring wildlife populations over time, monitoring genetic diversity, conducting inventories of biodiversity, gathering natural history data, and measuring water and air quality (Prysby 2001). In the UK, iSpot provides an example of a long-term project that involves 70 natural history societies whose members submit photos of species and identify them on the website. In the first 2 years, iSpot volunteers documented 66,000 observations of 500 species, including two species that had never been recorded before (Silvertown et al. 2013). A subsample of almost 3000 species included 10% with a conservation listing and 102 rare/scarce species on a country level. Once the observations were validated, these data become part of the biodiversity records in the UK. In South Africa, iSpot has been adopted by the South African National Biodiversity Institute, and an endemic species thought to be extinct was rediscovered (Silvertown et al. 2013).

The Protea Atlas Project aims to foster an interest in botany and South African conservation issues by collecting data about 370 different plant species in the Proteaceae in South Africa (Silvertown et al. 2013). In this 10-year project, organizers recruited volunteers by giving talks and visiting 42 annual flower shows where they provided training and also harnessed local knowledge about the locations of species and their common names. During the span of the project, 478 volunteers sent in data, representing 30% of the 1455 individuals who contacted the project managers and expressed interest in participating. Of note, ten volunteers collected 52% of the data. At least 1000 people have participated in this citizen science project.

While many citizen science projects focus on data collection, community-based research tends to involve community members in all aspects of the research, with an emphasis on the application of the findings in communities. With community-based research, the researchers often play the role of facilitator, rather than director, although these roles can vary depending on the project (Hacker 2013). Historically, community-based research has often been applied in fields such as community-based forestry, development, and public health. In the Sustainable Solutions Initiative, researchers from the University of Maine, USA, worked with tribal members and basketmakers to address an invasive beetle species, the emerald ash borer (*Agrilus planipennis*), which threatened ash populations in states surrounding Maine (Silka, 2012). The research project attempted to respond to the arrival of the emerald ash borer, which will disrupt the livelihoods of local basketmakers.

Community-based research in the Philippines addressed the crisis of a decreasing supply of high-quality water in the watershed of the Manupali River. Community members received training in water quality monitoring and analyzed the results of thousands of water quality samples, which revealed clear connections between degradation of the water supply and clearing of land for roads and agriculture. Local governments incorporated the community findings and recommendations into their natural resource management plan. With these findings, the community members took the lead and formed a NGO whose president served on the Natural Resource Management Council of the municipality (Deutsch et al. 2005).

In Benin, West Africa, a United Nations program uses community-based research with local fishing communities to compare the effectiveness of two fishing methods. The FAO's Sustainable Fisheries Livelihood Program sponsored this study to compare the effectiveness of 2-inch mesh that leaves undersized fish behind with the current 1-inch mesh that catches juvenile fish which would otherwise mature (afrol News 2003). The method chosen for the research was to enlist one fishing group to test the new nets for 18 months while a technician lived in the community to measure the size and value of the catch. With additional room in the seine for larger fish, the nets catch higher-value fish.

Preliminary results in the Aido Beach community showed that the group using the new nets caught 24 tons of fish in nine outings (US$140), while the control group using the small mesh pulled in 30 tons in nine outings but only earned US$75. Representatives of the experimental group said the difference convinced them firsthand of the value of the new nets (afrol News 2003).

Implementation of public participation in scientific research does not require a global online system and extensive funding. Some of the most successful projects have involved one group of students or adults helping scientists monitor the quality of soils or water in a creek in their watershed. Local non-profit organizations like Riverkeepers can help provide the necessary training for research, such as water quality monitoring. If you have funding from an external source, ensure you meet all the reporting requirements. Follow your plans for data analysis and validation, publication, and reporting to partners. Ensure that decision-makers have access to your data analysis and recommendations for action. Your results can create positive change for science, social–ecological systems, and individuals.

7.4.3 Evaluation

Your evaluation can range from a simple survey with participants to a pre- and post-visit evaluation with follow-up surveys a year and more after the program. Your evaluation should also assess the process of data collection to ensure data quality at all stages from collection to analysis. Your evaluation tools should address your educational objectives for your participants. Issues that you could consider in your evaluation include:

- How well were the educational and research objectives met?
- Which target groups participated in the research?
- How satisfied were community members and the researchers with the process?
- What aspects of the project would they change? What would they keep?
- How useful were the collected data? How well were the results disseminated?

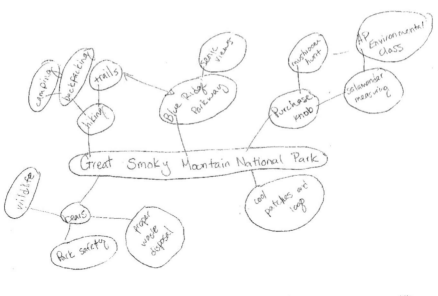

Now, you get to create your own concept map on the main topic of *Great Smoky Mountains National Park.*

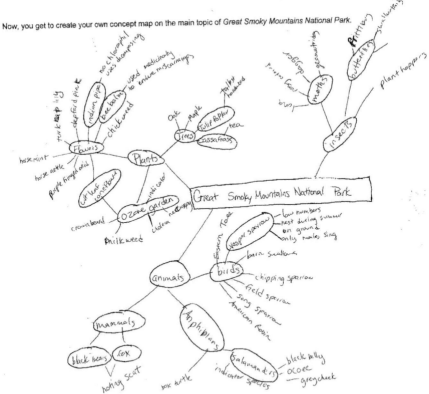

Fig. 7.5 Compare the pre- (top) and post-program (bottom) concept maps, used as a tool to assess the impacts of internships at a citizen science center in the Great Smoky Mountains National Park. (Photo by the US National Park Service.)

- Did the data influence conservation decision-making?
- How cost-effective was the project? Is it sustainable?
- How adequate was the timing, funding, and other resources?
- How effective was the training of participants?

The Appalachian Highlands Science Learning Center in the Great Smoky Mountains National Park uses multiple evaluation tools, such as pre- and post-program tests, questionnaires, journals, interviews, photos, and concept mapping. Concept maps are visual representations of a learner's knowledge on a given topic. Teachers often use concept maps to understand the connections students are making among concepts, as well as any misconceptions. Environmental educators asked high school interns to draw concept maps for the topic "Great Smoky Mountains National Park," before and after their internship at this center for citizen science. Analysis of the pre- and post-internship maps showed a change from general knowledge of the park and its resources to an in-depth understanding of connections between multiple resource groups (Fig. 7.5).

Another tool for evaluating public participation in scientific research is a logic model (see Chapter 1), which allows project organizers to identify the following (Shirk et al. 2012):

1. *Inputs* to the project, which includes the balance of interests between public and scientific interests.
2. *Activities*, such as sampling strategies, trainings, communication, recruitment.
3. *Outputs*, including recorded data and the experience of recording and analyzing observations.
4. *Outcomes*, for science, for social–ecological systems, and for individuals.
5. *Impacts*, which are generally long-term and more challenging to measure, but can include stewardship, knowledgeable publics, and responsive science.

7.5 Mapping

People have used maps throughout history to record the past and chart decisions for the future. Mapping is a structured activity that allows individuals or groups to create visual representations of their resources, communities, region, country, and world (Feuerstein 1986). Mapping can reveal differences in perceptions and uses of resources among different groups of people in a community, as well as changes over time in land use, resources, and social structures. Imagine asking a group of senior citizens to draw maps documenting open spaces or clean water sources in the community during their youth and sharing those results with students or members of a city planning commission. With the help of a smartphone, mapping by volunteers can also provide invaluable humanitarian information during catastrophic environmental disasters such as flooding and earthquakes (Soden and Palen 2014).

When working with multiple stakeholder groups, mapping can become a springboard for discussing resource use, understanding environmental issues in a community, and building support for conservation initiatives. Mapping can be important for developing mutual understanding among groups, such as local land users, administrators, politicians, and elders—residents who share resources but may not share perceptions or priorities.

In a mapping activity, members of the community usually create the maps but can use existing maps of scientific data to generate discussion about conservation issues and actions in the past and future. Because mapping is a visual activity, this tool can be used with participants who do not read or write, due to age or language barriers. Paper and pens are not even required for mapping, as community members can create maps on the ground using sticks for drawing and rocks, leaves, and grasses as symbols.

7.5.1 Planning

Mapping can achieve many different objectives, from identifying priorities for land use and wildlife conservation with adults to developing a sense of place with children. The first task is to identify the objectives of your mapping session and its participants. If you are using mapping to compare perspectives, group participants to reflect the comparisons, such as dividing into groups of men and women or older people and youngsters.

Mapping generally falls into two categories: (1) mapping of knowledge and perceptions and (2) scientific maps. When you use mapping to document perceptions about natural resources, the map produced is not right or wrong; rather, the facilitator uses the map to understand different perceptions. Scientific maps, on the other hand, document the identified location of natural resource features in a community and are often used to inform decision-making.

The objectives of a mapping session can include the following (Pretty et al. 1995; Slocum et al. 1995; Sobel 1998; Soden and Palen 2014):

- Demonstrating that different people have different mental maps of where they live.
- Showing that different groups of people, such as men and women, or young and old, use and value different resources in a community.
- Developing a sense of place among children and adults.
- Reflecting changes, such as land use, social structure, wildlife diversity, and resources over time.
- Identifying on-the-ground locations to aid in disaster relief in both remote and urban areas.
- Increasing knowledge and access to scientific data about conservation issues, such as maps of hydrology, wildlife, development pressures, air quality, and deforestation, or measuring changes in knowledge before and after a conservation education program.
- Using environmental and social data to influence environmental and land-use planning.

Content of a mapping session

The content of the maps will stem from the objectives of the mapping session. Maps can help show (Feuerstein 1986):

- Social structure, such as the location of neighborhoods, ethnic groupings, social centers, governance, and communication and transportation networks, including roads, bridges, trains, and paths.

- Geographical features, for example rivers, oceans, mountains, forests, deserts, and natural resources like wildlife, trees, plants, and pastures.
- Physical features, including the size of the town, location of houses, schools, factories, and farms.
- Health and medical features, such as hospitals, water sources, sanitation facilities.
- Changes over time, which can be shown with overlays to compare changes with the original map.

The complexity of maps can range from maps drawn in the dirt to maps created using geographic information systems (GIS) and online platforms like OpenStreetMap. With GIS you can create digital maps showing different features and overlay these "layers" to create a rich picture of an area. The Wombat State Forest in Victoria became Australia's first community managed forest, resulting in the development of issue-based working groups to tackle management issues such as invasive exotic species. Prior to the establishment of working groups, the region's Blackwood community had struggled for 10 years to obtain assistance to control invasive weeds. The newly established Weed and Pest Animal Working Group (WPAWG) helped the community obtain university assistance in developing maps showing the distribution of weed species. Community members walked the bush to map the location and densities of weed species. The resulting GIS maps were used as evidence in the Blackwood Weed Management Strategy, a funding proposal to the government (Baral et al. 2004). For indigenous groups in Venezuela, community maps created using global positioning systems (GPS) have been used as documentation for claims to legal title of land. Two local communities received training from researchers in reading and recording GPS data. Over a period of 3 years, community members then recorded geographic coordinates of significance to them, place names, and descriptions of cultural significance (Zent 2010).

After an earthquake struck Haiti in 2010, volunteers mounted a community-mapping response using OpenStreetMap, a free world map built by users that emphasizes local knowledge using a crowd-sourcing platform, much like a wikimap of the world (Soden and Palen 2014). By providing geospatial data from remote areas, volunteers supported aid efforts and launched an organization called the Humanitarian OpenStreetMap Team. With climatic change, such on-the-ground mapping may prove invaluable in responding to environmental disasters. Contributors to OpenStreetMap use GPS devices in smartphones, field maps, and aerial imagery to verify the accuracy of information.

7.5.2 Implementation

This subsection presents four examples of implementation, including mapping the neighborhood, mapping the town, mapping to compare stakeholder perceptions, and mapping with young people.

Mapping the neighborhood

One strategy for beginning a mapping session is to give participants the opportunity to create their own maps of the neighborhood using paper and pen. Ask participants to think about where they live and to draw major landmarks and natural resources of importance to them. After 10 minutes post the maps on the wall and allow everyone to observe differences in the maps. Ask follow-up questions such as: "What natural resources did you draw? What symbols did you use to represent features on the map? Who has lived here for more than 10 years? How does that knowledge of the natural resources compare with someone who just moved here? What changes in natural resources have occurred over time in this neighborhood? What conservation measures, if any, are needed to protect the resources portrayed in the maps?" (Pretty et al. 1995).

Mapping the town

Another strategy for implementation is to divide your participants by the relevant demographic variable in the group. For example, you could divide the group into men and women, farmers and city dwellers, community members who grew up in the town and those who recently moved to the area. Give each group a large sheet of paper and pens, and ensure that each person has access to a pen if you are using paper. You can photograph the drawing for documentation.

Ask the participants to create a map of the important natural resources in the town or city and give them about 45 minutes for their drawing. Emphasize that each group member should be involved in the drawing. Ask each group to present their map and explain the process of creating the drawing. Reflect on the maps using questions such as: "What did your group agree upon? What natural resources did you include? What did you exclude? What did you emphasize? What did you not emphasize?" Ask the community members to analyze what the maps reveal about the natural resources and conservation issues of the area (Pretty et al. 1995).

Comparing perceptions using maps

Maps can reveal perceptions about natural resource management between different stakeholder groups in a community; this can be an asset for generating conservation solutions that affect diverse groups. In Abaco National Park in the Bahamas, mapping was used with six different stakeholder groups to gather input and assess current and desired uses of the park for recreational management planning (Marks et al. 2004). Facilitators of the mapping session distributed topographical maps to all participants, who used colored pencils to identify areas for different activities in the park. After the individual mapping session, groups of stakeholders used a large topographic map to identify their preferred location for zoned activities, such as hunting and ecotourism, by gluing colored squares on the large map (Fig. 7.6). For the majority of groups, the maps revealed a combination of ecotourism and protection to be most important for the park's future.

Mapping with young people

Mapping with children can build a sense of place and a spatial perspective of the natural resources in a young person's community. Young children should begin mapping exercises by representing their home and then move to their neighborhood, corresponding

Fig. 7.6 A group mapping exercise in Abaco National Park in the Bahamas provided input for recreational management planning. (Photo by S. Jacobson.)

to their developmental level (see Chapter 2). As students get older, their maps can explore their country and even the world (Sobel 1998).

High school students in Fairhope, Alabama, USA, mapped growth and development in their community. They first drew maps of their neighborhood and then the entire town. Next, pairs of students interviewed elderly residents who grew up in the town. The students created maps with the senior citizens, drawing from their memories. Finally, the students compared historical maps of the town with the ones drawn by themselves and their elders. As a final mapping activity, the students drew an imaginary map of how they wanted to see their town in the future. This mapping exercise revealed the changes in land use—from rural to suburban—and the need for land-use planning to protect their natural resources.

You can also use mapping in combination with another technique, such as service-learning or issue investigation, described in this chapter. For example, the service-learning program ACT uses mapping exercises to begin the program that connects the study of civics with community involvement. Students first draw their community, and the maps highlight community issues that become a focus for their research and the service-learning project (Loney 2000).

7.5.3 Evaluation

Maps drawn by students or adults can show gains in knowledge as a result of time or an educational program. The urban program VINE (volunteer-led investigations of neighborhood ecology) asked young participants to draw and label what they had seen living in their schoolyard before and after the program (Fig. 7.7). The pre- and post-program drawings were scored based on change in three criteria: application of

Fig. 7.7 Mapping can show pre- and post-program gains in knowledge, as seen in these maps of schoolyard ecosystems drawn by children in the VINE program.

(From p. 57, in Hollweg, K. (1997). *Are We Making a Difference? Lessons Learned from VINE Program Evaluations*. NAAEE, (<http://www.naaee.net//>), Washington, DC.)

information presented in a VINE activity, organization and context, and complexity (Hollweg 1997). Thus, mapping can be an important evaluation tool for your conservation education initiative. (One constraint is that developmental changes may account for some of the observed changes in the post-program drawings.)

When evaluating a mapping activity itself, observe your participants and document the level of participation. Is everyone involved in the mapping and decision-making? Who is taking the lead in drawing and discussions? Who is holding back? At the end of the mapping session, ask participants to reflect on the process. What did they learn from creating a map with others? What differences did they observe from different maps?

If your participants create maps for land-use planning and management, follow the community to document how often the maps are used in decision-making. Are the maps sitting on a shelf or posted on the walls for planning purposes? City planner Elizabeth Teague in Fletcher, North Carolina, USA, posted brightly colored maps of a proposed greenway around the town hall during community visioning sessions. She invited community members to post their comments about the maps, which became focal points for a stakeholder-based planning process. "The maps were central to our planning," she said, "because the visuals gave people a reference point for describing the town they wanted to see in the future."

7.6 Summary

Effective conservation aims to integrate, rather than compete with, the needs of the human communities that share the landscape with biological communities. This chapter includes five techniques for connecting classrooms and communities with conservation. Techniques such as service-learning, issue investigation, and project-based learning were developed to connect conservation with classrooms. Although techniques such as service-learning originated in an academic setting, conservation educators can use service-learning with any group of learners, from teachers to senior citizens, if the goal is to impact learning and conservation in the community.

Public participation in scientific research and mapping are techniques developed to work with either community groups or students. The choice of which technique works best for your conservation education program depends primarily on your overall goal. If you have a field research project that would benefit from community involvement then public participation in scientific research could provide an educational technique to help your program. If you want to connect the work of your conservation organization with academic learning in local classrooms then service-learning can enhance learning while involving students in conservation work. The tips for each technique in this chapter offer important tools for building that connection with conservation. No matter what your objective, you can align it with one of these techniques to bring conservation issues to the forefront of communities and classrooms and ultimately help achieve your conservation goals.

8
Networking for conservation

If you have ever moved to a new town you may recognize the importance of networking to daily life. You learn to navigate grocery stores, markets, public transportation routes, and medical facilities. At work, you become familiar with your responsibilities and colleagues. If you have children, you meet teachers and other parents. In short, you become adept at learning about both people and places.

Effective conservation demands these same skills to build relationships in communities. People make decisions in relationship to other people. Therefore, decisions about conservation often hinge on our ability to network with other individuals and institutions—especially with unlikely partners we may perceive as the opposition.

Successful conservation can start with small-scale networking like an information booth at a conference and build to a larger partnership, such as the Sierra Club's Beyond Coal campaign in Los Angeles, California, USA. This example of networking resulted in the announcement by Los Angeles mayor Antonio Villaraigosa of strategic plans to end the city's dependence on coal by 2025. In addition to the Sierra Club, partners in this network included the Natural Resource Defense Council, the Los Angeles Business Council, the Los Angeles Alliance for a New Economy (LANE), and Strategic Concepts in Organizing and Policy Education (SCOPE), which all led efforts on energy efficiency and renewable energy. Networking for conservation allows you and your partners to become allies and find common ground between your interests, which can leverage more comprehensive changes over time.

The techniques for networking in this chapter begin with organizing environmental groups and clubs, conducting workshops and seminars, giving public presentations, developing professional posters and information booths, and hosting conferences and special events. These techniques can be used to share information, create synergy between groups, galvanize resources, and lay the foundation for partnerships (Box 8.1). To that end, the chapter includes tips for identifying potential partners, cementing strong partnerships in the community, and assessing the effectiveness of those partnerships. One take-home message from this chapter is that techniques for networking in conservation can be creative and productive, starting small to create alliances with possible long-term gains. Networking can be an adventure with positive outcomes, much like moving to a new town.

Conservation Education and Outreach Techniques. Second Edition. Susan K. Jacobson, Mallory D. McDuff & Martha C. Monroe © Susan K. Jacobson, Mallory D. McDuff & Martha C. Monroe 2015. Published 2015 by Oxford University Press.

Box 8.1 Techniques for conservation networking

Technique	Purpose
Environmental groups and clubs	Mobilize individuals into a group that shares a common interest or stake in a conservation issue
Workshops and seminars	Provide a structured forum where people come together to increase knowledge and skills, work on a common task, build consensus, and solve problems. Workshops use strategies such as discussions, small- and large-group activities, and reflection
Public presentations	Address a public audience to present the latest scientific data, influence attitudes and behaviors, respond to questions in a community, or clarify public misconceptions
Information booths	Provide information at a booth designed to raise awareness about a conservation organization or issue to people gathered at an event, such as a festival
Professional posters	Convey information in a visual format in order to share research results and network with professionals typically gathered at a conference
Conferences	Bring together like-minded people or members of an organization to share information, network, conduct business, and build skills
Special events	Provide an event, such as a festival or concert, centered on a conservation theme with goals such as raising funds, recruiting members, building awareness, and attracting publicity
Partnerships	Create an institutional arrangement between two or more organizations that provides mutual benefits and helps achieve conservation goals

8.1 Environmental groups and clubs

In 1958 in Kenya, 50 students gathered at Kagumo High School to create a national conservation organization, the Wildlife Clubs of Kenya (WCK). The students realized that tourists, rather than Kenyan citizens, had primary access to the national parks and wildlife that symbolized their country's resources to the world. These environmental clubs lobbied for and gained free entry into the national parks for their members. In the 1970s, the clubs rallied 5000 young people to protest against elephant poaching. Club members have marched in the streets of downtown Nairobi to encourage the use of baskets rather than plastic bags for shopping. The formation of WCK, the largest conservation organization for young people in Africa, prompted the growth of similar clubs that promote wildlife conservation across Africa, Latin America, Asia, and Europe (Fig. 8.1) (McDuff 2000).

Environmental clubs are a technique for mobilizing individuals with a common interest or stake in conservation. Environmental organizations can provide significant

Fig. 8.1 The Wildlife Clubs of Kenya is the largest grassroots conservation organization for young people in Africa. (Photo by M. McDuff.)

life experiences that help develop environmental interests and actions (Chawla 1999; Chawla and Cushing 2007). Conservation groups build motivation and skills to conserve natural resources by providing practical experiences in outdoor settings, developing hands-on conservation experiences, increasing knowledge of environmental issues, identifying roles in community environmental action, and developing environmental responsibility (Voorrdouw 1987).

Environmental groups are not only for young people. In the southeastern USA, congregations from different faith traditions came together to form the Creation Care Alliance, a network of faith communities working to promote environmental stewardship. Among its activities, the group has organized a Care of Creation Vigil, hosted a forum on climate change and faith, and presented a letter signed by 74 clergy to the CEO of Duke Energy Progress Co. calling for the decommissioning of a local power plant, a large source of climate-disrupting pollution in the region. Just as importantly, the group is sharing resources and knowledge between congregations that have installed solar panels or community gardens, for example, and those wanting to take similar actions (McDuff 2010, 2012).

An environmental group can be a rallying point for a conservation cause, a meeting place for people interested in environmental action, and a social group with a passion to make a difference. An active club at the Nanyang Technological University (NTU) in Singapore is Earthlink NTU, whose goal is to promote environmental awareness among students. Student activities include reforestation projects, a summer EcoCamp, and field trips such as the treetop canopy walk in Central Catchment Nature Reserve.

8.1.1 Planning

You may decide to start your own club or use existing organizations, such as the Audubon Society, Girl Guides, Boy and Girl Scouts, Rotary Clubs, and Kiwanis Clubs, to address a conservation need. Collaborating with clubs that have a large membership base saves resources and uses the existing infrastructure in your community. Many clubs have monthly speakers, so volunteer to present a program on your conservation issue or involve members in a special event for conservation. Wildlife conservation agencies such as the US Fish and Wildlife Service have worked with Boy and Girl Scouts to correlate activities in the Project WILD (2007) curriculum with the badges earned by Scouts. Environmental educators in Michigan, USA, have used 4-H youth development clubs to conduct conservation projects.

Common interests in outdoor activities often drive the creation of recreational clubs, such as garden clubs. Recreational groups like canoe and kayak clubs depend on the natural resources of rivers and estuaries, so their members can become strong partners for conservation. The Children and Nature Network (2014) co-founded by author Richard Louv, publishes a free toolkit on its website for starting nature clubs for families. These clubs connect children with nature through experiences like meeting other families in an urban park or taking walks focused on nature study. Published in English, Spanish, and Chinese, the toolkit includes planning sheets, invitations, checklists, and testimonies from families worldwide who have started similar clubs in their neighborhoods.

If you decide to start an environmental club, brainstorm objectives for your group (Box 8.2). Does the need exist for increasing awareness among members or will your club lobby for a specific environmental action, such as restoration of habitat or conservation of public lands? The Roots and Shoots Clubs, established by primatologist Dr. Jane Goodall, promote conservation in countries as diverse as Germany, Uganda, Tanzania, the UK, and China. The Shanghai Roots and Shoots Club, for example, raised money to create improved enclosures for chimps at the Shanghai Zoo.

8.1.2 Implementation

Once you decide to begin a new group, the next step is to build interest and excitement by talking with potential members and then initiating a kick-off meeting. Plan a time when you think most people in your target audience can attend. If you are working with an existing club, contact key members to ensure that people can attend your presentation or initial event, find out what type of presentation they prefer, and connect their mission to your information (Schulz 2000; Children and Nature Network 2014). Plan to serve food at the meeting as an incentive for participation. People will want to stay involved if the meetings are both fun and focused. Email the agenda in advance, and then post the agenda in the meeting room so everyone can see it.

For your initial meeting, give an introduction to the group and ask participants to introduce themselves. Plan an icebreaker such as a partner introduction to allow people to relax and get to know each other. Provide an overview of the proposed organizational structure and ideas for activities. Let the group brainstorm, and take notes on flipchart paper of their vision for the club and ideas for activities. When working with another club, you can ask members to brainstorm avenues for collaborating with conservation objectives. At the end of the meeting, discuss a schedule for future meetings. To end on a

---

Box 8.2 Six steps in planning an environmental club

---

1. Find a core group of people who want to help plan the start-up of the club.
2. Brainstorm objectives for your club or organization.
3. Conduct an informal needs assessment of your school or community:
   (a) How are other groups organized?
   (b) Do you have a solid group of potential members? Word-of-mouth and social media can help assess this need.
   (c) Are there other environmental groups with whom you could partner and learn?
   (d) Do you have potential sources or ideas for funding?
   (e) What are the major environmental issues or the needed vision in your school or community?
4. If you are working with a school, write a proposal for your environmental club to outline the purpose, activities, and needs from the administration. Identify an advisor for the club as well.
5. Work with your planning team to develop a draft organizational structure to present to the larger group of members at the first meeting. The entire group should decide the organizational structure by a decision-making process such as consensus, majority voting, etc.
6. Recruit new members. Ask yourself why someone would want to join this group? Plan and publicize your kick-off meeting as a recruiting tool.

Adapted from Schulz, C. (2000). *School Environmental Clubs in Wisconsin: 2000 and Beyond.* Wisconsin Center for Environmental Education, Stevens Point, WI.

---

fun note, consider giving door prizes, like a gift certificate from an outdoor store. Make sure to include some discussion and decision-making about organizational structure in the agenda for the next meeting.

Promote the environmental club through advertising that gives the group visibility and increases awareness and knowledge among students or community members. Create a Facebook group for members. Send press releases to the local newspaper to advertise club events and initiatives and make contacts with a reporter who tends to focus on environmental news. Unless you have outside funding, your club may need to plan fund-raising events for your activities. If you are using an existing club, advertise the environmental work of the group in the local media.

One environmental group, PARC (People Advocating Real Conservancy), was formed in direct opposition to the proposed sale of a downtown park in North Carolina, USA, to a resort hotel. The city proposed to sell part of the downtown park to the hotel owners who intended to build a 10-story condo, but there was little press coverage and no public announcement about the proposal. The city council then voted to sell the land, and the mayor ignored 1500 signatures on a petition opposing the sale on the grounds of loss of green space. Several months later, the local newspaper published a poll showing that 82% of readers thought the hotel would build the high-rise, despite public opposition.

But PARC prepared leaflets, signs, displays, email alerts, and a scale model of the proposed building. Their website showed a drawing of the building superimposed on the park. As word spread about the public opposition, a League of Women Voters forum on the sale of the park attracted a crowd of 400 people who confronted the president of the hotel. With such strong support, PARC proposed a boycott of the hotel. Shortly afterwards, the hotel called off the development due to the "financial feasibility" of the project. By targeting a specific objective for their group, PARC achieved a conservation victory despite obstacles from both the city government and a development project.

Other clubs, such as Friends of Nairobi National Park in Kenya and Friends of the Rocky Mountain National Park in the USA, have lobbied successfully for funding, and increased protection of the parks they aim to protect. The Friends of Sherwood Island State Park in Westport, Connecticut, USA, have created a butterfly garden, sponsored community cleanups, purchased equipment, and helped with ecological restoration. This group even spearheaded fundraising that resulted in the construction of a nature center through a public–private partnership with the Connecticut Department of Environmental Protection.

8.1.3 Evaluation

Many environmental clubs or groups experience a large membership at their initiation, with participation stabilizing or dwindling over time due to the departure of a charismatic leader or the end of a galvanizing issue. Monitoring and evaluation can help identify trends in membership and factors associated with these trends. There are a number of tools you can use to evaluate the effectiveness of your club, including:

- periodic verbal feedback sessions or focus groups with members,
- surveys to gather data from members and non-members,
- documentation of success stories and failures—document all projects to learn from past activities,
- accurate records of members to track trends in membership,
- interviews with members who left the club to gain insight into factors influencing the members, and
- interviews with community leaders to assess the effectiveness and support for your environmental actions.

In Kenya, the WCK records show that a total of 1800 clubs had registered since 1968, but only 25% had renewed their membership 30 years later. The national office had begun to focus on a target audience of adults and had accumulated substantial debts. In the 1990s, the office created an endowment fund and refocused on the local clubs with yearly themes such as young women and biodiversity conservation. The WCK also conducted a participatory evaluation to involve its stakeholders in evaluation of the program (McDuff 2000). The evaluation created criteria for assessing success and established membership registration as a priority for the organization. The evaluation, among many tools, allowed the organization to refocus on its values and regain traction, and it had a membership of 2200 clubs in 2014.

8.2 Workshops and seminars

Workshops and seminars are structured events at which people come together to increase knowledge and skills, resolve problems, and build consensus for action. Workshops use strategies such as large- and small-group activities, discussions, reflection, role-plays, and case studies with participants representing either a variety of stakeholders on an issue or a specific group, such as teachers or environmental planners. The organization 350.org (2014) has facilitated climate leadership workshops lasting from 1 to 5 days in more than 20 countries. The 350.org website includes all the materials required to facilitate its workshops, including an organizing toolkit for taking climate action. Typically, these workshops are facilitated by at least one 350.org staff member.

Workshops can bring together decision-makers who do not typically share information or network. The Appalachian Sustainable Agriculture Project in the southern Appalachian Mountains, USA, hosted a farm-to-school workshop that brought together 50 stakeholders including school nutrition directors, teachers, farmers, cooperative extension staff, environmental educators, and health department officials. The goal of the workshop was to take steps to improve childhood nutrition and conservation of farmlands by providing local schools with foods from local farms. Participants in the workshop tasted delicious foods—herbed goat cheese and homemade bread, fresh salads, and quiche made from local eggs—during breaks between sessions.

After 1 hour of a set agenda, the participants started asking each other questions, eager for information from others. The school nutrition directors explained their requirements for accepting local produce from the farmers, and the farmers explained the foods available during each season. The workshop resulted in a proposal for funding field trips for the school nutritionists to visit the farms, as well as talking points for explaining the concept of farm-to-school to school boards and county commissioners. This introductory meeting helped facilitate the process of establishing relationships between the diverse participants.

8.2.1 Planning

Proper planning for a workshop includes three phases—building support, designing the workshop, and selecting instructional strategies.

Building support

You need to build support from two groups: (1) the people with whom you will work, such as directors of your organization or school, supervisors, and donors, and (2) the participants in your workshop. Begin by identifying the funding, personnel, or resource materials you could receive from your partners or sponsors. Consider a broad range of sources for support, including for-profit, non-profit, private, and governmental agencies. Think about issues such as the philosophy of the supporting organization, a clear understanding of the goals and objectives of your workshop, and support for incentives for participants. Consider the connection between your goals and your venue, and if possible choose a location that can provide some opportunity for outdoor reflection (Braus and Monroe 1994; 350.org 2014).

Second, you must assess your audience. Conducting a needs assessment will give you the information to design the workshop to meet the needs and interests of your participants. You can gather this information from online surveys, by interviewing participants, or from questions on the registration form. These data will also help you refine your agenda and develop your goals and objectives for the workshop. Most participants appreciate the chance to express their ideas prior to the workshop. Ensure that you gather information from a representative sample of attendees.

Seven steps in designing an experiential workshop

This seven-step process builds on the experiential learning cycle (see Chapter 2) that involves interactive experiences, reflection, generalization, and application of learning. Use this model to design a 2-hour session or a 1-week course (adapted from Braus and Monroe 1994; 350.org 2014):

1. *Set the climate.* Begin with an activity that excites participants about the workshop. The opening can also explain the relevance of the subject to participants using data from your assessment. During this time make introductions, conduct an icebreaker or use a demonstration to pull people into the setting. Think about the impact of room arrangement on learning and interaction. You can arrange chairs in a circle with areas for break-out groups or have four to five people at each table, angled so everyone can see the front.

2. *Review goals and objectives.* Write the workshop goals and objectives on flipchart paper or project them on a screen and state the knowledge and skills you want participants to gain by the end of the workshop. Discuss how you used information from the needs assessment to develop the agenda. Give everyone a chance to ask questions. It is often helpful to ask participants to list their expectations on a flip chart so you can explain which ones will be met during the workshop.

3. *Conduct the activity.* During a workshop session, engage participants in an activity that gives them the opportunity to "experience" a situation relevant to the topic of the workshop. Common examples include role-plays, case studies, field experiences, and small-group activities.

4. *Process the experience.* Allow participants to share their reactions to the activity. Ask questions such as "What happened in this activity? What worked well? What was challenging for you or your group? What would you change?"

5. *Generalize.* Try to identify key generalizations about the experience, so participants can see how the activity relates to their own lives. Ask questions like "What insights did you get from the experience? What was the most important lesson for you and why?"

6. *Apply.* Help participants identify and share how they plan to incorporate these insights and lessons into their lives and work. Questions such as "Now what?" and "How can I use what I learned?" can help them begin to apply the lessons learned.

7. *Reach closure.* Summarize and make connections to the goals and original expectations. Also be sure to conduct a workshop evaluation to see if you have achieved your objectives and to gather reactions from participants.

If you are scheduling a 1-day workshop, plan at least 45 minutes for lunch and include opening and closing times. Include 15-minute breaks in the morning and afternoon, which leaves three or four blocks of teaching time. If your workshop lasts for less than a day, be sure to focus your objectives on a reasonable amount of material. Avoid the mistake of including too much material for a short workshop. Consider planning your workshop 2 or 3 months before an event where participants can apply their skills, as the workshop will generate practical collaboration. For workshops lasting longer than a day you can include out-of-class assignments, fieldwork, and more opportunities to practice new skills and get feedback from peers.

Selecting the instructional strategy

A variety of teaching techniques exist to accomplish your workshop goals. Role-plays, lectures, small-group discussions, videos, field trips, case studies, hands-on activities, and many other techniques (see Chapter 5) can get your participants involved in the material (Fig. 8.2). Think about your overall workshop design, and integrate multiple approaches to keep attention and enthusiasm high.

For small-group activities, decide how you want the large group divided (e.g., randomly, by assignment, by skill), how long they will work together, the roles of people in each group, and how small groups will report to the large group. You can divide your large group into pairs, threes, or larger groups. In general, groups of about five participants result in the most interaction.

Fig. 8.2 A workshop for teachers included hands-on experience using ozone biomonitoring gardens to assess the impact of ozone on plant species. (Photo by the US National Park Service.)

Logistics

Logistics are a large part of planning a workshop, including the food, venue, audiovisual equipment, nametags, transportation, and back-up plans in case of bad weather. A checklist for conducting the perfect workshop gives a concise overview of the logistical arrangements that need to be considered (Box 8.3).

Box 8.3 Checklist for conducting the perfect workshop or seminar

Initial planning

- Discuss the workshop with administrators, colleagues, students, donors, and other partners who should be involved from the start.
- Determine sources of funding for the workshop. Will participants pay? Will you have an outside sponsor?
- Identify your audience and conduct a needs assessment.

Workshop design

- Develop workshop goals and objectives, incorporating the results of the needs assessment.
- Decide if you need a co-facilitator. Plan the agenda and workshop sessions, including objectives for each session. Include a variety of techniques and activities to hold the interest of the group and appeal to different learning styles.
- Choose the date, time, and location, and make sure these work for your target audience.
- If you are inviting special guests, make arrangements for their participation, including their roles and compensation.
- Determine the materials you will distribute during the workshops and who will gather, develop them, and make copies.

Logistics

- Reserve the room or area appropriate for the workshop. It should have enough floor and wall space, outlets, tables, comfortable chairs, good ventilation, etc. The area also should provide access to the outdoors. Organize the room in a way that best suits your needs.
- Determine what incentives, if any, you will offer participants.
- Decide how you will publicize the workshop.
- Determine how you will evaluate the workshop. What type of follow-up efforts will you ask of participants?
- Decide what kinds of food and drink you will provide. Have them delivered to a separate room at least 30 minutes before you need them.
- Order workshop supplies, such as pencils, resources, notebooks, curriculum packets, at least 2 months before workshop.

Box 8.3 *Continued*

- Determine which audiovisual equipment you will need (flipcharts, iPads, a lap-top computer and projector, extension cords) and reserve them well in advance. Make field trip arrangements. Check on costs, special clothing, and transportation. Pack a first-aid kit and have an alternative plan in case of bad weather or other complications.
- Send introductory materials to your participants—a map of the site, travel directions, parking information, phone number, agenda, and items they should bring. Decide if you want to include a pre-workshop survey to gather additional information from confirmed participants.

Last-minute reminders

- Set up early so you can talk with participants when they arrive. Display posters, charts, and other materials.
- Put signs along the route and in the building so participants can locate the site.
- See that food and drinks are ready. Set out name tags and wear one yourself.
- Make sure goals and objectives are written on flipcharts or projected on a screen before you start. Write small-group tasks on flipcharts to post for individual sessions.
- If you are using flipcharts, tear off masking tape in advance and stick the pieces along the easel for easy access.
- Write down questions you want to ask participants. You also can write reminders or notes to yourself on prepared flipcharts using a pencil—you'll be the only one who can see them.
- Before everyone arrives, make sure all equipment works. Make sure all handouts are ready to go, including the evaluations.

During the workshop

- Greet participants warmly when they arrive. Point to name tags and handouts as you mingle with the group.
- Start on time. After your welcome and icebreaker, give an overview of the entire workshop, including the agenda and goals. Highlight breaks, meals, and restroom locations. Introduce yourself and allow participants to do the same.
- Stay on schedule, give breaks as indicated, and go over the scheduled finishing time of the workshop.
- Leave time in each session for asking generalization and application questions and for closure.
- Leave enough time for evaluation at the end. Collect all evaluations before participants leave.
- Record participants' names, addresses, phone numbers, emails. Distribute the list via email before everyone leaves. If you already have this list, late registrants can add their names.

Box 8.3 *Continued*

After the workshop

- If you are working with co-facilitators, meet at the end of the day to review what worked well, what didn't, and what needs revision for the next day or the next workshop. Keep debriefing sessions brief, upbeat, and focused.
- Identify how you plan to follow up with participants. Remind them of any post-workshop assignments. You may wish to conduct a follow-up evaluation to see if they have implemented changes or practiced their new skills.
- Give yourself time to clean up room at the end after you've answered questions and seen your guests to the door. Congratulations, you're finished!!

Adapted from Braus, J.A. and Monroe, M. (1994). *EE Toolbox: Workshop Resource Manual: Designing Effective Workshops*. Kendall Hunt Publishing, Dubuque, IA.

8.2.2 Implementation

After designing the workshop and planning logistics, turn your attention to facilitation skills. An effective facilitator can put the participants at ease, help them clarify their thinking, and build their understanding. Four key facilitation skills can help implement an effective workshop (adapted from Braus and Monroe 1994):

1. *Asking questions.* The ability to ask good questions is critical to guiding any discussion. The best questions are open-ended and help participants reflect on activities. Write down questions and practice them, such as "What are some different ways this activity could be used?"
2. *Paraphrasing.* This skill is important for clarifying and highlighting a comment. With paraphrasing, you rephrase what someone else says. For example, you might say, "Did I understand that you said ..." or "I hear you saying that ..." Avoid overusing paraphrasing though, so you are not constantly repeating every comment.
3. *Summarizing.* Summarizing allows you to guide a discussion, draw similarities and differences between participants' comments, or transition to the next session. You can note, "It sounds like we all agree that having green space in our town is important, but we differ on how to get there. Is that correct? Does anyone want to add anything?"
4. *Offering encouragement.* You can use many techniques to encourage discussion. Maintain eye contact with participants. Use encouraging body language by paying attention when individuals are talking. Give people time to think by waiting 5 seconds before calling on respondents. Call people by name.

The checklist includes other helpful hints for implementing the workshop and ensuring smooth facilitation. During the workshop, make sure you stick to the schedule, especially by ending on time, and be sure to say, "I don't know" when appropriate.

Building ongoing support

A concern about short-term workshops is the long-term value for the sponsoring organization and participants. People often need more than a 1-day program to make a difference in their behaviors or practices. However, strategies exist to build support and ensure that the workshop is just one step in a sustained initiative for change. Ongoing support may include funding for new programs, resources, newsletters, email correspondence, a Facebook group, and other networking opportunities. Think about how you plan to interact with the participants after the workshop, and how they can interact with each other.

One strategy is to register participants in pairs, and design the workshop so they can continue to work together at their site or via email. Give partners an assignment to do after the workshop with publicity for their efforts in local newspapers, and offer incentives for participants who complete action plans. Organize participants to collaborate on a community action that draws on skills gained in the workshop (Braus and Monroe 1994; 350.org 2014).

To provide ongoing information and reminders, schedule a follow-up meeting, webinar, or conference call to check on their progress. Stay in touch via email. Ask participants to write a postcard to themselves documenting their commitments and mail it to them in several months. The Leopold Education Project, an environmental education program focused on the writings of Aldo Leopold, conducts 10-hour workshops for educators. The workshops include a homework component where participants must complete an assignment such as teaching or correlating a lesson to the state education standards. Such simple incentives ensure that participants do not leave their new skills and resources behind when they leave the workshop site.

8.2.3 Evaluation

Evaluation is a critical part of any conservation education workshop, providing feedback about what works and what needs improvement. One strategy is to break down the evaluation of a workshop into four categories (Kirkpatrick and Kirkpatrick 2007):

1. *Reaction*: how much did the participants like the workshop?
2. *Learning*: what principles, skills, facts, and techniques did they learn?
3. *Behavior*: what changes in participants' behavior, if any, resulted from the workshop? (Behavior changes may not be an objective of your workshop.)
4. *Results*: what were the tangible results of the workshop in terms of learning, collaboration, networking, or environmental conservation?

To assess reactions to the workshop format, ask participants: What were your favorite parts of the workshop? What were your least favorite parts? What improvements would you make to the workshop? You can also use written evaluations, an online survey, or small-group interviews to collect reactions.

A typical strategy for documenting changes in learning is a pre-test/post-test design or a comparison with a control group. Other tools include performance assessments, focus groups, or interviews. To evaluate changes in behavior, you can observe the participants or ask them to measure and report their own behavior. If the participants include teachers, get them to document how often they incorporated the conservation education lessons into their teaching in the 2 months after the workshop. Include incentives for reporting these behaviors.

Lastly, to evaluate results, conduct a survey or interviews 3–6 months after the workshop. Schedule interviews with a representative group of participants on the phone or via an online survey. Make sure you keep good records of paperwork, lesson plans, evaluations, and your own debriefing of the workshop. These records will prove invaluable as you prepare for future events!

8.3 Public presentations

Public presentations are a part of most workshops, seminars, conferences, and meetings. In the field of conservation, public presentations offer the chance to present the latest scientific data, address public misconceptions, influence attitudes and behaviors, and respond to questions affecting the lives of community members. If your audience has a stake in the issue, a public presentation can speak to the heart of their concerns. In Rocky Mountain National Park, USA, researchers funded by the US Environmental Protection Agency spent 2 years assessing the effects of climate change on factors such as the local economy, hydrology, and wildlife. Public presentations of the findings to local stakeholders gave community members insights into the impact climate change might have on their home towns.

When audience members are divided on a conservation issue, public presentations can become lightning rods for opposing political stands. In cities across the world, opponents and supporters of proposed developments often collide at public presentations. During these forums, speakers may present the costs and benefits of extractive industries or new construction in terms of destruction of habitat for wildlife, growth of the local economy, and the demise or revitalization of small businesses. The stakes are often high in terms of conservation of land and small businesses, and public presentations touch the core of community concerns.

8.3.1 Planning

Singer Patti Scialfa, a member of Bruce Springsteen's E Street Band, overcame her fear of performing in front of thousands by focusing on singing to one person in a crowded auditorium or stadium. Public speaking can evoke similar fears, but time-tested strategies exist for delivering effective public presentations.

Think about what makes you pay close attention to a friend or family member talking at a loud, crowded party. Typically, a good story with a personal connection can help you focus on the details of the tale, rather than the background noise. With public presentations, good stories also hook the audience by weaving the key points of the talk into meaningful anecdotes, supported by substantive data. Remember that effective presentation styles are individualistic and natural. An audience can tell if you are affecting mannerisms that do not fit your speaking style.

When you begin practicing your talk, construct notes that will cue you, rather than deliver your lines word for word. You can write out your talk, but then construct notes in outline form. Nothing bores an audience more than listening to a speaker read a prepared text without engaging with the audience. Practice your talk aloud and in front of a small group of colleagues. Videotape yourself or record your voice on your computer or phone so you can review it later.

Publicity is another key to planning a public presentation to ensure you have an audience. For some talks you will be the invited speaker on a predetermined agenda, such as an Audubon Society meeting or the local zoning board. But if you are organizing your presentation to attract a variety of stakeholders, publicize the presentation through multiple channels used by your audience, including flyers, email lists, a Facebook event, newspapers, and word-of-mouth.

Organization

Presentations generally use the structure of an introduction, main body, and conclusion. The three-step mantra repeated in many high school debate teams still holds true: tell them what you are going to tell them; tell them; then tell them what you told them. The introduction should draw the audience into the talk through a "hook" that can include revealing anecdotes or surprising facts. Highlight the key points of your talk during the introduction, and present a concise thesis statement.

The body includes the key points that support your thesis statement. Limit the body of your talk to the most significant points related to your primary topic, and support your points with evidence, such as personal experience, research, expert testimony, and historical data (Meany and Shuster 2002). Make sure you rehearse the transitions between the main points. The National Park Service in the USA trains its interpretive staff to develop audience connections to both tangible and intangible resources to make the presentation relevant to the audience. Tangible resources are those that can be seen, such as props, photographs, or charts. Intangible resources are universal and apply to diverse cultures, such as values like love, safety, and family. Lastly, the conclusion should summarize the main points, and create a memorable message to leave with the audience. After concluding the talk, plan to take questions from the audience as well.

Audiovisual aids

Presentation aids—from a flip chart to a YouTube video—can enhance a presentation, but bear in mind the following tips:

- Visit and set up the room or outdoor space prior to your talk. Consider all equipment you need, such as a laptop, iPad, flipchart stand, and computer projector. Practice with the equipment you plan to use. Check for electric outlets, or bring an extension cord.
- Set up chairs so all audience members can see the audiovisual aids. Consider arrangements for the hearing and visually impaired, if relevant.
- Consider the languages spoken by your participants, and whether or not you need an interpreter or digital equipment for interpretation from English to Spanish or vice versa.

- Evaluate the lighting in the room. If using computer-projected images don't plunge your audience into darkness at the beginning of your talk. Address the audience before dimming the lights.
- The use of Power Point, Prezi, and Keynote have become ubiquitous in presentations. There are many advantages and conveniences of these tools, but you should heed some guidelines so slides enhance, rather than overpower your talk (Jacobson 2009; Young Entrepreneur Council 2013).
- Plan for one graphic slide every 15 seconds, but vary the time from a few seconds to a minute.
- Limit the amount of information on a slide, so the text does not overwhelm the audience. Aim for key phrases rather than complete sentences. Some presenters only use images, such as photographs, to illustrate talking points, without including any text on the slide.
- When preparing your stories to accompany the images, think about writing a Tweet of 140 characters for each slide. This format will enforce brevity and a focus on your main point. (And you could even send the Tweets to your audience after the talk.)
- Prepare text and graphic images that contrast with the background. Dark text on a light background is easy to see, such as black on ivory. Light text on dark background is also easy to read. Use conservative colors such as blue and green. Avoid using reds for people who are color-blind.
- Select clear and simple fonts. Limit the variety of fonts.
- Eliminate distracting and unnecessary words, graphics, or transitions between screens.
- Have a back-up plan, such as outline notes or text handouts, in case the technology fails you.

8.3.2 Implementation

Practice, practice, and more practice before your actual presentation will boost your confidence during your talk. This practice also will help you eliminate any distracting mannerisms, such as saying "uhm" or "you know," and using vague and imprecise words such as "these things." During your talk, use expressive body language, dress appropriately, and maintain eye contact with your audience. Most people have heard a presentation where the speaker faced the flipchart or screen rather than the audience. Avoid this trap by using notecards or an outline of speaking points. You may want to choose one or two members of the audience in different places in the room to focus on during the presentation. Use your normal conversation or speaking style, articulate clearly so the audience can understand you, and vary the pitch of your voice. And remember that audience members will recall the stories you told more than the facts, so focus on your key story!

At the beginning of your talk, do not worry if you are nervous. You can use that nervous energy to appear excited and focused for your presentation. Another strategy for reducing nervousness is to anticipate "presentation disasters." Try visualizing how you will react to "worst-case" scenarios such as losing your train of thought or arriving at the talk to find ten times more people than you expected (Box 8.4).

Box 8.4 How to anticipate and handle presentation disasters

How do you deal with a disaster during your presentation? Most disasters are not life-and-death situations, and you can handle them by following a few helpful hints. Above all, try to keep smiling and remain calm. So what should you do if . . .

- *You have 15 minutes instead of the 40 minutes you had prepared.* Think about your talk in three parts—the introduction, main body, and conclusion. Decide quickly what percentage of your time each part should take. Consider one or two key stories to illustrate your main point.
- *Someone asks a question about an issue you plan to discuss later.* Answer briefly and say you will go into detail later.
- *Audience members are focused on their tablets or smartphones, rather than your talk.* You can ignore the people who are on email or Facebook and trust that they will listen if and when they want. Or you can ask them to put down their electronic devices, as you need their full engagement. Explain that you will provide a link to all materials discussed in the talk. Sometimes a quick experiential activity can engage the audience as well.
- *You expect to talk to 15 people but 120 people are in the audience.* If you were planning on working from a set of handouts or curriculum materials, ask for a flipchart and make a sketch of key points for everyone to see.
- *You plan to discuss a handout, but people are reading ahead at their own pace.* If you give people handouts at the beginning of the talk, they usually read at their own pace. If possible, give handouts at the end of the presentation or provide a link to your resources and avoid handouts.
- *Several people start a side conversation while you are speaking.* Try these strategies in this order. Ask if there are any questions. Ask if you can do anything to clarify. If they will not stop talking, continue your presentation but move nearer to them. Lower your voice or pause. If absolutely necessary, ask them to continue their conversation elsewhere or ask the group if they want to schedule a new meeting time

Adapted from Meany, J., and Schuster, K. (2002). Presentational aids: A brief guide to effective practice. Retrieved April 20, 2015, from <https://www.uvm.edu/~asnider/IDAS_2011_CD/Teachers/Materials%20for%20Public%20Speaking/presentation%20aids_20040721105126.pdf>

Remember that you are probably the expert on the subject, so try to enjoy conveying your message to the audience. Presentations to a larger group should last 30–45 minutes with time for questions and discussion at the end. Always repeat any questions asked since other members of the audience may not have been able to hear.

If possible, avoid staying in one fixed position during the presentation, such as behind a keyboard or podium. Rather, you can step away from the podium at key points. Use your slides as back-up information or to illustrate your own speech, rather than talking

---

Box 8.5 A sample feedback form to document reactions from audience members on public presentations

---

Presentation evaluation

Name _____

Please rate the following:

1. Organization of presentation:	Poor	Fair	Good	Excellent
2. Logical sequence of presentation:	Poor	Fair	Good	Excellent
3. Knowledge of presenter:	Poor	Fair	Good	Excellent
4. Ability to answer questions:	Poor	Fair	Good	Excellent
5. Visual aids:	Poor	Fair	Good	Excellent
6. Professionalism:	Poor	Fair	Good	Excellent
7. Overall presentation:	Poor	Fair	Good	Excellent

8. What were the strengths of this presentation? Please explain.
9. What were the weaknesses? Please explain.
10. What suggestions do you have for improvement?

---

while your audience reads text from your slides. Remember that you can use blank slides during transitions as well.

8.3.3 Evaluation

One concrete strategy for evaluating your presentation is to videotape the talk and watch it to critique your own presentation style. Many speakers also prepare an evaluation form for their audience to solicit performance feedback immediately after the talk. Have a stack of business cards available or your contact information so people can get in touch with you after the event. Your presentation is an opportunity to open dialogue about the topic, and comments after the talk can shed light on your performance. Give colleagues a feedback sheet, and ask them to meet you after the presentation to share their opinions (Box 8.5).

8.4 Information booths

Information booths raise awareness about your conservation organization or issue with people gathered at an event, such as a festival, concert, exhibition, or conference. Information booths may be set up at a central location frequented by a specific target audience, such as a grocery store or university commons. Many environmental organizations use information booths, from the World Wide Fund for Nature with more than 5 million supporters worldwide to Earthaven Ecovillage, an intentional community of 65 people.

Information booths used for events typically include a portable exhibit such as a display board that sits on a table, leaving room for publications, sign-up sheets, and

Fig. 8.3 An information booth for the Strive Not to Drive campaign seeks commitments from the public to use alternative transportation. (Photo by Land of Sky Regional Council.)

demonstrations. An advantage of the information booth is that staff or volunteers can engage people, answer questions, and direct individuals to specific resources.

The Land of Sky Regional Council has an information booth to promote its annual Strive Not to Drive week (Fig. 8.3). The organization places the booth at local fairs and festivals. Volunteers also target an organic grocery store where many shoppers make the commitment to reduce their driving by car-sharing, biking, or taking public transport during that week. During a 2-hour time slot, for example, volunteers registered 70 people for the campaign to reduce their driving. The display includes publications about air pollution, global warming, local bus schedules, and an interactive website where people can type in the model of their car and find out its emissions. Volunteers also enter the names of people who make the commitment to reduce their driving in a drawing to win prizes such as a new bike.

Information booths can focus attention on an issue, increase awareness, and allow for different levels of sharing information with the public. If people are very interested, they may talk with you for 30 minutes about the issue, while those not as interested may just take a brochure. The challenges of using information booths, however, are that the staff or volunteer at the booth must encourage engagement from the public, who must be motivated to attend the event.

8.4.1 Planning

Planning for an information booth includes the design of your display as well as the research and preparation for interacting with visitors. People view an average exhibit for less than 60 seconds. Often, less than 1% of people read the whole text of an exhibit (Knudson et al. 2003). Therefore, the display for an information booth should be attractive, brief, and clear, and address the design principles of good exhibits (see Chapter 12).

Design

Themes

Your display should communicate a theme to the viewers. By stating the theme in the title, you increase the probability that even visitors who just glance at your information booth will take away your central message. The theme is the key point of any display (Ham 2013). Visitors to an information booth should be able to capture the essence of your organization with just one sentence, such as "Riverlink protects the French Broad River." Avoid displays that include only topics, such as "Riverlink," the name of the watershed protection organization.

Remember that topics are only the subject matter, while themes are the key message. Moreover, people remember and understand themes better than topics (Ham 2013). Think about that one sentence you would like visitors to remember from the booth, for example "Our community depends on us to conserve natural resources" or "Healthy human communities depend on healthy natural communities." Design the display to support this theme and four to five supporting points. Solicit feedback from others on the theme, messages, and design of your display. Chapter 12 includes more details on developing themes.

Attracting visitors

The design is important in attracting people to your information booth. Displays can include opportunities to get feedback from visitors, such as models, visual representations of community issues, maps for people to mark their favorite green spaces, and demonstrations of proposed community projects.

Designing opportunities for people to interact with the resources of concern to your organization can attract both young and old to your booth. The non-profit Riverlink, for example, sponsored an information booth at a music and art festival, which became one of the most popular sites at the entire festival. Riverlink secured permission from city officials to use a large downtown fountain for "whitewater" raft rides for children. In partnership with rafting outfitters, Riverlink used trained rafting guides who steered the boats right into the spray of fountains, to the delight of children during the hot month of July. While parents waited for their kids, they often picked up pamphlets and other information about Riverlink and conservation of the region's creeks and rivers.

Additional strategies for attracting people to your booth include: giveaways, such as tree seedlings, local food, or coloring books; raffle items or contests; movement from videos, mobiles, running water, or any demonstration; sound, from music to a recorded animal howl; giant objects that draw attention due to their scale; participation by pushing buttons, turning knobs, or anything that involves people in the display (Fazio and Gilbert 2000).

Remember that any technique you use to attract attention must have a direct connection to your theme. Otherwise the strategies will come across as gaudy gimmicks, rather than fun complements to your booth.

Your information booth should include publications, pamphlets, magazines, and other resources for people. Include a sign-up list for people who want more information or have questions.

Preparation of staff and volunteers

The personnel at an information booth are as important as the exhibit. If you are choosing staff or volunteers to work at the booth select these people carefully, with the goal of creating positive interactions between your personnel and the audience. Many organizations make the mistake of sending untrained volunteers or staff who don't have much investment in the organization. Avoid this mistake by training volunteers and providing them with adequate resources to answer the questions you receive most frequently. The last thing you want is to have a volunteer sitting with a smartphone behind the booth while avoiding questions during the entire event! Also, ensure that volunteers wear a uniform or T-shirt representing your organization, and avoid sunglasses or a hat that obscures their eyes.

Training for volunteers before they work at an information booth should present an overview of the organization, its successes, and its challenges, and familiarize volunteers with the publications. Provide a take-home tool, such as a handout of frequently asked questions with responses and tips for volunteers working information booths. You can use and adapt the helpful hints from the following list to any conservation group (Block 2003):

1. If you are a volunteer, learn about the organization or conservation issue by exploring the website and reading all brochures and handouts. If you have questions, call the staff or volunteer coordinator.
2. Think ahead about a few good opening questions to start conversations with people who stop to look at the display board or publications. For example:
   • Do you have concerns about water quality (or your conservation issue) where you live?
   • Have you heard about our organization?
   • Do you have questions about the organization?
   • Can you find where you live on this map? Here is a marker—make a dot.
3. Practice a short answer to the questions: "So what does your organization do?" For example: "We are a state wide non-profit that works with communities on environmental issues that affect human health. We especially support low-income communities and communities of people of color that may not have the resources they need" (Block 2003).
4. Learn about the festival. What is the theme of the festival? What are the goals?
5. Anticipate your audience. Whom do you expect to attend? What ages? What languages will people speak? What types of questions might they ask? For water quality issues, a rural audience may ask about septic tanks and agricultural run-off. An urban audience might ask about construction site runoff and industrial facilities.
6. If you are picking up supplies for the festival, make arrangements with the staff at least one week before the event:
   • standard supplies: box of brochures, organization banner, display board, maps, tablecloth, pens, nametags, mailing list sheets, duct tape
   • possible additional supplies: table, tent, chairs

7. Get directions, passes, and any special instructions from staff. Exchange your contact information with staff in case of weather changes or last-minute emergencies.

8. Allow extra time when going to an unfamiliar location. Plan to arrive on time or early. It is often helpful to arrive early so you can quickly check out the content of other booths and the demographics of attendees.

8.4.2 Implementation

You arrive at the site of the festival, hear the sound of bands warming up, and watch as organizers direct exhibitors to their assigned places. Now the fun begins, as you interact with people about your passion. For most events, individuals will sign up for 2- or 3-hour time blocks. If you are the staff member in charge or the volunteer doing the setup, plan to give yourself 30 minutes extra time to find the location of your booth and arrange the display and publications. When you transition with volunteers for the next shift, make sure you discuss any issues that have emerged, such as publications that are in short supply, interesting questions asked, or humorous stories to relate! The following additional guidelines will help implement a successful information booth (Block 2003):

- Before you head off to the festival, be sure you have any necessary parking passes, entrance passes, food tickets, directions, drinking water, site map, and the contact name for the event.
- Make the information booth as attractive and organized as possible. Restock depleted handouts. Put boxes under the table and out of sight. If there is a limited supply of one report, only place one out at a time. Pick up any coffee cups or trash from the table, and hide any valuables such as purses.
- Wear a nametag. Preferably, you will have printed/typed nametags, which you can reuse at the next event. If not, ensure the nametag is legible.
- Stand (or sit if necessary) to the side of the table toward the front and look alert and welcoming. Do not stand directly in front of the display or place chairs in front. Try not to pounce on visitors, but be ready to engage them with an opening question. Keep a clicker in your hand to record the number of people you talk to.
- Let visitors take what they want from the table rather than hand everyone a brochure. If they have a specific question, you can recommend a related handout.
- Ask if people want to be on a contact list. If so, get them write down their name, address, email, and phone number. Ensure that their email address is legible. Ask if they want to become a volunteer. Know that you won't be able to answer all questions and that's okay! You can respond by saying, "I don't know the answer, but I can take your name and number and have one of our full-time staff give you a call, or you could call the office directly".

8.4.3 Evaluation

If you are working the information booth, pack up all supplies at the end of the event and thank the organizers. To gauge the success of the information booth, many organizations use a volunteer evaluation form that allows volunteers and staff to document their concerns, impressions, and questions about the event. What questions did people ask? Were there any misunderstandings or common perceptions, and what were they? How many people wanted more information about the organization? Did the volunteers feel they had adequate training for the event?

To evaluate your display, ask visitors or colleagues to give feedback on the design, even before you attend an event. Ask them if they can tell you the main message of the information booth. At the event, choose a representative sample of interested visitors and ask them for their opinions on your booth. What do they like best? What do they like least? What are suggestions for improvement?

In their annual reports, many organizations report the number of people reached during festivals and events through information booths. You can also include feedback from people who visited the information booth. Be sure that you make changes to your display based on common recommendations for improvement.

8.5 Professional posters

The advancement of knowledge depends on effective communication of research findings to the scientific community as well as the wider public. Poster sessions are an important form of communication at many professional meetings as they allow you to highlight your main message—your research findings. Viewers can study your poster at their own pace and discuss the results with you in an informal and interactive setting. The Society for Conservation Biology's 26th International Congress for Conservation Biology in Baltimore, Maryland, USA, included displays for more than 200 posters.

Planning a poster follows the usual guidelines of determining your goal, audience, message, and evaluation process. The goal of a poster is to convey scientific information in a visual format to an audience comprising viewers such as other scientists, extension professionals, and students. Similar to a good oral presentation, an effective poster can help you make professional contacts, establish your reputation in the field, exchange information about research findings with similar researchers, and promote your department or agency. With some planning and preparation you can create an effective poster presentation and make a great impression (Jacobson 2009).

8.5.1 Planning

How do you attract viewers to your poster? The type of meeting you are attending will allow you to determine your audience. You'll be competing with scores of other posters and often a concurrent social gathering. The same principles for designing an effective brochure apply to posters (see Chapter 10). The qualities of attractiveness, brevity, clarity, and dynamism are crucial to hook your audience. The audience will want to briskly scan the important points of your poster to see how it relates to them. An inviting title, enticing graphics, and clear layout will encourage your audience to give your poster a closer look. Study other scientific or professional posters that catch your eye before designing your own poster (Fig. 8.4).

Fig. 8.4 Posters present research or program results and stimulate social interactions at meetings. (Photo by C. Morales.)

Content

Posters usually include a title, authors and institutions, abstract, introduction, methods, results, discussion, conclusions, and literature cited. You can also design a poster to highlight an educational program with headings that include the need for it, implementation, and evaluation. A good poster is organized around an introduction, a body with at least three main points, and a conclusion, similar to an oral presentation.

The title should concisely communicate your main message. It should catch the attention of the audience and arouse their interest in your subject. The introduction should briefly indicate why the topic is important, placing it in the context of other scientific literature. It should state the hypotheses and objectives of your project or study and briefly explain your methods. A photograph of your study organism or site helps illustrate this section. If a separate methods section is called for, briefly describe your experimental equipment and techniques and your statistical analysis. A flow chart or table can often be used to illustrate the research or project design.

Use visuals to present results, including graphs, photos, and other illustrations. Briefly describe whether the study supported your hypotheses or if the experiment worked. Figures should have legends that concisely state your major findings. These may be all that many viewers read. The main conclusions and implications should sum up the hypothesis and results, and explain why they are noteworthy relative to other studies and to the real world. Literature citations can be placed at the bottom of the poster, since only dedicated colleagues will want to peruse them.

Keep in mind that most people will spend about 10 seconds gazing at your poster, so you must catch their interest with your title and graphics. Few will spend more than 3 minutes. This limits your text to a total of 200–300 words. It is important to curb the urge to tell the viewer everything about your study. Instead, you must be satisfied if you communicate your messages. Colleagues who are involved in related research will no doubt spend time chatting with you at the poster session, allowing you to describe more details of the study.

Layout

A poster is made up of three components: text, graphics, and empty space. A rule of thumb is to have equal parts of these three elements. Just as in brochure design, the empty space helps make the poster look inviting and easy to read. Visual material such as photographs, drawings, diagrams, charts, graphs, and tables will make the poster attractive and help emphasize the main points. Charts and graphs are usually easier to absorb at a glance than tables. These should be simplified to enable the reader to understand quickly the major findings.

To create more empty space, avoid extraneous text and distracting graphics. Colors, graphics, and text should work together to make the poster easy to read. The size of the text and the colors selected for text and graphics can help orient the reader, and emphasize the main points. Larger text for headings and subheadings will help organize the poster and highlight important points. Choosing a light, unifying color for the background and two or three dark, contrasting, colors for your various sized text and graphics will make your poster stand out, and attract attention to your photographs and other visual materials. Color can be used to associate related text and graphics and to separate various sections. But beware, too many colors make the design look busy and confuse the viewer.

Conference organizers will usually specify the size of the posters. A vertical format that is about 120 cm high by 100 cm wide is common, although many posters also use a horizontal layout. The poster title should have lettering large enough to be read from 4 m away to reel in prospective viewers. Poster text should be legible from a distance of 2 m. This requires font sizes of 90–110 points for the title, 48–72 points for the section headings, and 24–36 points for the text. Some scientific posters use a minimum text font size of 18 points. Remember if you can't make out what it says, no one else can. Only the least important information, such as literature citations, should be printed in smaller fonts.

The layout should follow how people usually view material. A person's first glance at your poster will be at the center. Attract them with a succinct title and effective graphics. English speakers are used to reading from left to right and from top to bottom. Therefore, orient your poster accordingly. If the allowable poster size is large, think carefully before you fill all the space. Few people will kneel to read your conclusions if they are printed below eye level.

Many of the design elements for posters are common sense. Posters often display text and graphics in three vertical columns because of the size of the text font and the number of words (about 11) that fit across each column and make it easy to read. Lower-case print is more legible than all capital letters. This means capitalize only the first letters in your title and headings to maximize ease of reading. Bulleted lists are easier to read than full sentences or numbered items.

Many conservation educators and scientists resize PowerPoint files to design professional posters. By adding color, photos, text boxes, and other design features with PowerPoint, it is easy to create and print an attractive product to transport to a meeting or conference.

8.5.2 Implementation

Once you have prepared your poster, you can shift your focus to enjoying your interactions with colleagues at the poster session. Try to arrive early to the poster session to ensure you have a place to mount your poster. Typically, at least one collaborator in the research project should stay by the poster during the session to explain the findings and discuss results with viewers. This is your opportunity to engage colleagues in your research and make additional contacts. Be prepared to explain your work in one succinct sentence. Always have available a supply of business cards, the link to a website, or an abstract of your study to give viewers if they want more information about your research. Bring thumbtacks or some other mounting equipment in case it is not provided.

8.5.3 Evaluation

Similar to other communication materials, it is imperative to pilot test your poster with members of the target audience. Feedback is critical. Before you actually print your poster, make a small mock-up and ask your colleagues to critique it. Can some verbiage be eliminated? Do they understand your main points? Are your graphics clear? Fix it before you waste time and money printing your final poster. Also ask to see a proof of your poster before printing the final version. You may find that fonts, colors, or shading change from one computer to another. Then you can attend your meeting and enjoy the benefits of successful outreach. After the poster session, assess how many colleagues interacted with you, read your poster, and discussed the results with you. Keep track of individuals who were especially interested in your research and follow up via email if they had questions. During the session, check out the other posters, especially those that attracted many visitors, and get ideas for improving your own poster design (Jacobson 2005; Society of Conservation Biology 2014).

8.6 Conferences

Have you ever returned from a conference with renewed energy for your work, a creative idea, or a valuable contact with a new colleague? Well-organized conferences can generate enthusiasm, exchange innovations in education and outreach, and create partnerships. A conference usually brings together like-minded people or members of an organization to share information, network, conduct business, build skills, and make decisions together. The scale can range from a 1-day symposium with 20 local participants to a 1-week, large-scale international conference with 5000 attendees and a professional conference manager. Conferences can bring together individuals who live and work in different regions of a country or even the world, such as the International Wildlife Management Congress in Durban, South Africa or the International Outdoor Education Research Conference in Dunedin, New Zealand.

The North American Association for Environmental Education (NAAEE) convenes an average of 900 members to its annual conference with varied locations and themes. Past locations have included Anchorage, Alaska, USA, Cancun, Mexico, and Ottawa, Canada. The conference activities each year involve keynote speakers, concurrent presentations, affiliate meetings, poster sessions, exhibits and vendors, an authors' corner, social events, a service project, and field trips highlighting local ecological and conservation education issues. One NAAEE conference in Boston, Massachusetts, USA, for example, featured a 1-day workshop on environmental justice that included a field trip to meet local students working to eradicate environmental racism in their inner city neighborhood.

The setting for a conference should match the philosophy and membership of an organization, if feasible. The Gathering, a week-long conference for hikers and supporters of the Appalachian Trail meets in Hanover, New Hampshire, USA, with participants camping on the grounds. Through presentations and informal conversations, attendees exchange information on topics such as lightweight backpacking and conservation efforts affecting the Appalachian Trail, which extends from Georgia to Maine, USA.

The location also should consider factors for inclusiveness such as access for the disabled, childcare, interpretation for multiple languages, location near transit centers, and affordability. The Association for Experiential Education provides childcare at its international conferences and allows children and families at meals and evening entertainment. Such arrangements make conference attendance more feasible for many working parents. While the conference of the Association for Experiential Education is located at a large hotel or conference center, the marketing materials for the conference include information about affordable lodging, such as youth hostels and campgrounds. If conference attendees cannot convene in one location, videoconferencing is an option to bring people together to network and share ideas.

8.6.1 Planning

Planning a conference is an invitation to get creative, disseminate new information, help members of an organization or cause, and raise money for an organization. The standard menu of options for a conference can range from panel discussions to service projects. Many larger conferences have plenary sessions attended by most participants with concurrent presentations organized by topic. If you are planning a 1-day conference, you might decide to schedule a presentation and large-group discussion in the morning, followed by break-out groups with focused questions in the afternoon. Think about what activities would best serve your audience as you start to brainstorm with your organizing team for the conference, and don't be afraid to try something new. The Association for Experiential Education conference includes "consultations with experts," so members new to the field can sign up for 30-minutes consultations with a leader in experiential education. Scholarships may be a good way to attract students and younger professionals, and a session on Saturday may be required to recruit local teachers.

Before you begin, decide on a way to organize and document your planning with topics and tasks such as: timeline/schedule, initial proposal, contacts, committees, correspondence, budget, contracts, site, marketing, promotional materials, registration, food and reception, theme and program, and audiovisual.

Begin to talk to the people who have organized this conference or a similar conference in years past to get their tips, tricks, and suggestions. Form committees to help you shoulder the big-picture vision and the logistical details of the conference. The administrative committee will include any paid staff and will oversee the other committees. Depending on the number of volunteers and staff available, you can combine the committees listed below to cover the necessary tasks (Devney 2001). Remember to build in methods for your committees to communicate with each other and work together, through email updates, conference calls, webinars, Google docs, or periodic meetings.

- Administrative committee: coordinates all the committees, solicits donations, evaluates, and writes final report.
- Business: handles online payments, receives and deposits any checks, pays bills, solicits sponsors and exhibitors.
- Facilities: selects and reserves site, diagrams facilities (seating, table arrangements), contacts government officials, obtains permits, assigns rooms to presentations.
- Publicity: designs website and Facebook page, writes press releases, creates posters, designs advertisements, interacts with the media, and coordinates with keynote speakers.
- Reservations: tracks reservations, handles reservation desk and packets, and greets attendees.
- Kitchen and serving: plans menu, shops, cooks, or selects caterer; coordinates servers, explores opportunities for limiting and recycling waste.
- Programming: schedules programming, selects keynote speakers, presides over ceremonies, produces agenda and program.
- Setup/cleanup: assigns exhibit space, moves furniture, cleans and closes site.
- Theme and decorations: develops theme, decorates site.

Your next step is deciding the goals of the conference, researching the audience, and deciding on the content and activities. What type of conference appeals to your audience? What are their needs in terms of accessibility, programming, location, and cost?

An important piece of conference planning is outlining the budget and identifying potential sponsors. First outline an estimate of your budget to get an idea of the scale of conference you can afford. Use the budget worksheet in Box 8.6 to assess your income and expenses with categories typical for most conferences. As you calculate the budget and the estimated number of participants, try to include reduced registration costs or scholarships for students or members with financial needs in exchange for volunteer hours at the conference site.

Attendees at the annual Association for Experiential Education conference can choose to work with the service crew on tasks such as registering participants and

Box 8.6 Budget worksheet for a conference

Expenses

Site: $_____
Room and hall fees, site staff, equipment, tables and chairs
Refreshments: $_____
Food, alcohol (if included), staff, catering fee
Decorations: $_____
Flowers/plants, banners, candles, lighting
Prizes, awards, ribbons: $_____
Programming: $_____
Performers, speakers travel, lodging
Publicity: $_____
Photocopying, website, registration packets, graphic artist/photographer
Miscellaneous: $_____
Telephone, paper supplies, photocopying, transportation, postage
Add 20% for preliminary budget $_____
Total: $_____

Income

Admissions/attendees: $_____
_____attendees @ $____ each
_____attendees @ $____ each
Exhibitors/vendors: $_____
_____ booths @ $_____ each
Advertisements/programs: $_____
_____ 1/2 pages @ $____ each; _____ 1/4 pages @ $____ each
Sale of items: $_____
Total $_____
Total profit (or loss) $_____

Adapted from the book *Organizing Special Events and Conferences: A Practical Guide for Busy Volunteers and Staff* by Darcy Campion Devney (2001). Used with permission of Pineapple Press, Inc., Sarasota, FL.

setting up equipment for speakers. Working for 8 hours reduces the registration fee by 30%, while volunteering for 24 hours results in a 70% reduction. While most participants may not choose to work for 24 hours, the option sends a strong message that the organization does not want to exclude participation on the basis of financial resources.

Your goals, philosophy, and budget will help determine the conference site. The four basic criteria for site selection include location, cost, size, and facilities (Devney 2001). Calculate your site budget and programming needs and create a list of possible sites, which you can narrow to a smaller list of five to ten. Call these sites to screen for your needs, and then visit at least three sites in person. If your organization is planning a large conference for 1000 people, for example, the local chamber of commerce and visitor bureau may place a bid to host your event. From your shortlist, you can negotiate facilities, personnel, and cost with the site your committee likes best. Remember that some large organizations require proposals for sites several years in advance to lock in the dates. Once you select a site and sign a contract, you can work with the site manager to diagram the seating and tables for each event. More experienced conference planners know to negotiate for deals before they sign a contract. Ask for perks such as free audio-visual equipment, coffee, and complementary rooms.

The advantage of many conservation education organizations is a large pool of dedicated volunteers who can decrease costs by pitching in to help with these planning tasks. A list of conference planning tasks will help keep you organized and on track (Box 8.7).

Box 8.7 Schedule of tasks for a conference

When?	What?
5–12 months before conference	Recruit and meet with committees
	Decide purpose, goal, and theme
	Research audience needs
	Select site
	Announce conference theme, date, and location on website and via social media
	Invite exhibitors and vendors
	Post call for proposals if applicable
3–5 months before	Meet monthly with committee
	Make a preliminary budget
	Choose caterer or decide menu
	Outline schedule and program
	Diagram site (which event goes where)
	Apply for permits, licenses, insurance
	Contact entertainers and speakers
	Send publicity to newsletters
2–3 months before	Meet monthly with committee
	Send invitations
	Select entertainers and speakers
	Send publicity to external media
	Send program to printers
1–2 months before	Meet monthly with committee
	Collect reservations
	Confirm all contracts
	Collate registration packets
	Purchase prizes, decorations, etc.

Box 8.7 *Continued*

When?	What?
1 week before	Meet with committee
	Close reservation list
	Arrange tables and seating
	Print nametags
	Give final head count to caterer
	Purchase non-perishable items
	Order food items
	Borrow/rent any cooking and serving equipment
1 day before	Purchase perishable food
	Pack up equipment
	Deliver ingredients to cooks
	Pick up keys, transport items to site
	Call all committee chairs to confirm tasks
Conference day	Put up direction signs
	Meet with site staff
	Unpack equipment
	Set up registration table
	Open event officially and begin scheduled activities
	Informally interview participants
	Set tables and serve food
	End scheduled activities and clean
	Pack up supplies
	Check site for lost items
1 day after	Sign out, lock up, and celebrate!
	Take down outdoor signs
	Thank all volunteers
	Clean and return borrowed items
	Make notes on conference evaluation
2–4 weeks after	Meet with committee for evaluation session
	Summarize evaluation techniques
	Finish budget paperwork
	Calculate profit or loss
	Write final conference report

Note: this schedule also applies to planning a special event.

Adapted from the book *Organizing Special Events and Conferences: A Practical Guide for Busy Volunteers and Staff* by Darcy Campion Devney (2001). Used with permission of Pineapple Press, Inc., Sarasota, FL.

8.6.2 Implementation

The day of the conference is the culmination of months of hard work with the excitement of the actual event. Before people arrive to register, place direction signs on the main routes to the conference site. Hang your conference banner above the site or on the road leading to the conference. Unpack all equipment that you will need for the day, and touch base with the staff at the site.

Your registration committee should set up the registration tables in a configuration that allows a smooth flow for new arrivals. Standing in a long line with irritated newcomers is not the first experience you want people to have at the conference. Locate the registration tables near restrooms and coffee or snacks. For a large conference, many organizations use a registration service that handles reservations, registration, check-ins, online payments, and name tags (Devney 2001). Sometimes personnel from the convention and visitors center will be in charge of reservations for a large event. The registration site is the location of the master list of reservations and payments, information packets, nametags, notices, and announcements. Ideally, for a large conference, your registration site will include a separate information/questions desk and registration table, so attendees without complex questions can sail through registration.

Opening day will involve preparing meals and refreshments if you are providing the food. Try to include regional specialties and local foods, but remember to plan for diversity with your meals. Vegetarians visiting cattle country will be unhappy and hungry without some choices. If you are using a caterer, talk with the staff early in the day to ensure timely and sufficient preparation of appropriate food. Make sure the kitchen doesn't unwittingly support an unsustainable fishery, for example. During the conference, you will spend much of your time trouble-shooting. With organized planning, you can handle the unforeseen problems that will arise.

8.6.3 Evaluation

Attendance and profit margin are often the first measures many organizations use to assess the success or failure of a conference. Your evaluation must refer to the original conference goals—the drivers in your planning and implementation. As stated, during your planning, review your goals and identify the evaluation tools for measuring your effectiveness. Evaluate your conference using these methods (Devney 2001):

- During the conference, talk with participants to get informal impressions.
- Distribute evaluation forms or the link to a survey at individual workshops.
- Include an overall evaluation form or online survey in the registration packet. If possible, provide a small incentive for completing the forms.
- Hold a meeting with your administrative committee soon after the event. Debrief the conference in terms of attendance, registration, goals, and programming, and calculate your profits or losses.
- Make a backup copy of your documentation for future organizers.

- Write a final report of the workshop to include information such as budget, site selection criteria, program, menu and recipes, sponsor list, committee members, and evaluation summaries.

8.7 Special events

Special events can range from local to national, outdoor to indoor, or serious to silly. An event can be anything from a public meeting to promote discussion of a conservation easement, to a triathlon to raise awareness of public transit systems. A special event could involve a giant community board game of Monopoly to simulate changes in land use, a parade to celebrate a local harvest, or an educational forum about the health impacts of a coal-fired power plant.

Bat Night festivals occur every summer in more than 30 countries throughout Europe, including Bulgaria, Latvia, and Armenia, to celebrate bats and raise awareness about their plight. Festivals feature excursions, exhibits, children's workshops, and information booths about bat conservation. In Ecuador, the village of Ambato celebrates the annual blooming of fruits and flowers with the Fiestas de las Flores y de las Frutas de Ambato. In Japan, cherry blossom festivals have occurred for centuries and recent changes in flowering phenology have raised awareness of climate change. And in the USA, the organization RiverLink organizes river awareness days to connect the community with local rivers and watersheds (Fig. 8.5). You can create your own special event or integrate your conservation cause into an existing celebration, depending on your resources and needs.

Fig. 8.5 The organization Riverlink coordinates special events such as river awareness days and rafting rides in a downtown fountain, as a way to raise awareness about local rivers and watersheds. (Photo by Riverlink.)

8.7.1 Planning

The first step in planning is to decide the type of event that is appropriate for your goals, audience, and organization. A special event may have the following goals (Devney 2001):

- to raise funds for a cause or place,
- to build spirit among long-term members to solve a problem or initiate a new program,
- to distribute or exchange information,
- to recruit new members,
- to celebrate, or
- to attract publicity.

Given these goals, think about the desired interactions between participants at an event, between participants and a natural resource, or between performers/organizers and attendees. Do you want different stakeholders to share perspectives on a contentious issue? If so, you might use a community forum. Would you like to bring people together to mingle in a fun atmosphere? Then think about a game where you assign teams randomly. Do you want your target audience to learn about conservation of habitats for local species? How about a birdwatching hike? This planning can help develop the theme for a special event that is appropriate for the desired outcomes. To plan and organize your event, use the budget and timeline of tasks in Section 8.6 on conferences (Boxes 8.6 and 8.7).

As with planning conferences, you will want a strong committee structure to facilitate organization. First, convene an organizing or administrative committee to oversee planning of the entire event. Then create committees to delegate other tasks essential to the special event, such as committees for the theme, finances, facilities, publicity, food, reservations, serving, programming, and setup/cleanup (see Section 8.6 for details of committee tasks). The names and responsibilities of your committees will obviously differ depending on the nature of your special event.

Often your theme will drive the decision of the date, site, and logo, as well as your choice of sponsors. Consider connecting to existing celebrations of natural resources to streamline resources and organization. You can find published listings of national and international celebrations appropriate to your country and resource, such as *Chase's Calendar of Events: a Day-to-Day Directory to Special Days, Weeks and Months*. If possible, dovetail outreach efforts with existing community events focusing on nature:

- Istanbul, Turkey held Global PowerShift, a week-long summit for climate leaders.
- Bhutan hosts a Crane Celebration to celebrate their native species.
- Countries and cities around the world celebrate Earth Day on April 22 and World Environment Day on June 5.
- The organization 350.org organized a Global Work Party for climate change with 188 countries participating in 7000 events and sharing photos online.

If you choose an outdoor location, remember to have toilet facilities, drinking water, and a contingency plan in case of rain. Also, with many outdoor recreational events, such as a race or bike-a-thon, you will need insurance and a liability form for

> **Box 8.8** Creative ideas can connect special events to a conservation theme
>
> - Fundraisers, such as phone-a-thons, bike-a-thons, dance-a-thons, costume contests, or a local crafts fair.
> - Clean-ups, such as a beach, city, river, or road clean-up.
> - Games, including live board games, Twister, word games, or improvisational theatre.
> - Sporting events, such as triathlon, a running race, fishing rodeo, kayaking race, adventure race, ultimate Frisbee, soccer, golf, or putt-putt golf.
> - Exhibits or demonstrations, such as field days and farm tours.
> - Fairs and festivals, such as an Earth Day festival.
> - Public meetings to bring stakeholders together on a specific issue.
> - Dances and musical performances such as a concert for conservation.
> - Block parties in neighborhoods with a focus on an issue or community campaign.
> - Tours, such as the Girls on the Move Outward Bound cross-country bike tour.

participants. Consider organizing multiple events at different locations and sharing photos via social media.

The details of your planning will depend on the type of event you choose (Box 8.8). Your creativity is the only limiting factor in planning a special event that resonates with your target audience, and becomes a community tradition!

8.7.2 Implementation

Make sure you contact the heads of your committees the day before the special event to ensure that everyone knows their responsibilities on the big day. On the morning of the event, hang direction signs on the roads leading to the event and a banner over the site. Post any licenses or required permits for your site, and check in with security or site officials. Bring all your equipment for the day, such as tables, chairs, water, speakers, etc. Have copies of a site map with numbered locations for vendors, exhibits, educational displays, or performers.

As the event progresses, talk to participants about their perceptions of the event. You may even be able to tweak some details during the activities. Circulate with committee chairs to address unforeseen needs. Are the vendors satisfied with their locations? Did the videographer show up to record the public meeting? Volunteers and staff will appreciate your calm attention to detail and assurance that they have the necessary supplies and support. Make sure you have cellphone numbers of your committee coordinators or provide radios so they can keep in touch with each other during the event.

At the end of the event, work with the cleanup committee to pack up all supplies and check the site for any missing items. Take down all signage and banners. Now celebrate and sleep!

8.7.3 Evaluation

Keep meticulous records of your planning to assist future committees. Meet with your organizing committee after the event to document strategies that were successful, challenges, lessons learned, and unexpected outcomes. Write down remarks from your informal interviewing during the event and summarize your findings. Another useful tool is visitor feedback surveys, which you can distribute during the special event or share online via a link to ask for feedback on what worked well, what didn't work, and what could be improved. Use separate feedback surveys for vendors, volunteers, and visitors.

Your evaluation tools, such as observation, interviews, and surveys, should address these common evaluation questions for special events (Devney 2001):

- Did the attendees enjoy the event?
- Were participants engaged in activities at the event?
- Who was the best speaker or what was the best workshop?
- Did participants like the location?
- Did attendees enjoy the food? Was there enough food?
- Did participants feel the event was a good use of their time or money?
- Would they attend the event again?
- Was the event at a good time of year, month, week, or day?
- Would they recommend the event to other people?
- What was the most important part of the event?
- Did you meet your objectives?
- Are there any suggestions for improving the event?

8.8 Partnerships

To enhance conservation, we must build relationships with other groups to work as allies and meet mutual conservation goals. Environmental groups are often regarded as individual organizations with isolated causes, each with its own membership, messages, and lobbyists. Yet we are all working for the same end—the conservation of natural resources. Thankfully, there are success stories of impressive outcomes when environmental groups create partnerships within the conservation community and with other institutions, such as faith communities, corporate groups, and the medical community.

A partnership is an institutional arrangement between two or more organizations that provides mutual benefits, which in turn helps achieve common goals. It can range in scope from sponsoring a weekend special event to joint lobbying efforts that span decades. Challenges with partnerships often include communicating between partners, defining roles and responsibilities, navigating conflicting or poorly defined needs, and maintaining focus on shared goals. Clear communication and documentation can help address these challenges. As one example, SmartWood, the world's first independent forestry certifier, established formal partnerships with non-profit organizations to provide local expertise and certification services. As a program of the Rainforest Alliance, SmartWood works in Brazil with Instituto de Manejo e Cerificacao Florestal e Agricola, Brazil's leading certifier of sustainable forestry. In eastern Europe, SmartWood partners with NEPCon (Nature, Ecology, and People Consult), another non-profit consulting firm. These partnerships give a local perspective to a global sustainable forestry program.

8.8.1 Planning

Planning for partnerships first involves identifying the reasons for aligning your interests with another group. Why should you partner in the first place? When you partner for conservation, you can:

- share resources, strengths, strategies, and constituencies,
- discover mutual interests behind competing positions,
- build credibility within a community,
- increase media coverage,
- gain access to and influence political leaders,
- broaden your understanding of different stakeholder groups, and
- put your organization in a better position to leverage new funds.

The next step is identifying potential partners (Fig. 8.6). Consider the following groups in addition to your stakeholders, and think about how their issues of concern intersect with conservation: faith communities, such as synagogues, churches, mosques, spiritual retreats; civic and youth groups, such as Rotary International, the Girl Guides, and Boy Scouts; corporate groups, including local and even global businesses; hospitals, clinics, and others in the health community; resource extraction industries; other environmental groups; agriculture; the tourism industry; schools; municipalities; politicians; and unlikely partners, or any group that you may perceive as the "opposition."

8.8.2 Implementation

Environmental success stories often come about when conservation interests intersect with quality of life issues. One such example is the work of the Nobel Peace Prize

Fig. 8.6 Identifying your stakeholders and other potential partners is an important first step in planning partnerships. (Photo by M. McDuff.)

winner Wangari Maathai in networking at the community level in the Kenya, where she launched the Green Belt movement that integrated women's rights, conservation, and tree planting. The environment surrounds us and affects our everyday lives, from the water we drink to the air we breathe. When partnerships increase the scope and scale of an organization's reach, conservation can increase its impact on both the human and ecological communities.

Implementing a partnership can involve collaboration between non-profit organizations with similar goals, such as the network between The Nature Conservancy, Conservation International, and the World Wide Fund for Nature. Or a partnership can involve organizations with different institutional goals but overlapping interests, such as partnerships between public agencies and private groups (e.g., Aviles 2012). For example, the Poco das Antas Biological Reserve, created by the federal government in Brazil to protect the golden lion tamarin, collaborates in a partnership with the Golden Lion Tamarin Association, a non-governmental organization supported by international funds.

The same strategies for networking in business can improve your success in implementing effective environmental partnerships (Speisman 2005):

- Remember that partnerships are about being authentic, building relationships, and learning how you can help others.
- Define your own goals before you set up a meeting with another group. This exercise will help you choose groups efficiently, and define their interests.
- Develop a reputation as a powerful resource for others. Other groups and individuals will turn to you for suggestions and ideas when you are known as a resource in the community.
- Articulate your needs, the goals of your group, and how other organizations or people can help you. Develop responses to the question "How can our group help you?"
- Have a concrete understanding of the work of your group, your goals, target audience, and the necessity for and uniqueness of this work. Your staff and volunteers should have a clear understanding of your direction and mission before expecting others to sign on with you.

The opportunities for creating partnerships are only limited by your creativity in considering the interests of different groups. In this section, we examine the implementation and outcomes of partnerships with two potential partners: faith communities and the medical community, two groups that have increased their collaborations with conservation in recent years.

Faith communities

The spiritual foundations of the world's religions reflect care and concern for the Earth. Religious imagery is filled with symbols from the natural world, such as the Buddha achieving nirvana while sitting by the bodhi tree, or the Genesis story of the Garden of Eden. Across the globe, nature and religion are inextricably linked.

This connection bodes well for environmentalists who form partnerships with faith communities, from temples to meditation groups to churches. In an attack on gas-guzzling SUVs, the bumper sticker "What would Jesus drive?" used faith to prompt reflection on environmentally responsible choices for transportation (Fig. 8.7). As the leader of the Catholic Church, Pope Francis makes a biblical case for addressing climate change, calling on the world to protect creation as a moral calling. And Christians, Buddhists, Jews, and Muslims have joined the group Interfaith Power & Light and its religious response to global warming through education, worship, and advocacy across the USA (McDuff 2010; McDuff 2012).

Christian followers and environmentalists have not always worked together, with long-standing differences regarding the legacy of "human dominion over the Earth." Yet modern interpretations of the Bible view the word "dominion" to mean stewardship and care of the Earth, revealing a strong correlation between conservation and the biblical call for love and justice for all (McDuff 2010). With a foreword written by Archbishop Desmond Tutu, The Green Bible (2010) highlights biblical passages in green that reflect care of the earth and includes introductory essays by both Christian and Jewish theologians. Of note, some Christian groups refer to stewardship of the earth as "creation care" to avoid political connotations often associated with "environmentalism."

For conservation educators, it is important to recognize that educational resources, books, films, and organizations exist to support partnerships with diverse religious traditions, including Muslim, Jewish, Christian, and Buddhist faiths (e.g., Abdul-Matin and Ellison 2010; Bingham 2009; McDuff 2012; Hanh 2013; Neril and Marzouk 2013). Some of these religious-environmental groups include: Green Muslims, Buddhist Peace Fellowship, Coalition on the Environment and Jewish Life, Hazon, Earth Ministry, and the Evangelical Environmental Network. Diverse congregations exist within any faith tradition or denomination. In addition, interfaith groups like GreenFaith and Interfaith Power & Light bring people from different religious backgrounds together to work toward conservation.

Opportunities to partner with faith communities include organizing around issues such as food, energy efficiency, land conservation, consumerism, public health, green building, and climate change (McDuff 2010, 2012). The Episcopal Church of the Holy Family partnered with the Carolina Mountain Land Conservancy, for example, to place its land under conservation easements and restore habitat for wildlife. On a larger scale, the religious-environmental group Earth Ministry in Seattle, Washington, USA partnered with the Sierra Club to lobby the state legislature to pass the Coal-Free Future for Washington Act. This law retires the state's only coal-fired power plant in an effort to increase the state's reliance on renewable energy and reduce carbon emissions. The two groups have continued to work together in efforts to block the construction of

Fig. 8.7 The bumper sticker "What would Jesus drive?" united religious and environmental interests to promote fuel-efficient vehicles.

coal-export terminals in Washington State (McDuff 2012). In this campaign, the Sierra Club brought its national reputation and resources, while state-based Earth Ministry leveraged its regional membership, houses of worship, and the moral connection to the health of the state's people and places.

Medical and health communities

Environmental and health concerns often parallel each other. A study in the USA found that newborn babies have 300 industrial chemicals in their bodies (Environmental Working Group 2014). Toxic substances in our bodies accumulate from chemicals in the food we eat, skin creams we apply, air we breathe, water we drink, and plastic containers that hold our food. Some of these chemicals include phthalates in plastic, bisphenol A in food and beverage containers, and fire retardants in furniture.

Arctic people such as the Inuit have the highest concentrations of toxins in their bodies including polychlorinated biphenyls (PCBs), dioxin, DDT, mercury, polybrominated diphenyl ethers (PBDEs; bromine-based flame retardants), and perfluorooctane sulfonate (PFOS; a type of stain repellent). Since the Inuit diet relies on animals at the top of the food chain, they are getting a hefty dose of these chemicals (Guynup 2004; Burleson and Dougherty 2012). Many of these chemicals are hormone disrupters and carcinogens. Even additives in food such as high fructose corn syrup put a detrimental burden on our bodies. These alarming facts reflect a prime opportunity to work with doctors, medical researchers, public health officials, funding agencies, and families to improve both health and the environment.

Conservation education programs that use gardening as a context for learning have discovered success through partnerships with the medical and health community. School gardening programs take students outside to plant and grow food and then eat the produce. Many school-based programs, such as Growing Minds, aim to increase the local, fresh foods served in the school cafeteria. The Growing Minds program is a part of an organization called Appalachian Sustainable Agriculture Project that builds healthy communities through connections with local foods.

More than a third of the world's population is overweight, representing a staggering public health problem with long-term economic implications. The USA has the largest percentage of the world's overweight people, followed by China and India (Cheng 2014). As a result, school gardening programs have found that their conservation education goals resonate with the need to address the obesity epidemic. Emily Jackson, director of Growing Minds, says that they have collaborated with health professionals in schools to write proposals to fund nutrition and gardening programs. "Our programs address the obesity issues because we're taking students outside, feeding them healthy food instead of junk food, and providing exercise," she said. "And we're teaching them about gardening, plant ecology, and appreciation of the outdoors." The Growing Minds program also involves local chefs in cooking classes for students, as well as visits to local farms. These partnerships draw on resources from the National Farm-to-School Network, another coalition available to conservation educators.

8.8.3 Evaluation

When you begin work with a partnering organization you should collaboratively define criteria for judging the effectiveness of the networking and the partnership. Some indicators of an effective partnership include: agreement on goals and strategies; shared power and mutual trust; clear communication; flexibility; and alignment of interests and needs (Strand et al. 2003a).

Convene the partnership on a periodic basis to assess barriers and benefits to a successful partnership. How would you evaluate your progress on each of your criteria for a productive partnership? Brainstorm areas for improvement, make changes when possible, and continue to build a stronger partnership.

An early study of the partnerships in Brazil between protected areas and nongovernmental organizations used interviews to assess the effectiveness of three such partnerships. The research identified 26 benefits to the partnership and 30 problems, including bureaucracy, lack of a legal framework, and unclear definition of roles in the partnership (Rocha and Jacobson 1998). These findings helped frame recommendations, such as increased public involvement. A similar qualitative study examined communication and conflict with groups working for conservation of endangered species on military lands (Lee Jenni et al. 2012). The US Department of Defense (DoD) manages 12 million hectares of land with habitat for hundreds of at-risk species, but the goal of conserving endangered species sometimes can work at odds with the military mission. This study found that suppressing conflict between partnerships that involved military trainers and natural resource professionals employed by the DoD only escalated negative outcomes. The recommendation from this study was to acknowledge conflicts and allow dissent and resolution early in the decision-making process (Lee Jenni et al. 2012).

Whenever you bring together different people and organizations, there is the possibility for conflict. Historically, conservation has involved an increasing population of people competing for finite resources (Moser and Pollio 2012). But identifying and then leveraging the diverse perspectives from partnerships can help with networking to achieve conservation goals.

8.9 Summary

Networking involves aligning your interests with other individuals, groups, and communities to increase the success of a conservation effort. If you are talking with festival attendees or forming a long-term partnership, networking means making connections. In conservation, making connections can involve creating environmental clubs and groups, as well as promoting your conservation objectives through public presentations, workshops, and professional posters. The skills needed to organize conferences and special events promote networking with a larger audience. Finally, partnerships create institutional relationships to promote conservation. Used alone or to complement one another, the techniques in this chapter provide opportunities to network and attain success both within and beyond the conservation community.

9
Marketing conservation

A media campaign in Egypt promoted water conservation practices to farmers. An elementary school in Ontario, Canada, engaged students and their parents in trying to achieve a litter-free lunchroom. Signs in hotel rooms suggest that guests hang up their towels and use them for several days. The 10% Challenge encourages citizens and businesses to reduce their carbon emissions to help mitigate global warming.

These education and communication programs focus on a particular issue and set of behaviors. Rather than providing experiences that make concepts more meaningful (such as a field trip to investigate sources of water pollution) these efforts were designed to elicit a change. They used techniques of social marketing—the application of marketing principles, those techniques that companies use to sell toothpaste and shoes, to issues that will improve society. It has a long history in the field of health where it has been used to promote immunizations and oral rehydration therapy for toddlers and discourage cigarette smoking and drunk driving. Research in environmental behaviors began with the interest in increasing recycling and energy conservation practices and then moved into the realm of conservation education where the principles of social marketing have been applied to environmental issues in a purposeful fashion. Now we have a rich set of examples from around the world to draw upon (Day and Monroe 2000; Cialdini 2009; McKenzie-Mohr 2011; Rare 2015a).

Social marketing hinges on a complete understanding of the audience's motivations and perceptions so that very specific persuasive communication messages can be crafted. Like other education and outreach programs, social marketing techniques use the values and motives of the audience to appeal to their concerns. By knowing how information travels in a community, we can be more effective about where we target our outreach materials. Social marketing also uses psychological theory to suggest other techniques, such as incentives, feedback, modeling, and commitment.

Social marketing, however, is not just about communication. After exploring the perceptions about and barriers to a behavior, a social marketing program may suggest physical modifications to elicit the desired change, such as extending the hours of an office or placing additional waste receptacles at key intersections. In Sweden, there is a clear correlation between participation in waste recycling and the promotion of waste recycling opportunities. Those waste-reducing activities that are not supported by government policy and local organizations (e.g., repair shops and used clothing collections) are less frequented by the public (Lindén and Carlsson-Kanyama 2003).

Conservation Education and Outreach Techniques. Second Edition. Susan K. Jacobson, Mallory D. McDuff & Martha C. Monroe © Susan K. Jacobson, Mallory D. McDuff & Martha C. Monroe 2015. Published 2015 by Oxford University Press.

Some conservation educators may disagree with this type of programming. They are more comfortable with traditional environmental education programs that aim to provide audiences with the awareness, knowledge, and skills to make their own decisions. In fact, traditional education programs often take great pains to avoid the appearance of advocating one solution. But will the traditional approach result in significant change quickly enough? Those conservation educators whose ultimate goal is a behavior change may choose to design a program that targets and changes that behavior. Unlike traditional programs, they are less concerned about fairly representing the advantages and disadvantages of all possible outcomes; they are promoting one particular outcome, such as water conservation or carpooling. Then again, can we afford to create programs for each and every behavior, or is it more efficient to use limited resources to elevate consciousness so that citizens want to engage in multiple conservation behaviors (Crompton 2008)? Such debates are important as they help organizations and agencies develop conservation education programs that are most appropriate for their mission and budget (Monroe et al. 2007).

It may be helpful to consider situations where social marketing is *not* appropriate. During a heated controversial issue, for example, it may not be wise for one party to announce and "market" their version of a proper solution. Unless there is some urgency to act quickly, many communities will want to figure it out for themselves. If an issue is controversial because of the value positions held by opposing camps, such as with climate change, a persuasive appeal may backfire (Corner and Randall 2011). Where communities have decided what behavior is appropriate, such as recycling household waste, educators may be encouraged to change behavior and support that norm. Thus, community approval can be a prerequisite to using social marketing tools effectively.

Some agencies have begun to think about a type of decision architecture called "nudge" where the default condition is the one that is in the best interest of the individual or society at large. From the placement of candy at the grocery checkout line to whether a copy machine prints single or duplex pages, a variety of choices can be made if people take the time to do so thoughtfully, but if they don't a default condition will kick in for them (Thaler and Sunstein 2009). Why not make it easier for people to do the right thing? People will still have a choice, so goes this logic, but if they are too busy to make it, fruit will be at eye level instead of candy, or paper will be saved by two-sided copies. Again, when the default condition is one that the community prefers, this could be the most logical way to engineer conservation behavior.

Many programs combine these strategies by providing information and social encouragement. Australia's popular Sustainability Street is a program that enables friends and neighbors to inform and support each other's efforts to reduce waste, conserve energy and water, and engage in community projects to enhance sustainability. Websites provide information and examples of the changes participants have found to be effective (Sustainability Street Institute 2015). Local municipal councils help provide leadership and offer training programs on everything from compost bins and solar panels, to gardening and water recycling. Entertaining communication strategies, such as festivals or contests, appeal to families and get them thinking about issues they care about.

Working with neighbors helps create a social norm, reminds people that they are not alone in this venture, and offers participants a ready-made group of eager listeners with whom they can share their success. A "street" may be an actual street or any group of people who are willing to work together, such as a club or community group. People voluntarily register and decide how to participate, making a commitment to try something new. In a suburb of Sydney, for example, residents created a lovely garden along a public road and plan to continue by planting fruit trees (reduce your footprint 2015).

These and other social marketing techniques can be powerful tools for changing human behavior. That alone raises important questions: who decides which behavior should change and what role does the audience have in agreeing to it?

Such questions are rarely given a second thought when large corporations seek to change our behavior and encourage consumption; we recognize it is their job if they want to stay in business. But when natural resource agencies use social marketing tools to conduct their job of protecting endangered species, regulating water, or managing forests, some citizens are a bit nervous about being told what to do. In an era where public participation is a tool that improves program success, could social marketing work against this goal?

There are several considerations that could help organizers decide whether to use social marketing in conservation: (1) if the goal matches the publicly accepted mission for the agency or organization; (2) if the audience is involved in the design of the social marketing program; or (3) if the issue must be addressed quickly. This chapter suggests that community members could be engaged in every decision (Andrews et al. 2002), which could help communities feel more comfortable with a social marketing effort.

Where community participation is feasible, consider working with an existing group of community members. If one does not exist, you might develop your own advisory group of well-respected leaders. Once a relationship is established, there are many opportunities to involve them in the development of a behavior change program. If you represent a different cultural perspective from the community, or if the community consists of several cultures, consider teaming with their representatives. You may even hire and train local people as staff members. They can help define the goal, select the behavior, and make the barriers clear. They can work to design and field test messages. They can be featured in posters or social media posts to promote the new change. By giving community leaders access to the powerful tools of social marketing, conservation educators are partners to the process of change, not manipulators (McKenzie-Mohr 2011). The power of social networks or peer-to-peer learning is one of the most important characteristics of a good social marketing campaign (Corner and Randall 2011). Creating opportunities for your message to be spread among friends could be your goal.

Social marketing follows a process of asking key questions to understand the audience, developing tools, testing those tools with the audience, revising the tools so they are most effective, implementing the program, and evaluating the outcome. In many ways it is not different from the development of any other educational program that begins with a needs assessment and uses evaluation techniques to improve the product (see Chapter 1).

This chapter explains how to plan, implement, and evaluate a social marketing program, and then explores eight techniques common to social marketing programs, offering strategies for each. This information will help conservation educators use the power of social marketing techniques in an honest and reasonable way, to empower communities to conserve resources, and to offer opportunities to design an effective strategy for behavior change.

9.1 Planning a social marketing program

The process of developing a social marketing program involves working with community members, either through an existing group who can be advisors and partners or by meaningful data collection efforts, or both. The first step in social marketing is to identify the behavior that should be targeted.

9.1.1 Selecting a behavior

Identifying the action to change may involve meeting with the community, introducing or responding to their concern, and asking for their cooperation in designing a strategy to solve the problem. By starting with the selection of a behavior, you can help focus attention on how people can change a situation or solve a problem. Douglas McKenzie-Mohr, an experienced social marketer, trainer, and author of several useful manuals, encourages organizations to be deliberate as they consider how to approach behavior change since there are usually a variety of reasonable changes that could be made. The process begins by listing feasible activities, selecting one that would promote the intended behavior and one that would dissuade an existing behavior. Next consider the barriers and benefits for both activities. What might influence the audience to participate? Finally, try to ascertain the realistic impact this activity would have on the problem. This process may help reveal the most appropriate behavior for your project.

9.1.2 Assessing the audience

The second step is to collect information about why some people practice the intended behavior and why others do not. Initial community meetings may provide some ideas, but preconceived notions can be faulty. Furthermore, ideas and barriers are not the same from issue to issue. For example, knowing how people feel about wildlife is not likely to help design messages about water quality. It is best to conduct interviews, focus groups, or a small survey to better understand the reasons behind the action and inaction. Theories about human behavior (see Chapter 3) suggest some key questions that may assist this process:

- What do people know about the problem?
- How important is this problem and how does it affect their goals for the future?
- What motivates people to care about this problem or solution?
- Do people believe any change is likely to resolve the problem?
- Do people have the opportunity to make the change?
- Who is already conducting this behavior and are they respected?

- What do people think that others (particularly respected and important others) will think of them participating in this behavior?
- What barriers stand in the way of making the change and which are most important?

As an example of how these data might be used, consider the following. Many cities are installing bike share systems that allow residents and tourists to borrow bicycles and return them to docking stations in other parts of the city. When for-profit companies manage the service, they are likely to install the stations in places where people who are already motivated to use a bike live and work, guaranteeing high use. When cities control the service, however, they may also wish to make this form of transportation available to people who have not considered cycling as feasible. Focus groups with these residents will help organizers understand the barriers and benefits from their perspectives. A docking station under a bridge (Fig. 9.1) may be preferred because it will keep cyclists and bikes dry in the rain.

Fig. 9.1 A bike-share docking station near King's College London, UK, is sheltered from the elements. (Photo by M. Monroe).

In some cases community members may collect this information themselves, while in others you will present the results to the advisory committee. In either case, the community must have access to the information and should be involved in directing the program to the next step.

In some circumstances the data collected for designing the program can also be used to establish a baseline of public knowledge, attitudes, and behaviors. Several years later, a repeat of the same survey can help indicate the success of the program by measuring change in key factors. In this way, the planning phase can contribute to the evaluation phase. In Michigan, USA, the 6-year Rouge Project to build public awareness, knowledge, and behaviors in the Rouge River watershed documented that, prior to this program, nearly half the respondents thought business and industry were the source of poor water quality. A post-program survey revealed more accurate responses. Those blaming business and industry were reduced to a third, while another third believed water pollution was the result of combined sewer overflows, with the remaining third believing stormwater runoff was the major cause of water quality problems (Powell and Bails 2000). This increase in knowledge about the causes and solutions of water pollution was attributed to the program.

Some of the most commonly used tools for collecting information about an audience include interviews or focus groups which yield rich detailed explanations of experiences from a limited number of people. Questions asked in a survey format usually provide a set option of responses, making it easier to tally and interpret a large number of respondents. Direct observation is a useful method for documenting changes in the target behavior. More information about these data collection tools can be found in Chapter 1.

9.1.3 Communicating opportunities

An audience assessment is used to develop a plan for communicating information and reducing barriers. Once the results of the assessment have been presented to the community advisory group they can help identify the information that will help people adopt the new behavior by considering questions such as:

- What information about the problem or solution will change perceptions?
- What information about how to implement the solution is needed?
- What information about the consequences of the action is not well understood?
- What do people care about? What do they want to keep? What do they want to change?
- What will motivate them to support change?
- What changes in location, opportunity, and service will reduce barriers?

Sometimes a comparison of people who are already carrying out the behavior with people who have not yet adopted it will help identify the information and opportunities needed.

It is not surprising that many people care about the same priorities. These common motives can be used to attract a large audience to a program or workshop that can help them achieve their goals as well as yours. In general, people are concerned about:

- spending quality time with their family,
- health, for themselves and their family,

- status and public appearance,
- participating in community improvement,
- saving money or other resources for an uncertain future,
- freedom, equality, or justice,
- clean air and water, and
- nature.

In addition to motivations, the advisory group can identify barriers that should be reduced, new alternatives, more convenient solutions, and the community benefits that should be highlighted in the communication campaign. Messages that involve people who are respected in the community and those who already practice the target behavior may be useful.

The identification of these basic elements comes directly from the community assessment. A good understanding of the perceived barriers and benefits will suggest which social marketing tools should be used in the program. Although tools can be combined, it is more expensive to use multiple strategies. Since each technique has somewhat unique characteristics, it is important to carefully consider which tool will help achieve the program's objectives. The information on each technique provided in this chapter gives suggestions for how it can be most effectively used.

All the social marketing in the world won't help change behavior, however, if you are asking people to do the impossible. Listen to your audience and understand the barriers that prevent action and work to reduce those barriers. Heatherwood Elementary School, Boulder, Colorado, USA, more than tripled the number of students walking and bicycling to school on a regular basis by building a highway crosswalk with a grant for infrastructure improvements from the state of Colorado (National Center for Safe Routes to School 2011). It is doubtful that anything else could have been as successful.

9.1.4 Creating and selecting messages

The next step is where some might think "magic happens." Actually, it is the creative work of converting the information to messages that will be easily understood. In a community, you might want to say: "Stop eating these special birds," but you know from experience this will not help people find other sources of food. So you might present the message more subtly: "Will this bird live long enough to raise its own chick?" Complementary messages might reinforce the community's sense of responsibility to protect the birds and the importance of a more modest harvest to sustain the population. You can use the information from the audience assessment to create your message:

- Recall what people care about. How can you use the motives and values they have to make your information more acceptable? Because people care about wildlife, messages about forest fires may remind people not to play with matches because some animals might lose their home. Because people care about spending time with their family, a message about recycling might emphasize the role children can play in preparing and sorting materials.
- Recognize that most people do not want to be the first to try something new. Humans are social animals and like to be with the pack. Use respected community

leaders to convey the message that this is a good change, because they do it too. Movie stars and athletes are often courted to promote behaviors and environmental causes because they help define what society deems is appropriate.

- Choose one or more basic elements for the foundation of your message: (1) rational elements that provide factual information; (2) emotional elements that elicit a positive or negative response, such as pride or fear; (3) moral elements that refer to the audience's sense of right and wrong; (4) non-verbal elements that use visual cues and symbols to make their point (Kotler et al. 2002). Any element can be effective, and a message only needs one, although using more than one may help the message appeal to a wider audience. Adding either a lighthearted or serious tone to the element can also boost its appeal.
- Appeals to fear should be used only when followed by reasonable information about what people can do to reduce the threat. If the information is complicated or difficult to use, people could feel paralyzed by their fear and helpless. This does not lead to change.
- Humor is a good strategy and often makes the message more memorable. It is not useful, however, for a complicated message.
- If you know where your audience is on the path toward a new behavior, you can better target a message. For example, someone who is still thinking about the issue should get a message that promotes the positive outcomes and expectations. People who have already decided to change their behavior would be better served by a message that details how to conduct the behavior and how to know they are doing it correctly.

You may choose to hire creative people (such as an advertising agency) to generate possible messages or ask a group of staff and advisors to brainstorm suggestions, coming up with as many ideas as possible before winnowing them down (Jacobson 2009). Either way, a variety of potential messages should be generated. Some may be more appropriate for certain social marketing techniques (such as prompts or commitment) than others. Ask the advisory group to review, comment on, and choose the messages that resonate best. Use their information to help decide which are the most persuasive and memorable messages, and the materials that best fit the community. Which ones enable viewers to say, "Yes, this would work for me"? Then take the selection to a sample group of the audience to confirm that these materials are useful, appropriate, attractive, and relevant. The advisory group may be able to help you with this task.

It is critical to test the messages on the audience, although too often campaigns rely on just staff and experts to determine the best message. After one expensive failure, it is easier to remember to test the translation, to ask local people to review the images, or to make sure teachers will use the suggested educational materials. This pilot testing process is essential in the development of an effective campaign. Mistakes caught at this stage are much easier to fix than after the program is implemented. Revised tools should be pilot tested again to make sure the new version is acceptable.

It is generally easier to change behavior if there are many different reasons why someone would find it a good thing to do. Try to use all of those reasons in a campaign, since your favorite reason may not attract many people. Additionally, using a range of benefits will help promote the behavior to more people. Do not worry about which is the "right" reason, either. It does not matter if people ride bicycles to work because they do not want to pay for parking, because they want the physical health benefits, or because they want to improve air quality—what matters is that they do it. However, if you want this campaign to be part of a larger effort, consider how to help people try out a new behavior and then reinforce it with the message that will position them to more readily receive the next challenge. Relying on people saving money on utility bills, for example, may not be enough to change all the behaviors associated with creating a culture that mitigates climate change (Corner and Randall 2011).

9.1.5 Program implementation

When you are pleased with the results of your pilot test, you are ready to produce the materials and launch your outreach campaign. Implementing social marketing tools involves identifying what will be done, when, where, and how. Tasks and responsibilities should be outlined in an action plan with a timeline. Constraints, such as time and money, may restrict the activities that are conducted.

Complicated projects may evolve over time in phases that first target a geographic area and then spread to others, or that communicate one introductory message and then progress to more detailed ones. Continue to involve your advisory group and community members in the program delivery. Do not forget to establish strategies to monitor the results of the campaign. Once again, consult with community members to decide how to measure changes.

Programs will be implemented differently based on the social marketing techniques that are chosen. Research studies give us an idea of the effectiveness of techniques when used separately, but most effective social marketing programs use several techniques in combination. Since both communities and behaviors vary, there are few magic rules for the best combination of strategies. It is most important to test your ideas with your advisory group and in your community.

9.1.6 Program evaluation

Communities and agencies will want to know if their social marketing efforts have been successful, making program evaluation imperative. Since it is typical for social marketing programs to use several tools in a campaign to bring about behavior change, an evaluation should assess the entire program. Unlike some conservation education programs that only measure participant satisfaction or knowledge, social marketing programs are evaluated by measuring saturation (how many people saw and remembered the message) and actual behavior change (Box 9.1).

This is most often done using observation (counting the number of single-passenger vehicles, the lawns irrigated, or the homes with native plant gardens) or data-collecting systems that measure behavior, such as bar-code readers at grocery check-outs, electric and water meters, and traffic counters. Many studies have demonstrated the unreliability of asking people if they have changed their behavior; respondents are often generous

Box 9.1 Social marketing helps support change

Across Latin America's highlands, the cloud forests and grasslands play a critical role in the watersheds, filtering rainfall on its path to nearby rivers from which communities obtain water for cooking, washing, irrigation, and drinking. Changes in the upstream landscape can degrade the forest and water supply for those living downstream. Rare, an international conservation organization, works with local communities and water authorities to implement social marketing campaigns to encourage residents to protect their watershed. The basic tool is a reciprocal water agreement and payment incentive, where downstream water users agree to pay a small water fee to help ensure they receive water at a desired quality and quantity. Those fees are used upstream to provide landowners with an incentive to protect the watershed by maintaining the native forest and reducing off-road racing and road construction, for example (Rare 2015b).

The social marketing campaign included strategies to increase awareness of the watershed problems and cultivate pride in the community's role in protecting the quality and quantity of water. Organizers conveyed conservation messages through several mechanisms: radio spots and a campaign song played on radio stations and from a vehicle fitted with loudspeakers, posters on the agreement and forest protection, puppet shows, and sport or art competitions. The Pride campaign was evaluated with a survey that measured increased knowledge about the upstream land affecting water quality downstream (an increase from 35 to 41%) and increased willingness to sign the water agreement More than 250 landowners have signed contracts, protecting more than 15,000 hectares in 29 watersheds (Rare 2015b).

with their memory of good intentions and tend to over-estimate a desired behavior. It could be expensive to train and equip observers to watch and record behavior, but in some cases this will be the best way to achieve an unbiased record.

Another strategy is to design the program to collect evaluation data internally. If your brochure includes a coupon that can be collected or a downloaded form generates a registration link, you will be able to know how many people picked up the brochure and acted on the message. Coupons of different colors could be distributed in different venues, such as newspaper flyers, school newsletters, or door-to-door. When they are returned you have a record of which technique was the most effective at reaching and convincing the intended audience. Similarly, slight variations in social media announcements can help track what works.

Local universities may be able to help provide student assistants to collect and analyze data. It may be sufficient to measure behavior before and after your campaign with the population that you are addressing, unless you need to know which tool was most effective. A small pilot program, for example, may be used to compare several tools to decide how to expand the program in the next phase.

In many cases the results of the campaign can be assessed by actual environmental impacts without the need for a public survey. Social marketing campaigns have facilitated the creation of new reserves in Indonesia, Costa Rica, and the Philippines and the passage of new natural resource management legislation in Montserrat and Yap. After a campaign in Mexico's Sierra de Manatlán Biosphere Reserve promoting best practices for slash and burn techniques, forest fires were reduced by 50%. A social marketing campaign also helped the Palau Conservation Society launch itself as Palau's first homegrown environmental NGO and one of Micronesia's leading voices for conservation.

9.2 Social marketing tools

Every social marketing program needs to inform the audience about the targeted issue and the desired behavior. Most of the techniques mentioned in this book can be used for those goals. What might make a brochure or a workshop more likely to change someone's behavior, however, is the use of social marketing techniques (Box 9.2). A brochure that persuades by highlighting local leaders uses the technique of modeling; a workshop that asks for participants to sign an agreement uses commitment. These techniques could make the brochure and workshop more effective at changing behavior than those that just provide information.

Box 9.2 Social marketing tools at a glance

Tool	Value	Tip
Sign, billboard, poster	Raise awareness of an issue.	Keep the message short, simple, and positive.
Prompt	Provide a reminder to do an easy-to-forget action.	Use for habitual behaviors, after knowledge and intent are in place.
Feedback	Inform people that they are making progress toward a change.	Provide both personal and collective feedback.
Model	Creates a new social norm and provides procedural information.	Use to suggest how, when, and where after people already know what and why.
Commitment	Obtain the promise of future action from willing individuals.	Usually requires personal interaction.
Incentive and disincentive	Provide a different reason to stop or begin a new behavior.	Can be difficult to continue providing the incentive or sustaining the change but useful to kick-start a new behavior.
Press interview	Provide information to the public.	Provide background for the reporter but give a simple, clear short message for the public.
Advertisement	Raise awareness and provide testimonials.	Can reach a large number of people with a very simple message.

9.3 Signs, billboards, and posters

A variety of written communication tools can be used in a social marketing context if they are designed to inform and persuade. Brochures, posters, door hangers, stickers, news releases, exhibits, editorials, stories, and billboards are but a few of these. The basics of graphic design and writing skills needed to construct many of these tools are explained in Chapters 10 and 12, including how to achieve readability, direct eye movement, and develop and use a theme.

Signs, billboards, and posters are posted messages printed on flat surfaces that can be quickly understood. Because they can utilize images, they can communicate across language and literacy barriers. Some signs and billboards have moving parts and flashing lights, though some communities and nations actively discourage roadside messages that might distract drivers. They are less likely to be used by conservation outreach efforts because of expense.

Billboards are large, permanent structures usually designed to be read from moving cars. Signs are typically site-specific and smaller permanent structures. Posters are printed on paper for large-scale distribution. Scientific posters are not distributed but are used for professional meetings (see Chapter 8). A campaign to make resources available to others can include all these options in PDF format on a website for download.

9.3.1 Planning

You may wish to develop a summary of what you know from your audience assessment as you begin to plan your sign, billboard, or poster. Describe your audience and your ultimate goal. Then describe what you want them to know, believe, and do as a result of your campaign. Also list the benefits and the reasons why they may want to change their behavior.

A billboard is a mass media tool used to raise awareness (Fig. 9.2). Signs should be posted at the site where they can inform and change very specific behaviors. The sign shown in Fig. 9.3 is mounted on a platform for easy use and effectively tells hikers what they should do and why before walking in the specified area. Signs that provide too much information may be much less effective. With your advisory group, decide on a tone and basic element for your message. Do you want to be stern and moralistic, or lighthearted and emotional? Will you use a testimonial from someone who has already carried out the behavior?

Because posters are generally distributed for others to put up, it is difficult to know where they will be placed. Therefore, it is most important to design an attractive image that the audience will want to display. Consider your audience when you design your sign or poster. A survey of more than 500 small businesses in the USA suggests that the majority of younger business owners (age 18 to 34) value creativity in graphics and messages, whereas older owners (age 55 and up) prefer simple designs (Alexander 2014).

Try not to threaten or demand a behavior because people could feel coerced. Messages that are negative or threatening (e.g., "Don't litter") are more likely to be ignored or generate the opposite reaction than messages that reinforce the socially acceptable behavior or offer choices (e.g., "Keep your park clean"). If you need to present information about risk or negative consequences, it should be accompanied by helpful suggestions of what people can do to mitigate the problem (McKenzie-Mohr et al. 2012).

Fig. 9.2 Highway billboards can be eye-catching places for a short, memorable message designed to raise awareness (Photo by M. Monroe).

Fig. 9.3 To protect natural areas from the spread of *Phytophthora* root fungus, this sign effectively explains the risk, the consequences, and the action hikers can take. It contains more information than a road sign and is still graphically pleasing. (Photo by M. Monroe.)

In addition to your message, it is essential to have a good design for a sign, billboard, or poster because they stand alone as a communication technique. There is no accompanying presentation or explanation in a billboard, for example, just the visual image and minimal text. The layout of the sign, billboard, or poster will include several elements, often a headline or phrase and an image. These elements should be attractive and balanced so the eye moves through the whole design (see Chapter 12). The color scheme should be compelling and relevant to your message, such as green for forests or blue for water. Color contrast can help make the text more readable, such as very dark and very light colors. Although any contrasting combination is readable, light letters on a dark background appear bigger. In signs, size matters. The larger the letters, the easier they are to read. One rule of thumb is 10 feet per inch—a 3-inch letter can be read at 30 feet (Fell 2014). Large areas of open space are important to prevent the design from looking cluttered or tight (Walnut Creek n.d.).

When you have several ideas for your message and design, circulate drafts among your advisory group and collect their feedback. Ask them to describe the main message and the purpose of the sign, and how it makes them feel. Since your advisory group may be more knowledgeable about your goals than your audience, make sure you also ask the audience the same questions. With this feedback, apply necessary changes to images, colors, layout, and wording to improve the design.

9.3.2 Implementation

Posters usually require a distribution plan, whereas signs and billboards are erected by the campaign. A campaign may have one sign at a park entrance warning people of the consequences of feeding animals, or multiple copies distributed to every community in the vicinity. Consider how long you want the signs to be posted for and how you will distribute them. A statewide campaign in Florida to remind travelers about lands that are managed with prescribed fire produced and distributed 150 1.3-m² painted signs, made from 2-cm thick outdoor-grade plywood. Unfortunately the signs were so heavy that the organizers had to rent a large truck to carry them to workshops. The workshop participants were also informed of the need to arrive in a large vehicle so they could transport signs back to their work sites. Aluminum signs would have been equally sturdy and very lightweight, but more expensive.

Consider how fast people will be traveling when they read your sign or billboard. Highway travelers have 6–10 seconds to understand a billboard, so use fewer than 10 words and a large font (Fig. 9.2). If your audience is walking or the sign is placed at an intersection where they stop momentarily, your font can be smaller and have more words (Fig. 9.3). Brief messages, however, are generally easier to read and remember. Images and symbols can be understood very quickly and should be used on large signs and billboards. Remember to pilot test any symbols to make sure people comprehend the intended message.

9.3.3 Evaluation

You can determine if your signs, posters, and billboards are effective if a survey of the audience reveals they remember seeing your signs, can state your message, and perceive a problem, and if these results are greater than your baseline level of awareness.

9.4 Prompts

Sometimes people know what they should do and intend to do it, but just forget. Many of the habitual activities that we do every day are hard to change, even if we know we should. Conservation educators can use prompts to help people remember to do something they already know is an appropriate behavior. Prompts are brief reminders that tell people what to do and when to do it. The location of the prompt often tells them where or how to use a behavior. Stickers, magnets, posters, billboards, and signs are some of the opportunities educators have for prompts. All of these techniques share several common features—they contain a short phrase that is easily seen, quickly read, and strategically placed.

The popular wallet-sized Seafood Watch pocket guide and cell phone app (Fig. 9.4) are produced at the Monterey Bay Aquarium in California, USA, to remind consumers which seafood is harvested relatively sustainably and which should be avoided. The goal of the program is to shift consumption patterns toward species that are sustainably harvested. Several criteria are used to rank species, including bycatch, population size, and farming practices. The pocket guide is effective because a major barrier to making sustainable choices when buying seafood at a market or restaurant is a lack of information. A handy, portable prompt, carried in the wallet or pocket, is therefore a good strategy, and a cell phone app is even more convenient. From 1999 to 2010 over 34 million pocket guides were distributed to consumers through organizations, agencies, restaurants, and other venues (McKenzie-Mohr et al. 2012). The Seafood Watch program also includes workshops and opportunities for chefs to make commitments and win sustainable fishery awards, combining many social marketing tools.

9.4.1 Planning

Since location is one identifying characteristic of a prompt, a number of advertising opportunities are excluded. Ball caps, T-shirts, pencils, and bus advertisements are

Fig. 9.4 The Monterey Bay Aquarium Seafood Watch cell phone app enables consumers to buy fish from more sustainable fisheries. (Photo by M. Monroe.)

excellent choices for creative and memorable messages, but the program developer cannot control where these messages are seen. Therefore, these are best used in situations where the goal is to advertise to a large audience anywhere and everywhere. Because they are not likely to be associated with the ability to immediately perform the behavior, they are not prompts.

When planning your prompt, consider placing it strategically where a person would need a reminder. For example, you could place a "No compost" sticker on a garbage can to remind residents to take their organic waste to the compost pile. If the compostable waste were dumped into the garbage bin in the kitchen, however, this prompt is useless. An attractive pail on the kitchen counter might be a better prompt.

"Scoop the poop" is a popular slogan to remind dogwalkers to pick up after their pet, and when it is printed on a sign at a park entrance or on a plastic bag dispenser along a trail, it is a prompt. "Be bright, turn out the light" is a frequently used slogan for light switches. "Recycle this container" is a reminder printed on some beverage cans and bottles. Shelftalkers or signs on grocery shelves that inform consumers about the recycled content of the product have been effective in some communities. Prompts are usually visual reminders but can also be an auditory aid, as in the spoken message in airports to "mind your step" at the end of a moving sidewalk. Prompts do not convey enough information to convince someone to conduct the behavior, and therefore they are only effective when people already intend to do it (McKenzie-Mohr 2011).

Use your advisory group to give you ideas about where a prompt would effectively remind them to participate in a certain behavior. You might even ask each of them to give a prototype to a neighbor and see if it works.

9.4.2 Implementation

For prompts to be effective they must (McKenzie-Mohr 2011):

- Deliver the reminder close to the behavior—in time and space. Consider where you could put a prompt that would be appropriate, and how it would be affixed. A key chain message could remind people to measure tire pressure to improve their gas mileage, magnets can go on refrigerators, and stickers must be affixed to something that people will not mind being covered.
- Be attractive and interesting so that people notice them, but do not tire of seeing them. A clever message or logo is a good way to attract attention. A butterfly label on native plants in the nursery could remind people to consider wildlife when they landscape.
- Be self-explanatory and understandable. Prompts are reminders, not explainers. The message needs to be specific, clear, appealing, and simple (Fig. 9.5).

To achieve these goals, prompts should follow appropriate graphic design techniques (see Chapters 10 and 12) for color, white space, images, and fonts.

9.4.3 Evaluation

Studies show that prompts can be effective at increasing compliance. You can measure the effectiveness of your prompts by observing the behavior of people approaching

Fig. 9.5 This prompt reminds people not to use storm sewer drains for waste material. The campus mascot, an alligator, makes a good spokesperson for local water quality in Gainesville, Florida, USA. (Photo by M. Monroe.)

public prompts (on litter receptacles perhaps) or by asking a random sample of the public where they saw the prompt and what it means. That will help you know if the prompt is conveying the appropriate message. To know if it is achieving the behavioral goal, it may be necessary to use surveys or observations. These tools can compare the population that received the prompt with a population that did not. Since prompts are typically used in conjunction with other tools, such as persuasive information, it is often difficult to know how valuable the prompt is alone.

9.5 Feedback

People need to know that their attempts at a new behavior are both correct and worthwhile. They also like to know they are not the only people doing the new activity. Thus, providing feedback to participants is an important element of a social marketing program.

Writer Bill McKibben's experience with feedback indicates that when provided while the behavior is being conducted, feedback can be interesting, and even addictive. His hybrid vehicle has a gauge that tells him how many miles he gets to a gallon of fuel (McKibben 2003), and the feedback mechanism is so sensitive that he can see a difference when going downhill or slowing for an intersection. McKibben observes that his driving became a competitive game to maintain high mileage. Like an itch, he notes, you cannot help but pay attention to the feedback and try to better your last result. McKibben suggests that the ability to measure results on a host of environmental actions will help change behaviors.

OPOWER, a company that enables utilities to report to each consumer how well they do in comparison with their neighbors, effectively provides feedback to individuals on their own electricity usage in the context of the social norm of their community. In pilot projects across the USA this comparative billing program has resulted in 1.5–3.5% reduction in energy use per customer (Hummer 2010).

9.5.1 Planning

Collective and individual feedback are both effective at providing participants with information they need to continue their actions. Thus, feedback tends to be used only for actions that are repeated frequently. In a campaign to promote a one-time behavior, such as replacing a toilet with a water-conserving model, there is little opportunity to provide feedback to the participant. The number of water-conserving toilets installed can be used to help convey the social norm (Chapter 3) and attract interest among those who have not yet converted.

Feedback, as with prompts, is most useful when associated with the opportunity to change that behavior. Reminders of the important work of a local civic group and their request for donations may be more successful if people have recently pulled out their wallet (such as when leaving a grocery store). In addition, feedback may be most useful if the audience believes the information is relevant to their situation. If data are provided from a previous year, another village, or a different season, it may be harder for people to believe that the information is helpful to them.

Testing your ideas for feedback with your advisory group will help you choose the message and the location that will work the best for your community.

9.5.2 Implementation

Since the information provided may change daily or weekly, from individual to individual, or from home to home, it may not be practical to use printed communication devices to share feedback. Brochures and posters may be out of date too quickly to justify the expense. The exception, of course, is personalized utility statements, such as those provided by OPOWER. It may be feasible to use electronic forms of communication for providing feedback. Websites, social media sites, radio announcements, electronic signs, and television news programs could be considered for community feedback. For example, an electronic billboard tells the residents of Melbourne, Australia, the current level of their water reservoir and which category of water conservation rules applies.

For the effective use of feedback, consider these tips:

- Provide feedback for behaviors that are done repeatedly.
- If using personal feedback, try to include comparative information that is relevant to the situation so people have a realistic sense of how they are doing.
- If using collective feedback (e.g., how the town is doing), consider comparing data from other similar groups outside the target area.
- Add an incentive to encourage participation, such as a competition (see Section 9.8).
- Provide feedback through communication tools that are easily changed and updated.
- Provide feedback through communication tools that are easily noticed and understood.
- For complex or unfamiliar tasks, provide feedback in conjunction with procedural information so people remember what they are supposed to do.

• Consider how to display feedback so it is understandable in each medium. If announced on a highway sign, it must be read at high speeds. If announced over the evening news, a visual chart or graph could be included. If provided on a website, detailed pages could be included for those who wish to know more.

9.5.3 Evaluation

A survey is necessary to understand how feedback affects people's willingness to change behavior. A written or phone survey will help you know how many people changed their practices and if the feedback they received had any impact on their behavior. You could also conduct an experiment that compares several treatments in different geographic areas to determine which techniques are most effective for this behavior and audience.

9.6 Models

Models and other similar tools, for example cases, examples, or demonstrations, are important components of a social marketing program. Models typically involve the use of a few leaders or early adopters to model a behavior for others or using a physical example to act as a model. A demonstration (see Chapter 12), such as used at an interpretive site, demonstrates a certain process or action that others can employ at home or work. Models and demonstrations encourage changes in behavior by physically showing people how it is done or what the end result will be. They also help establish a new social norm by making this new behavior seem normal. A model paints a picture of what is possible by providing an example. Models are effective because people often like knowing that they are not the first to try something and can learn by watching others (see Chapter 3). Therefore, if you are persuading people to do something different, and that action or result can be witnessed, consider the power of models. Increasing the number of children who cycle or walk to school may be successful in part because of the increased visibility of "walking school buses" whose members sport bright vests and armbands and the commitment from parents who accompany their children. Bike sharing programs that have successfully enhanced public transportations systems in cities like Paris and Montreal depend on people noticing the bikes and riding them.

Project Porchlight is using these results in communities across North America where volunteers deliver free compact fluorescent bulbs, courtesy of the local utility. When people hear a message from a peer, they are more likely to listen. The volunteers are trained to talk about other ways to conserve energy and answer questions, providing residents with information not just about energy conservation but also about the social norm that says, "people like you and people like me care about energy" (Hummer 2010).

9.6.1 Planning

Research on models indicates that when someone is performing the "right" behavior, other people are more likely to do it too, even if they do not specifically talk about it. For research purposes, these models are paid and trained to perform the desired behavior. In the real world, models could be community members who have already made the switch to the new behavior. Seeing someone model the activity is an indication that new behaviors are possible and feasible. If the activity is observable, it is also a chance to find out how the activity is done, what one needs to do, or how long it takes. Polling place stickers proclaiming, "I voted" or water conservation stickers on home windows announce who in the community has participated in this behavior and lets others know how widespread the behavior might be. Not only might these adopters answer questions about their experience, but the frequency with which one sees these stickers helps change the notion of what is "normal."

To use models in your conservation program, think about the barriers to participation in the activity. If the behavior is so new that people are not sure how to do it, consider establishing a demonstration at a convenient location in the community (Fig. 9.6). Include brochures or signs so newcomers know what is being demonstrated and who to contact for more information.

If people do not know that community members have already begun to practice the new behavior, consider strategies that advertise who has already taken the plunge. Putting a large box of recycled materials on the curb helps tell everyone in the neighborhood "I am recycling" and could make non-participants feel guilty. It is more difficult to devise similar proclamations for behaviors that are personal or hidden. Consider simple but effective strategies to advertise participation. Some organizations use car license plate holders, T-shirts, ball caps, and bumper stickers to advertise membership (e.g., World Wildlife Fund member), behaviors (e.g., "I brake for snakes"), or beliefs (e.g., "Growing trees grows jobs").

Another strategy for using models is to organize an event or festival that engages people in conducting the behavior in public for fun. Making bird feeders, planting dune grass, or removing invasive vines are activities that can be done with a group of people

Fig. 9.6 This sign helps make obvious the landscaping techniques that reduce the risk of fire around these structures. (Photo by M. Monroe.)

in a festive situation. The act of participating creates an opportunity to learn how to do the activity from others and, furthermore, the social benefit of being with others is an important motive for volunteers who contribute time to conservation programs (Grese et al. 2000; Guiney and Oberhauser 2009). Additionally, the opportunity to have fun while starting a new adventure may help ensure the success of the behavior change program.

Finally, examples (a type of model) can be used easily in nearly every communication technique in this book. They portray details of "what" and "how" and suggest that others are doing it. Testimonials from community leaders can be powerful stories that model by example. They communicate not only that someone is doing the activity, but that they are also happy enough with the results to be quoted. Newspaper articles can feature demonstrations of organic gardens, brochures can provide quotes from people who returned from an ecotourism vacation, and a public service announcement can feature bicycle commuters. The more relevant, concrete, and vivid the example, the more memorable and useful the information will be.

Your advisory group can help to determine the examples that are best for communicating the appropriate message in their community and how models might be most effectively used. They might even become the models!

9.6.2 Implementation

Since models show concrete actions and behaviors, they are most effective when someone already has the background information and is interested in considering the new behavior. Thus, models should come after basic persuasion activities and provide the details people need to move from "I ought" to "I will." Models are most meaningful when they are personally experienced, so a model in each neighborhood may be more effective than one for an entire town. They are most useful when seen in person.

Testimonials and examples, which are a type of written model, can be used to make persuasive materials more effective in brochures, posters, stickers, public service announcements, and newspaper advertisements.

Characteristics that make models effective are:

- *Visibility*. Models should be located so they can be seen, such as a model garden at the entrance to a neighborhood, or at an intersection where people stop for traffic. If the action itself is not visible, indirect evidence that people are doing the behavior must be sought (McKenzie-Mohr 2011).
- *Information*. Models should have brochures or signs telling people what is going on, how the model was created, and what they can expect will happen as a result of the activity.
- *Vivid*. Models and examples are good communication tools because they are specific, concrete, and local.
- *Simple*. If the action is complex, a series of models may be needed to break the action into achievable steps.
- *Locally applicable*. Models demonstrate that the action is locally feasible. The essence of a model is communicating to people that this can happen here.

9.6.3 Evaluation

You can evaluate the success of your model by comparing compliance rates in areas with models to those in areas (or times) without models. Conversely, you can observe the behavior prior to and after the implementation of a model. Finally, asking people if they have seen and understood the model is helpful for knowing how well it conveys your message.

Using the power of social norms and modeling was one of the key components of the social marketing program at Pacific University Oregon, USA, to increase recycling rates and reduce paper use. A competition between departments to increase participation and win prizes was implemented along with a variety of prompts and informative flyers to increase awareness and knowledge about recycling opportunities and product purchases. Publication of participation rates and the winners helped create a new norm. One participant wrote in a post-survey, "Greening Pacific! became a good way for me to support ways we could do this in our office since many of my colleagues did not previously see the point in doing these things" (Cole and Fieselman 2013). For this individual, the visible campaign supported new behaviors that were not part of the previous social norm.

Models are effective tools for bringing about behavior change. In rural communities, the success of a modeling technique may depend on the closeness of the community and the level of comfort people have with each other. Extension workers often use this technique by including visits to models as part of their group tours and in workshops.

9.7 Commitment

Some interesting aspects of human behavior have been harnessed by social psychologists to help predict behavior. For example, if people *say* they will do something, they are more likely to do it. Voicing the commitment creates a self-image that people are likely to honor and reinforces the social norm for consistency (Gopinath and Nyer 2009). In fact, asking someone if they will do a behavior might be all it takes to obtain greater compliance.

Research on the power of commitment helped establish this technique years ago. In one study, registered voters were called the night before an election and asked "Do you expect you will vote or not?" Those who answered that they would vote were asked to provide the most important reason for voting. Since people tend to over-predict a socially desirable behavior, it was not surprising that more respondents thought they would vote than actually did. But there were a significantly greater number of voters among those who said they would vote compared with those who were not asked (Greenwald et al. 1987).

When home energy auditors were trained to include several different techniques in combination with visits to homeowners, residents were much more likely to retrofit their homes. The simple techniques included using vivid language and meaningful examples (all the cracks in your windows amount to a football-sized hole in your wall), describing the problem in terms of resources lost (money) instead of acting for resource gain (energy), and asking homeowners to make a verbal commitment to make the recommended changes (Gonzales et al. 1988).

Making a public commitment is a strategy that strengthens initial attitudes and makes people more resistant to conflicting information. A study with undergraduate students, for example, asked all of them to evaluate a billboard advertisement for a new restaurant. Half of them were asked to agree for their evaluation to be made visible to the other participants. After viewing peer evaluations that were opposite to their own, participants were asked to rate the billboard ad again. Students who made a commitment to share their evaluation were more likely to stick to their original evaluation—they were not swayed by additional information to change their rating (Gopinath and Nyer 2009).

Energy Smackdown is a game and television show that used a number of techniques to make household energy conservation visible, competitive, and fun. In 2009 organizers coordinated a pilot project with 120 households in three communities near Boston, Massachusetts, USA. A competition between teams formed a reality TV show. Organizers effectively used social norms, feedback, commitment, and incentives to engage homeowners. Community leaders helped recruit participants who made a commitment to join a team and bring in friends and neighbors; their activities and experiences were publicized, and they received prizes for team competitions. Participants received a comprehensive energy audit and suggestions for how they could reduce energy use. Participants also committed to use specific strategies to reduce greenhouse gas emissions, with the number of pounds of carbon dioxide reduced equaling the number of points earned in the game. By the end of the television show, participating households reduced their emissions by 17%. These early adopters (see Chapter 3) were able to provide viewers with examples of what regular people could do. The light-hearted competition made an interesting television show and helped encourage other residents and communities to reduce energy use (Kassirer 2010).

9.7.1 Planning

Most cultures value and promote the characteristics of honesty, trustworthiness, reliability, and consistency. This makes asking for commitment an important tool in a social marketing program.

Getting verbal or written commitment is almost always done in face-to-face conversations. This means your social marketing program must have trained helpers to knock on doors, to staff a booth at an event, or to intercept visitors at a public area. The conversation should be carefully scripted to include persuasive information about the problem and exact wording of key questions to ask for commitment. Many telephone sales people know how to do this very well by asking, "Can I put you down for a $50 contribution?" For a topic that is not something they care about, most people quickly say "no." Consider what you know about the audience and what kind of commitment is possible. Carefully word the kind of question people might agree to, and consider how much information about the resource problem they need in order to make a commitment. Would distributing a brochure or other tool help? Can you give them a prompt to remind them of their commitment?

Obtaining commitment was an important element of an anti-idling social marketing campaign, Turn it Off, that asked motorists to turn off their engines when waiting. In Toronto, Canada, idling cars are an air quality concern at locations where people wait to pick up family members—at schools and at public transportation stops. It is also a behavior that is more easily changed than commuting, for example. Local partners and agencies worked together on the steering committee to direct and guide the project (McKenzie-Mohr et al. 2012). Recognizing that freezing temperatures are one reason that people keep their engine on, the campaign focused on idling behavior in warmer months. The program helped establish a community norm for turning off an engine when waiting for more than 10 seconds.

To help remind people to turn off their car, signs were posted at idling locations. To help establish a community norm, volunteers provided motorists with an information card, explained the importance of turning their engine off, and asked them to commit to doing so. Those who agreed received a window sticker (Fig. 9.7). Over 80% of the drivers who were asked to make a commitment put the sticker on their windshield. These stickers served to demonstrate their commitment to others and to remind drivers to turn off their engine. In a pilot test, the signs alone did not reduce the incidence or duration of idling. When coupled with the commitment strategies, however, the incidence of idling dropped by 32% and its duration by 73%. This combination of personal contact, commitment, and prompts could significantly reduce engine idling in locations like Toronto, where over 50% of the motorists wait for family members with their engines idling (McKenzie-Mohr 2011).

9.7.2 Implementation

Commitment can be made an effective tool in your program by following these tips (McKenzie-Mohr 2011):

- The commitment must be voluntary. People must never feel they were pressured or coerced to commit.
- Commitment should be requested only after people express an interest in the activity. Therefore, plan to provide information and ask several questions to ascertain their interest before moving toward the commitment questions.

Fig. 9.7 This window sticker reminds drivers to turn off their engine while idling and lets others know of their good intentions. Graphics are available free of charge for use in anti-idling campaigns (Natural Resources Canada 2014).

- Written commitment is more effective than verbal commitment, as in signing a pledge card, a petition, or a form.
- Verbal commitment is more effective than no commitment at all.
- Publicly displayed commitments are effective, such as a poster or newspaper article about those companies that agree to a new behavior.
- Since commitments are usually obtained through personal presentations or conversations, it may be easiest to use opportunities that already exist to speak to citizens. Therefore, try to intercept visitors at check-out counters, entrance gates, or registration areas.
- Actively involving the participant in practicing the behavior increases their confidence, their ability to give a commitment, and their ability to carry it through.

9.7.3 Evaluation

Since using this technique involves contacting individuals, it is easy to develop a form to record each contact. If you are knocking on doors, your form might include date, address, whether or not a conversation happened, whether or not the person expressed interest, and whether or not the person made a commitment. You could contact those who made a commitment in 3 months to ascertain whether they carried out the behavior.

9.8 Incentives and disincentives

There are many different opinions about the use of incentives and disincentives (e.g., fines and punishment) to encourage or discourage certain behaviors. Some argue that if the ultimate goal is for citizens to maintain the behavior on their own, a program should not rely on an incentive to reward good behavior—such a practice cannot be sustainable. In addition, the use of financial incentives can undermine the intrinsic motives that may be reinforced by social norms to help people continue the behavior (Ariely 2009). The popularity of social incentives like awards programs, however, indicates that there may be cases where these public incentives work to generate a new awareness of a problem, increase the motivation for those who take some risk to change behavior, and help build a new norm. In some cases realizing the positive benefits of conservation can become an incentive. Conserving water and energy rewards residents with an immediate incentive: saving money. The experience of the Energy Smackdown game suggested that people can be motivated by prizes as simple as a dinner at a restaurant if they are well advertised and part of the overall campaign (Kassirer 2010).

As these examples indicate, incentives and disincentives can complement other tools as part of a behavior change program. They may be particularly useful when the motivation to change behavior is low (McKenzie-Mohr 2011) or when a significant financial investment is required.

9.8.1 Planning

Awards programs are an example of an incentive-based technique that culminates an educational effort, generates media attention, and can work to change a social norm. In some cases the award is a designation for achieving a new standard. Florida's Clean Marina Program (FDEP 2015), for example, designates marinas and boatyards that incorporate best management practices to protect water quality. A clear connection between clean marinas and economic profitability establishes a strong incentive for marina owners to consider voluntarily improving their environmental quality. Federal grants for sewage pumpout facilities prompted the Florida Department of Environmental Protection to design a holistic program that addresses water, air quality, waste, and land concerns. The marina business community participated in a statewide process to identify best practices and design the program. A workshop informs marina owners what they must do to achieve the Clean Marina designation and benefit from the grant program, and participants sign a pledge card committing them to reducing pollutants from local waterways. They conduct an assessment of their facility with worksheets and reference materials provided and have access to supporting mentors if they have questions. A visit from a third party will confirm that the marina has adopted the practices leading to designation, and recognition as a Clean Marina is given in an awards ceremony with a press release. The marina is then authorized to use the Clean Marina logo on its letterhead and advertisements, fly the flag, and hang the plaque (Fig. 9.8). The Clean Marina flag acts as a prompt to boaters and an incentive to marina owners to participate in the program and attract more business. This combination of training, incentives, commitment, and prompts has worked well.

In other cases the awards are prizes for winners of a contest. Keep America Beautiful sponsors an annual competition, the Recycle-Bowl, to increase recycling activity in schools. The program is advertised through chapter affiliates and partners who provide assistance to interested school staff. Interested schools register online and collect recyclables during the 4-week collection campaign. The schools report the type and amount of material collected during the following 4-week reporting period. Over 1440 schools participated in 2014 for prizes such as a recycled park bench and plaque (KAB 2015).

Planning a large awards program is a time-consuming process. Carefully consider what behavior you want to encourage, and whether a contest will encourage people to do it. Decide what rules and guidelines will support your goal. Is group participation necessary,

Fig. 9.8 The Clean Marina logo on a flag and other materials acts as a prompt to boaters and an incentive to marina owners to participate in the program and attract more business.

or can one person on a bulldozer be eligible for a cleanup award? Create categories so that different types of projects can win. Categories could be by entrant (e.g., school group, youth project, women's club, business) but also could by topic (e.g., water conservation, gardens, litter). Provide criteria for a "good" project. This may be difficult for your first contest, but it will define your program and give participants an idea of what they should strive for. Provide criteria for submitting the project. Will you require photos, testimonials, or evidence of accomplishment? Identify what the awards will be, and choose incentives that are relevant and desirable. Organize the judging process by identifying reputable and unbiased people to judge each category of submissions by standard criteria. A point system is often developed for each criterion. Finally, plan the awards ceremony where all of the submissions can be celebrated, the winners announced, and the awards distributed.

Other programs could incentivize participation, offering enhanced status or cost savings. People who reduce their quantity of weekly trash by recycling, reusing, or reducing consumption are rewarded with a smaller bill for trash collection. In communities that charge for the trash bag, the fewer bags used, the more money they save. People who invest in energy-saving appliances and insulation are rewarded with a reduced energy bill. Free bus tickets can be used to encourage increased bus travel, or coupons can be distributed to encourage people to buy native plants for their flower garden.

When changes in behavior require changes in business productivity or economic investments, a financial barrier can be overcome with monetary incentives. Federal programs in the USA have effectively used technical assistance and cost-sharing to help farmers plant trees in conservation areas, build composting facilities for animal waste to improve water quality problems, reduce water use by lowering the nozzles from pivot irrigation systems, or construct fences to keep cattle out of sensitive areas. These monetary supplements are incentives to encourage the use of technologies and behaviors that help improve environmental quality.

9.8.2 Implementation

An effective incentive program has a few key characteristics (McKenzie-Mohr 2011):

- The incentive must be desirable. It must be something people want otherwise they will not bother with the behavior change.
- The incentive must be the right size. It cannot be overwhelmingly large or people will be suspicious. It cannot be miniscule either, or people will not pay attention. The best incentives are reasonable rewards that get people to try something new, with the intent that maintenance of the new behavior will occur when people experience the benefits first-hand (De Young 1993).
- The incentive should be accompanied by a media campaign that: (1) announces the incentive, (2) helps people acknowledge the benefits of the behavior, and (3) provides an example of someone who has been pleased with the behavior and the incentive.
- The incentive should be closely associated with the behavior. Completely irrelevant rewards are not likely to help maintain the behavior because people may not link the action with the incentive.

- The incentive should actually reward the behavior that is being encouraged. This may require research to identify how people will react to the program. Bottle bills enable people who return beverage containers to receive a small monetary reward. The "rebate" is actually a deposit included in the increased cost of the beverage. The buyer who does not return the container is punished by paying an unclaimed deposit in the increased price of the beverage. Although this does not work to encourage recycling, it does work to encourage someone to pick up discarded bottles, resulting in less litter.

9.8.3 Evaluation

Incentive programs often have a built-in monitoring tool because you can count submissions for a contest, fines collected, or coupons distributed. This evaluation function can be quite useful when deciding whether to reduce, continue, or expand the incentive program. What is harder to determine, however, is the extent to which the incentive program will prompt people to continue practicing the behavior after the incentive period. Pairing incentives with other tools, like commitment or modeling, helps to make the program continue for long after the incentives are gone.

9.9 Press interviews

Many conservation educators are nervous about the possibility that someone from the press might interview them for a story. It is an honor to be interviewed, but it is also a risk since the journalist writes the story, not you. You can provide information along with a fact sheet (see Chapter 10), but exactly what is conveyed is not up to you. Therefore, you need to be prepared. It helps to have several brief, clear, easy to understand messages that you repeat several times to the journalist who is writing the story. The journalist can help distribute your message at virtually no cost to you. In some cases an agency message may gain credibility if it is carried by the news media and it helps to be prepared and to cultivate a good relationship with the local press.

One strategy for informing many journalists about an important story and providing material is to hold a press event. In an effort to halt the declining population of Russian sturgeon, the US Fish and Wildlife Service launched a campaign to let caviar eaters know the new limits on international trade and to inform illegal smugglers that DNA testing is used to determine the origin of eggs in a can of caviar. A press conference in New York City, USA, was held featuring a huge fish tank encasing a 7-foot Atlantic sturgeon. The director of the service said, "These magnificent fish survived the catastrophe that wiped out the dinosaurs and most of the other species existing 65 million years ago. But in the space of one century, we may do what nature could not—drive this fish to extinction."

The event took about 6 months to organize and included press kits, posters, stickers, and public service announcements. Journalists from television, newspaper, gourmet magazines, and a publication for cigar aficionados ran the story. Information was included in theatre playbills. Only one mistake marred the event: the midtown

Manhattan traffic was so bad that some media personnel could not reach the press conference that morning (NCTC 2004).

9.9.1 Planning

If you get a message that a reporter called the first thing to do is call back and find out what they want. It could be a simple question to clarify a term, or it could be a request for an interview about your work. If it's the latter, ask to schedule the interview in an hour and take the time to collect your thoughts. You should not start an interview unprepared. Ask about the audience that the reporter will reach with this story and think about how to frame your message for that audience.

If your communication campaign includes mass media, you already have a sense of your audience and message. Choose the messages that this journalist should convey to his or her audience and devise how to present them. Frame the messages in complete sentences, not phrases, to make it easier for you to use them in conversation. Instead of saying, "Cats: indoors" try, "Protect small birds and mammals and keep your pet safe from cars by keeping your cat indoors."

Although your message needs to communicate with the ultimate audience—the public listening to or reading the news—you first need to communicate with the journalist. Provide some basic background information about the importance of the issue the consequences, possible actions, and opportunities for involvement. Most communities do not have a journalist that specializes in science or environmental issues, so you should assume that the reporter needs this background. The words you use to explain the problem may be used verbatim in the story. In this way, you can have a major influence on the article.

Write out a few sentences that are most important to your story and practice them aloud. Use action verbs and do not ramble. Emphasize the key points that you want to make. Ask a colleague to review your statements with you; think about what the journalist is likely to ask and be ready with succinct answers. Journalists are trained to start their stories with who, what, why, where, when, and how. Make sure you have answers that connect back to your goals. Specific, concrete examples are usually helpful. Rather than saying, "Lots of plants are endangered," it would be better to state, "Here in the park we have six endangered plants and 30 others which are likely to become endangered."

The reason that resource managers complain about the media is that complicated stories become condensed into short phrases. That is particularly true for television. A TV reporter will be looking for about 15 seconds of your interview. So keep your sentences short and clear and give them a simple message they can use. Since they may not use the interviewer's question on air, provide your answers in a complete sentence. In response to the question, "Is the climate really changing?" you can use the question to start your answer, "Scientists have evidence that our climate is changing," and continue with the locally relevant details.

If you have advance warning, try to test the key messages on your audience. This is an important role for your social marketing advisory group. They can help collect information about how the various messages work and make sure that the examples are culturally appropriate.

9.9.2 Implementation

When you are being interviewed, try to relax. Sometimes it helps to pretend you are talking to a neighbor over a cup of tea. If you are on camera, do not look at the camera and keep your eyes focused on the interviewer. Comb your hair beforehand and refrain from fidgeting. Do not wear bright or busy fabrics; instead, stick to neutral colors and traditional styles.

Remember to use your assessment data to frame your story. You have an understanding about what the audience knows and understands. You can tell the journalist what is important based on your findings. The National Communication Association, USA, offers these tips for an effective media interview (NCA 2014):

- Do not wait for the journalist to ask the right questions. You can volunteer the information they need.
- Even if a hostile reporter asks a loaded question, keep your cool! Offer the most compelling facts you have to make your case, not your opinion. Let the listeners come to their own conclusions.
- Use stories that illustrate your points. Case histories and success stories are popular ways to attract attention and give the audience something they can understand. Your own stories are helpful too.
- There is no such thing as "off the record." It implies you know something that others should not know. Similarly, there is no reason to say, "no comment": merely say you do not have a response to that question and offer to get back to the reporter with more information.
- Never lie to a reporter. If you do not know the answer, just say so. Making up data is not helpful. In the media business, honesty really is the best policy. Similarly, avoid speculation and respond to "what if" questions with, "I am unable to speculate on that, however . . . " and provide the facts that support your message.
- Recast questions in the affirmative. Rather than saying, "No, our program does not kill cats," you might say, "Our program connects homeless pets with people who want to care for them."
- Keep your statements simple and concise. Edit out your expert jargon or acronyms.

9.9.3 Evaluation

The results of your press interview will be broadcast that evening or within a few days. The link to the story may then be shared via social media. You can review the story and decide if the main points you intended to make are apparent. You can also ask the journalist to give you some tips about your performance. It might help develop a professional relationship with the media if you appear to be interested in doing a better job and helping them do their job. Calls to your agency or organization and hits on your website or social media sites are additional strategies for learning about the effectiveness of your interview.

9.10 Paid and public advertisements

Paid and public advertisements use print (e.g., newspaper and magazine) and electronic media (e.g., radio, television, websites, and social media) to communicate brief messages. Fifteen or 30 seconds is quite a bit more time than a billboard gets, but it still is not enough time to explore the complexities of natural resource issues. A paid advertisement can be very expensive, depending on the cost of the professionals who design it, the size of the ad, and the market coverage you want, but this is one way to get your message out to large numbers of people. If your budget cannot support a paid advertisement, you may be eligible for a public service announcement. In some countries, newspapers, radio, and television stations air free announcements as a public service. These announcements usually promote activities of government agencies or non-profit organizations, or are seen to be in the community interest. In other countries it may be more common for a business to support the work of conservation education in exchange for mentioning their name as a sponsor.

Because of the limited time and space, most advertisements are designed to raise awareness. Some ads use powerful images to shock people into an action, such as sending money in support of an issue. The corporate world is quite adept at designing effective advertisements to increase their environmental appeal; the non-corporate world can learn from their successes!

Advertisements have been an important element of a multifaceted campaign organized by WWF-UK and TRAFFIC to deter trade in endangered species. They have worked for decades to raise awareness of the problem, improve enforcement and penalties in the UK, and reduce demand for products from endangered species (WWF-UK 2015). An early campaign used a variety of tools—press releases, media events, advertisements, television personalities, petitions, direct lobbying, and the release of key reports and findings to engage the public and convince parliamentarians to pass new legislation. Advertisements were used to alert members to urgent opportunities for communication with elected representatives and to support the more general press coverage.

Most campaigns strategically schedule the release of certain messages and the use of different tools, moving from general awareness to specific instructions about what one can do. In the case of the UK legislation, Members of Parliament were the target audience, but a public campaign was vital to show ministers the nature of support for the proposed legislation. In obtaining that support, the campaign was able to promote a large number of reasons why people should care about trade in endangered species and how wildlife products can be used sustainably, minimizing the impact of illegal trade.

The campaign was ultimately successful, with the UK government authorizing legislation to make illegal trade in endangered species an arrestable offence in the UK and increasing the length of a prison sentence from 2 to 5 years. In 2014 another campaign resulted in funding for the National Wildlife Crime Unit to provide police support to stop wildlife crime. Coordinator David Cowdrey explained, "We organized a campaign to win and offered good support for key changes; we didn't organize a campaign to protest the current state of illegal trade."

9.10.1 Planning

Think about the message you want to convey and your audience. How can you best reach that audience? What motives and values will attract their attention and move them toward a change? Your advertisement should have the following (Hampton 2013):

- one clear and memorable message that is easy to understand,
- public interest (if for a public service announcement),
- a focal point—either an image or a headline—action images and clever headlines are best,
- relevance to the audience—they should know why and how this message will help them,
- a specific directive of what listeners should do—call, write, volunteer, contribute, etc.
- brevity—for a 30-second message, limit your advertisement to 60–75 words or 150 syllables. A 15-second message should be limited to 30–35.

Consider which media channel(s) to use for your advertisement. Television, while popular and familiar, is expensive. Nevertheless, to reach a large audience with a basic, simple awareness message, a 30-second television spot might be helpful. Invest the time to make a creative, memorable message. Learn from both good and bad examples of product marketing advertisements. Some television ads end up on websites as YouTube files, increasing their lifespan with additional viewers.

A radio advertisement allows a campaign to target a more limited audience with a specific message. Who listens to classical music? What about the morning traffic report? Radio messages can be targeted by geographic area, program time, language, and sometimes profession and at a rather economical cost. Unfortunately, many radio listeners tune out the advertisements, or listen to a station without advertisements. In nations with multiple language groups, this means translating and recording the same message for everyone.

A magazine advertisement offers another opportunity to narrowly define the audience—people who subscribe to or read that magazine. Many conservation organizations sell advertising space in their newsletter or magazine. Other relevant magazines may be commercially available, such as *Backpacker* or *Organic Gardening*. If you want to reach a larger segment of the public, try a news or sports magazine. Large magazines will be able to tell you whom they reach. You can also use your audience assessment to find out what magazines and other media they use. Knowing about the audience, you can design an advertisement to inform, motivate, and appeal to them. A drawback to magazine advertisements, however, is that they are less helpful during crisis campaigns as there is a long lead time before printing.

Local organizations have newsletters that may be useful for your advertisement. Some employers will allow relevant notices to be placed in newsletters that go to all staff.

Newspapers reach national or local audiences on a daily or weekly basis. Simple ads, with limited text and graphics, can be placed quickly. Color ads or ads in national papers may reach a larger audience but can be much more expensive.

9.10.2 Implementation

Advertisements can play a strategic role in a campaign. Because they are expensive, they tend to be used sparingly, just at the moment when action is needed. A plethora of advertisements precede elections, for example. In Wooster, Ohio, USA, a failed campaign for a sales tax to fund a purchase of development rights program offers insights into the importance of the right message in advertisements. Although the campaign used a variety of tools (letters to the editor, yard signs, and a public forum), the newspaper was a key communication medium for this semi-rural population. Images that looked like the city of Wooster dominated the ads and mailers instead of photographs taken across the county. Similarly, although research indicated that the $4.00 increase in taxes was not a burden, campaign organizers thought mentioning the tax increase was too risky. Instead, they promoted farmland preservation. Opponents were able to exploit the fear of paying more taxes in their attack advertisements (Bostdorff and Woods 2003).

There is a great deal of competition for attention. For your advertisement or public service announcement to be noticed and remembered it should be interesting, professional, important, relevant, and appealing. Use the planning process and your advisory group to help you invest in the best advertisement possible.

The Community Toolbox offers these tips for implementing an effective public service announcement (Hampton 2013):

- Consider hiring a professional firm to help write a script, obtain a "voice," and record the product.
- Make multiple public service announcements so a station can cycle through a variety of messages that make the same point. Then people are more likely to pay attention.
- Ask your local stations how to provide a public service announcement. A good cover letter should be compelling and refer to conversations you had with their staff. Radio time is generally easier to obtain than television.

9.10.3 Evaluation

Try to link your advertisement to something else you can monitor, such as calls to a telephone number, attendance at a festival, or hits on a website. By matching the dates that you ran the ads with the records from the website, you can infer the impact of the advertisement.

9.11 Summary

You can increase the likelihood of designing a successful social marketing program by carefully combining the techniques described in this chapter. Prompts with commitment, incentives with demonstration, persuasive documents with feedback, or press interviews with an awards ceremony are a few of the possible combinations of techniques that can meet specific goals. Communication tools that convey messages through personal

contact help provide the audience with information, opportunities to learn how to perform the desired behavior, and a chance to commit to continuing the behavior. Mass
media tools (e.g., public service announcements, press events, advertisements, and social
media) are excellent ways to spread the word, increase awareness, and set the stage for
problem-solving. Group meetings, demonstrations, and workshops (see Chapter 8) are
usually good strategies for answering questions, providing details, offering concrete information, reducing the barriers to behavior change, and obtaining commitment. Group
activities and festivals (see Chapter 8) are other strategies that are helpful to communicate
information and increase the attractiveness of a new behavior.

Using multiple strategies to promote a behavior will increase the likelihood that a
greater variety of people will participate. Typically, there are several benefits associated
with a conservation behavior. Use all of them in your campaign as it does not matter which good reason people use for practicing the behavior. Family time together,
community participation, health benefits, and the satisfaction of helping may be used
to motivate people to participate in a new behavior (De Young 2000; Kaplan 2000).
Increased participation will support the development of a new social norm that favors
the conservation activity.

Getting your message out using
the written word

Conservation educators commonly use written materials to inform distant audiences, to provide information to visitors at preserves, or to build awareness about conservation issues among target groups, ranging from legislators to farmers. News editorials, stories, and blog posts released via the mass media, and brochures, flyers, guidebooks, and other written material can reach your audience with information and illustrations.

Publications are easy to produce, revise, and disseminate, and can be used how and when the audience desires. The PIE framework (planning–implementation–evaluation) can be used to create effective written materials for an education and outreach program. This chapter explores the design of written materials for a variety of audiences. Although the goals and audiences may differ, the basic concepts for producing effective written communication are similar. For any written material, following the ABCD of print communication—making your material attractive, brief, clear, and dynamic—will help ensure success (Jacobson 2009).

The design and format of publications largely dictates whether they will be read at all. Editorials and news releases have standard formats that must be followed to help ensure that reporters and editors print or post them. Similarly, it is critical to follow guidelines for graphic design and easy-to-read text if you are to attract readers to your materials. From an editorial or blog post about coral reefs and climate change to a guidebook on tropical plants, this chapter explores ways to develop successful written material to achieve your conservation objective. Chapter 11 provides more guidelines for using social media and the Internet to greatly expand your reach.

10.1 Opinion articles

Opinion articles are published daily in newspapers. These are also called op-eds because they often appear *op*posite the *ed*itorial page and they are an attractive technique for building awareness about a conservation issue among citizens and policy-makers. Op-eds average around 400 words in length, but succinct writing resulting in fewer words will help ensure your ideas get published and read. This means you will need to stay focused on one issue and make only three or four strong supporting arguments. If possible, talk to the op-ed editor before submitting your piece and see what interests and angles might be publishable. Cite your credentials for writing the piece and why it

Conservation Education and Outreach Techniques. Second Edition. Susan K. Jacobson, Mallory D. McDuff & Martha C. Monroe © Susan K. Jacobson, Mallory D. McDuff & Martha C. Monroe 2015. Published 2015 by Oxford University Press.

is newsworthy. Remember all four functions of the mass media—to inform, entertain, persuade, and educate—as you work on your piece. Facts are key, yet entertainment value will help ensure that editors print your article, and that readers finish it. Your first sentence must grab people's attention and entice them to keep reading.

Starting with a concrete example or image to illustrate your topic can arouse curiosity. Next state your opinion clearly and succinctly. If you cannot summarize your point in one sentence, think about it further before writing. Once you've made your point, briefly give any background needed. Then make your argument and back it up with a mix of facts, quotes from authorities, and specific examples. When possible, use anecdotes that support your opinion. People are more likely to remember stories than a lot of facts. The ending of your op-ed also should grab the reader. Restate what action should be taken, and make your last sentence, like your first, strong and memorable (Meadows 2000).

Op-eds should focus on local or regional angles for local newspapers and on broader topics for national papers. When possible they should be tied to current news or trends to appeal to editors. Relating your op-ed to an upcoming event, a historical anniversary, or a holiday provides an immediate hook to catch readers. Ecologist Gary Nabhan, at the Arizona-Sonora Desert Museum, published an op-ed timed for release at Thanksgiving. It promoted the museum's campaign to conserve pollinator species in order to protect rare plants and economically important food crops. Nabhan reminded readers that their Thanksgiving dinner could be devoid of traditional foods if the habitat of the "forgotten pollinators" that pollinate everything from pumpkins to cranberries is not protected (Jacobson 2009).

10.1.1 Planning

Planning an op-ed involves identifying your objectives, understanding the media, and targeting your audience, from policy-makers to a broad base of readers. Writing the op-ed involves deciding on a hook or angle for the piece and the key message(s), and delivering it in a clear manner. These are not the only challenges. Contacting editors and maintaining contacts with the media are an important aspect of getting out the written word.

A 500-word editorial written by Michael Beck, lead marine scientist of The Nature Conservancy (TNC), was published in the *Caribbean Journal*, the leading digital newspaper in the Caribbean region (Box 10.1, Fig. 10.1). The timing coincided with the warm summer months and the hurricane season. The goal of the op-ed was to raise awareness about the benefits of coral reef conservation in the face of global warming throughout the Caribbean, which will be greatly affected by storms and sea-level rise.

10.1.2 Implementation

Beck published his editorial in June, when people visit beaches and the hurricane season is on many readers' minds, thus providing a timely hook for both editors and readers. Note how Beck appeals to the reader's *self-interest* by presenting reasons for caring about coral reef issues—the disappearance of favorite beaches due to storms and climate change. The author presents both the threat of loss from the impacts of storms and an

Box 10.1 Op-ed article: Rebuilding Caribbean coral reefs

Headline: Rebuilding Caribbean Coral Reefs

Byline: By Michael W. Beck, PhD, *Op-Ed Contributor*

ELEUTHERA, Bahamas (25°8′22″ N; 76° 8′59″ W) is one of my favorite islands.

Unfortunately, storms seem to like it too. The eyes of both Irene and Sandy passed right over the island before coming to the United States.

Storms have always been a fact of life in the Caribbean, but their impacts are getting worse.

Global warming, poor development choices and the loss of protective coastal habitat, such as coral reefs, all increase risk.

Of the many actions needed to reduce these risks, a smart and cost-effective first step is to restore the coral reefs that provide our first line of coastal defense.

In a recent global study, we found that coral reefs are an extremely powerful tool for coastal protection.

On average, healthy coral reefs reduce wave energy by 97%—greatly limiting the force of waves that could otherwise hit coastlines causing erosion and flooding.

This defense is important to nearly 200 million people around the world who live in areas that receive risk reduction benefits from reefs or bear the costs if the reefs are lost or degraded.

In places where reefs have been degraded, it often means we have lost the living "skin" of corals from the top of these natural sea walls.

The corals have built and grown this wall of calcium carbonate over hundreds to thousands of years. The wall will not be lost immediately, but waves will erode it away over time if we do not act to restore the structure and the corals.

The good news is that we know that corals can recover.

There has been significant recovery in many places around the world from the severe coral bleaching that occurred in the extremely warm El Niño year of 1998.

Recovery was most sustained where other stresses on the reef, such as pollution, were managed well.

And there is reason for further optimism.

At a time when towns, cities and countries are making major investments in climate and weather-related hazard protection, we found that coral reef protection makes economic, ecological and practical risk-reduction sense.

The average cost of building artificial breakwaters is $19,791 per meter, compared to $1,290 per meter for projects focused coral reef restoration.

And of course healthy corals also provide significant benefits to the health of fisheries and tourism—industries that provide tens of billions of dollars annually across the Caribbean.

Toward this end, we have been working with community leaders in Grenville Bay, Grenada on reef restoration.

We have looked at the shoreline evolution in the bay and found that just a little loss of their coastal barrier reef explains 60 years of erosion and sedimentation.

Box 10.1 *Continued*

More importantly, using the same coastal engineering tools for designing artificial breakwaters, we can show how coral reef restoration would decrease erosion and likely even flooding.

In coastal communities from the Bahamas to Grenada, we shouldn't be investing just in built "grey" infrastructure like seawalls and breakwaters that will further degrade coastal habitats, and are typically more expensive to build and maintain. Instead, we should also be integrating investments in conserving and restoring "blue" infrastructure like our coral reefs—the sea wall nature built.

Michael Beck is lead marine scientist at The Nature Conservancy.
From: Beck, M.W. (2014). Rebuilding Caribbean coral reefs. *Caribbean Journal*, June 13, 2014. <http://www.caribjournal.com/2014/06/13/rebuilding-caribbean-coral-reefs/>

alternative bright future if we support coral reef conservation. He dispels myths about technological fixes and reaches right into readers' pocketbooks to promote good stewardship, coupled with strong economic return. Beck uses an active voice and opens with a sense of humor and a story to keep readers interested. Also, he is optimistic that we can find solutions, not just pessimistic about the problems.

When submitting an op-ed, it is helpful to call or email the newspaper and communicate with the editor of the op-ed page. If you are able to make contact, you can

Fig. 10.1 To attract attention and illustrate his op-ed, Beck submitted this photo showing outplanted staghorn coral after 1 year of growth. (Photo by Kemit Amon.)

discuss the piece with the editor to see what would be of interest. If you have relevant credentials, mention them again in a brief cover letter in your introductory email, and ask about the time required between submission and publication so you can anticipate the release date.

Another strategy is to convince a columnist to write about your issue. Read editorials by columnists in your news outlets to identify someone who covers the kind of issues you are involved with and who might have a similar opinion. A call or email to introduce the topic to the columnist to assess his or her interest is all that is required.

Beck gives the following advice for writing an op-ed:

- *Make one simple and clear point.* Focus on one issue with several supporting arguments.
- *Be clear about your "ask."* What do you want people or decision-makers to do?
- *Write short sentences and paragraphs.* Brevity is beautiful.
- *Make a personal connection.* I usually start with how the topic connects to something I have seen or done to make it real.
- *Get help.* I usually turn to a friend or colleague who writes professionally for a living. There are more than a few writers out there; find one. For this op-ed, I turned to my colleague Matt Barrett.
- *Read a lot of op-eds and find an author or style you like.* I like Paul Krugman. This does not mean you could expect to write like that person(s), but it gives you a feel for styles that resonate with you.
- *Be timely.* My op-ed topics are usually around recent scientific papers or reports. It is usually best to have something prepared to "sell" right when the paper is released, which means you must have prepared it ahead of time. If it is not about a paper release, then I am usually writing around an event (e.g., a storm, a spill, a legislative vote). If you are writing around events, then timeliness really matters.
- *Use your scientific editor or journal connection.* I'm lucky that I have colleagues who can help connect me to newspaper and magazine editors. If you are publishing in a journal, ask the publishing editor for help and connections (they will usually put you in touch with their media and marketing staff—if you have a clear message). Journals want people to hear and talk about and then cite their papers. They want to help you; use them.

10.1.3 Evaluation

Before submitting your op-ed, get several people to read it. If they have difficulty understanding any part of it, news editors and readers will too. Questions to ask include:

1. Does the lead sentence or paragraph address an audience need, concern, or interest?
2. Is the solution presented in a clear, concise manner?
3. Are the consequences of leaving the problem unresolved clearly presented?
4. Does the op-ed help the audience think through or mentally rehearse the action you want them to take?

Read the piece aloud to eliminate awkward wording. Keep revising until it is clear and organized. Avoid creating what an editorial page editor of the *Chicago Tribune* termed a "three bowler." The phrase refers to the possibility that a reader will be so bored by the dullness of a news article as he sits at breakfast that his face flops into his cereal bowl once, twice, or, if the article is especially boring, three times. Ultimately the goal of an op-ed is to serve as a catalyst to increase readers' awareness, foster positive attitudes, or stimulate pro-environmental behaviors. Some indicators of success would be the response to the op-ed, such as letters written to comment on your topic, re-posting the piece or comments on social media, direct comments to you from other members of the community, or increased interest from policy-makers.

Beck's editorial appeared in the *Caribbean Journal* shortly after he submitted it and highlighted findings from the TNC scientific publication. TNC media staff felt the piece contributed to their large-scale effort to draw attention to the ongoing issue of coral reef protection. Beck explains that the TNC media and marketing team use Google Analytics and send out monthly reports on media hits. In most cases, such as the Caribbean op-ed, the TNC team tracks the overall pick-up of the scientific paper in traditional and social media. TNC recognizes that op-eds in major, national, and international outlets are critical in reaching a wider audience, and they provide important "knock-on" opportunities. For example, Beck first Tweeted about the study and scientific paper, and then later Tweeted about the op-ed itself (which of course links back to the paper). For Beck, the op-eds and papers are always connected to a major conservation goal, and they are a part of a suite of strategic actions to reach that goal.

10.2 Blog posts

Over three-quarters of all Internet users read blogs; 6.7 million people blog on blogging sites, and 12 million people blog via social networks (Sprung 2013). Blog posts are an excellent device for commenting on conservation issues in the news and making a point about your program or activities. You can urge readers to support your fund drive, clean-up campaign, or special event. Blog posts can also increase awareness about management and policy, thank community organizations for help, and remind readers about the goals of your organization. For organizations that do not maintain their own blog (web-log) sites, posting pieces to popular blog sites provides a useful forum for getting your message out quickly and succinctly.

10.2.1 Planning

When composing your blog post, think about whether your readers know a little or a lot about your topic. As with all media activities, you must have a clear understanding of your audience. What will resonate with them? You can increase your chance of being published on blog sites of well-known news media, such as the *Huffington Post*, if your blog post addresses a recent news story or a current event. Addressed to the editor of established news or environmental blogs, your post should be brief and to the point.

For conservation organizations that host their own blogs, creating relevant and frequent material for your audience is critical: different staff members, for example, can contribute blog posts on a rotating basis to highlight their personal engagement with priority issues.

Your post should be relevant to the reader, state your opinion about the conservation issue or problem, give supporting facts and evidence, then conclude with an action you wish the reader to take. A striking title and a photo will help to spark interest in your blog post. For longer blog posts especially, the piece must be well organized. This can take multiple forms with headings, subheadings, sections, lists, or tips. Starting with an outline will allow you to organize the material. Once you have an outline, you can expand and fill in your points.

10.2.2 Implementation

A successful format for a blog post begins with an attention-getter: the first sentence should grab the attention of readers so that they will continue to read. What gets attention? A startling fact, an unusual example of the subject of your letter, an interesting piece of information, a provocative quote, a catchy or humorous phrase, an analogy, or a story will hook a reader. If the post is designed to be persuasive, start with an argument with which most people will agree.

Once you have readers' attention, present the main idea or argument of your post. Readers seldom have the patience to keep reading if they do not know the primary focus of the post. Some studies suggest that readers spend less than 90 seconds looking at a blog post (Sprung 2013). After presenting your main idea, provide supporting information. To persuade the reader, you should demonstrate your knowledge by providing facts and any relevant expert opinion. The post should indicate that you have a good reason for writing. If you have the support of other people or groups that support your cause, indicate this along with your own credentials.

Finally, request the action you desire (e.g., a positive vote on a land-planning initiative, or compliance with new water conservation measures). Ask readers to consider your arguments and take appropriate action.

Many sites have a word limit of a few hundred words or fewer, so you must deliver your message concisely. Make your point and stop. A short piece has a better chance of being posted, and read in its entirety, than a longer one. Meta descriptions and keyword tags that describe the post can allow readers to search for more information, and can help optimize your post on search engines.

If possible, include a photograph with your post. A compelling photograph can illustrate your point and catch the attention of editors and readers. A photograph will help focus the reader's eye on your post amid competing advertisements or other online material. Photos should be simple low-resolution images that will appear effectively on audiences' phones and other devices.

Posts should be clear and well written. They should be factual and rational. Tirades, personal attacks, or petty-sounding concerns will not be published. Posts should follow newspaper style, with terse writing and short paragraphs of only two to three sentences. It is helpful to read other blogs regularly to identify compelling styles. Notice how humor or catchy phrases can provide a change of pace and help attract attention.

In order to ensure maximum coverage of your post, make sure that social media buttons for sharing, liking, Tweeting, and emailing are available. Readers should be able to easily share your post using multiple social share buttons, regardless of whether they prefer Pinterest, Facebook, or other sites.

A blog post about the role of religion in combating climate change calls for a new approach to reach consensus on addressing this challenge (Box 10.2). The author,

---

Box 10.2 Blog post: Finding consensus on climate change through religion

---

With two children in public schools, I'm dismayed—but not surprised—to learn that the Heartland Institute, a conservative think tank, planned to pay $100,000 to a consultant to develop a school curriculum that would promote skepticism about the science of global warming.

In a karmic twist, this news came last week from leaked documents within the Heartland Institute, which spread false claims about climate scientists based on stolen e-mails in 2009. The drama sounds like a fictional plotline from the bestselling novel "The Girl Who Plays with Fire." Unfortunately such polarizing stories play with our future by hijacking facts, creating confusion, and delaying action on climate change.

Given the peer-reviewed research about global warming, why are we so confused as a national collective? And what can we do besides pray for a miracle to decrease our global carbon emissions?

This month, a study revealed that divisive political leaders drive our public confusion about climate change, an unfortunate finding given the overwhelming scientific consensus about global warming. The research showed that "elite cues"—statements from political leaders and advocacy groups—and the economy had the largest influence on public concern about climate change in the U.S.

Published in the journal *Climatic Change*, the study used data from 74 surveys conducted from 2002–2010 to construct measures of public concern about the threat of climate change. The research examined five factors that could contribute to changes in public opinion: extreme weather, media coverage, access to scientific information, elite cues, and advocacy efforts.

The authors found that the "elite partisan battle" about climate change was the most important factor in influencing public opinion about its threat. Specifically, when Congressional Democrats expressed their concern about human-generated global warming, support grew for initiatives to confront climate change. When Republicans cast anti-environmental votes, support decreased. In short, when political leaders were polarized about climate change, public opinion followed.

The media also played a role: "the greater the quantity of media coverage of climate change, the greater the level of public concern," the researchers wrote. So, if the public saw climate change on the front pages of newspapers, readers assumed the issue was important. If climate change wasn't in the news, it didn't seem like much of a problem.

At first glance, these findings seem downright depressing given the lack of political consensus on climate change. But despite this political polarization, there is one public

Box 10.2 *Continued*

---

arena with more agreement than discord, more action than argument about climate change. Surprisingly, that's among our religious leadership.

Religious voices have the power to influence both political leaders and public discourse. Think of the role of religious leaders in the civil rights movement or the earlier fight to abolish slavery. Unlike issues such as abortion and gay marriage that divide religious communities, climate change can be—and is—a unifying issue for many faith leaders.

Diverse religious groups—from evangelicals to Episcopalians—have issued public statements calling on congregations to address climate change as a moral issue.

"If we speak sincerely about our belief that climate change represents a real threat to our well-being and our planet's well-being, and that our faith compels us to respond, over time we can influence others," said the executive director of GreenFaith, the Rev. Fletcher Harper.

GreenFaith works with congregations on projects such as installing solar panels at the United Methodist Church in Red Bank, N.J., which now generate 30% of the congregation's energy and conducting an energy audit at Shiloh Baptist Church in Trenton, N.J., with $7,000 in annual savings. Economic savings provide a critical incentive, but the religious principle of loving your neighbor as yourself also drives these programs, given the disproportionate impact of global warming on the poor.

And on the frontlines of global warming, Alaska Interfaith Power & Light organized a panel discussion and call to climate action that featured climate scientists, Alaska native leaders and religious leaders from the Catholic, Protestant and Muslim faiths. More than 200 Alaskan towns risk having to relocate as the foundations of their buildings crumble due to the melting of frozen ground. According to the U.S. Army Corps of Engineers, moving just one town will cost between $150 million and $400 million.

Given such high stakes, religious leaders and their congregations shouldn't rely on politicians to shape opinions. As perhaps our most influential pastor, the Rev. Martin Luther King Jr. said, "A genuine leader is not a searcher for consensus but a molder of consensus." If we act with vision, we can create dramatic headlines to change the way the world thinks.

Blog post published in the *Huffington Post* by Mallory McDuff, author of *Sacred Acts* and *Natural Saints*.

Mallory McDuff, catches the reader's interest with her personal perspective as a mother of two children and then provides an intriguing story to entice the reader to continue.

10.2.3 Evaluation

Before posting your blog entry, ask colleagues or friends to critique it for you. Was the message clear? Did it catch readers' attention and awaken a concern? Did it clearly state what actions readers should take?

Of course the first stage of feedback you will get is from the editor of the blog. Once the piece is online, you can monitor whether it is shared, liked, and re-posted, and comments can stimulate additional interactions. Web metrics are available for tracking the response. Google Analytics offers a range of numbers, such as click-throughs, bounce rates, and average duration of visits. Blogs rely on a combination of volume and inbound links to effectively reach readers. Engaging your audience in relevant and new ways take time. The longer-term outcome, such as votes for energy conservation measures, a land preservation bill, participation in an event, or changes in local policy, will help provide data for the ultimate evaluation.

10.3 News releases

News releases, also called press releases, are a device for sending your message to the public via the news media. News releases are announcements that describe a newsworthy activity or event of interest to newspaper, radio, television, and Internet audiences. Depending on the scope of your news and the objectives of your outreach program, you can send news releases to local, state, national, or international media outlets.

For conservation organizations, having a story covered in the press translates into "free advertising" for the organization, and the ability to reach an enormous audience, depending on the amount of coverage. For example, a story picked up by major US newspapers might reach 2 million readers and for the *Nikkei* daily paper in Japan over 3 million (Nikkei 2009). One picked up by the British Broadcasting Corporation (BBC) can reach 388 million homes worldwide through its daily programs and online resources, including social media. Businesses pay millions for that kind of coverage. An added value is that the story is in the form of hard news, which is regarded by the public as a more legitimate channel for information than advertising (Jacobson 2009).

The catch is that your news release will compete for attention with releases from other organizations and industries. You will have to work hard to get your message out. It is important that your release is structurally correct and newsworthy. It must be brief and clear. You must attract editors, reporters, and readers to your news by appealing to their interests in topics ranging from your organization's important events and significant people to the relevance of conservation goals to financial, health, or security concerns.

10.3.1 Planning

Conservation organizations and agencies have many newsworthy activities. The World Wildlife Fund (WWF) ensures that new partnerships, people, programs, and activities make the news through their press releases (Box 10.3). They also look for ways to tie current events, from environmental legislation to celebrity endorsements, to their conservation goals.

10.3.2 Implementation

The guidelines in this subsection focus on news releases for written media, which do not require expensive equipment or technical expertise. Technical help for broadcast media releases can be hired, or sometimes obtained as donations from advertising agencies.

Box 10.3 Sample topics of press releases by the WWF, spring 2014

- New analysis: America's largest companies are jumping on clean energy bandwagon and saving more than $1 billion a year
- WWF: Australia must heed warning to protect Great Barrier Reef
- Major conservation win: Oil company backs off oil exploration in Africa's oldest national park
- WWF: Stiff sentence for rhino horn smuggler is game changer in wildlife trafficking fight
- New Federal conservation program rightly prioritizes grassland conservation
- Africa's longest-known terrestrial wildlife migration discovered
- Watercourses convention provides tools to defuse international water conflict
- Ghana steps up efforts to combat illegal tuna fishing
- Climate assessment drives home importance of US emissions reductions
- Jane Goodall, Leonardo DiCaprio and Dave Matthews join businesses and conservation groups to sign open letter supporting US ivory restrictions
- NRC report underscores risks of Arctic drilling
- White House plugs into the power of solar
- New research estimates more than $1.3 billion in illegally caught fish entering US annually
- Report: The renewable energy revolution is here

Source: <http://www.worldwildlife.org/>

The format of a news release for print media helps ensure that it is easy for reporters to use. Contacts, dates, and the five Ws—who, what, where, when, and why—must be carefully composed and structured for easy reading. The structure of a news release places the most important information in the first or "lead" paragraph. The five Ws that may be included in the lead paragraph cogently answer the questions: Who is the story about? What happened? Where did it happen? When did it happen? Why did it happen? And, finally, an H—How did it happen?

The lead paragraph must capture the essence of your story, and tell the reader something of value. It also needs to grab the editor, so that your story will be published. The remaining paragraphs flesh out the story by providing necessary details. The body of the story often uses quotes from the people involved, particularly the project leader, to give the story a human element and to add interest. The release should stay focused on your communications objective. If there is an action or behavior that you want from the reader, make sure your message states it clearly. Make an outline of the major points of your story and sequence them from most important to least important.

The structure of a news release can be diagrammed as an inverted pyramid (Fig. 10.2). The least important information is placed at the end. Editors will cut the article from the bottom up to fit the space available. By placing key material first, you minimize the risk of losing it. The closing paragraph often describes the mission of your organization

Fig. 10.2 The format for a news release resembles an inverted pyramid.

or agency. Often, but not always, this will be cut. Mention your organization's name and location near the beginning of the story to ensure that it is included. Sometimes a reporter will rewrite the piece, but often it will just be published.

The headline of your news release should get the editor's attention while also highlighting your message. Headlines must be accurate, brief, and tell the reader who did what. They may contain a humorous or dramatic statement. The headline that you write for your news release is unlikely to be used by the paper; its main purpose is to catch the editor's eye.

The story should be of interest to a wide range of people. Emphasize readers' needs, concerns, and desires, and make your message fill the needs or satisfy the desires. Self-interest compels attention. When possible, tell your message as a story and put people in it. Editors of local papers, in particular, must emphasize the local angle of a story. Readers want to know the relevance of a news story to their lives.

As you will notice when reading a newspaper, brevity is key. Sentences are short. Paragraphs also are short, made up of only a few sentences. News releases are seldom longer than one page. The trend toward lower reading abilities or lowered appetites for reading among the public means that your press release must use simple words and sentences to reach the maximum number of readers. Additional information can be included with the release in the form of fact sheets and background material for use by the media.

The professional appearance of your news release, with a double-spaced type, ample margins, and simple-to-read style, can help predispose the editor to react positively to its content. Send your news release to a specific person at the media outlet. Use his or her name, not just "Editor," and begin to establish a rapport with the people who may cover your activities. Check with colleagues at other organizations that get good press coverage for a recommendation of relevant reporters, bloggers, or editors.

The example in Box 10.4 demonstrates the format, with the release date, contacts, headline, and body of the text. If the news release is more than one page, write "more" at the bottom of the page. Indicate the end of the piece by typing "####" below the last line.

Box 10.4 Example news release announcing Earth Hour

Go Dark for Earth Hour, Saturday, March 29 at 8:30 p.m. Local Time

Date: March 25, 2014

   Media Contact: Lorin Hancock [phone]

   Links in Press Release: Climate Change, Keya Chatterjee

   Buttons to: Share on Facebook, Tweet on Twitter, Share on Google +

On Saturday March 29th at 8:30 p.m., millions of people across the world are switching off lights for one hour to celebrate their commitment to the planet. Participants in Earth Hour will include iconic landmarks like the Empire State Building and the St. Louis Gateway Arch; major cities around the globe including Chicago and Las Vegas; and individuals in more than 150 countries as part of the world's largest voluntary environmental action.

"Earth Hour is an annual display of how our imagination can inspire and engage hundreds of millions to focus on the one thing that unites us—our planet," said Keya Chatterjee, director of renewable energy and footprint outreach for World Wildlife Fund (WWF). "In addition to raising global awareness, we are also transforming that excitement into local action to prepare our communities for the impacts of extreme weather and climate change."

While turning off the lights for an hour serves as a symbolic gesture, participants can go beyond the hour with simple changes to reduce energy consumption year-round. Homeowners can make a huge impact by installing solar panels, but even small changes like switching to LED light bulbs, taking public transportation, or wasting less food can make a difference.

####

Source: Hancock (2014).

Whenever possible, a photograph or graphic picture should be included with the release to illustrate the story. As the saying goes, a picture is worth a thousand words. An intriguing, high-quality photo can help get your release published and catch the reader's eye. For example, charming photographs of monk seals and fishermen were available to accompany a press release produced by the Mediterranean office of the WWF to promote their conservation project in the Aegean Sea.

News releases are often a key part of an entire press packet that attracts and facilitates the media to cover your conservation program. The WWF organized a press trip to publicize the story of a fishing community that had turned into guardians of critically endangered monk seals (*Monachus monachus*) on the Turkish coast. The communications officer for the WWF-Mediterranean program, Sampreethi Aipanjiguly, made sure that the story of their work with a local NGO (SAD-AFAG), fishermen, and monk seals in Aydincik, Turkey, targeted international—French, German, Italian, and British— media that reached audiences in places with many people who take summer vacations to the Turkish coast and other Mediterranean destinations.

In order to make the press release interesting to readers, Aipanjiguly wrote it as a feature story (Box 10.5). She followed guidelines and (1) put specific people into the piece, (2) told a story, and (3) let the readers see and hear the situation for themselves through

---

Box 10.5 Fishermen and monk seals on the Turkish coast

[Feature news release from the WWF announcing their project with fishermen and monk seals on the Turkish coast.]

WWF-Mediterranean Letterhead Stationary

For Immediate Release

Date

Contact: Sampreethi Aipanjiguly, Communications Officer, WWF-Mediterranean

Yeim Aslan, Communications Contact, SAD-AFAG

[address, phone, and email listed]

Guardians of the monk seals: Fishermen are helping endangered seals through a WWF project on the Turkish coast

It's still cool at five in the morning. Ahmet "Charlie" Orhan steers his small boat across the glassy Mediterranean waters, glowing pink in the early morning light. He's heading for his fishing nets, laid the night before just off the rocky shoreline, and now hopefully full of fish.

All around the Mediterranean, thousands more fishermen are similarly fetching the night's catch. But although the scene is timeless, today is a special day for Charlie and the other fishermen from the small town of Aydincik, Turkey. Today the governor will open the new shop of their fishery cooperative—the latest achievement in ongoing work that's giving the fishermen, and the endangered Mediterranean monk seal, a better chance for survival.

Like some other artisanal fishermen around the world, he's concerned about declining numbers of fish.

"In the 1980s, there were so many fish," he says. But now we don't see the same number or variety.

The culprits are trawlers. These boats, which come from bigger cities and whose huge nets indiscriminately catch everything that crosses their path, are not supposed to fish closer than 3 miles from shore. The inshore area is reserved for artisanal fishermen like Charlie—locals who set a small number of nets to supply their town with fish.

But as they have fished out the deeper water, trawlers have—illegally—come closer and closer to shore over the past 20 years.

Fewer fish is bad news for fishermen. It's also bad news for the Mediterranean monk seal.

These shy animals once lived in colonies along the coasts of the Black Sea, the Mediterranean, and the Atlantic Ocean from Portugal to Senegal. But today they are one of the rarest mammals in the world.

"Only 500 remain," says Yalcin Savas, Head of Conservation at SAD-AFAG, a Turkish group that works with WWF on monk seal conservation issues.

quotes and descriptions. Of course, as for any news release, Aipanjiguly followed the rules to keep it short and clear. She wrote a good headline that captured attention, and included essential information. The press release provided the backbone of the story the journalists would experience on their press trip to the Turkish coast.

10.3.3 Evaluation

The extent of the distribution and reproduction of your news release provides immediate feedback about its success. The international media attention that the WWF stimulated helped build regional political support for their monk seal project and recognition of the illegal fishing crisis. Locally, the mayor increased his support for the fishermen, using patrol boats to halt illegal fishing activities. The WWF's partner organization received more attention for their model program and made plans to build on this experience in other areas. The fishermen reported that they appreciated the attention the publicity created for their new cooperative fish store. In the long-term, the WWF has reported program success: the fishermen developed more stable incomes through fisheries cooperatives and illegal fishing is declining. Monk seal breeding caves were protected, and the fishermen have become their guardians, patrolling against activities that may harm the animals. As monk seal populations stabilized, the project expanded to Greece and the Cilician Basin (WWF 2014).

10.4 Brochures

Brochures are typically produced to introduce a broad audience to an organization's goals and activities. Brochures can describe environmental management objectives, special facts about an agency or site, or details about an important conservation campaign. Text is combined with graphics or photographs to create an appealing publication. Brochures are often useful for increasing membership or raising funds. They can fit in an envelope or pocket, and can be easily downloaded from a website. They can be grouped in a dispenser to target different audiences. In some cases, reading a brochure may be the first way a prospective member or supporter learns about your organization.

Brochures are a commonly used written format for interpretation at parks and refuges. They are distributed as hand-outs at sites, exhibits, and trails, mailed to groups planning a site visit, and used for membership drives. Brochures also are dispensed at nearby hotels and at other public parks or agencies.

People can pick up brochures and read them at their leisure. This allows you to provide detailed information about a conservation activity—from steps to attract backyard birds or remove exotic plants, to measures to protect groundwater or maps of regional parks. People also can save brochures as a souvenir or a reference for future use.

10.4.1 Planning

Your communication goal and specific audience will dictate the design and content for a brochure. To attract most audiences, a brochure should have a catchy title, bright colors and design elements, and an inviting layout. Collect and study brochures from other organizations that catch your eye before deciding on a design for your own brochure.

For the lay public, if the cover of a brochure does not look inviting, few will make the effort to delve into the text, no matter how scintillating the writing. Beyond the cover, you need relevant and interesting content to keep their attention and accomplish your communication goals.

Careful planning will ensure that all the elements of a brochure—paper size, color, illustrations, layout, and text—all work together. Once you have identified the main goal of the brochure, consider the interests and concerns of the audience as you frame the message and design the brochure to attract them. Important considerations about the target audience will also dictate the format—from inclusion of more than one language and a reliance on illustrations for multilingual audiences, to large print for older audiences. For the general public, text written at a typical middle school reading level is appropriate, although draft versions of your brochure should be tested with the audience before proceeding to publication.

Your budget will influence your choice of colors and paper for your brochure. Full color photographs on glossy paper may be easiest to attract attention, but it is also the most expensive format. Careful use of space and catchy titles and graphic design can make even a single-color brochure practically irresistible. Most word processing programs include a function for creating different types of brochures. With these easy-to-use programs, you can experiment with different layouts and get feedback before publishing.

The Earth Sanctuaries Foundation of Australia produced a brochure to publicize their program to residents and tourists. The Earth Sanctuaries Foundation provides a refuge for wildlife by restoring native habitat and excluding alien predators such as foxes and cats. The brochure features an attractive montage of photographs of unusual-looking, endangered Australian wildlife, including platypuses and numbats, to catch their audience's attention. The cover solicits interest with their theme "Saving our wildlife from extinction." Like most organizations, this brochure describes their mission and objectives, concrete examples of achievements, and areas of funding need. After briefly describing the problems and solutions for Australia's threatened animals, the brochure suggests the action that readers should take. Brief text follows each of the following headings:

- The sad history
- Now—a life raft for our precious species
- Making a real difference
- Providing a long-term solution
- You can help us

A convenient membership form can be detached from the brochure and mailed in with a contribution—"Yes I want to help save Australia's threatened wildlife and their habitats!"

10.4.2 Implementation

Brochure cover

Keep the title brief and thematic. Short titles of fewer than 10 words attract more readers. For example "Farm birds: Nature's pest controllers" or "Water—lifeblood of the

Fig. 10.3 Brochure covers with exciting graphics and clear messages from the New South Wales (NSW) National Parks and Wildlife Service, the Wildlife Conservation Society, and the Bahamas National Trust.

Everglades" give a snappy overview of the theme of the brochure. Keep your target audience in mind; if the brochure is for recreational users, mention hikers, boaters, or other audiences in the title: "Birders' guide to seeing and protecting shorebirds" is tantalizing to birdwatchers, while "Native bees are valuable crop pollinators" targets a key concern of farmers. Draw readers into your text by emphasizing their personal interest.

A single photograph or illustration on the cover is usually more effective than multiple visuals (Fig. 10.3). Make the visual interesting by showing something happening. Action shots of a bear eating berries or people hiking through a forest have more appeal than a sleeping bear or a forest setting. Use bright colors or a high-contrast design to attract people. Select colors that help emphasize your theme, such as red for a brochure on prescribed fire or blue for aquatic ecology.

Body

The body of the brochure should make use of subtitles, photographs, and other graphics to break up the writing. Many people will only read the headlines, so you need to make it obvious why the reader should continue. Some tips for increasing readability include:

- Use wide margins and extra white space (empty areas) around the headlines and between sections to make the brochure look easy to read. Empty areas attract a reader's attention.

Box 10.6 Tips for effective writing

The following tips will ensure your story will be read. Classic writing guides such as Zinsser (1985) or Strunk and White (1979), and a variety of online editing programs can be consulted for further guidance:

- Write with nouns and verbs. Adjectives and adverbs seldom add vigor to a story. For example, "The wolf howled," is more compelling than, "The wolf called loudly."
- Use action verbs to keep a story moving and interest the reader, rather than "to be" verbs that show little action.
- Use the active voice ("The biologist darted the tiger") not the passive voice ("The tiger was darted by the biologist").
- Use simple, ordinary language. Avoid jargon and elaborate words; for example, write "use," not "utilize," and "now," not "at the present time."
- Avoid using qualifiers, such as very, rather, and little. They sap strength from your statements.
- Be clear. As Mark Twain admonished: Say what you propose to say, don't merely come near it.
- Choose the right word, not its second cousin.
- Know your reader: relay your message using elements of interest to the reader.
- Use personal words, where appropriate, like "you," "we," a person's name, or a direct quote to appeal to the reader.
- Be specific and provide details; do not be vague.
- Be concise. Short sentences and paragraphs are easier to read.
- Revise, revise, revise. The delete key is your best friend.

- Use a simple font to make the page look inviting.
- Try using direct quotes or question and answer approaches. These often entice people to continue reading.
- Use bullets or check-boxes to add interest and organize the text.
- Use simple graphics, maps, and charts.
- Put captions (in a different size or font from the text) under photos and graphics. People often read captions, second only to headlines.
- Follow the tips for effective writing (Box 10.6).

10.4.3 Evaluation

All education and outreach materials benefit from feedback. Get some members of your target audience to evaluate your brochure before you invest in publication. They can help you avoid the common mistakes in brochure design that reduce readership. The problem ABC's of the brochure reader include:

- *Aggravation*. The page is too jammed with information. The type is hard to read or too close together. Organization is poor or non-existent. The page lacks white spaces and does not provide breathing space for the poor reader.

- *Boredom.* Nothing in the brochure stands out; it looks like a page of gray. Headlines are too small. Columns are too wide. Text is too long. Paragraphs and sentences are too long or complex.
- *Confusion.* The reader cannot follow the flow of the text, visuals interrupt reading, or the headings and subheadings are indistinguishable.

Pilot testing a draft of the brochure with the target audience can help ensure its success. After publication, tracking the numbers of brochures taken or downloaded suggests their appeal or utility to the audience. Surveys of the audience, through a tear-out response sheet or formal sampling, can provide data on the particular impacts of the brochure. Some organizations include brochure-specific phone or electronic contact details for readers to receive further information. This allows an organization to track the number of inquiries related to a brochure.

10.5 Fact sheets and flyers

Fact sheets and flyers serve a variety of purposes. Many large conservation organizations have fact sheets available for the press and public that can be emailed to specific audiences or perused on their websites. Fact sheets or flyers can be sent to constituents or reporters with information about new study results, activities, and updates on projects. They can be used to answer questions from the general public. They can be posted on a bulletin board or pulled from an envelope.

As a result of their many functions, fact sheets and flyers come in a variety of styles and forms. However, good ones have several things in common. They are short (one or two pages) written messages that grab someone's attention. They are well-organized and easy to read. They generally focus on a specific topic and provide sufficient detail about an activity or issue so that the reader can understand the subject. Longer fact sheets can be designed to cover a complex topic, but breaking the information into several fact sheets is often preferable. People are more inclined to read brief materials.

Fact sheets and flyers are often used to give the press and the public a better understanding of a subject area in which they are already interested. The Wildlife Society, a professional organization established in North America in 1937, produces fact sheets on issues related to wildlife management and conservation, which may accompany position statements the Society adopts on a particular topic. Members of The Wildlife Society, as well as non-members, are encouraged to distribute the fact sheets in support of efforts to educate decision-makers, the public, and other stakeholders on issues that affect wildlife. Their fact sheets cover topics such as captive deer breeding, feral and free-ranging domestic cats, feral horses and burros, lead ammunition and wildlife, and North American wolves (see <http://wildlife.org/get-involved/policy/fact-sheets/>).

The design of a fact sheet or flyer must fulfill two purposes. First, it has to get the attention of the reader for your main message. Second, it has to help the reader absorb the information that you present. It will need to include information and data that readers will find interesting and engaging.

Visual displays of information, unlike plain text, encourage a diversity of individual viewer styles and types of understanding (Tufte 1990). Colors, graphic design, illustrations, and photographs can attract and invite the reader to engage with the information in an entertaining and thoughtful manner. Flyers that are posted and passed out at functions are characterized by a large, catchy title to convey the essence of the flyer, large type that is easy to read, a lot of white space to make it inviting, and a professional-quality photograph (see Chapter 6) or illustrations to enliven the page and emphasize the message.

Fact sheets and flyers are an economical and time-saving technique for communicating with multiple audiences. Good fact sheets help replace the time-consuming chores of sending detailed emails to interested individuals or providing long explanations on the phone. The information in fact sheets is clear and consistent. Also, it is easy to add new information to an organization's collection of materials and post the fact sheet online.

10.5.1 Planning

First, imagine the typical readers you need to reach. Like all communication techniques, keep this image foremost in your mind as you design a fact sheet or flyer with a message that is relevant to them. Similar to planning a brochure, you will need to consider online constraints or how many copies you will need, as well as other printing decisions about ink, paper, and color, dictated by your budget and audience. If you are designing a fact sheet to support a press release, think like a journalist and include historical, factual, and anecdotal information that could be used in an in-depth story.

The Xerces Society for Invertebrate Conservation produces a series of fact sheets targeting farmers in California, USA (Xerces Society 2014). A fact sheet targeting watermelon farmers, "Native bee pollination of watermelon," provides information about watermelon pollination, native bee ecology, and conservation. Because of the specific audience it was targeting, detailed information could be presented. The first sentence in the fact sheet touches the wallet of any farmer: "Pollination by bees is critical for a successful watermelon crop." The fact sheet continues with information about the effectiveness of native bees for pollination, how to recognize and protect native bees, and how to enhance pollinator habitat.

When developing a fact sheet or flyer, make a list of key ideas that are crucial for you and your audience. Prioritize them and select the one basic theme or idea for your written material. Develop three to five main points or examples that explain your theme. People have trouble remembering more than five main points (Jacobson 2009). Once you have focused on your message, you can consider pictures, illustrations, graphics, and layout to attract your audience. Make sure your call-to-action or the objective of the flyer is clear and that the reader can see these elements without having to search for them. If your organization intends to create more than one fact sheet, you will need to develop a standard format and to identify your organization with a logo or recognizable style. Remember to provide easily located contact information, including a name, phone or text number, email address, and website address.

The distribution of your fact sheet or flyer will influence the format. The planning process helps you determine the audiences, how you will reach them, how much money you can spend, what public places or online sites are available for distribution of your material, how many people will help with distribution, and how fast the information must be got out. You will need to decide if you are planning to hand out the material, send it in the mail, distribute it through literature shelves or bulletin boards, or post online via email, listservs, social media sites, or a website.

The format for your fact sheet or flyer will vary according to the chosen distribution method. A flyer destined for bulletin boards must have big, simple headlines, lots of space, little verbiage, and distinctive graphics to make it stand out from the myriad of other flyers posted. A mailed flyer must look attractive when it appears at the door. A graphic or provocative headline should attract attention on the cover and space must be left for addresses and stamps. Web pages demand equal care in their layout to ensure easy reading for the viewer (see Chapter 11).

10.5.2 Implementation

Your publication will need to attract a reader's attention, hold their interest, spark their desire to learn more, and lead them to action. To grab a reader's attention, the title should communicate the primary message of the fact sheet or flyer. It should highlight the theme and attract attention to the page. An effective title is short—fewer than eight words. If a longer title is needed, a smaller subheading can be used. A good photograph or graphic image should highlight your theme.

Once you have the reader's attention, you need to hold their interest with important relevant details about your activity, issue, or subject of concern. Short, simple sentences, and everyday language help to keep a reader interested.

Excite the reader about your topic. Awaken a desire to learn more about the subject. A beautiful picture or descriptive detail showing why the reader should care about the topic can help them focus on how it might affect or improve their lives.

Once you have people's interest and concern, you will want to lead them to action. Depending on the objective of your fact sheet or flyer, provide a compelling reason for the reader to act. Be clear and direct in exactly how they may take action.

The visual design of your fact sheet or flyer can help ensure you move the reader from attention to action. Pictures are important for telling a story. Even newspapers that were once composed mostly of text have increased their use of pictures and graphics to attract readers. Online sites can support multiple images, videos, and links to other informative materials. Headings and pictures are crucial for getting readers' attention on a website or a homepage like Yahoo.

The weekly news section of the *New York Times* used to be mostly text. Now pictures, drawings, big catchy headlines, and bold layouts with a lot of white space fill the pages as they are viewed online. Graphic designers recommend that you devote two-thirds of your publication to pictures, white space, and headings (Beamish 1995).

Good graphic design can help ensure your written material is read. A number of factors should be considered as you are designing your fact sheet or flyer, or almost any printed material:

- Have a dominant focus on the page to attract the eye. This can be a headline or a picture. Too many bold features can cause confusion. If you emphasize everything, you emphasize nothing. By creating a hierarchy of design elements emphasizing a bold title and photograph or illustration and de-emphasizing less important information you will help lead the reader through the brochure.

- Pictures do more than decorate your text. Choose the right photograph or graphic that will help make your point and hook the casual reader. Other pictures should illustrate key points, so readers can tell the general message at a glance. Remember, people like to look at other people in your pictures (Chapter 6), just as they like to read about them in your text.
- Clarity and simplicity are key to an effective page. Respect readers' time and attention by providing information as concisely and attractively as possible. If readers have to search for clues about the purpose of the flyer, or for the contact information for the organization, they probably will not bother.
- Stick to one or two varieties of typeface in a flyer. Although your computer might offer hundreds of fonts, refrain from using more than two. Designers use a large, bold type for headlines and key captions, and a smaller, easy-to-read typeface for text. Dark letters on a light background provide a stark, legible contrast. White letters on a dark background can highlight a headline, but are more difficult to read.
- Make it easy for people to read the text. If the type is too small, the columns too wide, or the paragraphs too long, few readers will want to work hard enough to read it. Blocks of text can be broken up by interspersing short paragraphs with longer ones, indenting paragraphs, and using bold subheadings and bullet points. Even better, rewrite your text to be more concise and use more photos, graphics, and white space.
- Use illustrations that are relevant to your theme and objectives. Drawings or photographs should draw attention to or dramatize your message.
- Use charts and pictures to help explain complex ideas. Make sure your audience recognizes any symbols, maps, or diagrams you use by pilot testing your visual aids with the target audience.
- Use color creatively. Color enlivens and decorates your printed material. Color can serve as a label, such as green for forest and blue for water, or as a measure of quantity on a chart, such as showing more and fewer whale sightings by varying the value and saturation of the color.
- Be aware that pure, bright, or very strong colors can have loud, unbearable effects when they spread over large areas adjacent to each other, but extraordinary effects can be achieved when they are used sparingly on or between dull background tones (Tufte 1990). Small, bright areas will stand out vividly against gray or neutral backgrounds.
- To maintain a sense of unity, use the same colors throughout the written material, repeating color combinations. The text, illustrations, graphics, and white space in-between should feel balanced visually.
- Allow the eye to move in one general direction when reading the flyer, instead of a serpentine type pattern. Make sure there are proper column breaks with pleasing, but not unnecessary spaces.

• Have a clear, visible logo or organization name so that readers will know who to contact and how.

10.5.3 Evaluation

Feedback from the target audience during the planning process should help with decisions about color scheme, font size, layout, and graphics. Your pilot test can ask the audience: Which is easier to read? Which communicates more clearly? Do they see themselves in the photos? Once published, feedback will reveal if your message, content, and design are doing the job. Organizations can track the number of "hits" on fact sheets appearing on their website, as well as requests from the target audience for further information about the environmental issue. Assessing whether journalists use your information in subsequent media articles will reveal if your material was appealing and useful. The ultimate sign that the fact sheets or flyers have been successful is by monitoring whether your specific audience takes the desired action. For the Xerces Society, an increasing number of watermelon farmers setting habitat aside for native bees would indicate success.

If there is little response to your material, your method of dissemination, content, and graphic design all need to be re-tested with the audience to determine how to make improvements. Expert review of your materials by public relations specialists or graphic designers can help you evaluate the quality of your fact sheet or flyer. Continual review of materials produced for similar audiences by other organizations and businesses can provide ideas for making your material more effective.

10.6 Guidebooks

What's that bird? Where are the hiking trails? How do I monitor my management program? Guidebooks serve many purposes, from identification of plants and animals to park guides for visitors. They have helped resource managers improve their management activities and landowners protect threatened species. Whether in print or online, from simple identification phone apps to complex field guides, they can target a variety of audiences. Guidebooks use text and illustrations to disseminate ideas from basic to technical.

Guidebooks can help people become aware of conservation targets and learn new information and skills. A study of the development of field guides to tropical forest plants was initiated by the Forestry Research Program at Oxford University, UK. They found that guidebooks could promote global exchange of information about plants from international to local grassroots levels. Information about tropical plant species allowed better use of plants by collectors of non-timber forest products and by tour guides. Plant guides also could help influence farmers not to burn a valuable tree on their farm. In Bolivia, older community members felt that young people would be an ideal target audience for guidebooks to help retain indigenous knowledge of plants and animals that was being lost (Hawthorne and Lawrence 2013).

The sale of guidebooks also can generate income for local organizations. A plant guide to the trees of Brazil, *Arvores Brasileiras*, was produced in Brazil by author Harri Lorenzi. Researchers use the book for reference, while the high-quality photographs and large format also make it popular among middle-class Brazilians with an interest in nature. Lorenzi directs a private research institute that produces the guides and the proceeds of book sales fund employment of four scientists and an airplane for botanical research in the Amazon (Hawthorne and Lawrence 2013).

10.6.1 Planning

Clear identification of the purpose and target audiences for your guidebook is a critical first step. No matter how good your writing and graphics may be, the guide will fail unless it serves the needs of your organization and the audience. Audiences for guidebooks have varying technical knowledge, ways of communicating, and levels of formal education. Creating a scientifically accurate guidebook that is usable by readers with different literacy levels or languages is a challenge.

The content, format, length, design, and size should be geared to achieving your objectives with the audience in mind. Who will use your guidebook and how will they use it? Examine guidebooks you like to provide models for layout, type, graphics, and writing style. Getting feedback from members of your target audience at this initial stage can help steer you in the right direction. Take some time to research what the audience might be looking for—what styles, formats, and approaches resonate with them. If your audience intends to use the guidebook in the field, a portable size or laminated cover might be most useful, or your audience may wish for a downloadable version.

Consulting the users of your guidebook during the planning process will help ensure its usefulness. The authors of a tree guide for agroforestry production in Bolivia selected the species to be included in consultation with local community members and botanists (Hawthorne and Lawrence 2013). The authors visited communities in the four regions to be included in their guidebook. In each community they asked men and women to rank the top ten species they felt should be included in a guide. Botanists added to this prioritized list to include species which they considered to have potential for agroforestry, but which were not yet well known to farmers. Thirty of the lowest priority species were cut from the list of 100 species to produce a guide that was within the available budget (Hawthorne and Lawrence 2013).

Once you have some ideas about the ideal guidebook design, talk with a printer to discuss the costs of various layouts, paper types, colors, and length. You may need to compromise on some choices to stay within your budget. Will the guidebook be for sale or provided free of charge? Or both? Will the guidebook be available to download via your website? Will you develop a parallel downloadable phone app? The Bay Islands Conservation Association in Honduras provided free copies of a full-color guidebook to the natural history of the islands to all school teachers through a grant from a development agency to produce 1000 copies; revenues from the sale of the guidebooks to tourists subsidized additional printings (Jacobson 1992) (Fig. 10.4).

Fig. 10.4 The cover of a guidebook about marine conservation shows people enjoying the marine habitat. (Cover photo by Rick Frehsee.)

Budgets will often force compromises in the size, quality, and format of your guidebook. Be sure that your skills are a match for the requirements of producing a guidebook. You or your organization's staff must have good writing skills, good photographic or illustration skills, and good layout and design skills. Keep in mind that you must also know what will appeal to the target audience, as well as the people writing the guidebook.

If particular expertise is missing in your organization, additional staff or volunteers may be available to supply the necessary skills. Businesses and community members may be willing to provide support to conservation organizations for a worthy cause, such as developing an educational guidebook. Photographers may be willing to donate pictures for the venture. Professional writers and artists can also be hired if your budget is adequate, or photographs purchased from stock photo agencies. Some businesses may underwrite your costs in exchange for the opportunity for free advertising in your publication, or the creation of good public relations. Students from a local secondary school could help do research and writing for a place-based community project.

Once you are clear about the type of guidebook you are producing, establish a realistic schedule for the dates to complete research, preparation, audience feedback, and finally publication.

10.6.2 Implementation

To maximize your resources, it is important to have a plan and follow a structured approach. Begin by planning the details of your writing and thinking through the information required. It may be beneficial to draft a working document that includes any special equipment you may need, expertise or illustrations you may need to obtain, a timetable for fieldwork, an itinerary, and time for writing. It is important to focus your attention on the goal of your guidebook and exclude material that does not contribute to the goal.

When you actually write the guidebook, always keep the reader in mind. The objective is to be clear and easily understood. The material should attract the attention and interest of the reader, and elicit the desired reaction. The aim may be the successful identification of a butterfly, understanding of a camping technique, or a new skill in native plant gardening.

In order to achieve these results, the writing must be concise, direct, and jargon-free. Follow the rules of good writing reviewed in Box 10.6. Define or illustrate new terms when needed. Glossaries, keys, charts, and illustrations can help simplify complex terms or concepts. An easy-to-read typeface, uncluttered design, and attractive photographs, drawings, or graphics, all help ensure that your guidebook will be used. Similar to other written materials, a thematic title for the guidebook should state its content and target audience. *Valuable Tree Species for Agroforestry on Small Farms* or *Guide to Aquatic Insect Ecology for Fly Fishermen* should pique the curiosity of the target audience of farmers or anglers.

Keep in mind the audience for the guidebook when you determine the design. The Education for Nature organization in Vietnam produces a guidebook about ecosystems in a comic book format (Fig. 10.5.). They incorporate student activities, games, puzzles, and stories with abundant illustrations to appeal to their young audience.

A team approach was required to produce the useful guidebook *Flora da Resera Ducke* [Flora of the Ducke Reserve] (Ribeiro et al. 1999). The audience for the guide was tropical biologists who needed to identify plants in the field. Thirty-seven specialists and several local experts on tree identification helped to identify plant material for the book. A group of Brazilian botanists and students helped integrate the knowledge from the specialists to design a user-friendly guide to their reserve in the Amazon Basin, where little information is available. Their decision to include photographs of the leaves, bark, and venation of each species allows users in the field to identify trees (Hawthorne and Lawrence 2013).

Fig. 10.5 A student activity guidebook about ecosystems uses a comic book format to attract the young audience (Education for Nature, Vietnam).

Once you have completed a draft of your guidebook, get colleagues and members of the target audience to review it for clarity and relevance, as well as interest. To be successful, guidebooks should provide accurate information that improves the capabilities of the reader. Some factors to test are listed in Box 10.7. Use audience and expert feedback to revise the guidebook. Test it again with the audience if many revisions are made.

You also need to decide on a strategy for marketing the book. The intended audience must be aware of the book, interested to read the content, and motivated to obtain it. Dissemination of the guidebook at a park headquarters, via your website, through an organizational membership list, or in conjunction with other guidebook markets, may help it to successfully reach your audience.

> **Box 10.7** Design considerations for developing guidebooks for specific audiences
>
> - The purpose and content of guidebook are clear.
> - The format is easy to understand.
> - The information is accurate.
> - The content is relevant for the target audience.
> - The language, amount of text, and themes are appropriate for audience.
> - Keys, indices, maps, captions, color codes, and other systems to guide readers are simple and easy to use.
> - The layout and graphic design are attractive.
> - The illustrations or photographs aid identification or description of the subject.
> - The number, size, scale, and quality of illustrations are appropriate for audience.
> - The guidebook is easy and enjoyable to use.
> - The size and durability of the guidebook are suitable for purpose.
> - If the guidebook is for sale, the audience is willing and able to pay for it.
> - Dissemination plans—in print and online—will ensure availability of the guidebook for the target audience.

10.6.3 Evaluation

Audience feedback and expert review during the production of a guidebook are key components in ensuring its ultimate success. Review by audience members of draft versions of the guidebook can identify unclear text, graphics, and illustrations. Ambiguous language, inappropriate material, or overly complex directions can be weeded out before you go to the expense of final production.

The World Conservation Union and WWF developed a guidebook for managers of marine protected areas (MPA), entitled *How is your MPA doing? A Guidebook of Natural and Social Indicators for Evaluating Marine Protected Area Management Effectiveness* (Pomeroy et al. 2004). The goal of the guidebook was to help managers assess the success of their management actions. The guidebook was developed, tested, evaluated, and revised over a 3-year period. Initially, the authors hosted a workshop to collect feedback on the MPA management indicators from 30 recognized experts on MPAs from around the world. A draft guidebook with proposed indicators was reviewed at a workshop for 22 volunteer MPA "pilot" sites. The revised indicators were tested by the pilot sites and reviewed again by experts. Box 10.8 shows some questions from the expert review forms and pilot MPA evaluation forms for the guidebook. The comments from peer reviewers and the pilot sites resulted in the production of a third, "working" draft of the guidebook. This draft was released by the IUCN at the Fifth World Parks Congress in 2003, along with an invitation for review comments from interested individuals. This feedback helped create the fourth version of the guidebook.

It is often difficult for authors to receive feedback about their guidebooks after publication. Monitoring the distribution and use of guidebooks, demonstrations of changes

Box 10.8 Sample questions from expert review forms and pilot MPA evaluation forms used for developing a guidebook to evaluate management of MPAs

Expert reviewers considered the following questions in their review:

1. Is the indicator described accurately and the layout a valid method for measurement?
2. Is the description of the indicator written clearly and is it easy to understand?
3. Is the indicator and related information user-friendly?
4. Is there any additional information on how to use the indicator?
5. Are there additional reference materials?

Pilot MPA managers evaluated items such as:

1. List the most relevant strengths and weaknesses of your selected indicators in measuring management effectiveness.

Indicator	Number	Strengths	Weaknesses/problems
Biophysical			
Socioeconomic			
Governance/administrative			

2. Please comment on problems that occurred in your site while measuring some of the indicators (specify the indicator and methods/instruments used).

Courtesy of John Parks, co-author of *How is Your MPA Doing?* (Pomeroy et al. 2004).

in audience knowledge or skills, and informal polling of readers can help indicate success. User evaluation forms can be used to elicit audience feedback if there is a convenient way for the user to return the form, such during a visit to a park or zoo or online at a website. Feedback is certainly needed before updating and reprinting a guidebook, or creating a new one based on an untested model.

The popularity and use of the MPA guidebook is one indicator of its success. Several thousand English copies of the guidebook are in circulation, and new versions in Spanish, French, and other languages have been released. Monitoring of the US National Oceanic and Atmospheric Administration (NOAA) website, with the free PDF version of the guidebook and information about the MPA pilot sites, recorded over 1200 hits per day when it was first released. According to John Parks, co-author of the guidebook from NOAA, the ultimate success of the guidebook will be viewed through two lenses: first, if in 5 years' time MPA managers and administrators have integrated the guidebook's management effectiveness evaluations seamlessly into their management actions and budgets; and second, if in 10 years' time the marine conservation community can more accurately gauge the degree to which management efforts are resulting in the desired biological and social impacts. Parks hopes that someday the guidebook will become obsolete because MPAs are routinely using the principles outlined in their book.

In this case feedback from the audience was crucial to developing a useful guidebook. "What really allowed us to produce a useful document were the three rounds of careful peer review and practical feedback from the 22 volunteer MPA sites, who tested a draft version of the guidebook," explains Parks. "This cumulative feedback was instrumental in making the publication user-friendly and logical. It helped us think about how to best design the guidebook for ease of use and navigation, particularly because there is a lot of material for the reader to get through, and much of it is somewhat dry. We realized the need to use full color and many photos, in addition to the navigation tools—color-coded tabs for the indicators, consistent indicator outlines and descriptions, and an easy-to-use flow diagram of the four steps in completing an MPA evaluation."

10.7 Summary

Using the written word for education and outreach is an essential technique for accomplishing the conservation objectives of many organizations and agencies. Harnessing the power of mass media through editorials, blogs, and news releases provides the means to get information to vast numbers of people in a trusted and reliable format. This type of free advertising is valuable to everyone dealing with critical conservation issues and tight budgets. Knowledge of the structure and format for producing these materials is necessary for success in the competitive mass media arena.

Fact sheets, flyers, brochures, and guidebooks can help conservation organizations to build audience awareness, increase knowledge, and foster new conservation skills. Producing effective written materials is hard work, but involving the audience in the planning process can help ensure that the content and format will be appropriate and useful. Studying how words, type, graphics, and space are used in other publications will help you determine why some materials succeed and others fail. The guidelines presented for clear writing and attractive graphic design should help guarantee that your target audience will notice, read, and act on your materials.

11
Taking advantage of technology

The introduction of any type of technology into a learning environment usually promises to revolutionize education by making it more efficient, more effective, and more powerful. Some innovative technologies, like the digital camera, are genuinely helpful to educators by supplementing and enhancing the learning process. But other technologies, such as websites or smartphones, have the potential to fundamentally alter how educational opportunities are designed. This chapter can help managers and program developers consider how to use technology effectively.

Classroom teachers, school administrators, and agency administrators have a number of important considerations when planning how to best use new educational technology. For educators of young people, one goal is to help students become proficient in using technologies that are meaningful and relevant to their interests. In some cases this will mean using an interactive model on a computer, in others it could mean measuring dissolved oxygen with electronic probes to assess water quality. In the USA, the International Society for Technology in Education offers a set of guidelines for increasing student confidence and productivity while using digital tools and other technology (ISTE 2015). Conservation educators can support this goal by creating programs that use the technologies with which learners should become familiar. In other cases, new technology is a tool through which information is conveyed to learners. Some of these tools may help us reach more people or new audiences; others can make class time more effective by assigning lectures as homework (Ferenstein 2013). Conservation educators may find themselves adapting programs to integrate the use of social media sites, such as using Facebook to reach an older audience (Duggan et al. 2014).

Before investing in new technologies, educators will also need to know the direct and indirect costs and how they might change over time. For some technologies, the costs change quickly. Talking to technology specialists may be necessary before you develop a program that relies on a type of technology; you want to be sure it will be available and repairable for a while. On the other hand, the speed at which technology improves could make currently expensive devices more accessible in just a few years.

Technology does not automatically make programs more effective, but it can open new possibilities (Saxena 2013). Educators can be effective users of the strategies and techniques outlined in the other chapters of this book. Videos or smartphones cannot replace satisfactory outdoor experiences or community service projects, but these and other technologies can enhance these programs, create interest, and have the potential to attract people who may not have previously expressed interest in conservation.

Conservation Education and Outreach Techniques. Second Edition. Susan K. Jacobson, Mallory D. McDuff & Martha C. Monroe © Susan K. Jacobson, Mallory D. McDuff & Martha C. Monroe 2015. Published 2015 by Oxford University Press.

Most educational technologies introduced to schools are available to non-formal educators. Rather than preparing learners to become familiar with the technology, however, their interest is more in the efficient and effective communication of information to build knowledge, attitudes, and skills in support of conservation goals. For example, using data that birdwatchers contribute to eBird (<http://ebird.org/content/ebird/>), a nature center could let others know where to find rare migrants. This bird data website also enables resource managers to access an enormous amount of information from recreational and professional birdwatchers. The questions in Box 11.1 can help conservation educators consider which technologies might be effective in their programs (Milone 1996; Kent and McNergney 1999; Garrison and Vaughan 2008).

This chapter introduces four techniques and their accompanying technologies that are commonly used to communicate with young and adult learners in schools and non-formal settings. Because each technique has many possible technologies for production, duplication, or dissemination, we focus primarily on the educational component of the technique. Because technology changes rapidly, we offer generalities that should hold true even as the technology advances.

Box 11.1 Questions for evaluating technology for education

- How available is the necessary equipment? How much training is needed to use the tools effectively? Do teacher training institutions prepare educators to use this technology?
- Do learners interact with the technology? Will the technology enhance the level of learner interaction and challenge, thus improving educational programs? Does this tool teach learners to become more technologically proficient? Would this make educators more likely to use the program? How can educators assure parents of student safety and oversight?
- What kind of expense does this technology entail at present and how is this likely to change in the future? Is extensive research necessary to choose which brand to purchase?
- How likely is the equipment to break; how soon can it be repaired or replaced? Is the equipment dedicated to one use, or can it be utilized for several purposes? What ancillary materials are required to make the technology educational?
- Does the technology make a complex educational message more consistent? Is the technology an efficient way to distribute your message? Does this technology enable you to update your message frequently? Will it help you reach new audiences or larger audiences?
- Can the technology make your message more memorable, relevant, visually appealing, and engaging? Are learners more motivated to learn the information if it comes via this technology?
- Does this technology enable educators to blend technology with traditional forms of instruction? How will educators be supported through the process of redesigning lessons and curriculum to accommodate the required rethinking?

11.1 The World Wide Web

Internet users today are familiar with the vast possibilities of information exchange and retrieval while online: posting pictures on Instagram, purchasing airplane tickets, checking for directions, finding reference articles, and accessing weather reports through computers connected by Wi-Fi, phone, cable, or direct lines. Smartphones and tablets make it possible for people to have constant contact with friends via blogs, Facebook, and texting as well as constant access to the Internet. There are connections to nature and conservation as well: people can download apps to identify birds by vocalizations or look up the environmental impacts of a cleaning product.

The Internet is a network of computers around the world. Because they are all connected to each other, individuals can access information stored on any of them. An Internet Service Provider (ISP) provides individuals with access to the World Wide Web (the web) through dial-up, cable, fiber optics or Wi-Fi connections. Cellphones connect to cell towers, which then connect to the Internet; this service is provided through a cell-phone plan. Wi-Fi is provided by some retail locations or entire cities, enabling users to connect to the Internet from their phone or laptop computer without a service provider. Box 11.2 provides a brief glossary for the most common web terminology.

As ubiquitous as the Internet is, however, it does not provide equal coverage everywhere. Only 5 miles from a major research university in the USA, for example, residents did not have the option of purchasing a plan for high-speed Internet access in 2015. Teachers of low-income students in rural and urban areas across the USA report that many students are not likely to have access to digital tools at home or at school (Purcell et al. 2013).

The Internet is changing the way we interact with and obtain information. A survey of 2460 public school teachers in the Advanced Placement and National Writing Project in the United States indicated that digital technology is both helpful and challenging (Purcell et al. 2013). Virtually all respondents use the Internet for their work, and 92% reported that the Internet has had a major impact on their ability to access resources for teaching. At the same time, 75% reported that these tools have increased the range of content they are responsible for knowing. Younger teachers are more likely to express confidence in using digital technologies and expect their students to use websites, online discussions, or blogs in their assignments. Even though this sample represents teachers of academically successful students in the USA, those from high-income areas reported more support, more training, and more student use of technology than those from low-income areas. The quantity and quality of information available on websites are also a concern; 83% of the respondents agreed that the amount of online information overwhelms their students and 60% agreed that such technology challenges students to use credible sources of information (Purcell et al. 2013).

A large study in North Carolina, USA, explored the racial and socio-economic gap in academic achievement among over half a million students aged 10–13 years and found the gap was not reduced by obtaining Internet access and a home computer (Vigdor and Ladd 2010). In fact there was a small negative impact on student scores in mathematics and reading. Students in this study self-report that less time is spent using the computer

Box 11.2 Selected web terminology

- *Blog.* A frequent, chronological publication of personal thoughts or expertise on the web, also called a web-log. Individuals create their own blogs; each entry is followed by a comment button that allows others to write a reaction. Blogs are open to the public.
- *Hypertext.* Web-based text that allows links between web pages. When users click on a colored phrase or button, a new page loads to their screen.
- *Listserv.* A communication sent to groups of subscribers by email. Messages are posted to the entire group and members can reply to the entire list. Organizers at WWF-UK used this technology to exert speedy and efficient pressure on parliamentarians to support legislation to restrict the wildlife trade.
- *MUD and MOO.* Interactive virtual worlds that are constructed by users. Many are games, but educators are creating them to engage learners in collaboration and problem solving. MUD is a text-based multiuser domain. MOO is a graphical, object-oriented MUD.
- *MOOC.* Massive open online course, often offered by universities at no charge to anyone with the Internet and a computer.
- *Podcast.* A brief audio or video message available on the Internet. They are easy to download and play. Users can register for a series of podcasts which are automatically delivered when uploaded.
- *Social media.* Internet-facilitated interactions among the public or between organizations and the public. Because they are readily shared, messages quickly move across a community of linked members. Popular social media tools are facilitated by YouTube, Instagram, Facebook, and Twitter.
- *Voice over Internet protocol.* Internet-facilitated conversation conveying visual and/or audio information. This can enable phone systems to be attached to the Internet as well as accommodate visual calls with Skype or Viber, for example.
- *Webinar.* A seminar held on the Internet. Presenters can be on a camera and speak with a slide presentation. Participants can ask questions by typing in the chat box or by speaking in their microphone.
- *Wiki.* A public or private log for individuals to work together on the same content.

Source: Kinsey (2010).

for homework; apparently the computer is used recreationally rather than for school work. The authors suggest that parental oversight is important when expanding access to technology.

Websites, of course, contain different types of information. They can passively present information, like an exhibit or display. They can provide digital videos, photographs, presentations, maps, charts, and text. Pages can be connected with hypertext links, enabling users to jump directly to a related location. Virtual field trips, a popular web phenomenon, are just as varied. Some field trips are actually tours of websites linked together in a logical and cohesive manner. Others have interactive maps, photographs, and text to explain beaches in Hawaii or castles in England. Virtual field trips at museum or aquarium sites may include a real time webcam, enabling virtual visitors to see what real visitors see, like otters at the Monterey Bay Aquarium in California, USA (Monterey Bay Aquarium 2015).

Flash technology enables websites to present complex animated information if the user has installed a Flash plug-in player. Templates are available that allow designers to add their own text and photographs. Since 2000, this multimedia platform has enabled websites to have sizzle without size. The Southern Center for Wildland–Urban Interface Research and Information located in Florida, USA, contracted with a consultant to develop a Flash presentation to describe a renovated fire-wise home (SCWUIRI 2005). The staff and consultant met together to develop the look and layout and discuss the content. Staff wrote text, assembled photographs, and developed captions while the consultant created the final product. Annie Hermansen-Báez, technology transfer coordinator for the center, recalls that the process required several months of interaction. The completed program is an important feature of the center's website. She says, "We've received a lot of positive comments on the program. It is an effective strategy for attracting attention and showing before and after changes to the home." New technology like HTML5, however, may replace Flash (Casale 2012). There are a number of advantages to this new technology, particularly compatibility with mobile devices.

As educators know, learning is more likely to occur when learners manipulate the information themselves. Some educators build Internet resources into interactive activities, such as complementing a study of wetlands with data on wetland loss from the Northern Prairie Wetlands Research Center, North Dakota, USA (Czerniak 2004). Some sites allow data entry from citizen scientists (see Chapter 7) that enable users to retrieve specified data and then facilitate conversations with other users from across the globe. This section will focus on designing websites, which can be the basis for achieving a variety of educational goals.

11.1.1 Planning

Conservation educators who are designing their own website should think about learners and what makes it easy for them to navigate a website. Basic rules of thumb include:

- Viewers should be able to get the important information on one computer screen without scrolling. If scrolling is necessary, the user should only have to scroll vertically not horizontally as well. People skim to get the information they need; make it easy for them to get what they want.
- Navigation should be clear and easy. Three clicks, or connections, should be the maximum needed to find information, and pages should download quickly.
- By increasing vividness (audio and animation), websites can create more positive and enduring attitudes (Coyle and Thorson 2001).
- Sites should function on any type of computer: desktop, laptop, or mobile devices. A separate site for portable devices will enable users with tiny screens to navigate to the most visited sections of your site.

- Sites should be accessible by all users, regardless of ability. Your agency may have web accessibility guidelines to govern options such as screen readers and the use of alternative descriptions for all images and buttons, labels for all tables, and blinking or scrolling text (WebAIM 2014).

Involve the webmaster or member of staff who will be maintaining the site during the design process. The site can be designed so that little maintenance is required. There are a variety of options for easy authoring tools, including some open source tools. When designing a website, consultants often talk about the front end (what visitors see) and the back end (what webmasters maintain). New tools have more user-friendly back ends so someone without web design skills can update the content.

The web, by design, is a mechanism for anyone to post anything. As a result, it can be difficult to sort fact from fiction. The Persuasive Technology Lab at Stanford University, California, USA, has conducted a number of studies over the years and assembled a list of criteria that will help improve the credibility and trustworthiness of websites. Some, like eliminating errors and making it easy to contact the source, are true for any communication tool. Other tips are more essential for websites (Fogg 2002, Kyrnin 2014):

- Make it easy for viewers to verify the accuracy of the information. Use citations, references, and third-party sources to demonstrate confidence in your material.
- Highlight your expertise. Provide the credentials of your experts and show there is a real organization behind your site. Include the date when the site was last updated, and review and update it frequently.
- Pages must load quickly. You can't rely on everyone having access to the highest-speed connection, so think about compressing photographs and limiting data. Links must work and be obvious.
- Design a site that serves you and your audience. Provide an easy way for them to reach you (e.g. phone, map, GPS coordinates, or a contact-us form). Add buttons for social media.
- Make the site attractive, professional, appropriate, and consistent. Websites are judged quickly by the design, so make yours easy to use and useful. Do not emphasize dazzle at the expense of content. Select an attractive color scheme with appropriate symbolism for your content.
- The minimal cost of posting on a website enables designers to use a larger number of pages than one would use in print. Step-by-step photos of a process make it easy for users to understand.
- Consider how to make your website easily found by search engines. Use keywords in your titles and page header—the words that your audience will use in a search. Add a sitemap and links to your own site so it can be easily searched by computers and people. Choose a URL that explains your site. Frames and Flash make it difficult for search engines to find your page, so consider not using them on your homepage. Caption your photographs since search engines look for words. Link to other related sites and ask them to link to you (Male 2010). And check for the newest strategies for search engine optimization (DeMers 2013).

Like other learning tools and techniques, the prior knowledge and understanding that a learner brings (including familiarity and the density of their cognitive map; see Chapter 2), greatly affects how people explore and learn from websites. A comparison of novices and experts found that greater topic understanding led to more goals and more complex searches for information (Corredor 2004). Given the same amount of time, novices set fewer goals and thus found less information than the experts. Since many websites are designed for the general public, it is critical to think about the users as novices. Sites that provide navigational information, describe interesting features in common language, and provide details relevant to users could help novices conduct a more rewarding search.

A consideration unique to the web is the speed at which your pages load and the size of the screen. Photographs may be stored as small thumbnail photos, additional graphics can be put on a separate page, and low-resolution images (72 pixels per inch, or ppi) can be compressed to reduce loading time. Frames are commonly used on websites to provide stationary information like a table of contents or organizational banner. Frames, however, limit the size of the screen that is available for subsequent pages and could make it difficult for search engines to locate your page. By linking to other relevant sites you can help create a network for users and save yourself the work of re-creating information that has already been posted by other organizations. People with specific questions often access more than one website as they compare information (Eysenbach and Kohler 2002); you can make it easy for them to find what they might need.

11.1.2 Implementation

Once a website has been designed and developed, it can be loaded on a computer that will act as a web server (a computer that stores all of your website files and makes them available to anyone on the Internet). To keep your site useful, it must be reviewed and updated frequently. Consider rotating feature stories that promote new information, exhibits, or timely happenings at your site. You might also add an RSS (rich site summary) feed to enable users to subscribe to your site and receive automatic notices when you update your site. If you want users to contact you, make sure your contact information is easy to find and easy to use. Add social media buttons to your site so that users can connect. If one address receives all emails from the site, make sure that address is checked frequently and responses are sent quickly. If a response requires significant work, let the requester know that you are working on it.

Like other learning technologies, educators know that the Internet can be distracting as well as motivating. One strategy for structuring learner interaction with websites is a WebQuest. Simple WebQuests involve acquisition of knowledge and skills, sending students on a web-type scavenger hunt for information. More complex WebQuests engage groups of students for several weeks as they solve a problem by synthesizing information from a variety of sites (Ikpeze and Boyd 2007). By incorporating relevant and meaningful questions and tasks, a WebQuest is highly motivating. By assigning roles in cooperative groups, students learn to work together and take advantage of the skills and interests of others. By providing links and a concrete task, students are able to use the Internet for information and transform that information to meet their needs. The most effective WebQuests engage learners in critical thinking, applying knowledge, cooperating in groups, and synthesizing information (Zheng et al. 2008).

11.1.3 Evaluation

Websites have been evaluated in a number of different ways. Users can suggest criteria that make the site easier to navigate and read, such as the following list from a group of fifth-grade students (MacGregor and Lou 2004–2005):

- Text is in concise sentences, with simple vocabulary, and headings.
- Information is relevant and broad in scope.
- Additional pages are one click away.
- Design includes colored text boxes, white space, and borders.
- Audio and video elements are present.
- There are photographs that provide clarifying information.

The world of commerce, however, has much at stake, since websites enable millions of business transactions. Using business websites as models may give conservation educators some good ideas. An evaluation form for government websites was designed in Australia and includes 106 questions, most of which have yes/no answers. The questions help developers assess whether a website has a security policy, help pages, opportunity for citizen interaction or comments, search capability, and appropriate readability, navigability, and style (Henriksson et al. 2006).

Awards are given to good websites. You might consider using the award criteria to help develop or redesign your site, or simply use award-winning sites as a model for developing your site. Wildscreen Arkive has won a number of prestigious awards such as Best Environmental Website in 2013 from Reality Drop and See the Bigger Picture from National Geographic in 2010. It archives photographs and information about endangered and extinct animals to raise public awareness for conservation. Naturalists and educators can find a treasure trove of information on animals, such as keas (*Nestor notabilis*) and quaggas (*Equus quagga quagga*). Parallel sites provide information for children, teachers, and parents (Wildscreen 2015).

Online surveys provide an avenue for extracting some information about users of websites. Such forms typically ask for demographic information, the purpose of accessing the site, and level of satisfaction. Because questions with pull-down buttons and predetermined checklists are easier to complete than open-ended questions, these surveys tend to provide only factual, simple data. Search engines and other services provide data tracking, so it is also possible to determine how many times and when a site was accessed, how long a user spent on a page, and whether files were downloaded. You can also determine if people might have landed on your page by accident—if the tracking data show they visited one page and left your site. This may be because the search engines are not accurately identifying your page (DeMers 2013). If website evaluators wish to discover what users think when they navigate a site, how sites compare, or what they cannot find on the site, other evaluation tools are needed. Observation of users searching for information can help identify what information is obtained by quickly scanning sites and how long it takes to locate the information (Eysenbach and Kohler 2002). Focus groups can provide important insights about navigation, content, and aesthetics. Consider asking questions as people use your website such as: What are you looking for? How easy is it to find? Where do you think you should go next? What was the first thing you noticed on this page?

By combining various goals, researchers have developed a model to evaluate websites for tourist destinations that is relevant to nature-based recreation (Li and Wang 2010). The model suggests that 47 factors are important, grouped into five categories: information, communication, transaction, relationship, and technical merit. Websites should enable users to understand the attractions and activities, obtain outreach materials and provide feedback on them, purchase or reserve products, build a relationship with the organization and other users, and be usable and innovative (Li and Wang 2010).

11.2 Social media

The Internet and mobile devices like smartphones and tablets have enabled communication practices to shift in new ways. With the popularity of social networking sites, these devices have empowered both grassroots communication and organization. By authoring blogs, posting comments, re-Tweeting a Tweet, or uploading a homemade podcast, citizens have entered the previously restricted world of the mass media.

Social media consists of various forms of electronic communication through which users create online communities to share information, ideas, personal messages, and other content (Bercovici 2010). Industries, organizations, and government agencies are taking advantage of social media. Not only has this become an important platform for conveying information, but social media sites can be designed to encourage people to establish communities and build relationships offline as well (Rich 2014). "Social media is not about what each of us does or says, but about what we do and say together, worldwide, to communicate in all directions at any time, by any possible means . . . " according to Michelle Chmielewski of Synthesio (Cohen 2011).

Conservation educators can take advantage of this world by understanding and harnessing its power. At the very least, organizations and agencies can broadcast announcements and share information through networks that allow recipients to forward them to friends and achieve a wider reach (Gharis et al. 2014). A 2012 survey found that the USA population spent 121 billion minutes interacting with social media in only a single month (Popkin 2012). Cleverly designed campaigns using social media can be far more effective than their conventional media counterparts. Ultimately, social media can build social capital within online communities and support efforts to strengthen environmental governance. Connections through social media have become a norm for networking and hold the promise of great power for conservation.

In 1997, the first popular social network site, SixDegrees.com, enabled users to make online profiles and create a friend list. By 2004 social media sites like Myspace, Facebook, and Twitter had emerged. In a US poll, 73% of adults have used social network sites, with Facebook being the most frequently used (Duggan and Smith 2013). For many people and organizations, social media has become an essential part of daily communications. For example, a social media project was organized in a rural Californian community to help wildlife researchers understand the distribution of a rare weasel, the Pacific fisher (*Martes pennati*). The researchers attract fishers to motion-activated cameras in the forest by placing bait in a sock and hanging it near a camera. Unfortunately for the researchers, the fishers chewed through about 200 socks a month. A flyer was distributed to local schools in the community that asked people to donate old socks; researchers collected a few hundred socks. Shifting the request to social media generated additional news releases, radio interviews, and newspaper stories within 2 weeks of the first appeal. Over 280 packages of socks were received within 6 weeks—enough to supply the fishers and researchers for 2 years. Of course it helped to have a humorous title, such as "This guy wants to eat your socks" along with a photograph of a fisher (Kocher et al. 2013).

Social media even supports educational, interactive games. On Facebook, "Trash Tycoon" teaches youngsters about upcycling as they collect garbage and convert it into a new product. Users play for points and the title of "garbage tycoon" and if they recycle in the real world they can obtain points from corporate partners that are good for buying environmentally responsible products. The organizer plans to make a donation to an environmental non-profit organization based on its in-game purchases (Fox 2011; Leichman 2012).

Government leaders are also harnessing the power of social media. Strong political views make it difficult for people to listen to opposing information, and traditional media outlets only makes the division greater, since people choose which version of the news to hear. In the USA, the Obama administration developed a program to enable the public to send the White House petitions, called "We the People." Anyone can launch a petition and circulate it through social media. Petitions have expressed concern over illegal shark harvesting and inhumane treatment of wild horses. The White House responds to every petition that reaches 100,000 signatures in 30 days, and in some cases begins the process of real policy change with additional discussions or assignments. But the real value of the petitions is that the White House captures the email addresses of people who care about specific issues and opens a communication channel directly to these individuals. In response to a petition about gun control, President Obama recorded a video message that was seen by over 400,000 people, and many would not have listened to him in any other forum. A follow-up poll revealed that 25% of the listeners learned something new, suggesting that social media can help create conversation and deliberation about public policy (Scherer 2013). The White House has made the software for public petitions available to other governments.

11.2.1 Planning

As a marketing tool, social media can help gain exposure for an agency or organization. Educators need to understand what type of media would best fit their mission, objectives, and the age and level of their target audience.

When creating social media accounts, the first step is to know exactly what you want to achieve in order to focus on the most strategic social network sites for your audience. Similar to any program planning strategy, educators need to identify their goals, understand the audience, and determine how to link the two together (Odden 2010). Business advisors suggest that one experienced staff member be designated as the social media campaign worker, no matter how big or small the company. Large organizations typically hire someone with extensive marketing experience to direct their social media. Smaller companies may delegate the job to a staff member who has personal experience. Social media can link you with your target audience, keep everyone connected with what they are doing, advertise and promote your programs for free, and motivate people to do something. An essential detail when planning your sites is to create each account with the same name, making it much easier for followers to find you. Each should have a similar look or logo, even though the basic layout will depend on the social media site. This will allow members and supporters to trust and recognize your logo and learn that you are a reliable source. Most smaller businesses initiate their marketing campaign in small steps, broadcasting their presence on one or two networks until it gains popularity. Find out what network is best for your organization by gauging your audience's use of different platforms. The more your organization and digital marketing budget grows, the more you can test and expand your networking to other social media sites.

The Nature Conservancy (TNC) followed similar guidelines and started their campaign gradually. As social media grew in popularity the organization formed a social media team of experts in about a dozen different departments of their organization, with each member bringing unique ideas to the planning table. After determining the target audience they built a presence in a large variety of sites from Facebook and Instagram to Tumblr. The manager of web analytics strategy and social media for TNC and associate director Amy Ganderson advises that one of the most important attributes for social media campaigners is "You need to enjoy networking. That's really what social media is all about—forming relationships" (Nonprofit Tech for Good 2010). Ganderson, along with the social media team, continues to expand the presence of TNC, participating in "text to give" campaigns, a tool designed to help organizations receive $10 donations that are added directly to a cellphone bill. A presence on Facebook has helped TNC stimulate donations and brought followers to the main TNC website with "Facebook causes" pages and personal fan pages (Nonprofit Tech for Good 2010). The focus remains on raising environmental awareness and promoting support for conservation. Their Green Gift Monday social media campaign focused on raising awareness for green gifting options and providing ideas during cyber Mondays.

In a similar fashion, the WWF started off small and grew to implement several forms of social media that follow the three goals of their plan: growing, engaging, and mobilizing. The WWF wanted to grow in such a way that they would achieve over a million supporters; engage with friends, governments, and other similar originations; and mobilize by finding a way to get people involved with conservation every day.

11.2.2 Implementation

Once the basic objectives and layout are established for your organization's new social media campaign, there are important processes to consider as you start the journey into the social media world. Start designing the layout for each social network that you plan to use. Use a creative, easy-to-remember logo and color scheme so that each site looks similar and gives a strong impression to viewers. The site needs to make your organization stand out and provide a good depiction of what you support. Social networking is all about community and building relationships, along with promoting your cause. This means that an organization should be consistently posting, following, and engaging with the audience.

Posts should spur on intelligent discussion, not backfire and offend the viewers. Picture posts are often popular (Doyle and Briggeman 2014), particularly on sites that have a strong visual component, like Facebook, Pinterest, and Instagram. Site managers must remember not to make social networking solely about their organization. As they post and keep the site up to date they must remember to inform and show interest in other organizations to create a strong network (Baer 2013). Lee Odden, the CEO of TopRank Online Marketing recommends that social network sites should be creative while still focusing on the message. "Great content isn't great until it's discovered, consumed, and shared," he said in a keynote speech to online marketers (Miller 2014). A mix of types of posts, such as photographs, videos, tips, and questions, can also provide sufficient diversity that your audience will stay interested and return to your site. With this in mind, stay on top of continually updating the page or account, engaging with viewers and keeping them interested.

Because your followers often check their social sites at different times randomly throughout the day, social media strategy consultant Amy Porterfield recommends around five posts a day on each social network that an organization company is involved with. "One post a day simply isn't enough because most of your fans won't see it simply due to timing" (Porterfield 2011). By staggering the posts, the company sites and the company itself become much more efficient. Along with posting, your social media manager should make sure to constantly follow more and more people. This is a guaranteed way to gain a larger online community because users normally follow back, particularly if your site looks well established and relevant. The whole point of social media is interaction: therefore responding and listening to your supporters is essential. Attractive, eye-catching images of your causes, programs, and behind-the-scenes snapshots of people at work can be effective choices for these visual platforms.

Hashtags are on almost every social media site and allow users to find related content. For example, a post with the hashtag #rideyourbike could be discovered by anyone who searched for posts with that hashtag on a given social media platform. Hashtags allow those interested in similar topics to find each other's posts. Often, an organization will coin a specific hashtag for a conference or campaign and encourage followers to use the hashtag in their posts about the topic. By clicking on the hashtag, users can view all the posts on that topic. While some social media platforms disseminate information through known friends, the hashtag enables social media to connect unknown people who share a common interest. Social media is fast becoming the most common platform for current and potential customers to interact with organizations and companies. The site manager should be prepared to deal with exponential growth—of posts, used socks for fisher bait, or complaints. Getting followers to financially support you is a challenge, but it can be possible on social media. You can also use social media to launch crowdfunding platforms, such as Kickstarter and IndieGoGo, to raise funds for specific projects. A cross-platform contest that ties in a group of various social networks like Pinterest, Twitter, and Instagram can be a good way to get users from one social platform to explore other platforms that your organization controls (Shandrow 2013).

Each year the WWF holds a photography contest across all of its social media sites allowing all applicants to automatically become a member of the WWF. Promoting the contest through Facebook, Zoom, and Twitter, and using Zoom.nl, they garnered 4086 supporting photographers in 2011, surpassing their original goal, increasing awareness, and connecting with new members. The media expert for the WWF said, "I see our website as our home base, the blog as our podium, and Twitter, YouTube, Flickr, and LinkedIn as our megaphone" (Khan 2011). The successful use of social media, with more and more site traffic every year, can help any organization mobilize followers to have an impact on the environment.

11.2.3 Evaluation

With social media it is easy to get a "like" or a supporter, but the challenge is to keep these followers active and interested. Once your social media sites are established, it is important to market them and evaluate their impact (Gharis et al. 2014). Analytical data, such as number of posts, average user views per post, and average engaged user views per post, where engagement is defined as liking, sharing, or commenting on posts, can be gleaned from the site and from viewers (Doyle and Briggeman 2014). Consider using additional metrics such as demographics of followers, the number of likes per type of post, changes in membership, and increases in donations. A critical part of this process is to track the same site metrics with data collected by your organization. This will help determine which tactics work and which need to change. Some sites, such as Facebook and LinkedIn, include their own metric data for free. Google Analytics allows you to see how effective your social media campaigns are at forwarding site traffic to your organization's main website. If you see social media sites such as Facebook, Twitter, or other active social platforms are a top referrer to your main website, then you are on the right track towards achieving a successful social media campaign.

Evaluation also requires getting feedback from your audience and staying current with which social sites remain popular among your target audience. The last thing you want is to be stuck in the past with a site that has few followers. Among younger audiences in particular, sites change in popularity all the time as new ones become established. For example, from its creation in 2003 Myspace was the most viewed social network site in the world, until it was topped by Facebook in 2008, and by 2013 it was barely in the top ten (eBiz 2013).

One reason why the Sierra Club is one of the largest environmental organizations in the USA might be their social media campaigns and well-planned marketing strategies. Their home site is linked to their large presence on just about every social media outlet—Facebook, Pinterest, Flickr, and their own personalized apps. Each local Sierra Club chapter was encouraged to start its own social media campaign and was given a guide with concrete tips and advice to that end. One of the important tips is to make sure to check inboxes on a regular basis and respond quickly, since the goal is to build connections (Sierra Club 2014).

Social media is constantly evolving, so continuous evaluation is needed to improve your organization's social media strategy. Evaluation and refinement on a monthly basis can help you identify which tactics are working and which ones to ditch. In this marketing climate, a social media plan is vital for connecting with people and connecting people with conservation.

11.3 Video

In the past, movies were produced by exposing and editing film. Today, many educational applications have migrated to digital formats because of the ease of editing and producing digital media.

Editing software is cheaper and easier to use than in the past, and enables the editor to work on portions of the product in any order. Today, one can use a digital camcorder to shoot a video, edit it on a computer, store it on an external hard drive or DVD, and play it on a computer, television with DVD, or website. Students can even create a video with a smartphone and edit it on a tablet.

Once a video has been produced, it is a form of one-way communication. The final product cannot be easily reorganized or regionalized by users. However, it can be regionalized easily in the production phase. Local elements can be added to a digitally produced video to produce a suite of different versions. When videos accompany a program that engages the audience in discussion or enables a presenter to answer questions, they promote two-way communication. Depending upon the purpose of the program, a stand-alone video may suffice, or a personal presentation with the video might be necessary.

The production of the video itself may be an educational program or may help reveal new information. In Nepal, rural communities expressed their experiences and thoughts about community forests in a video letter that was shown to decision-makers in Katmandu and helped influence forest policy (Grieser 2000). By providing an opportunity for people's voices to be heard, this technology can be a powerful strategy for communication. In Egypt, the production of a video was a key element to help the government agencies understand the complex issues surrounding the maintenance of local irrigation ditches. The camera became a tool that enabled both men and women to articulate their experiences. In particular, women were able to explain that there was no other place to put household garbage—information that had not been part of the previous understanding (Grieser and Rawlins 2000).

Video is an appropriate educational technique when the topic is visually appealing and interesting. It is often the tool of choice when the topic involves movement or demonstration of a skill. Teachers, for example, can share their own videos of science and mathematics lessons through the Massachusetts Institute of Technology's Blossoms website (MIT 2015), and agencies can provide short, visual messages, such as an introduction to conserving biological diversity (UNESCO 2012).

Professionally produced nature and science films broadcast on television or shown in visitor centers can still be powerful ways to convey the beauty and resilience of our natural world. The popularity of websites like YouTube enables video to reach an enormous number of people (Box 11.3). The availability of public television, cable channels,

---

Box 11.3 Exploring YouTube

YouTube has 1 billion unique visitors each month, receives 100 hours of video material every minute, and enables people to watch over 6 billion hours of video each month. This social media tool allows users to both watch and share original videos. Although anyone can view videos on the YouTube platform, they may not be allowed to download and use them unless they request permission from the creators. Creators of original work automatically own the copyright on that material. If that work contains clips of previously recorded information or music, they have the responsibility to verify that the material is in the public domain before uploading it to YouTube. Nations have different laws protecting copyrighted material and defining fair use, which allows copyright-protected material to be used under certain circumstances (YouTube 2015).

To find a video on YouTube, simply navigate to youtube.com and use the search bar on the top of the webpage. If you create a YouTube account, you will have access to more features, such as creating playlists, seeing previously viewed videos, and uploading your own videos. Once you have an account, you can use the "Upload" or "Video Manager" buttons to create and organize your videos. A playlist enables you to organize and access your videos more easily.

Some schools may block YouTube because of the risk of viewing inappropriate materials. Educators may prefer to use TeacherTube since it is often not restricted (TeacherTube 2014).

---

and the Internet makes it feasible for agencies to share their videos. In countries where the public is accustomed to watching television or movies, the expectation will be for high-quality shows. Viewers will also expect to be entertained by a video, which is an effective way to touch emotions and attitudes that play an important role in learning (see Chapter 2). The proliferation of channels in some countries, however, makes it less likely that viewers will find and watch your show amid the myriad sports, cooking, comedy, drama, travel, food, and movie programs. But if they know where to look for your videos, your message can be effectively shared with your target audience.

Given the strong social norms surrounding some behaviors, such as the personal decision whether or not to use birth control, televised soap operas, telenovelas, and reality shows have been successful at conveying information, raising awareness about opportunities, and changing behavior around the world. Population experts have associated the broadcast of such programs with declining population growth rates in Mexico, Jamaica, Kenya, and Brazil since the 1970s. A geographer recently correlated a decline in fertility rates with a rise in TV ownership in rural India (Pearce 2013). Popular shows, it appears, have the power to influence attitudes and social norms, launching a social revolution.

In areas of the world where television is not available, radio often fills this niche for entertainment, news, and information. Radio programs can be translated into different languages and broadcast to rural areas. This medium has been successfully used in the Congo, for example, to explain practices that can affect the health of both gorilla and human families. Working with students at the Tayna Center for Conservation Biology and local actors and musicians, the Gorilla Rehabilitation and Conservation Education Center developed a 10-part radio drama about human hygiene and its effect on the health of both species (GRACE 2015). The local radio station reaches up to 60,000 people within its 100-km radius broadcast range, making this medium an effective way to reach rural residents.

Regardless of the purpose of a video or the means by which it is distributed, consider these guidelines for making a high-quality product.

11.3.1 Planning

The development of a video should begin with a clarification of the objectives for this tool. Agreement on the purpose, the audience, and the message will help writers, planners, and funders move forward in the development of a coherent and meaningful video. It helps to have a one-sentence theme that clearly conveys your message, such as "Mosquitoes spread deadly diseases" or "Mangroves protect the land and create important wetland habitat." It may be helpful to sketch out the development of concepts in a video in preparation for script writing.

A two-column script is used to describe the progression of the audio and visual portions of the video (Fig. 11.1). The left half of the page describes the visual scenes and the right half the audio content, which also includes the script. The columns are synchronized so that a scene and its audio accompaniment are presented together. Onscreen graphics and text are noted on the left side. Directions to the producer and suggestions for background audio are also written into the script, such as "pull back to reveal landscape" or "dog barking."

Producers use their own language when referring to the components of a video. A long shot refers to an image from a distance; a close shot fills the frame with the subject. Cut is a sharp transition to a new scene, whereas fade or dissolve refer to more gradual transitions. Pan directs the camera to move across a scene, zoom slides the camera lens in and out. A narrator speaking the script without being shown in the video is called a voice-over, and using a voice-over is often cheaper than hiring someone to act as well as narrate the script.

The video script should be more similar to spoken communication than written, because the audience will be listening, not reading. Short sentences, vivid imagery, and easy-to-understand phrases will help communicate the message. Do not use numbers or dates, unless they are short. Consider using onscreen text to emphasize key words, new vocabulary, or phrases (Telg 2009).

The following should be considered while developing the video:

- How long will the video be? Most adult audiences pay attention for 8–10 minutes, and children for less. Changing the pace and context of the video can help to hold the audience's attention (Telg 2009). Videos shared over the Internet are typically less than 3 minutes long.
- What will the video include? Interviews can help the audience imagine their own experiences and allow the message to be conveyed by multiple voices. They can also be more expensive and time-consuming. A narrator can be used to link interviews together.

Wildland-Urban Interface Video Script –page 2		
	Graphics	**Script**
6	*INTERVIEW*: RESIDENT NAME LOCATION (About 15 seconds)	RESIDENT–Discussing how living in the interface improves quality of life and one or two different concerns or challenges. Something like, "We love that our kids can run and play in the woods, but we do worry about the potential for wildfires."
7	- ATTRACTIVE FOREST LAND - CHARISMATIC WILDLIFE - A RIPPLING BROOK. - TRASH-FILLED RIVER - PEOPLE IN WUI – GARDENING - RESIDENTS AND RESOURCE PROFESSIONAL WALKING IN THE FOREST, TALKING	NARRATOR: Living in the interface has its advantages and challenges, and as these residents have realized, their presence in the interface inevitably affects their surroundings. You can make choices that will help reduce your impact on natural resources and improve conditions that affect forest, wildlife, and human well being. Different issues require different approaches. Let's see how interface residents and natural resource managers across the south are working on these issues together.
8	- FIRE FOOTAGE IN THE WILDAND-URBAN INTERFACE (2–3 shots)	N: Fire is often the main wildland-urban interface issue people think about. Although most wildfires are caused by human carelessness, some happen naturally. If allowed to burn , they help maintain fire-dependent ecosystems. But with more and more houses scattered throughout the interface, almost every fire that occurs threatens human safety and property and becomes a major emergency.
9	FIREFIGHTERS SPRAYING BURNING INTERFACE HOMES	N: When fires are out of control, firefighters are forced to make split-second decisions about what's most important to save. Protecting fragmented interface areas where people's safety and property are top priority can be more difficult than defending large forested areas.

Fig. 11.1 A sample video script.

- What is the audience interested in? What do they already know? What specifics do they need to understand your message? The video script should supplement and not duplicate what people see on the screen. It is not helpful to have a play-by-play narration of what people can easily see. Instead, identify what will help support and explain the visual imagery.
- Will you use graphics or music? Both can enhance the message, make the video more interesting and enjoyable to watch, and signal topical changes in the program.

As you develop your ideas for the video, consider who will produce it. If you have access to cameras and editing equipment, learn to use them by attending a class or workshop, reading the manual or online tutorial, and practicing. Amateur productions with new digital technology can be just as good as professional productions and much less expensive. If you have an in-house production unit, get on their schedule. Conversely, if you plan to contract with a professional firm, look at their recent work, and shop around for someone you can afford and enjoy working with.

Once you have a script, ask others to read it to check for appropriate language, unnecessary jargon, simple explanations, and vivid descriptions. Make sure it will sound like a conversation rather than a lecture. It should sound like you are speaking to one person, even though the video may be broadcast to thousands. This is the easiest stage for making changes in the script—you should not expect to reshoot the video to make changes later.

When your script is approved, and before you begin production, contact agencies and organizations that might have the footage you need for scenes, explanations, and transitions. Gathering pre-shot material can significantly reduce the cost of your program. Adding the organizations that contribute footage to your list of partners and collaborators may make it easier for them to donate material at no charge.

11.3.2 Implementation

During production, you or the hired firm should consider equipment (camera, microphone, batteries, tripod, and memory card), site requirements, and lighting. No matter how steady your hands, tripods are essential in video work. Arrive early enough to test the equipment, set the microphones and lights, and organize the props. If you are recording outdoors, try to eliminate excess noise from cars or machinery, such as air conditioners. Stop recording each time a plane flies overhead. Natural light on an overcast day is often ideal for recording; strong sunlight may require supplemental lights to remove shadows. Check the results of your set-up frequently to make sure the light and sound are appropriate (Box 11.4).

Talking heads refers to a basic, newsy style where the interviewee talks to the camera. It may be more interesting to ask the person to do something that relates to the message—walk across a field, test water quality, or take a songbird out of a mist net. Ask the people on camera to wear comfortable clothes with solid, light colors, and no

---

Box 11.4 Checklist for conducting interviews and shooting video

---

- Listen for distracting noises.
- Pay attention to distracting backgrounds or people.
- Take many shots if you plan to edit later (better to have too much than not enough).
- Make sure to not give audible feedback as your interviewee answers questions or the camera will pick up your voice too.
- Have your interviewee re-state your questions so that their answers can be used independently. Unless you intend for the interviewer to have a role in the final product, the questions are not usually included.
- Use a tripod.

flashy accessories or jewelry. Research shows that most of an audience's perception of the people in the video comes from non-verbal body language. Actions such as reclining in a chair may signal laziness to viewers; therefore ask interviewees to lean forward, keep their eyes focused on the interviewer, and act as if they are interested (Gleason and Holian 1996).

During the taping, be sure to shoot a variety of additional footage that could be used to bridge between edited portions of the video. You may wish to convert a 15-minute interview to 5 minutes by linking several discontinuous pieces together. If the interviewee's head changes position when two portions are glued together, the final version will be jumpy. A "cutaway" to something in the scenery will enable you to continue the interview as a voice over and then return to the interviewee in a new position. Likewise, you may wish to shoot one scene with several possible transitions—zooming out, fading out, and cutting away to something else—so you can effectively transition to a new scene during editing. Your final product should look clean and simple.

Some common mistakes made by those with less experience in video production include: poor visuals (bad focus, poor lighting, poor color balance, jerky camera movement, too many zooms, repeating shots); not enough cutaways or too few shots of people in transition so that people mysteriously and suddenly appear in a new position; too many graphics; too much or poorly selected music; shots that are too short or too long; people talking too soon after the tape begins; two people speaking at the same time; people who appear nervous; and people who sound or look like they are reading. The most frequent problem is trying to include too much information.

Editors should begin the editing process by reviewing the goals for the video program. With a log of the footage, editors and producers can begin to select scenes to use. Begin by identifying the major scenes and then work on the transitions between edited pieces. It is typical to make changes to the script when editors see effective shots and comments. Graphics and sound can be added, as well as names and titles of those interviewed. The opening title and closing credits are among the last details added.

When the video is completed, implement a distribution plan. This may include posting a digital version on your website and social media sites, advertising an order form on your website, mailing copies to members or educators, distributing copies with a training workshop or program, or showing it at your workshops and to visitors.

11.3.3 Evaluation

An important criterion for evaluating a video is technical accuracy. Long before any cameras roll, you should ask experts to review your script or storyboard. They should review the information carefully for what is said, what is implied, and what is missing. It is possible for a video to convey a message that is not carried by words. Therefore, how images are linked together, the type of background music, and the visual scenes should be considered.

Whether the video "works" will depend on its original purpose. A video intended to raise public awareness and concern should be evaluated differently from one designed to train employees on specific procedures (Box 11.5). A site-orientation video to a state park in Texas was evaluated with a short pre- and post-questionnaire. Responses after

---

Box 11.5 Research with videos helps suggest strategies for effective communication

---

To better understand how to convey information about climate change and forest management opportunities to forest landowners, four videos were created with slightly different messages to see if landowners' attitudes toward and intention to adopt forest management practices to adapt to potential climate changes were affected. Two videos stressed economic values (with and without mentioning climate change) and two videos stressed stewardship values (also with and without mentioning climate change). Private forest landowners in the southeastern USA were sent an email request to participate in the study, and, if they agreed, viewed one of the four videos that they accessed through a link to a survey.

The results of the survey suggested that all four videos were able to motivate intention to act, but if the goal of the video is to increase the landowners' sense that they could successfully adopt these behaviors, communicators should emphasize stewardship values. Perceived similarity between the viewer and the speaker in the video was important for the viewer to trust the speaker, and when values portrayed in the video aligned with viewers' values, they were more likely to like the videos, trust the speakers, and feel an intention to act. Rather than holding values for either economic success or stewardship, a majority of the respondents held both concurrently.

Source: Krantz (2014).

---

viewing the video scored significantly higher than the initial responses for all categories of questions: general information about conservation and recreation, history of the site and local culture, and regulations governing human impact on the heritage sites and vandalism (Akers et al. 2005), indicating that the audience obtained the intended information from the video.

The following tips are suggested for those who wish to attract a large number of viewers on YouTube (Kinsey and Henneman 2011):

- Use interesting subject matter and a short, catchy title.
- Keep it short—2 to 5 minutes.
- Engage the senses with lively music and eye-catching colors.
- Market your video with messages on social media sites (see Section 11.2). Distribute a message with the video link broadly.
- Provide a code to colleagues and partners that allows them to link their websites to your video.
- Include a link to the video in your email signature.
- Select a small photograph or graphic to represent the video and market this image with your message.
- Track the number of views your video receives and let others know how popular it is.

11.4 Distance education

Online learning or distance education often refers to courses offered by degree-granting universities in which technology mediates communication between the teacher and learners. The same techniques can be used by agencies and organizations to reach and engage their audiences as they learn new information and skills. Conferences, webinars, and professional development programs can be offered through the Internet to learners who are not physically in the same room—or even the same time zone—as the instructor.

Across Florida, USA, for example, residents are invited to join the Florida Seafood webinar series, broadcast live over the lunch hour. Although seafood is nutritious and tasty, consumers are often confused about which species have a stable population, which are harvested sustainably, which carry health risks because of ocean contaminants, or even how to prepare the items appropriately. Sea Grant agents in south Florida developed 18 30-minute webinar programs between 2011 and 2013. Over 420 participants tuned in for the live broadcast, and several hundred more viewed the recorded webinars. In 2012, fact sheets that accompanied the webinars were downloaded nearly 5000 times. According to Sea Grant agent Bryan Fleuch, planners, teachers, and seafood eaters appreciated the information: most people reported more favorable opinions about the sustainability of Florida's fisheries and also increased their consumption. Perhaps timing the broadcasts for the lunch hour was key to this program's success!

There are a number of reasons why institutions promote distance education. In some rural locations, travel time and costs for instructors and learners are prohibitive, making any form of distance education preferable. Specialized instruction that is useful to a dispersed population is another good candidate for distance education, such as a program evaluation course for environmental educators. Institutions striving to build larger programs are finding that the non-traditional student population—people who are raising families or building careers—could be enticed to enroll in degree programs if the courses are offered locally and more conveniently. Sometimes institutions are willing to make information available. The rapid rise of MOOCs, both in terms of offerings and participation, suggests that people are interested in learning over the Internet. A number of universities around the world have collaborated to create and offer interactive courses and materials, such as Udacity and EdX.

The growth in online education has generated a wealth of research into its quality and usefulness from which conservation educators can benefit. The following summary of findings comes from a meta-analysis of online learning studies (US Department of Education 2010), the vast majority of which were with adult learners:

- In studies comparing online learning with traditional in-person instruction, students in the online treatment performed somewhat better, on average.
- Instruction that blends online and face-to-face elements was more effective than face-to-face instruction, and usually comparable to purely online learning.
- Online learning can be effective with many different strategies and learners, though there is great variation in quality.
- Videos and online quizzes do not seem to be more effective than other strategies that provide information and engage learners, such as assigned homework.

Good instruction in any format, of course, takes thoughtful planning and understanding of the learners. Facilitating experiences, guiding inquiry, developing cooperative groups, and meeting individual needs must all be planned in advance when using an online format. The challenge in distance education is to use technology to create high-quality, effective instruction that engages learners in experiences, inquiry, cooperative groups, or any other desirable learning theory. It will not be the same as an in-person environment, so it is also important to change expectations; it can be just as effective, however. The technology itself can present a challenge to first-time distance learners and instructors. Both may benefit from training, mentors, models, and the availability of assistance when they need it. Like everything else on the Internet, sites require maintenance and are subject to technological glitches. A number of technologies and software tools can be used to create and enhance distance education programs, allowing learners to upload photographs, add verbal or written comments to posted materials, or work in small groups to complete an assignment. In addition to the webinar already described, two other examples of distance education are described in the next two subsections.

11.4.1 Online training and resources

New instructional resources for educators are often posted online to make them easier to distribute and access. Those same websites can also provide training resources to introduce the new material to educators. Targeting high school science teachers, the website Southeastern Forests and Climate Change offers narrated video "tours" of each activity to introduce the materials to educators (Monroe and Oxarart 2014). While brief, they convey the essence of the activity and the resources needed to successfully conduct it with students. A set of quiz questions enables teachers to check how much they know about the topics in each activity and directs them to additional resources if they answer incorrectly. Additional introductory material guides teachers through the website and provides links to resources and references. Teaching tools, such as slide presentations, handouts, answer keys, and videos, are also posted for each activity. Comments from teachers about the activities are received and posted to emulate the interaction that typically occurs at an in-person workshop.

11.4.2 Internet conferences

Teleconferencing (with or without video) can also occur over Internet lines with a variety of programs like Adobe Connect. Participants use their personal computers with a microphone headset (headphones) attached. Because users are talking instead of typing, the conversation can cover more territory in a limited period of time, and with small groups the use of a camera facilitates interaction and familiarity. In addition to audio and video capacity, many teleconferencing systems include an electronic whiteboard that allows users to write or draw figures that can be viewed by everyone. Several types of software provide audio and whiteboard capabilities.

When agency budget cuts eliminated travel for conferences, rather than cancel a planned event one enterprising coordinator converted the format from an in-person to an online, or virtual, symposium. According to Susan E. Moore, extension associate professor at North Carolina State University, more planning was required in advance of the event. Planners had to consider structure, time zones, firewalls, access to computers and headsets, how to incorporate both plenary and breakout sessions, and the amount of time a participant could reasonably be expected to stay online. Speakers had to participate in pre-event training to familiarize themselves with the software and had to be comfortable presenting without a physical audience in front of them. Attendees needed a computer with speakers (or a headset) with which they could access the webinars in real time. Instead of the 70 participants the agency had expected to fly to the conference, the online version engaged 556 individuals over the 12-session series. Discussion occurred at the end of each session, led by a moderator who read questions submitted by the audience. In some cases, discussions continued afterwards by email. Speakers reflected on the convenience of presenting from their own desks.

Organizers believe that the online conference was as informative and as interactive as in-person conferences typically are, and in fact allowed them to engage more high-profile presenters who might not be available to travel to a 2-day event but were able to lead a 90-minute session from their office. One missing element in the conversion, however, was the casual interaction that occurs when people meet over coffee or meals. Coordinators could facilitate this important interaction online by organizing special chat sessions and encouraging participants to answer get-to-know-you questions.

11.4.3 Planning

Like every other educational technique, planning for distance education begins with understanding the audience, including their needs, initial knowledge, constraints, and interests. Unique to distance education, however, is a simultaneous need to know about the available technology, budget, and access for your audience. Advance planning is needed to match the best technologies to the needs of your audience. If students are more likely to participate in online discussions after having a chance to reflect on the material and compose a response, for example, an asynchronous system may be most appropriate.

Planning for distance education requires that one pay special attention to how the instructional program can overcome the challenges of time and space. Three key considerations are: (1) generating an atmosphere conducive to learning, (2) engaging learners in the learning process, and (3) allowing learners to respond with comments about the content or the technology.

Planning for interaction is one of the most challenging aspects of distance education. Choose a learning theory that best fits your teaching style, the learners, and the content, and work to incorporate good teaching into distance technology (see Chapter 2). One strategy is to form cooperative groups at each site or among distant learners; another is to ask people to find a partner and work together on a task. If the program is to be synchronous, consider asking individuals to report their experiences and ideas or answer questions. It may take practice for learners and instructors to become accustomed to the way conversations flow over distance because of the lack of non-verbal cues and the changing technology.

Guidelines for developing multimedia learning change as new programs and technology become available. Some tried-and-true basics, however, are offered in Box 11.6

> **Box 11.6** Guidelines for designing effective multimedia instruction
>
> - Words and graphics on the screen are better than either alone, as long as the graphics help convey the relationships between elements, show change over time, or demonstrate function. Simple graphics are often better than complex images as extraneous detail can be distracting. Animations are not more effective than a series of still frames.
> - Audio narration can be helpful if the material is unfamiliar or technical. It need not be duplicated with text, but should be available in captions. A conversational and personalized tone leads to increased understanding.
> - Dividing the lessons into segments and allowing learners to click through screens at their own pace enhances their ability to process and understand each concept.
> - Planning a distance learning course or program requires substantial effort prior to any contact with learners. Lectures must be recorded without the benefit of people watching, nodding in agreement, or even nodding off in public. Discussion questions must be developed and assignments described with utmost clarity. Instructors who are accustomed to using student questions to provide information may find the distance format challenging and difficult to plan.

(Clark and Mayer 2011). Janice Easton, an instructor who helped create an online course on evaluation of environmental education programs, explained that it was difficult to decide how much information was enough, and what should be included, expanded, or left out. "Finding the balance that would give participants enough information through readings, examples, and assignments so they can apply the information to their setting was the biggest challenge," she said.

11.4.4 Implementation

The type of distance education will determine how it will be implemented. Most programs require some type of marketing to attract learners. Consider your ideal learner and how this type of person can be reached. A training program for program volunteers can be managed internally since the population is stable and known: people express interest, register for a session, and the program is offered when a group can be assembled. Offering a distance programming on a rolling basis means that someone will be answering questions, providing resources, or grading assignments in addition to everything else staff have to do. Small organizations find it easier to offer training once or twice a year.

Professional development programs can be advertised through professional associations and networks to a larger or less well-defined population. A course administrator who can handle marketing, registration, the uploading of course materials, and answering questions about technology will allow instructors to focus on providing content information to students.

The first interaction should be designed to orient participants to the technology and each other. This all-important introductory session will set expectations for learning, sharing, and exploring for the course. This perception of the presence of the instructor and other students was found to correlate positively with cognitive and affective outcomes (especially student satisfaction with their own learning) in a study of attitudes of graduate students to a synchronous distance education course in genetics (Russo and Benson 2005).

Instructional materials for distance education suggest that content should be presented in chunks—a 15-minute lecture, or three webpages. After one chunk of content, the teaching style should change to an assignment, conversation, video, or panel presentation (Telg 2012). The distance course for evaluation of environmental education programs achieved that balance by offering readings, reflective questions, examples on the web, examples from past course participants, and exercises with each unit.

11.4.5 Evaluation

Distance education programs can be evaluated with a thoughtful approach to the objectives of the program, the needs of the learners, and the ways stakeholders may need to use these data. Distance courses are typically evaluated by measuring student knowledge through quizzes, assignments, and exams and with evaluations of the instructors completed by students. Those who do not complete the course are another source of important data—try to find out why they gave up and explore how the program could be adjusted to retain more participants.

The first time an online environmental education training program was offered to volunteer youth group leaders, the organizer noticed that people were more likely to drop out just before an assignment or public post was due. The provision of explicit instructions for using technology to post and upload assignments could help overcome technological barriers. In the next offering of the program, the organizer made the requirements more explicit, reduced the number of assignments, and redesigned the program so participants gained more experience and benefits before the first assignment was due and thus improved the rate of completion (McConnell and Monroe 2012).

Webinar programs can collect information on participants' location, employment, and preferences while they are online with a few introductory questions. At the end of the program, a few more questions asking people to describe how they could use the webinar information or to offer ideas to guide the selection of future presenters could make a useful evaluation. Another viable option is to send evaluation questions to participants at their email address.

11.5 Other technologies

A number of technologies have been developed to measure, record, convey, and analyze various features of our planet. When used by educators, these technologies can greatly enhance conservation education and outreach programs. In many cases the technology accompanies or complements an educational technique mentioned elsewhere in this book: an exhibit, a presentation, or a website, for example.

Still other technologies may have been created to serve one purpose (e.g., make a phone call), but as cellphones developed into tiny computers their functions have increased exponentially. Downloadable apps enable people to identify and report a host of plants and animals, data which can then be incorporated into management decisions. The possibilities and opportunities are limitless, but for the purpose of illustrating diversity, we shall mention only a few examples.

11.5.1 Computer simulation and modeling

Computer models, a type of simulation, can enable scientists to test assumptions and predict how plants might grow in an environment rich in carbon dioxide or how forest biodiversity will respond to increases in global temperatures. Decision support systems, another type of simulation, enable farmers to determine the best time to plant, based on weather and climate projections (Southeast Climate Consortium 2015), for example. With the help of computer simulations, adults can see the impact that their food shopping might have on economic and environmental variables in Switzerland (Hansmann et al. 2005). Computer simulations are an intriguing educational technique for agencies and organizations to use in exhibits, to post on their websites, or distribute through an app to educators or adult learners.

Simulations, sometimes called "toy universes," extract important bits of the real universe, enable learners to control variables, and test learners' responses and skills. Computer simulation offers an educational technology that is repeatable, consistent, and available on any computer. Good simulations, like other educational techniques, are engaging enough to hold learners' attention; enable learners to stop and start from any point; are authentic, realistic, and important, though somewhat random and unpredictable; allow learners to gain meaningful goals in a reasonable period of time; and focus on higher-order thinking skills (see Chapter 2) because they typically are not used to memorize information (Norton and Sprague 2001). Students using the Brazilian program Carbopolis were more motivated to think about environmental problems and chemistry after simulating pollution problems and thinking about air quality (Eichler et al. 2005).

11.5.2 Podcasts

A podcast is an audio or video (sometimes called vodcast) segment streamed from the Internet to a computer or portable media device where it can be played offline. Consumers can search the web for interesting items through podcast directories and use a podcatcher to automatically download updates from the series. This feature makes it appear to users that the material is being broadcast to their player. A number of public radio programs are converted into podcasts, as well as music and news programs that are created just for this medium.

People can make their own podcast with a computer, an Internet connection, and some audio equipment, namely a microphone, a recorder/mixer, soundcard, and audio software to delete out the gaps or edit mistakes (an open-source product called Audacity is available for this). Files are saved in MP3 format and uploaded to the web. Existing podcast networks will generate the RSS feed that will allow people to subscribe to your program—you will need to put the small orange button on your website for people to click on (Grabianowski 2014).

At the University of Florida, an aquatic health specialist and Extension veterinarian hosts a number of podcasts for an international audience about maintaining an aquarium and healthy fish. In 2012 Roy Yanong reached over 250,000 listeners a month with sound scientific information on the Aquariumania website (PetLifeRadio 2014). From GloFish® to coral reefs, Yanong hosts discussions and answers questions in a talk show format, which also inspires familiarity. One listener wrote: "Hey there, Dr. Yanong. Just stumbled upon your podcast and wanted to let you know how much I like it. You get awesome guests and do a great job interviewing them. . . Since I don't have a community of fish keepers here, it's also great for learning about new resources (new to me). Thanks, Sean." Thus a podcast can create a learning community for diverse listeners on a scale that would be impossible to replicate in a traditional classroom.

11.5.3 Apps

Apps—short for applications—turn a smartphone into a library of resources and references due to the ability of phones to link to the Internet. In addition to identifying birds, leaves, and flowers, apps can enable citizens to report sightings of invasive species (IveGotOne) or migrating birds (eBird). That information can be used by agencies to concentrate efforts on removing invaders or by organizations to flood rice fields to create instant wetlands to feed the new arrivals (Robbins 2014).

An organization or agency can hire a company to create an app or create their own by learning basic coding skills and an account with Buzztouch. Consider whether the app should be available on both iPhones and Android phones, or just one or the other by assessing the audience you wish to reach. Also, determine whether you wish to make the app available for free or charge for each download. You may wish to make two versions, paid and free, and see how successful they are. You can even make money from a free app by adding advertisements (Heney 2013).

11.5.4 Geocaching

This high-tech version of orienteering is becoming a popular activity for friends and families in natural areas. Geocaching involves finding hidden (but not buried) containers in a park, nature center, or other facility, using the GPS coordinates of the container, which are posted on a geocaching website. Anyone can access the website, record the coordinates, and then hunt for the cache with a GPS unit. Caches contain trinkets, a logbook, or small toys, which can be taken by a finder, as long as another item is left in its place. An online form enables anyone to place and record a geocache. The activity utilizes technology to encourage the geocaching experience in real locations (Neustaedter et al. 2013). Some items, such as Travel Bugs, are geocached around the world, building mutual trust and social capital among strangers.

In Manatee County, Florida, USA, a geocaching program called Taking Flight GeoTour encourages families to explore local natural areas and bird habitats. Each cache has a theme, such as sea-level rise or invasive exotics, and in order to complete the tour, users must not only find the cache but also complete the educational activities. The Parks and Natural Resource Department office added a geocache on a small urban preserve that is managed with prescribed fire. The cache includes photographs of the site before and after the burn and asks users to take their own photographs and submit them online to continue to record vegetation growth. Coordinator Melissa Nell said, "One of the most useful aspects about geocaching is that each individual must log their visit and leave some sort of feedback. We quickly discovered that this was a wonderful way to receive both compliments and criticisms about the individual caches and the tour itself. This instant feedback has helped us adjust everything from cache locations to the format of our cache descriptions, providing for clearer communication and ease of use for geocachers. The majority of the logs are positive—geocachers thanking the county for creating the tour or remarking that they had never been to the location before."

11.5.5 Environmental monitoring

Educators have encouraged learners to monitor different aspects of the environment for decades. Collecting data on water quality, lichen, or traffic helps people witness changes that may be too small to detect by casual observation. High-quality data can be used by resource management agencies to document detrimental activities such as chemical spills. Water quality monitoring with chemical test kits, electronic probes, and sophisticated testing equipment occurs from Italy to Australia; results are often shared with others in the same watershed or around the world through interactive websites. Projects that involve public participation in scientific research (see Chapter 7) may ask adult volunteers to assess seed preference of birds at their feeder and report data on a website. GLOBE, an international monitoring program, established protocols for students to collect data on weather, air quality, water quality, ground cover, wildlife, and other aspects of the local environment (Fig. 11.2). Students can access the international data and answer their own questions about the relationships between variables or similarities among sites (GLOBE 2015). Journey North is another highly acclaimed website that engages young people in monitoring and reporting seasonal changes in plants and migrating animals. The website allows any user to access the results and witness the biological responses to environmental change.

Fig. 11.2 The GLOBE program uses a website to provide information and allow participants to share observations.

11.6 Summary

Educational technology includes a variety of devices that can help conservation educators reach a larger audience or share messages more effectively. Video can bring distant images home, demonstrate skills, and lend a realistic element to the message. A high-quality website can provide information, build skills, and launch campaigns. Distance education can take advantage of video, print materials, and websites to engage place-bound learners. Social media can be used to share information with followers and their friends and reach new audiences.

As technology continues to advance, more tools will be available to educators, but only those that are genuinely useful and simple to operate will survive. These are likely to be technologies that echo and support what we know about learning and education—the ones that enable learners to grapple with and apply new information in a way that makes a lasting impact on their mental models.

Designing on-site activities

First-hand experiences with wildlife or the outdoors are an effective way of increasing people's interest and concern for conservation. Informal settings, such as nature centers, parks, zoos, museums, camps, and farms, have natural advantages over formal school settings. On-site activities at informal settings can nurture curiosity, increase knowledge, improve motivation and attitudes, and engage the audience through participation and social interaction. Education and outreach techniques are needed to orient, inform, and engage visitors. Signs, guided walks, exhibits, demonstrations, nature studies, and visitor centers help people understand their surroundings, explore their personal feelings, and acquire new skills. From guide books or phone apps to a state-of-the-art visitor center, many techniques can enhance visitors' experiences.

This chapter provides guidelines for developing on-site activities and resources. An initial planning process at a site paves the way for designing a variety of materials, activities, and areas to achieve the goals of your organization. Components to consider include the total audience experience, from pre-visit materials to follow-up activities to support the on-site programs.

12.1 Laying the foundation: initial steps for designing on-site programs

Detailed planning is the best way to ensure successful on-site activities as part of your overall conservation program. The design process guides the orderly development of an education and outreach strategy in which you review and select from a variety of alternative actions to achieve your goals.

Since the site is managed by an agency or organization, the design phase starts with an institutional review to determine and articulate why on-site education and outreach activities are needed and which of the site's goals they can address (NAAEE 2004; Jacobson 2009). From a review of your organizational mission and policies, you can construct the specific objectives for the on-site program.

Once the objectives have been established, educational planners can describe the available resources and potential for the program. An inventory of biological and cultural resources helps determine what is available for supporting learning activities and

Conservation Education and Outreach Techniques. Second Edition. Susan K. Jacobson, Mallory D. McDuff &
Martha C. Monroe © Susan K. Jacobson, Mallory D. McDuff & Martha C. Monroe 2015.
Published 2015 by Oxford University Press.

for selecting major themes you wish to convey (Brody 2002; Veverka 2011). These steps include inventories of:

- site accessibility, habitat types, unique features, demonstration areas for management or restoration, geological resources, scenic vistas, waterfalls, gardens, and facilities;
- orientation available on the internet and on-site areas for contacting visitors, such as road intersections, boat launch areas, or campgrounds;
- regional interactions with nearby sites interpreting related material and regional impacts based on traffic flow;
- facilities and services needed; and
- actions needed to minimize the impact on natural or cultural resources and to protect sensitive areas.

As in all education and outreach programs, you must gather baseline information about the target audiences to design appropriate activities and materials and for later program evaluation. These data paint a portrait of the potential audiences for whom the programs are developed. Key audience information includes:

- specific target groups (visitors and non-visitors),
- visitor motivations and perceptions,
- visitor demographics,
- visitor orientation systems (pre-visit, on-site, post-visit),
- patterns of visitor use (time of visit, seasonality), and
- mechanisms for audience participation in the planning process and in an ongoing advisory capacity.

Based on the available resources and potential audiences, the design of education and outreach materials considers questions of how, when, and where the activities will be conducted. During this phase, a thematic concept is developed for each area, including:

- site-specific objectives, content, and context,
- recommended media and services,
- preliminary program, budgets, and justification,
- draft design for educational activities, and
- flexibility to incorporate new materials and themes in the future.

Once the planning phase is complete, the education and outreach designs need to be pilot tested with the target audience and the final materials developed. Contractors or in-house experts are engaged to assemble the program or physical structures for public presentation. Then the site is opened to the public. A management plan governs long-term care and maintenance of the materials.

Monitoring and evaluation of the activities will assess whether the goals and objectives of the program are being met and whether there are any unanticipated outcomes. In the classic text *Interpreting Our Heritage* (Tilden 1956), park interpreters are instructed to search for the gleam in a visitor's eyes to determine the effectiveness of their program. Counting gleams, however, does not provide accountability to managers and decision-makers, nor does it pinpoint problem areas in education and outreach materials so they can be modified accordingly. Methods used for the evaluation of materials and activities commonly include observational measures of visitor behavior, quantitative surveys and questionnaires, focus group studies, and long-term tracking. Staff may collect comments from a suggestion box or record visitor feedback from letters, calls, and online surveys (see Chapter 1).

The following types of information are generally collected and evaluated for on-site activities:

- The impact of the activity or materials on visitor knowledge, attitude, or behavior.
- The long-term impact of the activity or materials on visitors after they leave the site, measured through latent effects on schoolwork, homeowner activities, vocational interests, repeat visits, or website visits.
- Feedback for designing future activities or materials.
- The cost-effectiveness of activities.
- The time spent on site and money spent at the gift shop.
- Unexpected outcomes (both desirable and undesirable) that were not part of the original objectives.
- The broad impact of the activity or materials on the larger community, as measured through attendance/visits to natural areas or community trends.
- Restoration and environmental improvement activities in the community.

Evaluation not only improves programs but also helps meet agency requirements for reporting and cost accounting. It can provide marketing ideas to administrators who make decisions about program continuation and budgets.

Typical on-site education and outreach techniques can be grouped into personal (person-to-person) activities and self-guided activities. Personal services include talks and presentations, information desks, ranger help, guided walks, campfire programs, nature awareness activities, and environmental studies. Self-guided learning activities include exhibits, such as museum displays, signs, and kiosks; demonstration areas; publications, such as maps, brochures, trail guides, and books (Chapter 10); and audiovisual presentations, such as films, pre-recorded short lectures, self-guided audio tours via mobile devices and interactive computer activities (Chapter 11). This chapter describes several examples of personal and self-guided techniques to provide a framework for developing on-site activities.

12.2 Guided walks

On-site guided walks and other tours led by an interpreter offer audiences an opportunity to interact with your facilities and with natural and cultural areas. Guided walks can lead visitors along a forest trail, through a zoo or botanical garden, aboard a tour boat, or almost anywhere you wish to help your audience interact with your setting (Fig. 12.1). Tours of a demonstration area can show efforts at habitat restoration, such as the effects of prescribed burning on a pine forest, the management of rare wildlife species, or integrated pest management on a farm.

Fig. 12.1 A guided walk allows visitors to interact and search for rare birds. (Photo by S. Jacobson.)

Guided walks vary according to the site, educational objectives, and cultures and needs of the audience. In Denmark, two types of guides are available in natural areas (Ulstrup 2001). Nature guides are well versed in biology. They share their knowledge in the field with participants, essentially conducting an outdoor biology tour with a focus on cognition. In contrast, *friluftsliv* guides offer a different experience. The focus of the *friluftsliv* guide is on hiking. The hike may stretch over the course of a day and include an overnight stay. The goal is to teach people to feel comfortable and enjoy nature. The *friluftsliv* guide provides facilitation in basic areas, such as clothing, food, equipment, and tools used in backcountry travel. They share basic outdoor skills with their participants (Ulstrup 2001).

Most on-site guided tours have elements in common with effective public talks (see Chapter 8). They are entertaining, relevant, meaningful, and organized around a central theme. Making a guided walk entertaining involves the audience in actively observing, searching, thinking, or conducting an activity guided by the educator's narrative and theme.

12.2.1 Planning

Planning a trail for your guided walk should include an understanding of the needs of the visitors, the potential of your site, and your learning objectives. When designing a trail through a forest follow specific guidelines to ensure a unique and refreshing adventure for your audience (Box 12.1).

Guided walks have an identifiable introduction, body, and conclusion, like all public presentations. In addition, guided walks have a staging period before the tour starts.

Staging period

About 15 minutes before your tour you can begin to greet your audience as they gather at the departure point. This is your opportunity to learn something about their interests and background, and answer any questions they may have. Your friendly greeting and

---

Box 12.1 Design tips for an inviting forest trail

- Plot the trail past large trees, areas of plant succession, water features, and other unusual or unique sights.
- Plant or maintain native trees and shrubs with different leaf shapes, bark textures, and growth forms.
- Plan lookouts to enable visitors to get views of lakes, mountain peaks, river valleys, or other vistas.
- Create easy access to trails and manage vegetation to facilitate entry and movement.
- Provide benches, boardwalks, pergolas, or other structures to promote visitors' comfort and reflection.
- Screen unpleasant views or built structures.
- Use winding trails to draw visitors onward with the mystery of what may come next.
- Provide open areas for group activities or tour stops

---

enthusiasm for the tour helps build rapport with the audience and makes a good first impression. You can mention any physical or safety requirements, the availability of food or bathrooms, and suggestions for sun or bug protection at this time.

Introducing the walk

Begin at the designated time and introduce your program. Your introduction must capture the audience's attention (otherwise they may disappear!), create interest in the topic, and orient them (Jacobson 2009; Ham 2013). The specific needs of a school or tour group should be incorporated into the walk. Tell them how much time the tour will take and repeat any physical or safety requirements. Most importantly, introduce the theme of your tour and the general organization of the trip and your commentary. Set the stage for what they will see along the way by giving a brief overview of the tour. It is appropriate to keep a few tidbits for a surprise, however, and you may even want to hint at a bit of a mystery with which they can assist. As you walk along, stay in the lead and make sure that you can see the entire group behind you. As you reach each stop, wait if necessary, or walk back into the line, to make sure that you are talking to the entire group.

Body of the walk

The body of the tour comprises the stops that you make along the way. During this period, develop your theme by describing specific sites, plants, animals, or objects that you pass. Do not talk about "everything," stick to your theme. Remember, your audience will remember only about five main points.

Each stop may take 1–6 minutes, depending on the focus and the group. Larger groups take longer to assemble and move. Your narration generally will follow a four-step format in which you:

1. Get the group to focus their attention on a specific scene or object of interest. This can be done with a question: "What do you notice about this flower that would

make it easy for a bat to pollinate?" Make sure the question is something they can answer with observation.

2. Next provide your explanation or description: "The white, fragrant (encourage group to take a sniff later) flower attracts bats flying at night . . ."

3. Now connect the stop with your overall theme, such as: "We depend on pollinators to maintain our landscape." This makes it clear why you stopped there and why the point is important.

4. Lastly, provide a transition sentence to the next stop. A foreshadowing of what will follow or a suggestion of what to look for along the way to the next stop will reorient the audience to the tour. "Have you ever wondered where bats live?"

Experienced guides make their stops more dynamic by involving the audience at each stop in thinking or doing specific tasks. Some tour guides carry a backpack with visual aids, such as animal skins, pressed flowers, bird nests, owl pellets, binoculars, thermometers, photographs, or other objects that might not be seen or used on every tour but which would enhance or illustrate the theme at certain stops. Encouraging the use of all five senses, such as smelling leaves for identification or listening to frog calls, can make the audience enjoy and remember specific points.

Many guides rely on provocative questions to stimulate the group and encourage interaction. Asking creative questions is an art. Different types of questions solicit a variety of thoughts and answers. Questions may compare differences and similarities between things, such as, "What do bees and people have in common?" Questions can stimulate the group to think about the implications of something, such as: "What might this forest look like in 30 years if timber management remains unchanged?" Follow-up questions can elicit opinions or personal feelings, such as: "What would be a fair solution to address both the forest ecosystem and forestry jobs?" Questions also may enhance analytical skills, such as: "What needs to happen to keep this species from becoming extinct?"

Like all forms of communication, your questioning techniques and descriptions will depend on your audience. Not everyone will respond to contrived objects from your backpack or want to be questioned about personal beliefs. Differences in cultural backgrounds must also be considered (Whatley 2011). Some international tourists visiting US parks find direct questions posed by young rangers to be rude or discomforting based on their own cultures. Children in a group may make long stops or explanations unfeasible. At the same time, children's innate curiosity, lack of inhibition, and size can provoke observations in nature that adults might miss.

The length of the tour also must be geared toward your audience. You may have 20 planned stops along the tour, and anticipate a few unplanned stops to take advantage of serendipitous scenes or sightings that help illustrate your theme. If you have a large audience, you will have to eliminate some stops to stay on schedule. Do not forget that the audience will probably remember only five or fewer main points. Make sure that your stops do not cover much more than can be retained, and that several stops may relate to the same point.

Concluding the walk

The conclusion is given after the last stop of your tour. Like the conclusion to a talk, it should reinforce the theme. The conclusion reminds the audience of the relationship between the stops they made and the items you discussed during the tour and the significance of the theme. Good conclusions are brief and to the point. They reaffirm the take-home message for the audience and let them know that the tour is definitely over. Thank the group for their participation.

12.2.2 Implementation

Once you have carefully planned all elements of the guided walk, implementation involves a number of components. First, the design and content of your walk should be reviewed by colleagues or outside experts. Second, it should be pilot tested with members of the target audience. After giving a pilot tour, provide a feedback checklist or carefully question the participants about the content, duration, themes, topics, and props of the tour. Also ask about your voice, manner, delivery, language, and interactions with the audience. Make revisions and practice again. You also may want to ask a colleague to accompany you and provide additional feedback. Consider asking them what they think they will remember in 3 months. Is that what you hope they will remember?

Successful implementation also is dependent on having a strategy for advertising and scheduling the guided walks. How will the audience learn about them—how will they be marketed? Are staffing and budget needs fulfilled? Finally, consider how you will sustain long-term maintenance of the trail and ongoing operational needs in the way of equipment or materials.

Guided walks should be designed to meet the needs and interests of the target audience. A group of students at the Singapore American School teamed up with the Nature Society of Singapore and the Singapore Association for the Visually Handicapped to implement a sensory nature trail. The goals were to develop a trail on the island of Pulau Ubin, an important area for biodiversity conservation, and to make nature accessible for the visually impaired (Frazier 2002). The design of the trail incorporated advice from biologists about plant identification and ecological references. Students then selected interpretive stations along the trail and created descriptive accounts that visually impaired visitors would find interesting. They incorporated input from their target audience to better understand the range of visual impairments of their visitors.

During the walks, sighted guides helped the visually impaired visitors explore the textures, shapes, and smells of interesting wild plants (many that are used in popular foods and medicines). Shells, rocks, birdcalls, sounds of the sea, and the odor of the mudflats became features of the tour as well. The tours consisted of two student guides for each visually impaired visitor. One student interpreted the natural features of the trail, while the other served as a physical guide. The success of the initial outings led to a commitment by the students to continue to offer their guided walks for the next 5 years. Partnering with the outside groups provided continued advertising, scheduling, and maintenance for the tour and trail.

12.2.3 Evaluation

Evaluation provides feedback to remedy any problems with design or content that might be reducing the effectiveness of your guided walk. Direct feedback from visitors provides immediate data to help determine the strengths and weaknesses of the activity. By asking visitors questions or directly observing them, educators can find out whether the visitors used and learned from the interpretation (Ambrose and Paine 1993).

Asking visitors questions about the interpretation determines:

- If the guided walk got its message across.
- Which activities visitors found most interesting or stimulating, and why.
- What improvements and changes visitors would suggest.
- What message and information visitors remember.
- If visitors found the guide and walk effective.

Observing visitors at a site determines:

- How many people engaged in the guided walk.
- How many visitors stayed and interacted with the guide or asked for further activities after the walk (often measured by time spent at activity or site).
- How visitors reacted emotionally to the activity (e.g., smile, frown, talk, or laugh).
- How many visitors talked to each other about the activity (record positive and negative remarks).
- How many visitors asked questions.
- If visitors followed suggested activities or appropriate behaviors.

12.3 Exhibits

An exhibit is generally defined as a strategic presentation of ideas or themes with the intention of educating, informing, or orienting an audience. Exhibits are usually presented in informal settings, such as nature centers, outdoor areas, trails, visitor centers, museums, and building lobbies, where the majority of visitors are exposed to non-personal or self-guided interpretation. Visits to informal facilities are self-paced, voluntary, and exploratory, so exhibits reach visitors at their own speed and level of interest. Exhibits engage an audience in non-linear and creative kinds of learning, as opposed to the more orderly, linear, and verbal learning that goes on in classrooms and seminars.

Types of exhibits include self-guided trails, visitor center displays, educational kiosks, viewpoint markers, natural feature signs, special events displays, campground bulletin boards, regulatory signs, labeled trees or specimens, artistic statements, and three-dimensional models. Exhibits can encompass devices like quiz boards, audiovisual programs, continuous radio broadcasts, interactive websites, phone apps, talking animal displays, models, and computer simulations. Because exhibits often incorporate real objects, such as petrified wood or collections of shells, visitors can respond to "the real thing." Many exhibits also include take-home materials, such as brochures or other publications (Chapter 10), and links to websites (Chapter 11).

In many cases, exhibits reach more people than personal approaches, making them an important part of an overall education and outreach plan. Because of their importance, cost, and durability, care must be taken to design exhibits to be effective channels for a conservation message. Exhibits can be effectively used in a number of settings and to accomplish a variety of goals. They may inspire viewers to contemplate beautiful vistas, objects, or quotations. They can demonstrate a story or relay an educational message. Or they can simply encourage visitors to make their own discoveries and subtly direct viewers to follow their own interests (Ambrose and Paine 1993).

Exhibits take many physical forms. Indoor exhibits may be free-standing dividers, wall-mounted signs, objects on tables, or displays in cabinets, while outdoor exhibits may be free-standing signs or displays under weather-resistant structures. Exhibits in any situation may be either flat or three-dimensional, such as a model, diorama, object, or outdoor scene (Fig. 12.2). Exhibits are primarily visual, usually including illustrations, maps, graphics, charts, and other explanatory artwork. In addition, effective exhibits strive to excite more than one of the audience's senses, for example, providing an audio explanation and something to touch along with visuals and text. Some exhibits include smell to arouse the interest of an audience, by instructing them to sniff the surrounding air or a particular plant. Other exhibits involve live animals, which are exciting to people yet require careful attention to animal welfare and safety considerations (Fig. 12.3).

Self-guided tours along forest trails, bikeways, automobile drives, demonstration areas, and historic sites follow the same guidelines as for other types of exhibits. Self-guided tours lead people sequentially along a series of interpretive stops.

Fig. 12.2 Museum artisan Bob Leavy creates a life-size diorama of a mangrove swamp for the Florida Museum of Natural History. (Photo by S. Jacobson.)

Fig. 12.3 Live animal exhibits attract a crowd, such as this demonstration of the feeding behavior of an alligator at the St Augustine Alligator Farm in Florida. (Photo by S. Jacobson.)

The tour flows from an orientation and introduction to the site through 15 to 20 stops that elaborate on the theme. Most self-guided walking tours are about 1 km long and take half an hour to complete. Depending on the specific characteristics of the site and the audience, self-guided tours use signs, brochures, and audio and video information to communicate with visitors. Technology such as Quick Response codes, phone apps, and other electronic features can be used to enhance the visitor experience.

12.3.1 Planning

The best exhibits attract attention and effectively communicate a message or theme within the attention span of the target audience. Exhibits that use several media are stronger than exhibits that rely on a single medium (such as text) because they better reach audience members who have varied learning styles and tastes. Researchers have summarized characteristics of effective exhibits into the "ABCD" of exhibit design (Ham 1992):

- *Attractive*: attention-getting exhibits that use appropriate colors and interesting graphics and visuals.
- *Brief*: well-organized and simple exhibits that contain five or fewer main ideas, only enough text to develop the theme, and graphics to help communicate with viewers.
- *Clear*: the theme of the exhibit is obvious and can be immediately understood by the audience. Additionally, the exhibit is easily visible with adequate lighting and unobstructed viewing.
- *Dynamic*: the exhibit communicates the message by arousing curiosity, inviting participation, and providing entertainment (Fig. 12.4).

Fig. 12.4 Dynamic exhibits spark people's curiosity and engage their senses. Visitors are encouraged to tug a toy eel from its rock cranny at the Monterey Bay Aquarium in California. (Photo by S. Jacobson.)

The exhibit development process

Planning includes writing text and labels and developing and testing a mock-up exhibit. It entails working with staff or contractors to get the final exhibit produced and installed. Most of the time needed to develop an exhibit is spent in the planning stage, with less time spent in each subsequent phase in the process. The following describes specific steps that might be included in each of the exhibit development stages (Knudson et al. 2003).

During the development of an exhibit, educators set goals, identify and assess audiences, develop objectives, and research and conceptualize the design. Audience research at the San Diego Wild Animal Park, USA, includes the following qualitative methods (Trapp et al. 1994):

- Listen to visitors' conversations at an animal display.
- Ask visitors what they would like to know.
- Install a voice recorder or comment board at a display.
- Ask animal keepers and other employees what visitors ask about.
- Ask tour guides what visitors ask them.
- Brainstorm questions and topics with external educators and graphic artists.

Exhibit planning and preparation can take a long time. It can take weeks or months to develop a small exhibit, and over a year for a major exhibit. In addition, the exhibit work plan must allow for adequate time to test a mock-up exhibit and text with audience members, and for a final evaluation to determine whether the exhibit has met the interpretive objectives (see Chapter 1).

The exhibit design phase concerns the more practical and applied tasks of determining orientation, panel layouts, lighting, and other design details for the exhibit. Evaluation is used during this phase to test the opinions of audience and experts about exhibit design ideas. During the planning process your exhibit team must consider a number of design criteria. These describe the "powers" an exhibit should embody (Bitgood and Patterson 1987):

- Attracting power: does the exhibit get people to stop?
- Holding power: does the exhibit keep people and for how long?
- Teaching power: do people learn from the exhibit?
- Motivating power: are people motivated to find out more or take action?

Box 12.2 provides a summary of how to make your exhibit more powerful.

Getting an audience to stop and read or listen is an important function of exhibit design. The exhibit design is what initially attracts people, but the text and visuals must keep their attention in order for them to learn something. Visitors usually stop for less than 1 minute at an exhibit—long enough to read only a fraction of the text. Long text discourages many visitors. When preparing text, keep in mind the aim of the exhibit and the characteristics of the audience. These same guidelines apply equally to any non-personal or self-guided program—visitor center exhibits, trail signs, computer and cellphone applications, driving tours, and audiovisual programs. Besides having accurate content, correct spelling, good grammar, and understandable language, exhibit text should convey a theme that the audience can understand, no matter what the medium.

Box 12.2 Factors leading to effective exhibits that result in longer viewing times

- Indicate the flow of exhibit by including an exhibit title, an introductory panel, and a conclusion at the end. Use lines and angles to lead the eye where viewer should look; provide a clear pathway to follow.
- Identify a theme and story line in titles and headings.
- Match the exhibit to the demographic characteristics of your visitors, including languages; connect stories to visitors' interests and backgrounds.
- Keep the text short, concise, and thematic; use short sentences and bullets, personal pronouns, and the active voice.
- Feature unusual or rare information, and enhance perceptions of beauty or danger in the exhibit to provide variety and freshness.
- Make features easy to view by placing subjects directly behind signs, and main titles at or above eye level.
- Use large size graphics and text; isolate the main elements and make sure they stand out from the background.
- Express ideas visually through artifacts, illustrations, photographs, and videos; dominate panels with visual images.
- Create balanced graphic design using edge borders or boundaries, much empty space, harmonious colors and shapes, and consistent and clear typestyles and illustrations.
- Use intrinsically interesting visuals, such as baby animals, rather than a data chart.
- Engage other senses, for example touch or sound, in addition to vision.
- Provide interactive and participatory activities, such as having visitors answer questions, search for something, solve a puzzle, make a prediction, or confront a misconception.
- Ensure that interactive devices can be easily manipulated and provide immediate feedback to the visitor.
- Stimulate interaction among visitors.
- Make the exhibit easy to view by providing adequate lighting, and use lighting to focus attention on key themes or objects.
- Place information in the visitor's line of sight, close to viewer.
- Demarcate materials for children by special colors or lower placement.
- Eliminate visual interference from neighboring exhibits and auditory barriers from entrance/exit noise.
- Cater to different audiences with audio and video materials.
- Provide comfortable amenities, such as rails, seats, temperature control, and rest rooms.
- Enhance positive social pressures, such as attraction to crowds, walking speeds adjusted to other visitors, and comfortable waiting times.
- Accommodate visitors with disabilities.

Source: Caputo et al. (2008) and Jacobson (2009).

Planning an exhibit also requires consideration of the actual space available for the exhibit, for example, allowing space in the exhibit area for visitors to sit and comfortably contemplate exhibits and electronic devices to providing adequate lighting by windows or artificial light. An inventory of space requirements ensures the comfort of visitors and effective use of the area. Access and facilities for people with special needs, such as limited mobility, or the very young or elderly may require ramps, wide aisles for wheelchairs, or other accommodations. Safety elements, such as emergency exits, fire extinguishers, and first-aid equipment, are often dictated by government codes, and need to be followed.

In planning a new monkey exhibit at the San Diego Zoo, the design team included staff from exhibition, public relations, education, architecture, and maintenance departments to determine how to make the best use of the limited space available. The team realized they could create access to a vertical exhibit. This would provide more opportunity for viewing the animals, help portray the monkeys' natural, arboreal habitat, and increase the space available for information signs and displays. Aerial boardwalks would bring visitors into the tree canopy, yet remain accessible to wheelchairs.

Wayside exhibits located outdoors have other design concerns. They must be integrated into the landscape. A landscape designer can help with placement decisions: while exhibits need to interpret the scene, they should not intrude. Exhibits can be designed into pedestrian turnouts on boardwalk trails or blended into railings, hedges, or other unobtrusive borders. Quick Response codes posted on traditional signs can be useful at distant sites. They can provide audio or video information in areas where facilities do not have the budget to hire interpreters to provide programs.

12.3.2 Implementation

Guidelines for text include: writing simply, avoiding jargon and technical terms, putting the main point at the beginning, keeping it short, and using vocabulary that visitors use. Similar to the guidelines for good writing (see Chapter 10), these tips are easier said than done. Biologists and technical staff members often have a difficult time conveying their knowledge to the public in understandable language. It is important to write as if you were a friend of the visitor, rather than as a scientist or program administrator. External educators, copywriters, or journalists can be hired to assist with exhibit text. An outside person also may provide a fresh and unbiased perspective of your exhibit text and design.

The story told by exhibit panels is generally presented in three parts: the title, subtitles, and body text (Fig. 12.5). Most exhibits start with an introductory panel, giving the exhibit title and purpose. The audience should be able to grasp what the exhibit is about and why it is worth viewing. It may also be useful to give some information about where the exhibit or program will take the viewer. The direction of the exhibit may be obvious in a small visitor center or museum, but less obvious for a trail, discovery center, or computer simulation.

The introduction is followed by the body of the exhibit, often a series or network of panels. Section panels should follow an obvious order, such as chronology, cause and effect, problem/analysis/solution, or from part to whole or whole to part. Section panels

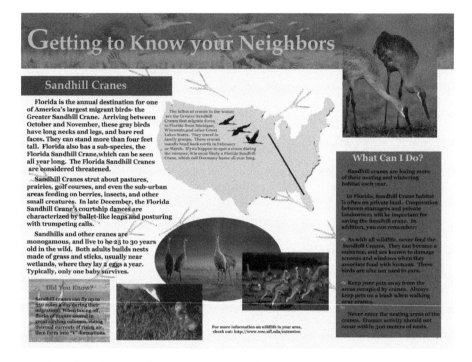

Fig. 12.5 This exhibit panel tells the story of sandhill crane conservation using graphics, titles, subtitles, and text. (Courtesy of M. Hostetler, University of Florida.)

should include thematic headings and give more background information about the exhibit topic.

Museum experts note that since most viewers only read a fraction of the text, the title and subtitles of interpretive panels must communicate the theme quickly. Instead of giving the panel a label that identifies a topic, it is better to use a title that relates the theme, uses an active voice, and is interesting and fun. Thematic, rather than topical, titles help get your message across. A topical title might be "Trees," but the thematic title developed from it could be "Our lives depend on trees" or "The forest is our pharmacy." An exhibit explaining biological research on ungulates in Alaska catches visitors with the title: "Poop: a valuable research tool." Studies of exhibit titles at the Birmingham, Alabama Zoo predator house revealed that thematic titles, such as "Animals that eat animals," were very good at attracting and holding visitors' attention. However, researchers have found that few people take the time to stop and read an entire exhibit.

A thematic title and strong graphic design can attract audience members to your exhibit, but it is the subtitles and body text that exert the holding power on the audience once they are near. Subtitles should be smaller than the main title, but they must clearly relate several separate ingredients of the theme. There should be fewer than five subtitles on any given exhibit panel. A coherent graphic design that physically separates the components of the theme, while maintaining a consistent look, will aid the viewer in finding the subtitles and understanding the theme. The body text is placed near each subtitle. More detailed text and object labels may also be added, but should be placed away from the main themes and text of the exhibit panels.

Exhibit text for general audiences should be written at middle school level (12–15-year-olds), and lower for younger audiences. Many computer software programs and free websites can test the level of your text, using indices like the Flesch–Kincaid readability test. This can involve simply uploading text to a website.

One easy method for calculating readability yourself is to use the Fry test to see if your text meets the middle school level guidelines. For the Fry test, use a sample of several passages of your exhibit totaling about 300 words. Count the number of words, sentences, and syllables in that excerpt. For text to target the level of 12–15-year-olds there should be between 5 and 10 sentences per 100 words (10–20 words per sentence) and between 120 and 150 syllables per 100 words. It is better for text to fall at the lower end of these guidelines.

Other factors also affect readability. The lighting and layout of the exhibit must be good, and the typeface must be large enough to read at an appropriate distance. For indoor exhibits, main titles should be a minimum of 2–3 cm tall and subtitles should be at least 1–2 cm tall. For outdoor exhibits to be read at a distance, titles should be 10–13 cm tall and subtitles 7–12 cm. Remember that these are *minimum* sizes—larger sizes will always be easier and more attractive for the audience to read (Fig. 12.6).

Fig. 12.6 Large lettering and a bold image attract attention to this outdoor exhibit placed in moose habitat at Yellowstone National Park. (Photo by S. Jacobson.)

Many exhibits convey a conservation message that encourages people to seek further information or take action. Audience members may be asked to think about a question, pick up trash during their trail hike, avoid trampling a rare species, write to a legislator, volunteer for a conservation project, visit a website, or get more information at the front desk of a visitor center. The additional information also may take the form of a marketing device—for example as a request for support or membership of an organization.

By following the guidelines for text development, readability, style, content, and exhibit development during the planning stage, you should be able to implement a display that has the power to attract and hold your audience and to deliver your conservation message. Once the exhibit is opened to the public, maintenance requires an ongoing plan. This ensures that interactive displays continue to work, signs are clean and legible, and buildings and landscaping are maintained as anticipated. Any problems with litter, vandalism, or other negative visitor behaviors must be addressed immediately to ensure long-term success.

12.3.3 Evaluation

Evaluation should be infused into every stage of exhibit development. Methods of getting information to improve the exhibit design at the planning stage include portfolio reviews and focus groups with members of the audience and with experts. Ongoing monitoring during implementation helps ensure smooth functioning of the program. The completed exhibit should be assessed to determine its effectiveness and make the required modifications. Methods used for the evaluation of exhibits include observational measures of behavior, before-and-after-surveys, visitor interviews, and electronic data tracking. While problems can arise at any stage of development, many can be corrected, taking into account visitor characteristics and exhibit objectives. Fixing problems depends on good evaluation data. For example, text cannot be worded for the interests of visitors if those interests are unknown, and major eye contact points and visitor pathways must be observed by testing a mock-up exhibit or through observational techniques in order to design an effective exhibit.

Box 12.2 can be used to check the style, content, and structure of your exhibit to assess how to better attract and hold your target audience. A wayside exhibit at Glacier National Park's Bird Woman Falls, Montana, explains the geology of the specific hanging valley that can be seen above the waterfall. An evaluation of the effectiveness of the exhibit revealed that visitors learned to recognize this glacial feature and looked for other hanging valleys during a tour of the park (Hoffman 1999). In a more quantitative assessment of an exhibit about the Great Bay Estuary in New Hampshire, visitors were surveyed after exposure to the material. They were asked to describe characteristics of an estuary, and list reasons why the Great Bay is valuable (Heffernan 1998).

12.4 Demonstrations

Demonstration areas are used to show visitors the results of a variety of conservation activities. Urban dwellers can see for themselves how and what to plant for a small butterfly garden. Farmers can observe the benefits of leaving habitat for birds that eat pests.

Forest owners can view improved silvicultural practices. Demonstration areas provide an opportunity to show the effort required and the results of management actions in a more convincing manner than vicarious methods such as reading or listening. A demonstration butterfly garden can provide signs that identify suitable plants, and explain the butterfly life cycle and the steps for planting native plants to attract butterflies. Visitors then can watch a myriad of butterflies sipping nectar or laying eggs, and make decisions about the aesthetic and financial impacts of developing their own butterfly garden (see Chapter 9).

12.4.1 Planning

The American River Parkway Foundation collaborated with Sacramento Suburban Water District and Carmichael Water District, California, to plan a native plant demonstration garden. The goal was to demonstrate the many benefits of native plants, particularly for water conservation. Many of the plants native to the Sacramento region are adapted to long periods of drought and intense heat. The objectives of the demonstration garden were to:

- promote the beauty of native California plants
- reduce water consumption in residential areas and decreases utility costs,
- reduce water withdrawals from the American River watershed,
- decrease the cost and time it takes to replant and maintain traditional gardens,
- limit the amount of non-native plants within the Sacramento area,
- reduce the amount of chemicals, fertilizers, and pesticides used in traditional landscaping, and
- support the native animals that evolved alongside the plants that are native to this area.

The garden was created in 2007, making use of the many volunteers active with the Parkway Foundation and using seeds from plants found in the American River Parkway and native to the greater Sacramento region. Real and virtual (via an interactive map and web page) visitors to the garden can gain specific information on exposure, growth, and naturalization of the many plants in the demonstration garden and can gauge exactly how and where to plant them in their own yards.

Demonstration areas are often planned to demonstrate forestry practices. Extension foresters at Clemson University, South Carolina, established three forest stewardship demonstration areas as an educational technique to help protect sensitive and rare coastal plain forests. They promoted three strategies: conversion to native longleaf pine, increase in the use of prescribed fire, and improved management of bottomland hardwoods. The demonstration areas were the setting for a series of workshops targeting private forest landowners in coastal South Carolina. An important component of the demonstration areas was the calculation of financial information and other benefits, such as wildlife and aesthetic values, based on changing forestry practices, a key concern for private forest owners (Straka and Franklin 2008).

The planning of demonstration areas requires careful attention to the goals, the audience, and the site itself. The initial expenditure for labor and materials is a key concern of any organization planning a demonstration area. The ongoing and long-term staff and funding requirements to properly care for the area are equally important constraints. Sometimes partnering with organizations that have similar interests can help provide long-term labor or funding needs. For example, local garden clubs may be willing to volunteer to maintain a demonstration butterfly garden. Water management agencies in the Parkway example were willing to design demonstrations of native plants and xeriscaping for home landscapes in order to promote reduction of water use in their district. Parents and local plant nurseries may volunteer labor and materials for the development of a schoolyard ecosystem demonstration.

Planning a demonstration site generally entails a team of individuals with expertise in the practical aspects of developing the site, educators with knowledge of how to use the site, members of the target audience to ensure the usefulness of the site, and individuals who can bring to bear other resources, such as funding, marketing, and other organizational support. The following steps were taken to create a schoolyard wildlife habitat demonstration (Flint 2002):

1. Meet the principal, teachers, students, parents, school officers, and maintenance staff to discuss using the school grounds for a demonstration area.
2. Form a project team and involve as many groups as possible in the labor, as well as in the fun and learning.
3. Include the maintenance staff in every step of the planning and implementation to ensure the area is designed for easy maintenance.
4. Obtain or draw a map of the school and demarcate all the existing wildlife features, such as sources for food, shelter, and water.
5. Choose a site that is easily accessible to the target audience: students, teachers, and staff.
6. Have the team decide on wildlife habitat improvements or additions that should be made.
7. Plan the implementation phase, including a detailed diagram of the project, a comprehensive list of materials, a description of how to build the project, and a schedule of maintenance requirements.
8. Incorporate walkways, tables, shaded areas, and other elements into the demonstration area that will maximize the comfort and safety of visitors to the site to promote an environment that is conducive to learning.
9. Develop safety and use procedures with input from appropriate groups.
10. Schedule the necessary steps to build the project, from gathering materials to assigning workdays.
11. Plan and draft the education and outreach materials—guides, signs, brochures, exhibits, QR codes, and websites—that will support the demonstration area.

12.4.2 Implementation

Implementing a demonstration area involves establishing a daily and seasonal maintenance schedule. Implementing the pedagogical activities for your demonstration area include pre- and post-visit activities as well as on-site activities and seasonal signage.

Student activities associated with a demonstration pond may vary from observing aquatic life to learning about their regional watershed. The North Carolina State Museum of Natural Sciences, Raleigh, suggests the following learner activities focused on a demonstration pond in a schoolyard (Flint 2002):

- Observe aquatic animals on the surface of the water and answer questions such as: what do you see, what is it doing, how does it move, eat, or breathe?
- Record and discuss observations about underwater organisms using underwater viewers.
- Catch aquatic animals with dip nets and identify them using guides and keys, then report interesting facts about them to the class.
- Make your own field guide to aquatic insects or plants.
- Compare water, air, and ground temperatures, or water pH over time, and develop hypotheses to explain differences.
- Study aquatic plants by measuring their growth over time and relate it to changes in water chemistry and temperature.
- Discuss natural wetlands and learn about the watershed in which students live.
- Tie the science-based exercises to other subjects, such as language arts and social studies, with environment-themed exercises in other classes (see Chapter 5).

Demonstration sites can also amplify their impact through networks and online resources. Web-based programs, such as the Global Rivers Environmental Education Network, allow students to share data and experiences among many sites. GPS programs (e.g., Google Earth) can help students explore the broader watershed. Web cameras and other electronic devices allow demonstration areas to reach larger audiences remotely.

Demonstration areas for all audiences—students, landowners, consumers—provide opportunities for first-hand observation and experiences. Depending on the goals, these sites provide information about the species present, equipment needed, and other logistical support to enable visitors to emulate the demonstration at home or work or to support similar activities in their communities.

12.4.3 Evaluation

A number of techniques can be used for collecting data to evaluate demonstration areas. Ultimately, evidence should indicate if visitors use the information or apply the skills learned at the demonstration site to different settings, such as visiting students applying new techniques in their own backyards. The subsequent actions of the visiting students could be compared to the practices of students in a control group who were not exposed to the demonstration site, to help determine the program impact. Data about the number of visitors attracted to a site, the length of time spent at a site, visitor understanding of the information and objectives of the demonstration, and whether they act upon the information, provide feedback for assessing the program and making improvements. Qualitative feedback from teachers implementing a schoolyard demonstration program reported: "[We] were very surprised that this lesson had spilled over to the students' own yards. They went home and returned the next day so excited about the bugs they had found in their own backyard" (Flint 2002). For visitors to web-based programs or social media linked to a demonstration site, the analytics discussed in Chapter 11 can be used for evaluation.

Informal interviews with visitors can be used to reveal if they understand

- the main point of the demonstration,
- how to duplicate the demonstration should they choose to,
- aspects that are unclear or confusing,
- whether the demonstration is interesting, attractive, and relevant to them,
- the usefulness of any supporting material, or additional materials needed, and
- factors that would make their family, friends, or colleagues more likely to visit the demonstration area.

Managers of forest demonstration areas have used a variety of qualitative and quantitative data to evaluate efficacy. The Hopkins Demonstration Forest in Oregon recorded more than 2000 volunteer hours, 1125 participating students, and 70 educational programs annually to help measure the success of their demonstration (Hopkins Forest 2013). Feedback from visiting teachers with their students stated that they were able to: "Discover the forest in my own terms," and had "Found a new lens to teach students about the subjects that are close to my heart." Visitors to conservation forest demonstration areas in South Carolina included more than 385 forest owners who controlled over 100,000 hectares of forest. Before and after surveys helped document impacts. Nearly 90% of the participants rated the experience as good or excellent and 86% indicated they would change their forest management practices. As a result of the program, the level of knowledge of forest management practices among participants increased by an average of 56% over pre-program levels (Straka and Franklin 2008).

12.5 Nature awareness and study

Remember the curiosity of young children drawn to watching a bee hover over a flower? Nature awareness activities build on this appreciation of the natural world. Nature awareness ranges from energetic activities where young children simulate a bat and moth to reflective experiences for adults, such as a silent hike or sharing circle in the outdoors. Whether you work in a primary school in Kenya or for the USDA Forest Service, nature awareness activities will allow you to explore the environment with your participants and create a sense of joy in the outdoors. The theory behind nature awareness activities developed from the nature study movement in the early 1900s. But the practice of nature awareness builds on the innate curiosity and joy that children experience playing outdoors (Cornell 2015), which can impact on their physical and mental health (Louv 2005).

On-site programs associated with parks and natural areas often offer a range of activities, from nature awareness games to in-depth nature study and citizen science activities, for people seeking a scientific understanding of the natural environment. Nature study programs may focus on increasing knowledge or skills in a particular subject area targeted to a specific audience, such as botany for gardeners or bird identification for photographers. On-site awareness and study programs enhance visitors' experiences and simultaneously help build support for the specific site or park system. Programs can last from an afternoon to an entire summer and offer activities for which visitors and community members are often willing to pay, especially if experienced staff plan the activities or recognized experts teach the courses.

12.5.1 Planning

Planning on-site nature awareness and study activities involves identifying goals and objectives, identifying audiences, and developing or marketing the programs. Scheduling, staffing, and budgeting must all be determined and planned well in advance. Some on-site classes operate with the assistance of a cooperating association or "friends" group. Others are self-supporting, non-profit organizations. The Teton Science School offers a range of residential programs for school groups in Grand Teton National Park, Wyoming. Their typical 3–5-day session includes activities such as a natural history hike or ski, canoeing on a nearby lake, a lesson on animal tracks and signs, wildlife observation, assisting in ongoing field research in the park, and use of field guides and map-reading skills. Planning these activities for school groups involves coordination with teachers and adherence to state academic standards.

Whether you are an educator planning a field trip to a natural area or a park staff member hosting schools and other groups at your site, planning usually requires consideration of the following steps, which are discussed in more detail in Chapter 5 (Giacalone 2003):

1. Get approval from the principal, teachers, parents, students, school board, or other participants. For school visits, this often entails showing how the trip is an integral part of the broader curriculum and addresses education standards.
2. Arrange transportation and housing.
3. Estimate total costs.
4. Obtain parental permission slips and medical information.
5. Provide a list of recommended clothing and equipment.
6. Develop fundraising activities if needed.
7. Design a detailed trip itinerary.
8. Clarify expectations of behavior and activities for participants.
9. Plan pre-trip activities to introduce new concepts to be covered, equipment to be used, and landscapes to be experienced.

The novelty of a field setting affects learning. Settings that are too novel cause fear or nervousness; settings that are too familiar lead to boredom. Learning is maximized when the field trip setting is of moderate novelty (Falk and Balling 1980). This can be accomplished by briefing participants in advance. Provide participants with pictures or a video of the site, locate the field trip route on a map, and provide details of the learning activities and information about possible weather conditions, safety hazards, restrooms, meals, and other logistical support (Athman and Monroe 2002).

Pre-trip activities are key to accomplishing the educational objectives. Teachers planning a field trip to Yellowstone National Park in Wyoming tied almost every element of their year-long science curriculum to the final field trip destination (Giacalone 2003).

They studied geology, volcanoes, earthquakes, glaciers, erosion, food webs, ecosystems, succession, microbiology, chemical reactions, minerals, energy transfer, animal life, and the scientific method in the context of Yellowstone. Students created their own guide to focus their study while visiting the park. The field guides contained plant keys, animal tracks, scavenger hunt questions, Yellowstone facts, an animal observation checklist, thermal feature comparisons, trail maps, questions for each stop, travel times between stops, and blank journal pages to draw and describe features. The students worked on the field guides together before the trip and received grades based on thoroughness and creativity.

Planning on-site activities at natural areas requires time regardless of whether the program involves in-depth study or a basic awareness activity. Planning on-site nature awareness activities requires careful attention to the sequencing of specific activities. Most people have experienced a facilitator who ignored the learning process, beginning a lesson with complex concepts and losing the audience shortly after. You can avoid that mistake by using a system for sequencing nature awareness activities, such as the four stages of flow learning (Cornell 2015). Each stage provides general guidelines for choosing activities to ensure the activities build upon each other (Cornell 2015):

- Stage 1. Awaken *enthusiasm*—building enthusiasm creates the alertness and interest critical to learning.
- Stage 2. Focus *attention*—channeling that enthusiasm into a focused attention primes the participants for learning.
- Stage 3. Direct *experience*—calm attention allows a direct experience with nature.
- Stage 4. Share *inspiration*—this direct experience opens the door to a deeper awareness and inspiration.

The concepts of flow learning were initially used for planning an entire sequence of complementary activities and lessons. You can use these four stages, however, as flexible principles for planning almost any nature awareness activity.

12.5.2 Implementation

Many environmental awareness activities emphasize sensory experiences—seeing, touching, hearing, smelling, and tasting. This encourages learners to develop a personal awareness of nature. Sensory experiences help participants "experience" nature in addition to studying it. An outline of activities (adapted from Van Matre 1972 and Cornell 1979) to explore a forest habitat might include the following stages:

1. Awaken enthusiasm:
   (a) Provide participants with blindfolds and explain that they are going to "lose" one of their senses in order to increase perceptions of their other senses. Explain how blind people often have more acute senses of hearing and touch than sighted people. Lead blindfolded participants to the site for exploration using a rope or railing to guide the way. This should stimulate participants to concentrate on their other senses and create a feeling of alertness and enthusiasm (Fig. 12.7).

Fig. 12.7 A sensory awareness game allows participants to explore the natural environment using a fun blindfold experience. (Photo by S. Jacobson.)

2. Focus attention and direct experience:
   (a) Give participants something to smell, such as an aromatic leaf or twig, as they begin their walk in the forest. This gets them to start using non-visual senses.
   (b) Ask participants to stand still and just listen. Ask them to think about how the noises change as they do this in several spots. They can notice changes in air temperature, hardness of the ground, and other things that stimulate their senses.
   (c) Get participants to dig a hole and sift the soil through their fingers. They should notice the grainy feeling of the soil. They can check for moisture content, temperature, and smell—a sensory recognition of the soil. This can be compared with drier, sandier soil in other areas.
   (d) Ask participants remove their blindfolds and look at the soil they have just felt. Have them look around the forest. They will notice that their vision, too, is more acute.
   (e) Get participants lightly touch and rub their fingers around a flower or a mushroom without crushing it. They *feel* what the flower or fungus is like while handling it with care.
3. Share inspiration
   (a) Ask participants to discuss their feelings about the results of these experiences. They also can continue their walk in the forest. When an animal, plant, or rock draws their attention, ask them to stop and write their impressions in a journal, for their own reflection and inspiration or to share with the group later.
   (b) Another activity for sharing inspiration involves providing cards with inspiring sayings related to nature written on them. Include a brief activity with each meditation. Turn the cards over and get each participant to choose a card and find a quiet place to be alone. For example, a card might say: "Holy

Earth Mother, the trees and all nature are witnesses of your thoughts and deeds.—Winnebago Indians. Go on a walk and repeat these words of thanks for the Earth" (Cornell 1979).

Nature study programs take advantage of natural areas as outdoor classrooms. Many on-site programs offer classes about a variety of subjects and activities. Mammoth Cave National Park, Kentucky, cooperates with Western Kentucky University's Center for Cave and Karst Studies to offer a series of 1-week summer courses focusing on caves and karst landscapes. These intensive field courses combine daily lectures with field observations and excursions. Visiting professors who are authorities in caving and karst science teach the classes. Some courses require previous subject knowledge, while others are designed for people who are merely curious about caves and caving.

The Kent Wildlife Trust offers an assortment of walks, talks, and classes at their visitor centers in the UK. On their "Walk with a warden," visitors join the warden to see how managers assess the flora and fauna. On one of their study days, visitors learn to identify trees in winter by using the buds, twigs, bark, shape, and size for identification. The North Cascades Institute works in cooperation with North Cascades National Park in Washington to provide over 60 programs for children and adults, offering a blend of science, natural and cultural history, literature, and the arts (Box 12.3).

Other settings, such as zoos and aquaria provide on-site study activities for a variety of audiences. The Tennessee Aquarium in Chattanooga, Tennessee, offers a program

---

Box 12.3 Example of nature courses offered at North Cascades Institute, Washington

Skagit Valley foodshed: wild edibles

Rediscover the ways Northwest cultures have sustained themselves physically and spiritually using resources near at hand. Join two local naturalists for a weekend of learning about wild plants. There will be lessons on plant identification, ethical gathering practices, and traditional use of plants for food, fiber, medicine, and shelter. We'll explore meadows and woodlands, forage in nature's well-stocked pantry, and learn how to collect in a safe and legal manner while preserving plant habitats. In the evening we'll share the tasty task of creating nettle lasagna for our potluck dinner.

Native plants: wild and restored

With more than 1600 native species, North Cascades National Park harbors some of the most diverse plant life in North America. Spend the weekend studying native flora with the Institute's restoration coordinator and a plant specialist for the National Park Service. Focusing on the area, we'll learn how to assess the terrain, treat soils, sow plants, and monitor for biodiversity. Examining projects to replace exotic species with natives, we'll also tour the Park's greenhouse and investigate wetland sites threatened by reed canary grass. We'll camp in North Cascades National Park.

Source: North Cascades Institute (<http://www.ncascades.org/>).

to enhance the high school science curriculum taught to home-schooled students (Matherly 2000). Through this program, students meet for a total of eight 2-hour sessions during the year. Laboratory sessions give students a chance to learn basic science skills using equipment and live specimens not available at home. Students observe the characteristics and behavior of live animals, participate in a dissection, learn how to use microscopes, and key out various plants and animals.

The outdoor sessions of the aquarium program give students a chance to discover the science in their everyday lives and to interact with nature. Students collect and identify macro-invertebrates that are later used to determine the health of a local water source. Students practice observation skills on a guided hike and test soil samples and vegetation at different locations.

12.5.3 Evaluation

Each nature awareness activity should include some form of debriefing to evaluate the immediate impact of the activity. Even simple activities, such as the sensory exploration of a tree, can evoke a rich response from participants (see Chapter 5). Debriefing is a method of asking questions to allow reflection and processing after the activity. When you first ask participants about an activity, start by asking questions that allow them to talk about what happened during the experience: "What did you just experience? What did you observe?" Then move to questions that allow the group to reflect: "So what does that mean?" Finally, prompt discussion from the group about applications of the activity to their lives. You can use debriefing as a quick check-in for evaluation or a more lengthy discussion. This method of debriefing follows the experiential learning cycle (see Chapter 2).

Another form of evaluation suited to nature awareness activities is the use of pre- and post-drawings (see Chapter 7). Drawings are simple to administer and easy to use with young participants. Drawings also provide direct feedback to students on their learning (Padua and Jacobson 1993). Before your activities, ask participants to draw the setting in which you will be conducting the lessons, such as the schoolyard or national park, or the concept you are exploring, such as ecosystems. Then ask them to draw the same setting or concept at the conclusion of your curriculum or workshop. Changes in the details and elements included in the drawings can reveal specific changes in the level of awareness of students before and after the activities.

Evaluation of informal courses usually includes an assessment form for participants to comment on course content, instructor interaction, and whether the objectives were met (Box 12.4). For long courses, it can be helpful to pass out an evaluation form halfway through the course to collect immediate feedback about the program. Results help guide any modifications needed during the remainder of the program. Peer review of a course by colleagues in the field, records of return attendees, and longer-term course popularity also provide information about the success of a class.

The Tennessee Aquarium collected feedback from students and their parents to assess their program. Parents felt their children gained technical skills in using laboratory and field equipment. They also felt the students had developed leadership skills as they worked together with other students on the activities, a positive, though unplanned, benefit of the program.

Box 12.4 Open- and close-ended questions for course evaluation

Examples of open- and close-ended questions included in a course evaluation form for an on-site nature class. Responses help assess if the class objectives are achieved.

1. On a scale from 1 to 5 (1 = very unsatisfied to 5 = very satisfied), please circle the number that corresponds to your satisfaction with the class:

A. Coverage of subject matter	1	2	3	4	5
B. Learning environment	1	2	3	4	5
C. Facilities for class	1	2	3	4	5
D. Class organization	1	2	3	4	5
E. Personal learning experience	1	2	3	4	5
F. Knowledge of instructor	1	2	3	4	5
G. Presentation by instructor	1	2	3	4	5
H. Group leadership	1	2	3	4	5
I. Take-home materials	1	2	3	4	5

Please provide a few details in response to each of the following.
2. What were the main strengths of the class?
3. What were the main weaknesses of the class?
4. How can we improve the class?

12.6 Facility design

The development of site plans for visitor centers is a key element for enhancing the quality of experience and learning opportunities for the visitor while preserving the ecological and cultural integrity of the site. Although the design of this infrastructure requires the expertise of architects, engineers, recreational planners, educators, biologists, and audience members, the basic principles related to the land, buildings, and people are useful when considering almost any kind of structures on your site. Many parks and outdoor education facilities have visitor centers. From small community nature centers to large museums, visitor centers can play an essential role in connecting people with special places and/or experiences. Visitor centers make visitors feel welcome; provide for their basic comforts and needs; and orient, inform, and inspire them. At some national parks, visitors spend as much time in the visitor center as they do in the rest of the park!

12.6.1 Planning

The design of a visitor center includes attention to parking and walkways, basic visitor information needs, and educational media and programs. First you must answer universal planning questions, such as:

- Who are the intended audiences, and what are their needs and interests?
- How might needs vary between distant and nearby visitors?

- What are the organizational mission, educational objectives, and outreach goals for the visitor center?
- What is significant about the site and what stories will convey its attributes and uniqueness?
- What are the staffing, budget, and other resource needs and constraints?
- What energy or resource conservation measures are possible?
- Will the facility also serve as a meeting place or site for events?

The budget includes not only capital outlays for land, buildings, and equipment, but also annual operating costs, which include personnel services, utilities, supplies, and items such as insurance. A design team including staff with specific expertise as well as professionals and community members can provide a full range of ideas for consideration. Workshops bringing these various groups together during the planning stage help ensure implementation is as effective as possible.

The style of the entrance and building convey meaning to visitors (Bitgood 2002). The basic design elements that need to be considered are outlined in the rest of this section (Gross and Zimmerman 2002).

Parking and entrance

- Design the road to the parking lot to follow the natural contours of the site and maintain the native vegetation.
- Unify the style of entrance signs with other signs on site that reflect the center's themes.
- Place the parking lot to avoid detracting from the building, trails, and views.
- Provide a drop-off loop for buses and people with physical disabilities; a separate entrance for deliveries and an emergency drive may be needed for large centers.
- Plant shade trees and native landscaping in the parking lot.
- Ensure the visitor center is visible or its direction clearly marked.
- Construct buildings and associated visitor services so that they do not degrade the natural site.

Building design

- Design the entrance and architecture to fit into the environment and culture of the site (Fig. 12.8).
- Research and select sustainable building materials to save money and resources over time, or to serve as a demonstration of locally appropriate materials.
- Use low-maintenance materials and structures.
- Plan for additions and easy updates or repairs.
- Focus on function to ensure maximum use of the building.
- Invest in water- and energy-saving technologies.
- Site the building to optimize sunlight for heating and light, and shade for cooling.
- Consider restoring or renovating existing structures.
- Consider sustainability goals and requirements to meet various materials, energy and resource use certifications.

Fig. 12.8 The entrance to the Rome Biopark in Italy uses classical sculptures of animals to reflect the history of the area. (Photo by S. Jacobson.)

Visitors' basic needs

- Ensure orientation and current information are available on the website for access prior to the visit.
- Provide after-hours information, maps to orient visitors, and an emergency phone or numbers on an information kiosk or introductory signs.
- Clearly mark trailheads.
- Provide the basic comforts that visitors expect, such as convenient toilets and bench seating for tours.
- Design the lobby so that it is open and inviting with an information desk and other important destinations easily visible.
- Make signs concise and easily viewed, using international symbols where appropriate.
- Provide personal services at the information desk to complement brochures, maps, and interactive computers to meet the requirements of most visitors.

Education and outreach activities and programs

- Design the exhibit area to entice visitors to hike the trails and see interesting features.
- Clearly advertise activities, such as guided walks, family games, special lectures, and other interpretive activities.
- Design areas between panels to provide adequate spacing for crowds during busy times and to allow both rapid pacing and in-depth viewing by visitors with different interests.

- Design the auditorium or multi-purpose room to serve the educational objectives and audience needs.
- Place sales areas for souvenirs and educational materials to avoid impeding the traffic flow of visitors seeking information.
- Include transitions between the visitor building and outdoors using observation windows, birdwatching stations, overlooks, and porches.
- Lead visitors from the building with exciting, inviting trailheads or outdoor exhibits.
- Ensure the traffic flow of visitors within exhibits follows cultural norms for the region, such as the inclination of visitors to turn in a specific direction, move along a straight-line path, and exit out the first open door.
- Follow the guidelines for effective exhibits discussed earlier in Section 12.3.
- Provide additional information, such as web camera viewing and other outreach materials, on websites or phone apps to encourage participation and future visits.

12.6.2 Implementation

Once the planning process is complete, constructing a visitor facility can take from months to years, depending on the complexity. To create the Zion National Park Visitor Center in Utah, the National Park Service worked with the Department of Energy's Renewable Energy Laboratory to design a sustainable building that incorporated the area's natural features and energy-efficient building concepts into an attractive design (US Park Service Zion NP energy <http://www.nps.gov>). This building has saved energy and operating expenses while protecting the environment, and served as a model in the region. The 2.8 million people who visit Zion National Park every year are awed by the park's natural sandstone canyons, mesas, and rock sculptures. Since the time of the ancestral Pueblo Indians, the narrow canyon has provided shade and cool breezes in the summer and warm rock surfaces in the winter. The visitor center capitalizes on these features and serves as a model of how to protect precious resources through energy-saving activities and technologies.

The implementation of the visitor center involved redesigning the transportation and parking experience as well as creating a new building and environs. Because Zion exists in a narrow canyon, automobile traffic causes air and noise pollution as well as congestion that are detrimental to the park's resources and visitor experience. With the new center, the park invested in efficient propane buses to shuttle visitors to nine stops within the park and six stops in the nearby town. Visitors are asked to leave their vehicles at parking facilities outside the park.

The visitor center incorporated low-energy design and renewable energy technologies, based on plans made by a multidisciplinary design team of engineers, architects, energy experts, and park staff. Some of the features of the building include:

- *Lighting*: the primary source of light in the center is daylight. The building's energy management computer adjusts high-efficiency electric lights as needed.
- *Windows*: windows placed high in the building are part of the lighting system as well as a part of the heating and cooling systems. Computer simulations helped size the windows to collect the right amount of light. The sun enters in the winter,

helping to keep the space heated (passive solar heating), and roof overhangs shade the glass from the high summer sun. A coating on the glass reduces heat loss in the winter. The high windows help cool the building by allowing hot air to escape. Low windows near the doors allow cool air in. The building's energy management computer controls the opening of windows and provides continuous natural ventilation.

- *Location*: the building was located to block the west windows from the summer sun. A tree canopy minimizes heat gain on summer afternoons. Windows on the west side of the building have glass that diverts the sun's heat.
- *Insulation*: the building is well insulated, designed to use 70% less energy than a typical building without costing more to build. The roof was made from structural-insulated panels of foam and strand board. Foam insulation in the wall cavities and insulated windows help keep the heat out in summer and retain it in the building in winter.
- *Cooling and heating*: when natural ventilation is inadequate, cool towers help lower the temperature. Water sprayed on pads at the top of the tower evaporates, cooling the air, which is directed down and into the building or patio. A Trombe wall provides most of the heat for the building by trapping solar heat between a pane of glass and a black coating on a masonry wall. The stored heat is released into the building to provide radiant comfort to visitors.
- *Energy*: photovoltaic panels on the south roof provide the majority of the electricity needed by the building. The efficient building design minimizes lighting needs and eliminates the need for air-conditioning, two major electric loads for the area. Excess power produced by the solar panels is stored in batteries as well as being sold back to the power company for use elsewhere. A computer ensures that all the energy-efficient features work together, and collects weather data and makes energy decisions about the building. Additionally, it controls the cool towers, radiant ceiling panels, lighting, and windows.
- *Landscaping*: landscaping helped create an extension of the visitor center with shade structures and existing trees. These outdoor rooms display permanent exhibits and allowed for a smaller building design. Irrigation ditches provide most of the water needed for landscaping, saving pumping energy, and water treatment.

Concomitant with planning a model energy-efficient building, the park service also planned their exhibits to create an appealing, inspirational, and informative experience for the visitor. The inside space of visitor centers must be designed to ensure that the placement of doors, windows, columns, and other permanent fixtures will complement exhibits, sales, information, basic needs, and educational activities for the projected number of visitors.

12.6.3 Evaluation

Evaluation of a facility design includes an assessment of its structural design as well as the visitor experience. In the case of the Zion National Park Visitor Center, the changes in transportation and building design resulted in significant improvements. The buses dramatically reduced automobile traffic in the park, protecting the park and providing a pleasant experience for visitors. Performance data collected after the completion of the building helped document the savings. Low energy demands have reduced operating costs and provided a model for other agencies to emulate. Initial reactions from visitors were overwhelmingly positive. The structural elements, such as lighting for clear visibility and a floor plan that provided easy circulation by visitors, were monitored by staff. More formal types of feedback discussed in Section 12.3 on exhibits will continue to help with evaluation of the themes, content, and graphics filling the building.

12.7 Summary

On-site education and outreach activities can enhance first-hand experiences in natural areas by orienting, informing, and stimulating visitors. The development of on-site activities considers the visitor experience, the resources of the site, and the education and outreach objectives of the organization. An initial planning process at a site paves the way for developing trails, exhibits, demonstrations, nature awareness and study activities, and visitor centers to achieve the goals of an organization.

The expertise of educators, artists, architects, engineers, recreational planners, maintenance staff, and target audience members is often needed to plan and implement on-site activities. The activities and techniques discussed in this chapter help visitors relate the site to their personal experiences and prior knowledge. This is an important feat to accomplish if learning is to be long-term and meaningful. From private forest owners at a demonstration forest to family groups at a state-of-the-art visitor center, on-site activities help audiences to understand their surroundings, explore their personal feelings, and acquire new skills.

References

350.org (2014). 350.org Workshops. Retrieved May 25, 2014, from <http://workshops.350.org/>

Abbey, E. (1968). *Desert Solitaire: Season in the Wilderness*. Ballantine, New York, NY.

Abdul-Matin, I. and Ellison, K. (2010). *Green Deen: What Islam Teaches About Protecting the Planet*. Berrett-Koehler Publishers, San Francisco, CA.

Adams, T.R. (2013). Overcoming barriers to teaching action-based environmental education: A multiple case study of teachers in the public school system. Masters Theses and Specialist Projects. Paper 1230. Available at: <http://digitalcommons.wku.edu/theses/1230/>

Adger, W.N., Barnett, J., Brown, K., Marshall, N., and O'Brien, K. (2013). Cultural dimensions of climate change impacts and adaptation. *Nature Climate Change*, 3, 112–117.

afrol News (2003). Community-based research nets results in Benin. Retrieved January 9, 2005, from <http://www.afrol.com/articles/10547>

Aipanjiguly, S., Jacobson, S.K., and Flamm, R. (2003). Conserving manatees: Knowledge, attitudes, and intentions of boaters in Tampa Bay, Florida. *Conservation Biology*, 17, 1098–1105.

Ajzen, I. (1985). From intentions to actions: A theory of planned behavior. In: J. Kuhl and J. Beckman (eds), *Action-control: From Cognition to Behavior*, pp. 11–39. Springer, Heidelberg, Germany.

Ajzen, I. (2002). Theory of planned behavior diagram. Retrieved January 4, 2015, from <http://www-unix.oit.umass.edu/~aizen/tpb.diag.html>

Akers, C.L., Segrest, D.H., Kistler, M.J., Smith, J.H., Davis, C.S., and Baker, M. (2005). Evaluating the effectiveness of Texas Parks and Wildlife Hueco Tanks State Historic Site orientation/conservation video: A media systems dependency theory perspective. Presentation to the Southern Association of Agricultural Scientists, Little Rock, AR, February 5–9, 2005. Retrieved January 9, 2015, from <http://agrilifecdn.tamu.edu/saas/files/2011/02/akers.pdf>

Alaska Native Knowledge Network (1998). *Alaska Standards for Culturally Responsive Schools*. University of Alaska Fairbanks, Fairbanks, AK.

Alexander, H. (2014). Small business sign survey reveals generational differences. Market Watch. *The Wall Street Journal*. Press release May 7, 2014. Retrieved April 23, 2015, from <http://about.van.fedex.com/newsroom/united-states-english/small-business-sign-survey-reveals-generational-differences/>

Allen, W. (2015). Social learning, governance and practice change. Retrieved January 13, 2015, from <http://learningforsustainability.net/social_learning/>

Ambrose, T. and Paine, C. (1993). *Museum Basics*. International Council of Museums (ICOM) supported by the Cultural Heritage Division of UNESCO and Paine, New York and London.

Andrews, E., Stevens, M., and Wise, G. (2002). A model of community-based environmental education. In: T. Dietz and P. Stern (eds), *New Tools for Environmental Protection: Education, Information, and Voluntary Measures*, pp. 161–182. National Academy Press, Washington, DC.

Ardoin, N.A., Clark, C., and Kelsey, E. (2013). An exploration of future trends in environmental education research. *Environmental Education Research*, 19, 499–520.

Ariely, D. (2009). *Predictably Irrational: The Hidden Forces That Shape Our Decisions*, 2nd edn. Harper Collins, New York, NY.

Armstrong, D.M. (1992). *Managing by Storying Around: A New Method of Leadership*. Bantam Doubleday Dell Publishing Group Inc., New York, NY.

Armstrong, E. (2012). *The Folklore of Birds*. Collins, London.

Ash, S.L. and Clayton, P.H. (2009). Generating, deepening, and documenting learning: The power of critical reflection in applied learning. *Journal of Applied Learning in Higher Education*, 1(Fall), 25–48.

Athman, J. and Monroe, M. (2002). Enhancing natural resource programs with field trips. *University of Florida IFAS Extension Publication* No. FR135. Retrieved April 6, 2005, from <http://edis.ifas.ufl.edu/FR135>

Athman, J. and Monroe, M. (2004). The effects of environment-based education on students' achievement motivation. *Journal of Interpretation Research*, 9, 9–25.

Audubon (2011). *Tools of Engagement: A Toolkit for Engaging People in Conservation*. Retrieved January 16, 2015, from <http://web4.audubon.org/educate/toolkit/pdf/the-toolkit.pdf>

Avery, E., Lariscy, R., Amador, E., Ickowitz, T., Primm, C., and Taylor, A. (2010). Diffusion of social media among public relations practitioners in health departments across various community population sizes. *Journal of Public Relations Research*, 22, 336–358.

Aviles, H. (2012). Chapter six: Partnerships with other NGOs and government. *IIP Digital*. Retrieved October 7, 2014, from <http://iipdigital.usembassy.gov/st/english/publication/2012/09/20120925136559.html#axzz3FU0P9ykD>

BBC (2014). BBC world news: Reach and advertising audience. Retrieved August 8, 2014, from <http://advertising.bbcworldwide.com/home/mediakit/reachaudience/bbcworldnews>

Baer, J. (2013). 7 critical elements of your social media strategy. Retrieved on June 16, 2014, from <http://www.convinceandconvert.com/social-media-strategy/7-critical-elements-of-your-social-media-strategy/>

Bandura, A. (1997). *Self-Efficacy: The Exercise of Control*. W. H. Freeman and Company, New York, NY.

Bandura, A. (2001). Social cognitive theory: an agentic perspective. *Annual Review of Psychology*, 52, 1–26.

Baral, H., Petheram, R.J., and Liffmann, P. (2004). A community–university–GIS partnership for weed mapping. *Agricultural Research and Extension Network Newsletter*, 50, 9.

Barlow, Z. (2000). *Ecoliteracy: Mapping the Terrain*, pp. 13–18. Learning in the Real World, Berkeley, CA.

Basu, S. (2010). 10 environmental games that teach kids about earth, ecology, and environment. Retrieved June 10, 2014, from <http://www.makeuseof.com/tag/10-environmental-games-teach-kids-earth-ecology-conservation/>

Bauer, R. (2005). How we learn from the viewpoint of cognitive neuroscience. Seminar presented at University of Florida, January 31, 2005 through the University Center for Excellence in Teaching.

Beamish, R. (1995). *Getting the Word Out in the Fight to Save the Earth*. Johns Hopkins University Press, Baltimore, MD.

Beck, M.W. (2014). Rebuilding Caribbean coral reefs. *Caribbean Journal*, 13 June. Retrieved July 30, 2014, from <http://www.caribjournal.com/2014/06/13/rebuilding-caribbean-coral-reefs/>

Beldon, N. and Russonello, J. (1995). Communicating biodiversity: Focus group research findings conducted for the Consultative Group on Biological Diversity. Beldon and Russonello Research and Communications Report, Washington, DC.

Bender, W. (2012). *Project-based Learning: Differentiating Instruction for the 21st Century*. Corwin, Thousand Oaks, CA.

Bennett, D.B. (1988–1989). Four steps to evaluating environmental education learning experiences. *Journal of Environmental Education*, 20(2), 14–21.

Bercovici, J. (2010). Who coined "social media"? Web pioneers compete for credit. Retrieved June 16, 2014, from <http://www.forbes.com/sites/jeffbercovici/2010/12/09/who-coined-social-media-web-pioneers-compete-for-credit/>

Berensohn, P. (2002). Environment and the arts: Interview on Earthbeat, June 1, 2002, ABC Radio National, Australia [transcript]. Retrieved March 25, 2015, from <http://www.abc.net.au/radionational/programs/earthbeat/environment-and-the-arts/3642930#transcript>

Berry, W. (1985). *Collected Poems*. North Point Press, San Francisco, CA.

Berry, W. (2002). *The Art of the Commonplace: The Agrarian Essays of Wendell Berry*. Counterpoint, Berkeley, CA.

Biedenweg, K. and Monroe, M. (2013). Teasing apart the details: How social learning can affect collective action in the Bolivian Amazon. *Human Ecology*, 41, 239–253.

Bingham, S. (2009). *Love God, Heal Earth*. St. Lynn's Press, Pittsburgh, PA.

Bishop, J. (ed.) (2012). *The Economics of Ecosystem and Biodiversity in Business and Enterprise*. Earthscan, New York, NY.

Bitgood, S. (2002). Environmental psychology in museums, zoos, and other exhibition centers. In: R. Bechtel and A. Churchman (eds), *Handbook of Environmental Psychology*, pp. 461–480. John Wiley and Sons, New York, NY.

Bitgood, S. and Patterson, D. (1987). Principles of exhibit design. *Visitor Behavior*, 2, 4.

Blatner, A. (2009). Role-playing in education. Retrieved April 24, 2015, from <http://www.blatner.com/adam/pdntbk/rlplayedu.htm>

Block, L. (2003). Helpful hints for Clean Water for North Carolina festival volunteers. Unpublished document. Clean Water for North Carolina, Asheville, NC.

de Bono, E. (2015). Thinking tools—the art and science of thinking. Lateral thinking. Edward de Bono. Retrieved January 14, 2015, from <http://edwdebono.com/>

Bostdorff, D.M., and Woods, J.L. (2003). Lessons from a failed PDR (purchase of development rights) campaign in Wayne County, Ohio. *Applied Environmental Education and Communication*, 2, 169–175.

Boudourides, M.A. (2003). Constructivism, education, science and technology. *Canadian Journal of Learning and Technology*, 29(3). Retrieved September 14, 2014, from <http://www.cjlt.ca/index.php/cjlt/article/viewArticle/83/77>

Braus, J.A. and Monroe, M.C. (1994). *Designing Effective Workshops*. EE Toolbox, Workshop Resource Manual. National Consortium for Environmental Education, Ann Arbor, MI.

Braus, J.A. and Wood, D. (1993). *Environmental Education in the Schools: Creating a Program that Works*. Peace Corps Information Collection and Exchange, Washington, DC.

Brehm, S. and Brehm, J.W. (1981). *Psychological Reactance: A Theory of Freedom and Control*. Academic Press, New York, NY.

Brew, A. (2003). Writing activities: A primer for outdoor educators. *ERIC Digests*, ED475390. ERIC Clearinghouse on Rural Education and Small Schools, Charleston, WV. Available at: <http://www.ericdigests.org/2003-5/writing.htm>

Bringle, R.G. and Clayton, P.H. (2012). Civic education through service learning: What, how, and why? In: L. McIlraith, A. Lyons, and R. Munck (eds), *Higher Education and Civic Engagement: Comparative Perspectives*, pp. 101–124. Palgrave MacMillan, New York, NY.

Brody, M. (2002). Park visitors' understandings, values and beliefs related to their experience at Midway Geyser Basin, Yellowstone National Park, USA. *International Journal of Science Education*, 24, 1119–1141.

Brooks, J.G. and Brooks, M.G. (1993). *In Search of Understanding: The Case for Constructivist Classrooms*. Association for Supervision and Curriculum Development, Alexandria, VA.

Brown, T. (1983a). *Tom Brown's Field Guide to Wilderness Survival*. The Berkley Publishing Group, New York, NY.

Brown, T. (1983b). *Tom Brown's Field Guide to Nature Observation and Tracking*. The Berkley Publishing Group, New York, NY.

Brown, T. (1984). *Tom Brown's Field Guide to City and Suburban Survival*. The Berkley Publishing Group, New York, NY.

Brown, T. (1985). *Tom Brown's Field Guide to Wild Edible and Medicinal Plants*. The Berkley Publishing Group, New York, NY.

Buck Institute for Education (2013). Rubrics. Retrieved June 21, 2014, from <http://bie.org/objects/cat/rubrics>

Burleson, E. and Dougherty, S.D. (2012). Arctic justice: Addressing persistent organic pollutants. *Law and Inequality*, **30**, 57.

Busch, A. (2013). *The Incidental Steward: Reflections on Citizen Science*. Yale University Press, New Haven, CT.

Bybee, R.W., Taylor, J.A., Gardner, A., Van Scotter, P., Powell, J.C., Westbrook, A. and Landes, N. (2006). *The BSCS 5E instructional model: Origins and effectiveness*. A report prepared for the Office of Science Education, National Institutes of Health. Retrieved September 14, 2014, from <http://sharepoint.snoqualmie.k12.wa.us/mshs/ramseyerd/Science%20Inquiry%201% 2020112012/What%20is%20Inquiry%20Sciecne%20%28long%20version%29.pdf>

Cable, T. and Ernst, T. (2003). Interpreting rightly in a left-brain world. *Legacy*, **14**(5), 27–29.

Caduto, M.J. and Bruchac, J. (1989). *Keepers of the Earth: Native American Stories and Environmental Activities for Children*. Fulcrum, Inc., Golden, CO.

Caduto, M.J. and Bruchac, J. (1994). *Keepers of the Night: Native American Stories and Nocturnal Activities for Children*. Fulcrum, Inc., Golden, CO.

Caduto, M.J. and Bruchac, J. (1997). *Keepers of the Animals: Native American Stories and Wildlife Activities for Children*. Fulcrum, Inc., Golden, CO.

Caine, R.N. and Caine, G. (1990). Understanding a brain-based approach to learning and teaching. *Educational Leadership*, **48**(2), 66–70.

Cairn, R. (2003). *Partner Power and Service Learning: Manual for Community-based Organizations to Work with Schools*. ServeMinnesota! and Minnesota Department of Education, Minneapolis, MN.

Camp Silos (2002). Why take field trips? Silos and Smokestacks National Heritage Area. Retrieved February 25, 2005, from http://www.campsilos.org/excursions/hc/fieldtrip.htm

Campus Compact (2014). Campus Compact. Retrieved May 28, 2014, from <http://www.compact.org>

Campus Ecology, National Wildlife Federation (2014). Campus Ecology. Retrieved May 19, 2014, from <http://www.nwf.org/campus-ecology.aspx>

Capra, F. (2000). Ecoliteracy: A systems approach to education. In: *Ecoliteracy: Mapping the Terrain*, pp. 27–35. Learning in the Real World, Berkeley, CA.

Caputo P., Lewis, S., and Brochu, L. (2008). *Interpretation by Design: Graphic Design Basics for Heritage Interpreters*. National Association for Interpretation, Fort Collins, CO.

Carlton, S.J. and Jacobson, S.K. (2013). Climate change and coastal environmental risk perception in Florida. *Journal of Environmental Management*, **130**, 32–39.

Casale, C. (2012). HTML5 v. Flash—What do you need to know? Accusoft's Blog. Retrieved June 27, 2014, from <http://blog.accusoft.com/2012/october/html5-vs-flash-what-do-you-need-to-know-part-1>

Case Studies in Science (2003). Case studies in ecology/environment. National Center for Case Study Teaching in Science. Retrieved February 25, 2005, from <http://sciencecases.lib.buffalo.edu/cs/collection/>

Cawthorn, M., Leege, L., and Congdon, E. (2011). Improving learning outcomes in large Environmental Science classrooms through short-term service-learning projects. *Journal of Environmental Studies and Sciences*, **1**, 75–87.

Chang, H.-C. (2010). A new perspective on Twitter hashtag use: Diffusion of innovation theory. *Proceedings of the American Society for Information Science and Technology*, 47, 1–4.

Chawla, L. (1998). Significant life experiences revisited: A review of research on sources of environmental sensitivity. *Environmental Education Research*, 4, 369–382.

Chawla, L. (1999). Life paths into effective environmental action. *Journal of Environmental Education*, 31, 15–26.

Chawla, L. and Cushing, D.F. (2007). Education for strategic environmental behaviour. *Environmental Education Research*, 13, 437–452.

Cheng, J.C-H., and Monroe, M.C. (2012). Connection to nature: Children's affective attitude toward nature. *Environment and Behavior*, 44, 31–49.

Cheng, M. (2014). 30 percent of the world is now fat. Retrieved April 19, 2015, from <http://www.huffingtonpost.com/2014/05/28/obesity-_n_5407038.html>

Children and Nature Network (2014). Research and resources. Retrieved April 19, 2015, from <http://www.childrenandnature.org/documents/C124/>

Cialdini, R.B. (2009). *Influence: Science and Practice*, 5th edn. Pearson, Boston, MA.

Clark, R.C. and Mayer, R.E. (2011). *e-Learning and the Science of Instruction: Proven Guidelines for Consumer and Designers of Multimedia Learning*, 3rd edn. Pfeiffer, San Francisco, CA.

Clayton, P.H. (2013). Defining service-learning. Retrieved June 14, 2014, from <http://curricularengagement.com/handouts/>

Clayton, P.H. (2014). The DEAL model for critical reflection. Retrieved May 28, 2014, from http://curricularengagement.com/handouts/

Clayton, P.H, Bringle, R.G., and Hatcher, J.A. (eds) (2013). *Research on Service Learning: Conceptual Frameworks and Assessment*, Vols. 2A and 2B. Stylus, Sterling, VA.

Cohen, H. (2011). 30 social media definitions. Retrieved June 16, 2014, from <http://heidicohen.com/social-media-definition/>

Cole, J. and Deagan, B. (2010). *The Magic School Bus and the Climate Challenge*. Scholastic Press, New York, NY.

Cole, E.J. and Fieselman, L. (2013). A community-based social marketing campaign at Pacific University Oregon. *International Journal of Sustainability in Higher Education*, 14, 176–195.

Commonwealth of Australia (2014). *Sustainability Curriculum Framework: A Guide for Curriculum Developers and Policy Makers*. Retrieved May 20, 2014, from <http://www.environment.gov.au/resource/sustainability-curriculum-framework-guide-curriculum-developers-and-policy-makers>

Cornell, J. (1979). *Sharing Nature with Children*. Dawn Publications, Nevada City, CA.

Cornell, J. (2015). *Sharing Nature: Nature Awareness Activities for All Ages*, 35th anniversary edition. Crystal Clarity Publishers, Nevada City, CA.

Corner, A. and Randall, A. (2011). Selling climate change? The limitations of social marketing as a strategy for climate change public engagement. *Global Climate Change*, 21, 1005–1014.

Corredor, J. (2004). General and domain-specific influence of prior knowledge on setting of goals and content use of museum web sites. *Computers and Education*, 47, 207–221.

Coyle, K. (2005). *Environmental Literacy in America: What Ten Years of NEETF/Roper Research and Related Studies Says about Environmental Literacy in the U.S.* The National Environmental Education and Training Foundation, Washington, DC.

Coyle, K. (2010). *Back to School: Back Outside!* National Wildlife Federation, Washington, DC.

Coyle, J.R. and Thorson, E. (2001). The effects of progressive levels of interactivity and vividness in web marketing sites. *Journal of Advertising*, 30(3), 65–76.

Creighton, J., Simon-Brown, V., and Sulzmann, J. (2004). *Saving Eden Creek: A Play about People and Forests*. OSU Extension publication EM 8858-E. Available at: <https://catalog.extension.oregonstate.edu/sites/catalog.extension.oregonstate.edu/files/project/pdf/em8858.pdf>

Crimmel, H. (2003). *Teaching in the Field: Working with Students in the Outdoor Classroom.* University of Utah Press, Salt Lake City, UT.

Crompton, T. (2008). *Weathercocks and Signposts: The Environmental Movement at a Crossroads.* Report of WWF-UK's Strategies for Change Project. WWF, Godalming, UK. Retrieved January 14, 2015, from <http://www.wwf.org.uk/wwf_articles.cfm?unewsid=2224>

Culen, G.R., Hungerford, H., and Volk, T. (2000). *Coastal Marine Environmental Issues: An Extended Case Study for the Investigation of Issues of the Gulf Coast and Florida Peninsula.* Stipes Publishing, Champaign, IL.

Curtis, D. (2003a). Initial impressions on the role of the performing and visual arts in influencing environmental behavior. *Proceedings of The Australian Sociological Association 2003 Annual Conference (TASA 2003): New Times, New Worlds, New Ideas: Sociology Today and Tomorrow,* p. 1–11 [CD-ROM]. Australian Sociological Association and the University of New England.

Curtis, D. (2003b). The arts and restoration: a fertile partnership? *Ecological Management and Restoration,* 4, 163–169.

Czerniak, C.M. (2004). Wetlands: An interdisciplinary exploration. *Science Activities,* 41(2), 3–11.

Daigle, J.J., Hrubes, D., and Ajzen, I. (2002). A comparative study of beliefs, attitudes, and values among hunters, wildlife viewers, and other outdoor recreationists. *Human Dimensions of Wildlife,* 7, 1–19.

Davis, R. (2005). 16: Is it too young to drive a car? *USA Today,* March 2, 2005, p. 1B.

Day, B. and Monroe, M. (eds) (2000). *Environmental Education and Communication for a Sustainable World: Handbook for International Practitioners.* Academy for Educational Development, Washington, DC.

Dearing, J. (2005). Accelerating the diffusion of effective techniques. Presentation at the International Conference on Transfer of Forest Science Knowledge and Technology, May 10–13, 2005, Troutdale, OR.

Decker, D.J., Brown, T.L., and Siemer, W.F. (2001). *Human Dimensions of Wildlife Management in North America.* The Wildlife Society, Bethesda, MD.

DeHaan, R. (2011). Teaching creative science thinking. *Science,* 334, 1499–1500.

DeMers, J. (2013). The three pillars of SEO in 2013: Content, links, and social media. *Forbes.* Retrieved July 14, 2014, from <http://www.forbes.com/sites/jaysondemers/2013/05/23/the-3-pillars-of-seo-in-2013-content-links-and-social-media/>

Department of Education, Training, and Employment, Queensland (2014). About the Queensland Environmental Sustainable Schools Initiative. Retrieved May 20, 2014, from <http://www.sustainableschools.qld.edu.au/Default.aspx?tabid=574>

DesMarais, J., Yang, T., and Farzanehkia, F. (2000). Service-learning leadership development for youths. *Phi Delta Kappan,* 81, 678–680.

Deutsch, W., Busby, A.L., Orprecio, J.L, Bago-Labis, J.P., and Cequina, E.J. (2005). Community-based hydrological and water quality assessments in Mindanao, Philippines. In: M. Bonell and L.A. Bruijnzeel (eds), *Forests, Nature, and People in the Humid Tropics,* pp. 134–150. Cambridge University Press, Cambridge, UK.

Devney, D.C. (2001). *Organizing Special Events and Conferences: A Practical Guide for Busy Volunteers and Staff,* 2nd edn. Pineapple Press, Inc., Sarasota, FL.

De Young, R. (1988–1989). Exploring the difference between recyclers and non-recyclers: The role of intrinsic motivation. *Journal of Environmental Systems,* 15, 281–292.

De Young, R. (1993). Changing behavior and making it stick: The conceptualization and management of conservation behavior. *Environment and Behavior,* 25, 485–505.

De Young, R. (2000). Expanding and evaluating motives for environmentally responsible behavior. *Journal of Social Issues,* 56, 509–526.

Dillard, A. (1988). *Pilgrim at Tinker Creek.* Harper, New York, NY.

Dillman, D.A. (2007). *Mail and Internet Surveys. The Tailored Design Method. 2007 Update with New Internet, Visual, and Mixed-Mode Guide*, 2nd edn. John Wiley & Sons, Hoboken, NJ.

Disinger, J. and Monroe, M.C. (1994). *Defining Environmental Education*. EE Toolbox, Workshop Resource Manual. National Consortium for Environmental Education, Ann Arbor, MI.

Dobbins, R. and Pitman, B. (2001). *GreenWorks! Connecting Community Action and Service Learning Guide*. American Forest Foundation and Project Learning Tree, Washington, DC.

Doyle, M. and Briggeman, B.C. (2014). To like or not to like: Social media as a marketing tool. *Journal of Extension*, **52**(3), 3IAW1. Retrieved June 27, 2014, from <http://www.joe.org/joe/2014june/iw1.php>

Driver, B.L., Tinsley, H.E.A., and Manfredo, M.J. (1991). The paragraphs about leisure and recreation experience preference scales: Results from two inventories designed to assess the breadth of the perceived psychological benefits of leisure. In: B.L. Driver, P.J. Brown, and G.L. Peterson (eds), *Benefits of Leisure*, pp. 261–286. Venture Publishing, State College, PA.

Duggan, M. and Smith, A. (2013). Social media update 2013. Pew Research Center. Retrieved on June 16, 2014, from <http://www.pewinternet.org/2013/12/30/social-media-update-2013/>

Duggan, M., Ellison, N.B., Lampe, C., Lenhart, A., and Madden, M. (2014). Social media update 2014. Pew Research Internet Project, Pew Research Center. Retrieved on January 9, 2015, from <http://www.pewinternet.org/2015/01/09/social-media-update-2014/>

Dungy, C. (2009). Black Nature: Four centuries of African American poetry. University of Georgia Press, Athens, GA.

Dunwoody, S. (2003). Explaining popular science. Unpublished presentation at Florida Museum of Natural History, November 10, 2003, Gainesville, FL.

Eadens, L.M., Jacobson, S.K., Stein, T.V., Confer, J.J., Gape, L., and Sweeting, M. (2009). Stakeholder mapping for recreation planning of a Bahamian national park. *Society and Natural Resources*, **22**, 111–127.

eBiz (2013). *Top 15 Most Popular Social Networking Sites June 2014*. Retrieved on June 16, 2014, from http://www.ebizmba.com/articles/social-networking-websites.

Ehlert, L. (1987). *Growing Vegetable Soup*. Harcourt, Inc., Orlando, FL.

Ehrlich, G. (1985). *The Solace of Open Spaces*. Penguin Books, New York, NY.

Eichler, M.L., Xavier, P.R., Costa Araújo, R., Castro Forte, R., and Del Pino, J.C. (2005). Carbopolis: A Java technology-based free software for environmental education. *Journal of Computers in Mathematics and Science Technology*, **24**, 43–72. [The simulation, Carbopolis, can be found at <http://www.iq.ufrgs.br/aeq/carbopp.htm>]

Elder, J.L. (2003). *A Field Guide to Environmental Literacy: Making Strategic Investments in Environmental Education*. Environmental Education Coalition, Rock Springs, GA.

Ellis, E.S. and Worthington, L.A. (1994). Research synthesis on effective teaching principles and the design of quality tools for educators. *Technical Report* No. 5. National Center to Improve the Tools of Educators, University of Oregon. Retrieved January 10, 2015, from <http://people.uncw.edu/kozloffm/ellisressynth.pdf>

Environmental Working Group (2014). Ten Americans. Retrieved May 25, 2014, from <http://www.ewg.org/news/videos/10-americans>

Enviroschools Foundation (2014). Enviroschools. Retrieved January 24, 2015, from <http://www.enviroschools.org.nz/enviroschools-programme/enviroschools-is>

Ernst, J. (2009). Influences on U.S. middle school teachers' use of environment-based education. *Environmental Education Research*, **15**, 71–92.

Ernst, J. and Monroe, M. (2004). The effects of environment-based education on students' critical thinking skills and disposition toward critical thinking. *Environmental Education Research*, **10**, 507–522.

Ernst, J., Monroe, M., and Simmons, B. (2009). *Evaluating Your Environmental Education Programs: A Workbook for Practitioners*. North American Association for Environmental Education, Washington, DC.

Eyler, J. and Giles, J. (1999). *Where's the Learning in Service-learning?* Jossey-Bass, San Francisco, CA.

Eysenbach, G. and Kohler, C. (2002). How do consumers search for and appraise health information on the World Wide Web? Qualitative study using focus groups, usability tests, and in-depth interviews. *British Medical Journal,* **324,** 573–577.

Faber Taylor, A. and Kuo, F.E. (2009). Children with attention deficits concentrate better after walk in the park. *Journal of Attention Disorders,* **12,** 402–409.

Faber Taylor, A., Kuo, F.E., and Sullivan, W. C. (2001). Views of nature and self-discipline: Evidence from inner city children. *Journal of Environmental Psychology,* **22,** 49–63.

Facione, P.A. (1990). Critical thinking: A statement of expert consensus for purposes of educational assessment and instruction. *ERIC Document* ED 315 423. Available at: <http://eric.ed.gov/?id=ED315423>

Facione, P. (1998). *What it is and Why it Counts.* The California Academic Press, Millbrae, CA.

Falk, J. and Balling, J. (1980). The school field trip: Where you go makes a difference. *Science and Children,* **17**(6), 6–8.

Fallon, M. (2010). 350.org's global climate art project. *UTNE Reader.* Retrieved January, 2014, from <http://www.utne.com/arts/350-earth-climate-change-art-project.aspx#ixzz3ourduryo>

Fazio, J.R. and Gilbert, D.L. (2000). *Public Relations and Communications for Natural Resource Managers.* Kendall Hunt Publishing, Dubuque, IA.

FDEP (Florida Department of Environmental Protection) (2015). Florida Clean Marina programs. Retrieved January 5, 2015, from <http://www.dep.state.fl.us/cleanmarina/>

Fell, J. (2014). 3 design tips for creating signs that attract customers. *Entrepreneur.* Retrieved on July 23, 2014, from <http://www.entrepreneur.com/article/233961>

Ferenstein, G. (2013). The flipped classroom boosts grades 5%. Why that's as big as we can expect. *TechCrunch.* Retrieved January 12, 2015, from <http://techcrunch.com/2013/09/18/the-flipped-classroom-boosts-grades-5-why-thats-as-big-as-we-can-expect/>

Feuerstein, M.T. (1986). *Partners in Evaluation: Evaluating Development and Community Programs with Participants.* Macmillan Education Ltd, Hong Kong.

Fien, J., Scott, W., and Tilbury, D. (2002). Exploring principles of good practice: Learning from a meta-analysis of case studies on education within conservation across the WWF network. *Applied Environmental Education and Communication,* **1,** 153–162.

Flint, C. (ed.) (2002). *Nature Neighborhood: Creating a Place for Wildlife and Learning.* North Carolina State Museum of Natural Sciences, Environmental Media Corporation, Port Royal, SC.

Fogg, B.J. (2002). *Stanford Guidelines for Web Credibility.* A Research Summary from the Stanford Persuasive Technology Lab. Retrieved May 1, 2005, from <https://credibility.stanford.edu/guidelines/>

Ford Foundation (2005). *Ford Foundation Report Winter.* Retrieved January 28, 2015, from <http://www.fordfoundation.org/pdfs/library/ar2005.pdf>

Fox, Z. (2011). "Trash Tycoon" brings eco-responsibility to social gaming. *Mashable.* Retrieved July 4, 2014, from <http://mashable.com/2011/09/09/trash-tycoon-social-gaming/>

Frank, L. (2013). *Journey to a Caring Classroom: Using Adventure to Create Community.* Wood 'N' Barnes, Bethany, OK.

Frazier, R. (2002). Singapore sensory trail. *Legacy,* **13**(3), 12–17.

Freire P. (1970). *Pedagogy of the Oppressed.* Herder and Herder, New York, NY.

Friedrich, M.J. (1999). The arts of healing. *Journal American Medical Association,* **281**(19), 1779–1781.

GLOBE (Global Learning and Observations to Benefit the Environment) (2015). The GLOBE Program. Retrieved on January 16, 2015, from <http://www.globe.gov>

GM GREEN (2009). *GM GREEN Annual Report 2009.* Retrieved June 25, 2014, from <http://earthforce.org/sites/default/files/GM_GREEN_2009_AnnualReport.pdf>

GRACE (Gorilla Rehabilitation and Conservation Education Center) (2015). Community outreach. Radio drama. Retrieved January 10, 2015, from <http://gracegorillas.org/programs/community-programs/community-outreach-2/>

Gardner, H. (1999). *The Disciplined Mind: What All Students Should Understand*. Simon and Schuster, New York, NY.

Garrison, D.R. and Vaughan, N.D. (2008). *Blended Learning in Higher Education: Framework, Principles, and Guidelines*. John Wiley, Jossey-Bass, San Francisco, CA.

Geller, S. (2002). The challenge of increasing proenvironment behavior. In: R. Bechtel and A. Churchman (eds) *Handbook of Environmental Psychology*, pp. 525–540. John Wiley and Sons, New York, NY.

Gelmon, S. (2003). How do we know that our work makes a difference? Assessment strategies for service-learning and civic engagement. In: Campus Compact (ed.), *Introduction to Service-Learning Toolkit: Readings and Resources for Faculty*, 2nd edn, pp. 231–240. Campus Compact, Providence, RI.

Gharis, L.W., Bardon, R.E., Evans, J.L., Hubbard, W.G., and Taylor E. (2014). Expanding the reach of Extension through social media. *Journal of Extension* 52(3), 3FEA3. Retrieved June 27, 2014, from <http://www.joe.org/joe/2014june/a3.php>

Giacalone, V. (2003). How to plan, survive, and even enjoy an overnight field trip with 200 students. *Sciencescope*, 26(4), 22–26.

Gleason, J. and Holian, P. (1996). Video productions. In: Agricultural Communicators in Education, *The Communicator's Handbook: Tools, Techniques, and Technology*, 3rd edn, pp. 153–193. Maupin House and Agriculture Communicators in Education, Gainesville, FL.

Gonzales, M.H., Aronson, E., and Costanzo, M.A. (1988). Using social cognition and persuasion to promote energy conservation: A quasi-experiment. *Journal of Applied Social Psychology*, 18, 1049–1066.

Gopinath, M. and Nyer, P.U. (2009). The effect of public commitment on resistance to persuasion: The influence of attitude certainty, issue importance, susceptibility to normative influence, preference for consistency and source proximity. *International Journal of Research in Marketing*, 26, 60–88.

Grabianowski, E. (2014). How to create your own podcast. *How Stuff Works*. Retrieved July 11, 2014, from <http://computer.howstuffworks.com/internet/basics/how-to-podcast.htm>

Grace, C.O. (2004). Medicine and metaphor: poetry as prescriptive. *Duke Magazine*, Nov.–Dec, 42–47.

Grant, P. (2001). Wild art at the world's end. *Artlink*, 21(1), 14–18.

Grant, T. and Littlejohn, G. (eds) (2001). *Greening School Grounds: Creating Habitats for Learning*. New Society Publishers, Gabriola Island, BC, Canada.

Greenwald, A.G., Carnot, C.G., Beach, R., and Young, B. (1987). Increasing voting behavior by asking people if they expect to vote. *Journal of Applied Psychology*, 72, 315–318.

Grese, R.E., Kaplan, R., Ryan, R.L., and Buxton, J. (2000). Psychological benefits of volunteering in stewardship programs. In: P.H. Gobster and R.B. Hull (eds), *Restoring Nature: Perspectives From the Social Sciences and Humanities*, pp. 265–280. Island Press, Washington, DC.

Grieser, M. (2000). Participation. In: B.A. Day and M.C. Monroe (eds), *Environmental Education and Communication for a Sustainable World*, pp. 17–22. Academy for Educational Development, Washington, DC.

Grieser, M. and Rawlins, R. (2000). Gender matters. In: B.A. Day and M.C. Monroe (eds), *Environmental Education and Communication for a Sustainable World*, pp. 23–31. Academy for Educational Development, Washington, DC.

Griggs, B. (2004). From Arctic refuge to Utah deserts, a focus on wild lands. *Salt Lake Tribune*, October 31, 2004.

Gross, M. and Zimmerman, R. (2002). *Interpretive Centers: The History, Design, and Development of Nature and Visitor Centers*. UW-SP Foundation Press, Inc., Stevens Point, WI.

Guiney, M.S. and Oberhauser, K.S. (2009). Conservation volunteers' connection to nature. *Ecopsychology*, 1, 187–197.

Gurevitz, R. (2000). Affective approaches to environmental education: going beyond the imagined worlds of childhood? *Ethics, Place and Environment*, 3, 253–268.

Guynup, S. (2004). Toxins accumulate in Arctic peoples, animals, study says. *National Geographic News*, August 27, 2004. Retrieved February 26, 2005, from <http://news.nationalgeographic.com/news/2004/08/0827_040827_tvarctic_toxins.html>

Hacker, K. (2013). *Community-based Participatory Research*. Sage Publications, Thousand Oaks, CA.

Ham, S.H. (1992). *Environmental Interpretation: A Practical Guide for People with Big Ideas and Small Budgets*. North American Press, Golden, CO.

Ham, S.H. (2013). *Interpretation: Making a Difference On Purpose*. Fulcrum Publishing, Golden, CO.

Ham, S. and Sewing, D. (1987/88). Barriers to environmental education. *Journal of Environmental Education*, 19(2), 17–24.

Hammond, D. (2013). *Go Out and Play! Favorite Outdoor Games from KaBoom!* Candlewick Press, Somerville, MA.

Hampton, C. (2013). Section 7. Preparing public service announcements. The Community Tool Box. University of Kansas. Retrieved on July 23, 2014, from <http://ctb.ku.edu/en/table-of-contents/participation/promoting-interest/public-service-announcements/main>

Hancock, L. (2014). Go dark for Earth Hour, Saturday, March 29 at 8:30 p.m. local time. March 25, 2014, Retrieved January 28, 2015, from <http://www.worldwildlife.org/press-releases/go-dark-for-earth-hour-saturday-march-29-at-8-30-p-m-local-time>

Hanh, T.N. (2013). *Love Letter to the Earth*. Parallax Press, Berkeley, CA.

Hansmann, R., Scholz, R.W., Francke, C.A.C., and Weymann, M. (2005). Enhancing environmental awareness: Ecological and economic effects of food consumption. *Simulation and Gaming*, 36, 364–382.

Harris, R. (1998). Introduction to creative thinking. *VirtualSalt*. Retrieved September 4, 2004, from <http://www.virtualsalt.com/crebook1.htm>

Hassrick, P. (2002). *Drawn to Yellowstone: Artists in America's First National Park*. Autry Museum of Western Heritage, Los Angeles, CA.

Haury, D.L. and Rillero, P. (1994). What is hands-on learning, and is it just a fad? In: *Perspectives of Hands-On Science Teaching*. The ERIC Clearinghouse for Science, Mathematics, and Environmental Education, Columbus, OH. Retrieved January 24, 2015, from <http://www.ncrel.org/sdrs/areas/issues/content/cntareas/science/eric/eric-toc.htm>

Hawthorne, W. and Lawrence, A. (2013). *Plant Identification: Creating User-Friendly Field Guides for Biodiversity Management*, Vol. 8. Routledge, New York, NY.

Heffernan, B.M. (1998). Evaluation techniques for the Sandy Bay Point Discovery Center, Great Bay National Estuarine Research Reserve. *Journal of Environmental Education*, 30, 25–33.

Heffernan, K. (2001). *Fundamentals of Service-Learning Course Construction*. Campus Compact, Providence, RI.

Henderson, K. and Tilbury, D. (2004). *Whole-school Approaches to Sustainability: an International Review of Sustainable School Programs*. Report prepared by the Australian Research Institute in Education for Sustainability (ARIES) for the Department of the Environment and Heritage, Australian Government. Available at: <http://citeseerx.ist.psu.edu/viewdoc/download?doi=10.1.1.231.7017&rep=rep1&type=pdf>

Heney, E. (2013). Making an app: 6 things you should consider before getting started. *udemy blog*. Retrieved July 3, 2014, from <https://www.udemy.com/blog/making-an-app/>

Henriksson, A., Yi, Y., Frost, B., and Middleton, M. (2006). Evaluation instrument for e-government websites. *Internet Research 7.0: Internet Convergences*, 28–30 September, Brisbane, Queensland, Australia. Retrieved June 27, 2014, from <http://eprints.qut.edu.au/3113/>

Herreid, C.F. (2007). *Start with a Story: The Case Study Method of Teaching College Science.* National Science Teachers Association, Arlington, VA.

Hoffman, R. (1999). Wayside exhibit planning: Focusing on significant terrain. *Legacy*, **10**(2), 17–19, 32.

Hollweg, K.S. (1997). *Are We Making a Difference? Lessons Learned from VINE Program Evaluations.* NAAEE, Washington, DC.

Hopkins Demonstration Forest (2013). *2013 Annual Report Forests Forever, Inc.* Retrieved October 15, 2014, from <http://www.demonstrationforest.org/sites/default/files/pdfs/annual_reports/annual_report_2013.pdf>

Huitt, W. and Hummel, J. (2003). Piaget's theory of cognitive development. *Educational Psychology Interactive.* Valdosta, GA: Valdosta State University. Retrieved January 5, 2015, from <http://www.edpsycinteractive.org/topics/cognition/piaget.html>

Hummer, J. (2010). Using social marketing to promote energy efficiency and conservation. *Environmental Leader.* Retrieved July 9, 2014, from <http://www.environmentalleader.com/2010/03/22/using-social-marketing-to-promote-energy-efficiency-and-conservation/>

Hungerford, H.R. and Volk, T.L. (1990). Changing learner behavior through environmental education. *Journal of Environmental Education*, **21**(3), 8–22.

Hungerford, H.R., Volk, T., Ramsey, J.M., Litherland, R.A., and Peyton, R.B. (2003). *Investigating and Evaluating Environmental Issues and Actions: Skill Development Program.* Stipes Publishing, Champaign, IL.

Ikpeze, C. H. and Boyd, F.B. (2007). Web-based inquiry learning: Facilitating thoughtful literacy with WebQuests. *The Reading Teacher*, **60**, 644–654.

Illeris, K. (2003). Towards a contemporary and comprehensive theory of learning. *International Journal of Lifelong Education*, **22**, 396–406.

Inwood, S.M., Sharp, J.S., Moore, R.H., and Stinner, D.H. (2009). Restaurants, chefs and local foods: insights drawn from application of a diffusion of innovation framework. *Agriculture and Human Values*, **26**, 177–191.

IPCC (2014). *Climate Change 2014 Synthesis Report.* Retrieved December 10, 2014, from <http://www.ipcc.ch/report/ar5/syr/>

Ireland, J.T., Monroe, M.C. and Oxarart, A. (2010). Should we use wood for energy? A high school education program. *EDIS Document* FOR 270. Institute of Food and Agricultural Sciences, University of Florida, Florida Cooperative Extension Service, Gainesville, FL. Retrieved July 21, 2014 from <http://sfrc.ufl.edu/extension/ee/woodenergy/index.html>

ISTE (International Society for Technology in Education) (2015). ISTE Standards. Retrieved on January 13, 2015, from <http://www.iste.org/standards>

Jackson, E. (2005). Literacy beds. Unpublished document by the Appalachian Sustainable Agriculture Project, Asheville, NC.

Jacobson, S.K. (1992). *The Bay Islands: Nature and People/Las Islas de la Bahia: La Naturaleza y la Gente.* Bay Island Conservation Association Publication, Roatan, Honduras.

Jacobson, S.K. (2005). Communications for wildlife professionals. In: C.E. Braun (ed.), *Techniques for Wildlife Investigations and Management*, 6th edn, pp. 24–42. The Wildlife Society, Bethesda, MD.

Jacobson, S. (2009). *Communications Skills for Conservation Professionals*, 2nd edn. Island Press, Washington, DC.

Jacobson, S.K., Monroe, M.C., and Marynowski, S. (2001). Fire at the wildland interface: The influence of experience and mass media on public knowledge, attitudes, and behavioral intentions. *Wildlife Society Bulletin*, **29**, 929–937.

Jacobson, S.K., Carlton, J.S., and Monroe, M.C. (2012). Motivation and satisfaction of volunteers at a Florida natural resource agency. *Journal of Park and Recreation Administration*, **30**, 51–67.

Jacobson, S.K., Mueller, R., and Seavey, J.R. (2013). Creative climate change communication. North American Association for Environmental Education Conference, Baltimore, MD.

Jensen, E. (1998). *Teaching With the Brain in Mind*. Association for Supervision and Curriculum Development, Alexandria, VA.

Jensen, E. (2000). *Brain-based Learning*. The Brain Store Publishing, San Diego, CA.

Jensen, E. (2008). A fresh look at brain-based education. *Phi Delta Kappan*, **89**, 408–417.

Johnson, D.W., Johnson, R.T., and Holubec, E.J. (1994). *The New Circles of Learning: Cooperation in the Classroom and School*. Association for Supervision and Curriculum Development, Alexandria, VA.

KAB (Keep America Beautiful) (2015). Recycle-bowl competition. Retrieved January 3, 2015, from <http://recycle-bowl.org/>

Kahan, D., Peters, E., Wittlin, M., Slovic, P., Ouellette, L.L., Braman, D., and Mandel, G. (2012). The polarizing impact of scientific literacy and numeracy on perceived climate change risk. *Nature Climate Change*, **2**, 732–735.

Kaiser, F. and Shimoda, T. (1999). Responsibility as a predictor of ecological behavior. *Journal of Environmental Psychology*, **19**, 243–253.

Kaplan, S. (1978). Attention and fascination: The search for cognitive clarity. In: S. Kaplan and R. Kaplan (eds.), *Humanscape: Environments for People*, pp. 84–90. Doxbury Press, North Sciuate, MA.

Kaplan, S. (2000). Human nature and environmentally responsible behavior. *Journal of Social Issues*, **56**, 491–508.

Kaplan, R. and Basu, A. (eds) (2015). *Fostering Reasonableness: Supportive Environments for Bringing out our Best*. Maize Books, Michigan Publishing, Ann Arbor, MI.

Kaplan, S. and Kaplan, R. (1982). *Cognition and Environment: Functioning in an Uncertain World*. Praeger, New York, NY.

Kaplan, R. and Kaplan, S. (1989). *The Experience of Nature: A Psychological Perspective*. Cambridge University Press, Cambridge, UK.

Kaplan S. and Kaplan R. (2009). Creating a larger role for environmental psychology: The reasonable person model as an integrative framework. *Journal of Environmental Psychology*, **29**, 329–339.

Kassirer, J. (2010). Energy smackdown uses game play to involve community members. *Tools of Change*. Retrieved on July 21, 2014, from <http://www.toolsofchange.com/en/case-studies/detail/643/>

Kaye, C.B. (2010). *The Complete Guide to Service Learning: Proven, Practical Ways to Engage Students in Civic Responsibility, Academic Curriculum, and Social Action*. Free Spirit Publishing, Minneapolis, MN.

Keeley, B. (2007). *Human Capital: How What You Know Shapes Your Life*. OECD Publishing, Paris. Retrieved January 14, 2015, from <http://www.keepeek.com/Digital-Asset-Management/oecd/education/human-capital_9789264029095-en#page1>

Kellert, S.R. (1996). *The Value of Life: Biological Diversity and Human Society*. Island Press, Washington, DC.

Kenney, J.L., Militana, H.P., and Donohue, M.H. (2003). Helping teachers to use their school's backyard as an outdoor classroom: A report on the Watershed Learning Center program. *Journal of Environmental Education*, **35**(1), 18–26.

Kent, T.W. and McNergney, R.F. (1999). *Will Technology Really Change Education?* Corwin Press, Thousand Oaks, CA.

Khan, M. (2011). Are trees social—nonprofit environmental groups use of social media. *Sustainability, Journalism and Media Regeneration Conference University of South Carolina October 2011*. Retrieved on June 16, 2014, from <http://www.slideshare.net/iftagon/are-trees-social-nonprofit-environmental-groups>

Kinsey, J. (2010). Five social media tools for the extension toolbox. *Journal of Extension* 48(5), 5TOT7. Retrieved June 27, 2014, from <http://www.joe.org/joe/2010october/tt7.php>

Kinsey, J. and Henneman, A.C. (2011). Making your online video viral. *Journal of Extension* 49(4), 4TOT3. Retrieved June 27, 2014, from <http://www.joe.org/joe/2011august/pdf/joe_v49_4tt3.pdf>

Kirkpatrick, D. and Kirkpatrick. J. (2007). *Implementing the Four Levels: A Practical Guide for Effective Evaluation of Training Programs*. Berrett-Koehler Publishers, San Francisco, CA.

Klingemann, H.D. and Rommele, A. (2002). *Public Information Campaigns and Opinion Research*. Sage Publications, Thousand Oaks, CA.

Knudson, D.M., Cable, T.T., and Beck, L. (2003). *Interpretation of Cultural and Natural Resources*, 2nd edn. Venture Publishing, State College, PA.

Kocher, S., Lombardo, A., and Sweitzer, R.A. (2013). Using social media to involve the public in wildlife research—the SNAMP fisher sock collection drive. *Journal of Extension*, 51(1), 1IAW3. Retrieved June 27, 2014, from <http://www.joe.org/joe/2013february/iw3.php>

Kollmus, A., and Agyeman, J. (2002). Mind the gap: Why do people act environmentally and what are the barriers to pro-environmental behavior? *Environmental Education Research* 8,(3), 239–260.

Kotler, P., Roberto, N., and Lee, N. (2002). *Social Marketing: Improving the Quality of Life*, 2nd edn. Sage Publishing, Thousand Oaks, CA.

Krajnc, A. (2002). Conservation biologists, civic science and the preservation of BC forests. *Journal of Canadian Studies*, 37, 219–238.

Krantz. S. (2014). Message framing to affect forest landowners intention to adapt to climate change. Unpublished Masters Thesis, University of Florida, Gainesville, FL.

Krathwohl, D.R. (2002). A revision of Bloom's taxonomy: An overview. *Theory into Practice*, 41, 212–218.

Kraus, J. and Boss, S. (2013). *Thinking Through Project-based Learning: Guiding Deeper Inquiry*. Corwin, Thousand Oaks, CA.

Kumler, L.M. (2009). People matter: Secondary students social and natural world knowledge, actions, and potentials in the context of land use decisions. Unpublished PhD Thesis, University of Michigan, Ann Arbor, MI.

Kyrnin, J. (2014). 10 tips to a great web page. *about.com*. Retrieved July 5, 2014, from <http://webdesign.about.com/od/webdesignbasics/tp/aa112497.htm>

Landgraf, G. (2013). *Citizen Science: Guide for Families*. Huron Street Press, Chicago, IL.

Larner, J. and Mergendollar, J.R. (2012). The 8 essentials for project-based learning (by BIE). Retrieved June 21, 2014, from <http://bie.org/object/document/8_essentials_for_project_based_learning>

LeFevre, D. (2012). *Best New Games*. Human Kinetics, Campaign, IL.

Learning To Give (2014). The five stages of service learning. Retrieved June 2, 2014, from <http://learningtogive.org/lessons/institute/service_learning/page2.asp>

Leave No Trace (2014). Leave No Trace principles. *Leave No Trace Center for Outdoor Ethics*. Retrieved May 24, 2014, from <http://www.lnt.org>

Lee Jenni, G.D., Peterson, M.N., Cubbage, F.W., and Jameson, J.K. (2012). Assessing biodiversity conservation conflict on military installations. *Biological Conservation*, 153, 127–133.

Leichman, A.K. (2012). Trash Tycoon—even recycling can be fun. *Israel 21C*. Retrieved on January 12, 2015, from <http://www.israel21c.org/headlines/trash-tycoon-even-recycling-can-be-fun/>

Lenton, P. (2002). Tapping music to encourage environmental literacy (or why we do what we do!). *Connections: The Newsletter of the Global, Environmental and Outdoor Education Council of Alberta*, 26(1), 1–5.

Leopold, A. (1966). *A Sand County Almanac*. Ballantine, New York, NY.

402 | References

Levinthal, C. (1988). *Messengers of Paradise: Opiates and the Brain*. Doubleday, New York, NY.

Li, X. and Wang. Y. (2010). Evaluating the effectiveness of destination marketing organizations' websites: Evidence from China. *International Journal of Tourism Research*, 12, 536–549.

Lieberman, G.A. (2013). *Education and the Environment: Creating Standards-based Programs in Schools and Districts*. Harvard Education Press, Cambridge, MA.

Lieberman, G.A. and Hoody, L.L. (1998). *Closing the Achievement Gap: Using the Environment as an Integrating Context for Learning*. State Education and Environment Roundtable, Science Wizards, Poway, CA.

Lindbergh, A.M. (1978). *Gift from the Sea*. Vintage, New York, NY.

Lindemann, E. and Anderson, D. (2001). *A Rhetoric for Writing Teachers*, 4th edn. Oxford University Press, New York, NY.

Lindén, A. and Carlsson-Kanyama, A. (2003). Environmentally friendly disposal behavior and local support systems: Lessons from a metropolitan area. *Local Environment*, 8, 291–301.

Liu, C.H. and Matthews, R. (2005). Vygotsky's philosophy: Constructivism and its criticisms examined. *International Education Journal*, 6, 386–399.

Liu, T.-C., Peng, H., Wu, W.-H., and Lin, M.-S. (2009). The effects of mobile natural-science learning based on the 5E learning cycle: A case study. *Educational Technology and Society*, 12, 344–358.

Loney, B. (2000–2001). Middle school and high school students map a community: Using service-learning to meet and measure standards. *Continuance*, Fall/Winter, 26.

Louv, R. (2005). *Last Child in the Woods: Saving Our Children from Nature-Deficit Disorder*. Algonquin Books, Chapel Hill, NC.

Louv, R. (2011). *The Nature Principle: Human Restoration and the End of Nature-Deficit Disorder*. Algonquin Books, Chapel Hill, NC.

Lozano, R. (2010). Diffusion of sustainable development in universities' curricula: an empirical example from Cardiff University. *Journal of Cleaner Production*, 18, 637–644.

Luvmour, J. and Luvmour, S. (2007). *Everyone Wins!: Cooperative Games and Activities*. New Society Publishers, Gabriola Island, BC, Canada.

McConnell, L.C. and Monroe, M.C. (2012). Making online professional development work for Florida Project Learning Tree. *Applied Environmental Education and Communication*, 11, 148–156.

McDuff, M.D. (2000). Thirty years of environmental education in Africa: The role of the Wildlife Clubs of Kenya. *Environmental Education Research*, 6, 383–396.

McDuff, M.D. (2001). Building the capacity of grassroots conservation organizations to conduct participatory evaluation. *Environmental Management*, 27, 715–727.

McDuff, M.D. (2010). *Natural Saints: How People of Faith are Working to Protect God's Earth*. Oxford University Press, New York, NY.

McDuff, M.D. (2012). *Sacred Acts: How Churches are Working to Protect Earth's Climate*. New Society Publishers, Gabriola Island, BC, Canada.

MacGregor, S.K. and Lou, Y. (2004–2005). Web-based learning: How task scaffolding and Web site design support knowledge acquisition. *Journal of Research on Technology in Education*, 37, 161–175.

McKenzie-Mohr, D. (2011). *Fostering Sustainable Behaviour: An Introduction to Community-Based Social Marketing*, 3rd edn. New Society Publishers, Gabriola Island, BC, CA.

McKenzie-Mohr, D., Lee, N.R., Schultz, P.W., and Kotler, P. (2012). *Social Marketing to Protect the Environment*. Sage, Los Angeles, CA.

McKeown-Ice, R. (2000). Environmental education in the United States: A survey of preservice teacher education programs. *Journal of Environmental Education* 32, 4–11.

McKibben, B. (2003). My mileage is better than your mileage. *Orion*, 22, 80–81.

Maclean, N. (1983). *A River Runs Through It*. University of Chicago Press, Chicago, IL.

McNeil, L. (2001). Goodbye honeybuckets. Retrieved May 24, 2014, from <http://serc.carleton.edu/introgeo/icbl/strategy1.html>

Male, B. (2010). 10 basic SEO tips to get you started. *Business Insider*. Retrieved April 23, 2015, from <http://www.businessinsider.com/10-basic-seo-tips-everyone-should-know-2010-1>.

Manoli, C.C., Johnson, B., Hadjichambis, A.C., Hadjichambi, D., Georgiou, Y., and Ioannou, H. (2014). Evaluating the impact of the Earthkeepers Earth education program on children's ecological understandings, values and attitudes, and behaviour in Cyprus. *Studies in Educational Evaluation*, 41, 29–37.

Markham, T., Larmer, J., and Ravitz, J. (2003). *Project-based Learning Handbook*, 2nd edn. Buck Institute for Education, Novato, CA.

Marks, L., Stein, T., Jacobson, S., Gape, L., and Sweeting, M. (2004). Recreational management planning for Abaco National Park: Initial results from stakeholder meetings. Unpublished report to the Bahamas National Trust.

Maslow, A. (1954). *Motivation and Personality*. Harper, New York, NY.

Matherly, C. (2000). Exploring nature from the inside out: Homeschooling opportunities at informal-learning facilities. *Legacy*, 11(4), 14–20.

Matsuoka, B.M. [executive producer] (2004). Concept to Classroom, Inquiry-based Learning. Educational Broadcast Corporation, New York, NY. Retrieved January 5, 2015, from < http://www.thirteen.org/edonline/concept2class/inquiry/index.html>.

Matthews, C. and Bennett, K. (2002). Naturalist writers and environmental sentiments. *Sciencescope*, 26(3), 22–27.

Meadows, R. (2000). Tips from the media committee: how to write and place an op-ed. *Society for Conservation Biology Newsletter*, 7(3), 13.

Meany, J., and Schuster, K. (2002). Presentational aids: A brief guide to effective practice. Retrieved April 20, 2015, from https://www.uvm.edu/~asnider/IDAS_2011_CD/Teachers/Materials%20for%20Public%20Speaking/presentation%20aids_20040721105126.pdf.

Melchoir, A. and Ballis, L.N. (2002). Impact of service-learning on civic attitudes and behaviors of middle and high school youth: Findings from three national evaluations. In: A. Turco and S.H. Billig (eds), *Service-Learning: the Essence of the Pedagogy*, pp. 201–222. Information Age Publishing, Greenwich, CT.

Miller, M. (2014). Creative Content marketing at scale: Lee Odden at #SESNY. Retrieved on July 21, 2014, from <http://www.toprankblog.com/2013/03/creative-content-marketing-sesny/>

Milone, M. (1996). *How to Use Technology to Improve Student Learning: Problems and Solutions*. American Association of School Administrators, Washington, DC.

Mintzes, J.J., Wandersee, J.H., and Novak, J.D. (2005). *Teaching Science for Understanding: A Human Constructivist View*. Elsevier Academic Press, Burlington, MA.

MIT (Massachusetts Institute of Technology) (2015). MIT BLOSSOMS: Math and science video lessons for high school classes. Retrieved on January 13, 2015, from <http://blossoms.mit.edu/home>

Monmoto, J. (1991). *Kenju's Forest*. Harper Collins Publishers, New York, NY.

Monroe, M.C. (2003). Two avenues for encouraging conservation behaviors. *Human Ecology Review*, 10, 113–125.

Monroe, M.C. (2008). Addressing misconceptions about wildland–urban interface issues. *University of Florida IFAS Extension Publication FOR108*. University of Florida, Gainesville, FL. Retrieved January 5, 2015, from <http://edis.ifas.ufl.edu/fr155>

Monroe, M.C. and Cappaert, D. (1994). *EE Toolbox—Workshop Resource Manual. Integrating Environmental Education into the School Curriculum*. Kendall Hunt Publishing Company, Dubuque, IA.

Monroe, M.C. and Krasny, M. (2013). *Across the Spectrum: Resources for Environmental Educators*. NAAEE, Washington, DC.

Monroe, M.C. and Oxarart, A. (2012). Etoile Firewise: Youth working with communities to adapt to wildfire. *Research Note NRS-159*. US Department of Agriculture, Forest Service, Northern Research Station, Newtown Square, PA. Retrieved October 17, 2014, from <http://www.nrs.fs.fed.us/pubs/42536>

Monroe, M.C. and Oxarart, A. (2014). Southeastern forests and climate change: A Project Learning Tree secondary module. University of Florida and American Forestry Foundation, Gainesville, FL. Retrieved October 1, 2014, from <http://sfrc.ufl.edu/extension/ee/climate>

Monroe, M.C., Andrews, E., and Biedenweg, K. (2007). A framework for environmental education strategies. *Applied Environmental Education and Communication*, **6**, 205–216.

Monroe, M.C., Oxarart, A., McDonell, L., and Plate, R. (2009). Using community forums to enhance public engagement in environmental issues. *Journal of Education for Sustainable Development*, **3**, 171–182.

Monroe, M.C., Plate, R., and Oxarart, A. (2013). Intermediate collaborative adaptive management strategies build stakeholder capacity. *Ecology and Society*, **18**(2), 24. Retrieved August 24, 2014, from <http://www.ecologyandsociety.org/vol18/iss2/art24/>

Monterey Bay Aquarium (2015). Sea otter cam. Retrieved January 13, 2015, from <http://www.montereybayaquarium.org/animals-and-experiences/live-web-cams/sea-otter-cam>

Morgan, J. (2001). Popular culture and geographic education. *International Research in Geographic and Environmental Education*, **10**, 284–297.

Morris, J.K., Jacobson, S.K., and Flamm, R.O. (2007). Lessons from an evaluation of a boater outreach program for manatee protection. *Environmental Management*, **40**, 596–602.

Moser, C. and Pollio, C.A. (2012). *Resolving Environmental Conflicts*, 2nd edn. CRC Press, Taylor and Francis, Boca Raton, FL.

Muir, J. (1911). *My First Summer in the Sierra*. Penguin, New York, NY.

Murray, J.A. (1995). *The Sierra Club Nature Writing Handbook: A Creative Guide*. Sierra Club Books. San Francisco, CA.

NAAEE (North American Association for Environmental Education) (2004). Nonformal environmental education programs—guidelines for excellence. Retrieved October 14, 2014, from <http://resources.spaces3.com/b85e2c0a-f321-40c2-9857-19a5f29d750b.pdf>

NAAEE (North American Association for Environmental Education) (2009a). Environmental education materials: Guidelines for excellence. National Project for Excellence in Environmental Education. Retrieved May 21, 2014, from <http://eelinked.naaee.net/n/guidelines/posts/environmental-education-materials-guidelines-for-excellence>

NAAEE (North American Association for Environmental Education) (2009b). Nonformal environmental education programs: Guidelines for excellence. National Project for Excellence in Environmental Education. Retrieved May 21, 2014, from <http://eelinked.naaee.net/n/guidelines/posts/nonformal-environmental-education-programs-guidelines-for-excellence>

NAAEE (North American Association for Environmental Education) (2010a). Guidelines for the preparation and professional development of environmental educators. National Project for Excellence in Environmental Education. Retrieved May 21, 2014, from <http://eelinked.naaee.net/n/guidelines/posts/nonformal-environmental-education-programs-guidelines-for-excellence>

NAAEE (North American Association for Environmental Education) (2010b). Early childhood environmental education programs: Guidelines for excellence. National Project for Excellence in Environmental Education. Retrieved July 21, 2014, from <http://eelinked.naaee.net/n/guidelines/topics/early-childhood-ee-programs-guidelines-for-excellence>

NAAEE (North American Association for Environmental Education) (2011). Developing a framework for assessing environmental literacy: Executive summary. North American Association for Environmental Education, Washington, DC. Retrieved January 6, 2015, from <http://www.naaee.net/sites/default/files/framework/EnvLiteracyExeSummary.pdf>

National Center for Safe Routes to School (2011). Two schools recognized for safe routes to school top honor (Press release). Retrieved April 19, 2015, from <http://www.saferoutesinfo.org/about-us/newsroom/two-schools-recognized-safe-routes-school-top-honor>

National Center for Case Study Teaching in Science (2014). Case collection. Retrieved May 24, 2014, from <http://sciencecases.lib.buffalo.edu/cs/collection/>

National Park Service (n.d.). Retrieved April 6, 2005, from <http://www.nps.gov/museum/exhibits/>

National Youth Leadership Council (2015). National Service-Learning Clearinghouse. Retrieved April 15, 2015, from <https://gsn.nylc.org/clearinghouse>

Natural Resources Canada (2014). A ready-made vehicle idling campaign. Transportation Initiatives, Natural Resources Canada. Retrieved January 20, 2015, from <http://www.nrcan.gc.ca/energy/efficiency/communities-infrastructure/transportation/idling/4469>

NCA (National Communication Association) (2014). Media interview tips. Retrieved July 23, 2014, from <https://www.natcom.org/uploadedfiles/more_scholarly_resources/media%20interview%20tips.pdf>

NCTC (National Conservation Training Center) (2004). *Public Outreach and Education: Overview and Planning*. Division of Education Outreach, National Conservation Training Center, US Fish and Wildlife Service, Shepherdstown, WV.

NEETF (National Environmental Education and Training Foundation) (2000). *Environment-based Education: Creating High Performance Schools and Students*. NEETF, Washington, DC. Retrieved January 14, 2015, from <http://www.neefusa.org/pdf/NEETF8400.pdf>

Neril, Y. and Marzouk, E. (2013). *Uplifting People and the Planet: Eighteen Jewish Lessons on the Environment*. Confei Nesharim, Roseland, NJ.

Neustaedter, C., Tang, A., and Judge, T.K. (2013). Creating scalable location-based games: lessons from geocaching. *Journal of Personal and Ubiquitous Computing*, 17, 335–349.

New South Wales Department of Education and Training (2001). Environmental education policy for schools. Retrieved January 28, 2015, from <https://www.det.nsw.edu.au/policies/curriculum/schools/envir_educ/PD20020049.shtml>

Newell, R.J. (2003). *Passion for Learning: How Project-based Learning Meets the Needs of 21st Century Students*. The Scarecrow Press, Inc., Lanham, MD.

Nikkei (2009). Unique positioning of newspapers in Japan. Retrieved July 30, 2014, from <http://adweb.nikkei.co.jp/english/newspapers_in_japan/>

NME (2013). Why do certain songs give you goosebumps? Retrieved December 6, 2014, from <http://www.nme.com/blogs/nme-blogs/why-do-certain-songs-give-you-goosebumps#rwrthqcsopirldt1.99>

No Child Left Inside (2014). No Child Left Inside. Retrieved May 22, 2014, from <http://www.cbf.org/ncli/landing>

Nonprofit Tech for Good (2010). [Book interview] Nonprofit example of social media excellence: The Nature Conservancy. Retrieved on June 16, 2014, from <http://www.nptechforgood.com/2010/12/13/book-interview-nonprofit-example-of-social-media-excellence-the-nature-conservancy/>

Norton, P. and Sprague, D. (2001). *Technology for Teaching*. Allyn and Bacon, Boston, MA.

Null, E.H. (2002). East Feliciana parish schools embrace place-based education as a way to lift scores on Louisiana's high-stakes tests. Rural Trust featured project. ERIC No. ED463136. The Rural School and Community Trust, Washington, DC. Retrieved January 24, 2015, from <http://eric.ed.gov/?id=ed463136>

Odden, L. (2010). Six critical steps to take before starting your social media monitoring initiative. Retrieved June 16, 2014, from <http://www.toprankblog.com/2010/09/6-steps-social-media-monitoring/>

Orleans, D. (2004). Earthsinging: The use of music in environmental education. *Folksong in the Classroom*, 9(1, Fall), 28–29. Retrieved January 28, 2015, from <http://www.geocities.ws/envirosongs/earthsinging.html>

Padua, S. and Jacobson, S.K. (1993). A comprehensive approach to an environmental education program in Brazil. *Journal of Environmental Education*, 24(4), 29–36.

Pardee, M. (2005). River of words. *Volunteer Monitor* (Winter), 17–19.

Pashler, H., McDaniel, M., Rohrer, D., and Bjork, R. (2008). Learning styles: Concepts and evidence. *Psychological Science in the Public Interest*, 9, 106–199.

Pearce, F. (2013). TV as birth control. *Conservation*, 13(3), 30–37.

Pennock, M.T., Bardwell, L.V., and Britt, P. (1994). *Approaching Environmental Issues in the Classroom*. EE Toolbox Workshop Resource Manual. Kendall Hunt Publishing, Dubuque, IA. Retrieved January 24, 2015, from <http://www.naaee.net/sites/default/files/publications/eetoolbox/ApproachingEnvIssuesClassroom.pdf>

Pennsylvania Department of Education (2014). Pennsylvania Department of Education environment and ecology academic standards. Retrieved May 21, 2014, from <http://www.education.state.pa.us/portal/server.pt/community/environment___ecology/7534>

PetLifeRadio (2014). Aquariumania. PetLifeRadio. Retrieved June 20, 2014, from <http://www.petliferadio.com/aquariumania.html>

Petty, R.E. and Cacioppo, J.T. (1981). *Attitudes and Persuasion: Classic and Contemporary Approaches*. Wm C. Brown, Dubuque, IA.

Petty, R.E. and Priester, J.R. (1994). Mass media attitude change: Implications of the elaboration likelihood model of persuasion. In: J. Bryant and D. Zillmann (eds), *Media Effects: Advances in Theory and Research*, pp. 91–122. Lawrence Erlbaum, Hillsdale, NJ.

Pigozzi, M.J. (2003). UNESCO and the International Decade of Education for Sustainable Development (2005–2015). *Connect*, 28, 1–7.

Plate, R. and Monroe. M. (2014). A structure for assessing systems thinking. *The Creative Learning Exchange*, 23(1), 1-6. Retrieved October 17, 2014, from <http://clexchange.org/ftp/newsletter/clex23.1.pdf#page=1>

Pomeroy, R., Parks, J., and Watson, L., (2004) *How is your MPA doing? A Guidebook of Natural and Social Indicators for Evaluating Marine Protected Area Management Effectiveness*. IUCN—The World Conservation Union, Gland, Switzerland.

PON (Program on Negotiation at Harvard Law School) (2014). Program on negotiation at Harvard Law School. Teaching negotiation resource center. Retrieved May 24, 2014, from <http://www.pon.org>

Ponto, C.F. and Linder, N.P. (2011). *Sustainable Tomorrow: A Teachers' Guidebook for Applying Systems Thinking to Environmental Education Curricula*. Retrieved October 17, 2014, from <http://www.fishwildlife.org/files/ConEd-Sustainable-Tomorrow-Systems-Thinking-Guidebook.pdf>

Popkin, H.A.S. (2012). We spent 230,060 years on social media in one month. Retrieved June 13, 2014, from <http://www.cnbc.com/id/100275798>

Porterfield, A. (2011). How to strategically dominate the Facebook news feed. Retrieved on June 16, 2014, from <http://www.amyporterfield.com/2012/01/how-to-strategically-dominate-the-facebook-news-feed/>

Powell, J. and Bails, J.D. (2000). Measuring the soft stuff: Evaluating public involvement in an urban watershed restoration. *Proceedings of the Watershed 2000 Management Conference, July 9–12, 2000, Vancouver, BC, Canada*. Water Environment Federation, Alexandria, VA. Available at: <http://www.rougeriver.com/pdfs/education/watershed2000-05.pdf>

Powell, R.B. and Ham, S.H. (2008). Can ecotourism interpretation really lead to pro-conservation knowledge, attitudes, and behavior? Evidence from the Galapagos Islands. *Journal of Sustainable Tourism*, 16, 467–489.

Pretty, J.N., Guijt, I., Scoones, I., and Thompson, J. (1995). *A Trainer's Guide for Participatory Learning and Action*. IIED, London, UK.

Pringle, R., Hakverdi, M., Cronin-Jones, L., and Johnson, C. (2003). Zoo school for preschoolers: Laying the foundation for environmental education. *Annual Meeting of the American Educational Research Association (AERA), Chicago, IL, April 21–25.* ERIC No. ED475663. Available at: <http://files.eric.ed.gov/fulltext/ED475663.pdf>

Pritchard, A. (2014). *Ways of Learning: Learning Theories and Learning Styles in the Classroom.* Routledge, New York, NY.

Pritchard, A. and Woollard, J. (2010). *Psychology for the Classroom: Constructivism and Social Learning.* Routledge, London.

Project WET Foundation (2011). *Project WET Curriculum and Activity Guide,* Generation 2.0. Project WET Foundation, Bozeman, MT.

Project WILD (2007). *K–12 Curriculum and Activity Guide.* Council for Environmental Education, Houston, TX.

Project WILD (2013). *Aquatic Activity Guide.* Council for Environmental Education, Houston, TX.

Projects International (2002). Mekong River: Education for sustainability project. Retrieved January 24, 2015, from <http://www.e-o-n.org/Projects_International/mekongefsproj.htm>

Prysby, M.D. (2001). Temporal and geographical variation in monarch egg and larval densities (*Danaus plexippus*): An ecological application of citizen science. Master's Thesis, University of Minnesota.

Prysby, M.D. and Super, P. (2006). Best practices in citizen science for environmental learning centers. A collaborative document produced from the Citizen Science Forum, November 13–16, 2003, Great Smoky Mountains Institute at Tremont, TN.

Purcell, K., Heaps, A., Buchanan, J., and Friedrich, L. (2013). How teachers are using technology at home and in their classrooms. Pew Research Center's Internet and American Life Project. Retrieved June 2, 2014, from <http://pewinternet.org/reports/2013/teachers-and-technology>

Ramsey, J. (1993). The effects of issue investigation and action training on environmental behavior. *Journal of Environmental Education,* 24(3), 31–36.

Ramsey, D. (2002). The role of music in education: Lessons from the cod fishery crisis and the dust bowl days. *Canadian Journal of Environmental Education,* 7, 183–198.

Ramsey, J. and Hungerford, H. (1989). The effect of issue investigation and action training on environmental behavior of seventh grade students. *Journal of Environmental Education,* 20(4), 29–34.

Ramsey, J., Hungerford, H.R., and Tomera, A.N. (1981). The effects of environmental action and environmental case study instruction on the overt environmental behavior of eighth-grade students. *Journal of Environmental Education,* 13(1), 24–29.

Rare (2007). *Rare Pride Handbook: A Guide for Inspiring Conservation in Your Community.* Rare, Arlington, VA. Retrieved January 26, 2015, from <http://www.rareplanet.org/sites/rareplanet.org/files/rare_pride_handbook_english_low_res.pdf>

Rare (2015a). Pride campaigns. Retrieved on January 3, 2015, from <http://www.rare.org/pride#.vkhxi8vjiuk>

Rare (2015b). Watersheds. Retrieved on January 3, 2015, from <http://www.rare.org/watersheds#.vkhh2svjiuk>

reduce your footprint (2015). Growing native. Rose Bay sustainability Street. Blog post of March 31, 2011. Retrieved January 3, 2015, from <http://reduceyourfootprint.com.au/blog/sustainability-street-takes-shape-in-rose-bay/>

Ribeiro, J. *et al.* (1999). *Flora da Resera Ducke: Guiade Identificacao das Palntas Vasculares de Uma Floresta de Terra-Firme na Amazonia Central.* INPA, Brazil.

Rich, C. (2014). The power of building offline connections in a digital world. *Entrepreneur,* October 1, 2014. Retrieved on January 9, 2015, from <http://www.entrepreneur.com/article/237961>

Riskowski, J.L., Todd, C.D., Wee, B., Dark, M., and Harbor, J. (2009). Exploring the effectiveness of an interdisciplinary water resources engineering module in a 8th grade science class. *International Journal of Engineering Education*, 25, 181–195.

River of Words (2005). River of Words contest. Retrieved June 19, 2005, from <http://www.stmarys-ca.edu/center-for-environmental-literacy/river-of-words>

Robbins, J. (2014). Paying farmers to welcome birds. *The New York Times*, Tuesday April 15, 2015. Available at: <http://www.nytimes.com/2014/04/15/science/paying-farmers-to-welcome-birds.html?_r=1>

Rocha, L.M. and Jacobson, S.K. (1998). Partnerships for conservation: Protected areas and non-governmental organizations in Brazil. *Wildlife Society Bulletin*, 26, 937–946.

Rogers, N. (1993). *The Creative Connection: Expressive Arts as Healing*. Science and Behavior Books, Inc., Palo Alto, CA.

Rogers, E.M. (1995). *Diffusion of Innovations*. Free Press, New York, NY.

Rogers, N., Tudor, K., Tudor, L.E., and Keemar, K. (2012). Person-centered expressive arts therapy: A theoretical encounter. *Person-Centered and Experiential Psychotherapies*, 11, 31–47.

Ross, A. (ed.) (2014). *Measuring Environmental Education Outcomes*. North American Association of Environmental Education, Washington, DC.

Roth, W-M. and Lee, Y-J. (2007). Vygotsky's neglected legacy: Cultural-historical activity theory. *Review of Educational Research*, 77, 186–232.

Rous, E.W. (2000). *Literature and the Land: Reading and Writing for Environmental Literacy*, pp. 7–12. Boynton/Cook Publishers, Portsmouth, NH.

Rowe, S.M. and Wertsch, J.V. (2002). Vygotsky's model of cognitive development. In: U. Goswami (ed.), *Blackwell Handbook of Childhood Cognitive Development*, pp. 538–554. Blackwell Publishers, Oxford, UK.

Russell, H.R. (2001). *Ten-Minute Field Trips: A Teacher's Guide to Using the Schoolgrounds for Environmental Studies*. NSTA Press, Washington, DC.

Russo, T. and Benson, S. (2005). Learning with invisible others: Perceptions of online presence and their relationship to cognitive and affective learning. *Educational Technology and Society*, 8, 54–62.

Ryan, R.M. and Deci, E.L. (2000). Self-determination theory and the facilitation of intrinsic motivation, social development, and well-being. *American Psychologist*, 55, 68–78.

SCWUIRI (2005). Firewise home. Southern Center for Wildland–Urban Interface Research and Information, USDA Forest Service, Southern Research Station, Gainesville, FL. Retrieved January 14, 2015, from <http://www.interfacesouth.org/fire/firewisehome/>

Sakurai, R., Jacobson, S.K., Matsuda, N., and Maruyama, T. (2014). Assessing the impact of a wildlife education program on Japanese attitudes and behavioural intentions. *Environmental Education Research*, doi: 10.1080/13504622.2014.898246.

Saxena, S. (2013). Using technology in education: Does it improve anything? *EdTechReview*. Retrieved January 12, 2015, from <http://edtechreview.in/news/681-technology-in-education>

Scherer, M. (2013). We the people. *Time Magazine*, 181(5), 34–37.

Schultz, P.W. (2002). Knowledge, information, and household recycling: Examining the knowledge-deficit model of behavior change. In: T. Dietz and P.C. Stern (eds), *New Tools for Environmental Protection: Education, Information, and Voluntary Measures*, pp. 67–82. National Academy Press, Washington, DC.

Schulz, C. (2000). *School Environmental Clubs in Wisconsin: 2000 and Beyond*. Wisconsin Center for Environmental Education, Stevens Point, WI.

Schusler, T.M., Decker, D.J., and Pfeffer, M.J. (2003). Social learning for collaborative natural resource management. *Society and Natural Resources*, 16, 309–326.

SEER (State Education and Environment Roundtable) (2000). California Student Assessment Project: the effects of environment-based education on student achievement. SEER, San Diego, CA. Retrieved June 1, 2005, from <http://www.seer.org/pages/research/CSAP2000.pdf>

Seng, P. and Rushton, S. (eds) (2003). *Best Practices Workbook for Boating, Fishing, and Aquatic Resources Stewardship Education*. Recreational Boating and Fishing Foundation, Alexandria, VA.

Shandrow, K. (2013). 10 questions to ask when creating a social-media marketing platform. *Entrepreneur*. Retrieved on June 16, 2014, from <http://www.entrepreneur.com/article/228324>

Shirk, J.L., Ballard, H., Wilderman, C.C., Phillips, T., Wiggins, A., Jordan, R., McCallie, E., Minarchek, M., Lewestein, B.V., Krasny, M.E., and Bonney, R. (2012). Public participation in scientific research: a framework for deliberate design. *Ecology and Society*, 17(2), 29. Retrieved June 25, 2014, from <http://dx.doi.org/10.5751/ES-04705-170229>

Sierra Club (2013). Stunning art made from trash. Retrieved December 2, 2014, from <http://sierraclub.typepad.com/greenlife/2013/11/trash-art-gyre-project.html>

Sierra Club (2014). Blogging guidelines. Sierra Club Policies. Retrieved on July 14, 2014, from <http://vault.sierraclub.org/policy/blogs.aspx>

Silka, L. (2012). Community-based participatory research: a rigorous approach to science. Public Participation in Scientific Research Conference, August 4–5, 2012, Portland, OR. Available at: <http://www.citizenscience.org/community/plenary-presentations/#silka>

Silverstein, S. (1964). *The Giving Tree*. Harper Collins Publishers, New York, NY.

Silvertown, J., Buesching, C.D., Jacobson, S.K., and Rebelo, T. (2013). Citizen science in nature conservation. In: D.W. Macdonald and K.J. Willis (eds), *Key Topics in Conservation Biology 2*, pp. 127–142. John Wiley & Sons, Hoboken, NJ.

Sischy, I. (2003). The Smithsonian's big chill. *Vanity Fair*, December, 242–256.

Slocum, R., Wichhart, L., Rocheleau, D., and Thomas-Slaytor, B. (1995). *Power, Process, and Participation: Tools for Change*. Intermediate Technology Publications, London, UK.

Smith, W.A. (1995). Behavior, social marketing and the environment. In: J. Palmer, W. Goldstein and A. Curnow (eds), *Planning Education to Care for the Earth. International Union for Conservation of Nature and Natural Resources*, pp. 9–20. IUCN, Gland, Switzerland.

Smith, G.A. and Sobel, D. (2010). *Place- and Community-based Education in Schools*. Routledge, New York, NY.

Snyder, G. (1974). *Turtle Island*. New Directions Publishing Co., New York, NY.

Snyder, C.R., Rand, K.L., and Sigmon, D.R. (2001). Hope theory. A member of the positive psychology family. In: C.R. Snyder and S.J. Lopez (eds), *Handbook of Positive Psychology*, pp. 257–275. Oxford University Press, New York, NY.

Sobel, D. (1998). *Mapmaking with Children: Sense of Place Education for the Elementary Years*. Heinemann, Portsmouth, NH.

Sobel, D. (2005). *Place-Based Education: Connecting Classrooms and Communities*. The Orion Society, Great Barrington, MA.

Society for Conservation Biology (2014). Designing a conservation science poster? Retrieved May 25, 2014, from <http://www.conbio.org/professional-development/advice-for-students/help-designing-posters>

Soden, R. and Palen, L. (2014). From crowdsourced mapping to community mapping: the post-earthquake work of OpenStreetMap Haiti. In: C. Rossitto, L. Ciolfi, D. Mertin, and B. Conein (eds), *COOP 2014: Proceedings of the 11th International Conference on the Design of Cooperative Systems, May 27–30, 2014, Nice, France*, pp. 311–326. Springer International Publishing, Switzerland.

Southeast Climate Consortium (2015). Agroclimate: Tools for managing climate risk in agriculture. Retrieved January 14, 2015, from <http://www.agroclimate.org/>

Speisman, S. (2005). Ten tips for successful business networking. *Business Know-how*. Retrieved January 24, 2015, from <http://www.businessknowhow.com/tips/networking.htm>

Splash! Animals (2014). Splash! Animals & WWF: Stop wildlife crime. Retrieved June 25, 2014, from <https://www.youtube.com/channel/UCOtX_5-0zvBqOTVdEJnpTWA>

Sprung, R. (2013). Compelling Stats That Make the Case for Smarter Site Design. Retrieved April 22, 2015, from <http://blog.hubspot.com/marketing/compelling-stats-website-design-optimization-list>

Stahl, R.J. (1994). The essential elements of cooperative learning in the classroom. *ERIC Digests*, No. ED370881. ERIC Clearinghouse for Social Studies/Social Science Education, Bloomington, IN. Available at: <http://www.ericdigests.org/1995-1/elements.htm>

Stanley, E. and Waterman, M. (2002). Using investigative cases. Retrieved January 24, 2015, from <http://serc.carleton.edu/introgeo/icbl/index.html>

Stapp, W.B., Cromwell, M.M., Schmidt, D.C., and Alm, A.W. (1996). *Investigating Streams and Rivers*. Kendall-Hunt, Dubuque, IA.

Stern, P.C. (2000). Toward a coherent theory of environmentally significant behavior. *Journal of Social Issues*, **56**, 407–424.

Straka T. and Franklin, R. (2008). Extension efforts enhance low country South Carolina conservation forestry. *Journal of Extension*, 46(3), 3IAW4. Retrieved October 14, 2014, from <http://www.joe.org/joe/2008june/iw4.php>

Strand, K., Marullo, S., Cutforth, N., Stoecker, R., and Donohue, P. (2003a). Principles of best practice for community-based research. *Michigan Journal of Community Service Learning*, 9(3), 5–15.

Strunk, W. Jr. and White, E. (1979). *The Elements of Style*, 3rd edn. Macmillan Publishing Co., New York, NY.

Sustainability Street Institute (2015). Homepage. Retrieved on January 3, 2015, from <http://www.sustainabilitystreet.org.au/>

Sutt, J.M. (2014). Assessing perspectives of goliath grouper fishery stakeholders. Unpublished Masters Thesis, University of Florida, Gainesville, FL.

Sylwester, R. (2010). *A Child's Brain: The Need For Nurture*. Corwin Press, Thousand Oaks, CA.

Te Kate Ipurangi (2003). Guidelines for environmental education in New Zealand schools. Planning environmental education programs within the New Zealand Curriculum Framework. Retrieved May 20, 2014, from <http://efs.tki.org.nz/curriculum-resources-and-tools/environmental-education-guidelines>

TeacherTube (2014). TeacherTube. Retrieved on January 13, 2015, from <http://www.teachertube.com/>

Teaching and Learning with Technology (2003). Using cases in teaching: Writing the case. Penn State University, PA. Retrieved January 24, 2015, from <http://archive.tlt.psu.edu/suggestions/cases/write.html>

Teed, R. (2003). Role-playing exercises. Starting Point—Teaching Entry Level Geoscience. Retrieved January 24, 2015, from <http://serc.carleton.edu/introgeo/roleplaying/index.html>

Teed, R. (2004). Game-based learning. Starting Point–Teaching Entry Level Geoscience. Retrieved January 24, 2015, from <http://serc.carleton.edu/introgeo/games/howtogbl.html>

Telg, R. (2009). Producing an educational video. *University of Florida IFAS Extension Publication AEC343*. Retrieved January 9, 2014, from <http://edis.ifas.ufl.edu/wc024>

Telg, R. (2012). Instructional methods for distance education. *University of Florida IFAS Extension Publication AEC 345*. Retrieved January 9, 2014, from <http://edis.ifas.ufl.edu/wc026>

Thaler, R.H. and Sunstein, C.R. (2009). *Nudge: Improving Decisions About Health, Wealth, and Happiness*. Penguin Books, New York, NY.

Thayer, R. (1989). *The Biopsychology of Mood and Arousal*. Cambridge University Press, New York, NY.

The Exchange Project (2007). Introducing students to environmental justice: A North Carolina case study. Retrieved June 10, 2014, from <http://www.exchangeproject.unc.edu/real-people_sub/by_county.html>

The Green Bible (2010). *The Green Bible.* Harper Collins Publishers, New York, NY.

The Nature Conservancy (2004). Wild New York: Creating a field guide for urban environments. Society for Conservation Biology Meeting, July 2004, Columbia University, New York, NY.

The Nature Conservancy (2005). Website homepage. <http://www.nature.org/>

The Millennium Development Goals Report. (2012). Retrieved April 22, 2015, from <http://www.un.org/millenniumgoals/pdf/MDG%20Report%202012.pdf>

Thoreau, H.D. (1854). *Walden.* Konemann Publishers, Boston, MA.

Thoreau, H.D. (1906). *The Writings of Henry David Thoreau.* Houghton Mifflin, Boston, MA. [Reprinted 1984, *The Journal of Henry David Thoreau*, Vol. 8. Gibbs M. Smith Inc., Layton, UT.]

Tilden, F. (1956). *Interpreting our Heritage.* University of North Carolina Press, Chapel Hill, NC.

Tinsley, H.E.A. (1984). The psychological benefits of leisure counselling. *Society and Leisure*, 7, 125–140.

Trapp, S., Gross, M., and Zimmerman, R. (1994). *Signs, Trails, and Wayside Exhibits: Connecting People and Places*, 2nd edn. UW-SP Foundation Press, Inc., Stevens Point, WI.

Sachs, S. (2013). Terrestrial Invertebrates. In Trautmann, N.M., Fee, J., Tomasek, T.M., and Bergey, N.R. (eds.), *Citizen Science: 15 Lessons that Bring Biology to Life, 6–12*, pp. 77–83. National Science Teachers Association (NSTA) Press, Arlington, VA.

Tufte, E. (1990). *Envisioning Information.* Graphics Press, Cheshire, CT.

Turner, K. and Freedman, B. (2004). Music and Environmental Studies. *Journal of Environmental Education*, 36(1), 45–52.

Ulstrup, S. (2001). Nature guidance and guidance in *friluftsliv. Pathways*, 13(3), 28–30.

US Department of Education (2010). *Evaluation of Evidence-based Practices in Online Learning: A Meta-analysis and Review of Online Learning Studies.* Office of Planning, Evaluation, and Policy Development, Policy and Program Studies Service, Washington, DC. Available at: <https://www2.ed.gov/rschstat/eval/tech/evidence-based-practices/finalreport.pdf>

UNESCO (1978). *Final Report. Intergovernmental Conference on Environmental Education.* United Nations Educational, Scientific, and Cultural Organization with United Nations Environment Program in Tbilisi, USSR, 14–16 October 1977. ED/MD/49. UNESCO, Paris, France. Available at: <http://www.gdrc.org/uem/ee/EE-Tbilisi_1977.pdf>

UNESCO (2012). Learning to protect biodiversity. Retrieved on July 10, 2014, from <https://www.youtube.com/watch?v=kHhspf5IfdE>

Union for Ethical BioTrade (UEBT) (2010). Biodiversity barometer 2010. Retrieved June 25, 2014, from <http://www.cbd.int/cepa/doc/uebt-barometer-2010.pdf>

US National Park Service (2005). Visitor Center, Zion National Park, Utah. Retrieved June 16, 2015, from <http://www.doi.gov/greening/energy/zion.cfm>

University of British Columbia Campus Sustainability (2014). University of British Columbia energy dashboard. Retrieved May 22, 2014, from <https://my.pulseenergy.com/ubc/dashboard#/overview>

Usher, A. and Kober, N. (2012). Summary paper: Student motivation—an overlooked piece of school reform. Center on Education Policy, Graduate School of Education and Human Development, The George Washington University, Washington, DC. Retrieved January 5, 2015, from <http://www.cep-dc.org/displaydocument.cfm?documentid=405>

Uzunoglu, E. and Misci, S. (2014). Building relationships through websites: A content analysis of Turkish environmental non-profit organizations' (NPO) websites. *Public Relations Review*, 40, 113–115.

Van Matre, S. (1972). *Acclimatization: A Sensory and Conceptual Approach to Ecological Involvement*. American Camping Association, Martinsville, IN.

Vaske, J.J. (2008). *Survey Research and Analysis: Applications in Parks, Recreation and Human Dimensions*. Venture Publishing, State College, PA.

Veverka, J.A. (2011). *Interpretive Master Planning: Volume 1—Strategies for the New Millennium*. MuseumsEtc Ltd, Cambridge, MA.

Vigdor, J.L. and Ladd, H.F. (2010). Scaling the digital divide: Home computer technology and student achievement. Working Paper 16078. National Bureau of Economic Research, Cambridge, MA. Retrieved on July 4, 2014, from <http://www.nber.org/papers/w16078>

Volk, T. and Cheak, M.J. (2003). Effects of environmental education on students, parents, and communities. *Journal of Environmental Education*, 34(4), 12–25.

Voordouw, J.J. (1987). *Youth in Environmental Action: An International Survey*. International Youth Foundation. International Union for the Conservation of Nature. United Nations Environment Programme, Gland, Switzerland.

Walnut Creek (n.d.). Sign design tips and guidelines. City of Walnut Creek California. Retrieved on July 23, 2014, from <http://www.walnut-creek.org/citygov/depts/cd/tdc/sign_design.asp>

Wals, A.E.J. and van der Leij, T. (2007). Introduction. In: A.E.J. Wals (ed.), *Social Learning Towards as Sustainable World*, pp. 17–32. Wageningen Academic Publishers, Wageningen, The Netherlands.

Warren, J.L. (2012). Does service-learning increase student learning?: A meta-analysis. *Michigan Journal of Community Service Learning*, Spring 2012, 56–61.

WCK (1997). *Trees, Myths, and Medicines: a Collection of Stories by Children of the Wildlife Clubs of Kenya*. Jacaranda a Designs Limited, Nairobi, Kenya.

WebAIM (2014). Web accessibility in mind. Introduction to web accessibility. Center for Persons with Disabilities, Utah State University. Retrieved on July 14, 2014, from <http://webaim.org/intro/>

Weick, K.E. (1984). Small wins: Redefining the scale of social problems. *American Psychologist*, 9, 40–49.

Weiss, R.P. (2001). The mind–body connection in learning. Retrieved December 2, 2014, from <http://www.trans4mind.com/counterpoint/index-health-fitness/weiss.shtml>

Wells, N.M. and Lekies K.S. (2006). Nature and the life course: Pathways from childhood nature experiences to adult environmentalism. *Children, Youth, and Environments*, 16(1), 1–25.

WGBH Educational Foundations (2000). Doing hands-on science with kids. Retrieved January 24, 2015, from <http://www.pbs.org/wgbh/buildingbig/educator/pla_hos.html>

Whatley, M.E. (2011). *Interpretive Solutions: Harnessing the Power of Interpretation to Help Resolve Critical Resource Issues*. InterpPress, Fort Collins, CO.

Wildscreen (2015). Wildscreen arkive. Retrieved January 10, 2015, from <http://www.arkive.org/>

Wilson, J.R. and Monroe, M.C. (2005). Biodiversity curriculum that supports education reform. *Applied Environmental Education and Communication*, 4, 125–138.

Winther, A.A. (2001). Investigating and evaluating environmental issues and actions. In: H. Hungerford, W.J. Bluhm, T.L. Volk, and J.M. Ramsey (eds), *Essential Readings in Environmental Education*, pp. 155–171. Stipes Publishing, Champaign, IL.

Withrow-Robinson, B., Broussard, S., Simon-Brown, V., Engle, M., and Reed, A (2002). Seeing the forest: art about forests and forestry. *Journal of Forestry*, Dec., 8–14.

Wondolleck, J.M. and Yaffee, S.L. (2000). *Making Collaboration Work: Lessons from Innovation in Natural Resource Management*. Island Press, Washington, D.C.

WWF (2013). Stop wildlife crime. Retrieved June 25, 2014, from <https://www.youtube.com/user/WWF>

WWF (2014). Monk seal project: Overview. Retrieved July 31, 2014, from http://mediterranean.panda.org/about/marine/monk_seal_project/project/

WWF-UK (2015). Wildlife trade in the UK. Retrieved January 7, 2015, from <http://www.wwf.org.uk/what_we_do/illegal_wildlife_trade/wildlife_trade_in_the_uk2/>

Xerces Society (2014). Native bee pollination of watermelon. Retrieved July 31, 2014, from <http://www.xerces.org/wp-content/uploads/2008/10/factsheet_watermelon_pollination.pdf>

YouTube (2015). What is fair use? Retrieved on January 13, 2015, from <https://www.youtube.com/yt/copyright/fair-use.html#yt-copyright-four-factors>

Young Entrepreneur Council (2013). 13 tips for giving killer presentations. *Huffington Post*, August 8, 2013. Retrieved May 25, 2014, from http://www.huffingtonpost.com/young-entrepreneur-council/13-tips-for-giving-a-kill_b_3728093.html

Young, J. (2010). *The Coyote's Guide to Connecting with Nature*. Owlink Media, Santa Cruz, CA.

Zent, S. (2010). Tools for biocultural diversity conservation: Community mapping of indigenous people's traditional lands in Venezuela. Retrieved June 21, 2014, from <http://www.terralingua.org/bcdconservation/?p=239>

Zheng, R., Perez, J., Williamson, J., and Flygare, J. (2008). WebQuests as perceived by teachers: Implications for online teaching and learning. *Journal of Computer Assisted Learning*, **24**, 295–304.

Zinsser, W. (1985). *On Writing Well: An Informal Guide to Writing Nonfiction*. Harper and Row Publishers, New York, NY.

Index